Discard
NHCPL

blog!

ALSO BY DAVID KLINE AND DAN BURSTEIN

Road Warriors: Dreams and Nightmares Along the Information Highway

ALSO BY DAVID KLINE

Rembrandts in the Attic: Unlocking the Hidden Value of Patents

ALSO BY DAN BURSTEIN

*Secrets of the Code: The Unauthorized Guide
to the Mysteries Behind The DaVinci Code*

Secrets of Angels & Demons (with Arne de Keijzer)

*The Best Things Ever Said About the Past, Present,
and Future of the Internet Economy*

Big Dragon (with Arne de Keijzer)

Turning the Tables

Euroquake

Yen!

blog!

how the newest media revolution is changing politics, business, and culture

David Kline and Dan Burstein

contributing editors:
Arne J. de Keijzer and Paul Berger

NEW HANOVER COUNTY
PUBLIC LIBRARY
201 CHESTNUT STREET
WILMINGTON, NC 28401

cds
BOOKS

IN ASSOCIATION WITH SQUIBNOCKET PARTNERS LLC

Copyright © 2005 Squibnocket Partners LLC.

All rights reserved. No part of this book may be reproduced or transmitted in any form or by any means, electronic or mechanical, including photocopying and recording, or by any information storage or retrieval system, without written permission from the copyright holder.

For information please address:

CDS Books
425 Madison Avenue
New York, NY 10017

ISBN: 1-59315-141-1

Orders, inquiries, and correspondence should be addressed to:

CDS Books
425 Madison Avenue
New York, NY 10017
(212) 223-2969 FAX (212) 223-1504

Printed in the United States of America

10 9 8 7 6 5 4 3 2 1

Blogging is cool, but nothing beats waking up in the morning to a family you love. For Sarah, Oliver, Charlotte, and Daniel.

—DAVID KLINE

For Julie and David, and all the ideas, articles, images, stories, snippets, and headlines we have shared, without even knowing we were preparing ourselves for life in the blogosphere.

—DAN BURSTEIN

CONTENTS

3 | THE COMMENTARY

APPENDICES

INTRODUCTION

FROM CAVE PAINTING TO WONKETTE: A SHORT HISTORY OF BLOGGING

by Dan Burstein

A four-letter term that came to symbolize the difference between old and new media during this year's presidential campaign tops U.S. dictionary publisher Merriam-Webster's list of the 10 words of the year. Merriam-Webster Inc. said on Tuesday that blog, defined as "a Web site that contains an online personal journal with reflections, comments and often hyperlinks," was one of the most looked-up words on its Internet sites this year. . . . Americans called up blogs in droves for information and laughs ahead of the presidential election. Freed from the constraints that govern traditional print and broadcast news organizations, blogs spread gossip while also serving as an outlet for people increasingly disenchanted with mainstream media. . . . Blog will be a new entry in the 2005 version of the Merriam-Webster Collegiate Dictionary, Eleventh Edition.

—From a Reuters report,
" 'Blog' Tops U.S. Dictionary's Words of the Year,"
November 30, 2004

Over the years, philosophers, anthropologists, and scientists have tried to define what makes Homo sapiens uniquely Homo sapiens. We are toolmakers, some experts tell us. We possess the capacity for complex language, others point out. We enjoy sex and engage in it for purposes other than procreation. We feel and express emotions. We experience wonder and curiosity, and we have the ability to contemplate why we exist and what the meaning of our lives may be. All of these statements are arguably true. But there is another distinguishing characteristic of human beings that has been unknown or underestimated until recently:

We blog.

I make this observation having just returned from a fascinating set of travel experiences through the Dordogne and adjacent regions of southwest France. There, my family and I wandered through magnificent caves whose walls showed off the brilliant engravings and paintings created fifteen to twenty thousand years ago at the dawn of modern human history. In learning about how these works developed, I discovered that in a number of places, the period of decoration of the cave walls went on for several generations—even, in some cases, for several hundreds or thousands of years. The paintings were often first inspired by the physical forms in the caves and were a kind of commentary on those forms. Then later painters and storytellers made subsequent commentaries about what they saw on the walls and what they had experienced in their lives. Having no written alphabetic language, they used the mysterious visual languages of the figurative and abstract—multicolored paintings and carved engravings—to describe their ideas and beliefs about the hunt; the spirit of bison, mammoths, deer, and various other animals; shamanism; the sacred feminine; initiation rites; sickness; mortality; the afterlife; the earth.

All of this was, of course, a very complex process, which I don't mean to oversimplify or trivialize here. Great thinkers have written hundreds of volumes describing the meaning and role in human development of these prehistoric art forms. But among the many mind-altering, paradigm-shifting ideas I took away from this experience was the observation that much of this art emerged as part and parcel of a long and highly compelling *conversation*: One member of the tribe initiating another, one generation speaking to the next, one group of humans inspired by and reacting to the ideas of those who came before. The conversation continues and is stored and archived for future access. The group memorializes and institutionalizes knowledge—and learns as a result.

Once you start to look for bloglike phenomena in the history of our civilization, you start to find them everywhere. The Talmudic tradition, for another example, is also a form of proto-blogging—scholars and thinkers debating the meaning of text passages from another era and creating commentaries, refinements, additions, and different shades of interpretation. Renaissance artists and thinkers were bloggers of a kind as well, commenting on what they found of interest and beauty from the cultures of Greece and Rome. Leonardo da Vinci probably wrote the greatest unpublished blog of all time in his more than thirty thousand pages of diary entries.

Tom Paine and the great American revolutionary zeal for political pamphleteering in the eighteenth century is another form: Passionate political rants, delivered in real time, designed to be read and discussed by groups of people who are then moved to action as a result. (Rereading these in the light of the twenty-first-century day, I marvel at the vocabulary, the cadence, the brilliance of the rhetorical style and the obvious intellect of the mass audiences that were capable of grasping the new ideas and the complex sentence construction. But if you think today's political bloggers are shrill, uncivil, or unobjective, they look reasoned and responsible by comparison to the Revolutionary War–era pamphleteers!)

The tradition of "commonplace books" provides another kind of example. These handwritten diaries were popular among Europeans, especially from the late Renaissance through the Enlightenment. The tradition continued to flourish into the nineteenth century in England and America. In these commonplace books, diarists collected and wrote down their favorite quotations and passages from a wide range of books, letters, and other sources. Sketches and hand-drawn illustrations were often included. Sometimes these diarists shared their notebooks with others and incorporated the reactions of their friends and colleagues, very much like a slow-moving, handwritten, in-person version of today's blogs.

So, although the word *weblog*, contracted into *blog*, may have first appeared in 1997, and there may have only been a few hundred blogs in 1999 around the time that Pyra Labs launched its Blogger software to make it easy for the rest of us to blog, I believe we are dealing with a phenomenon that has ancient antecedents and deep cultural roots. That is why, in my humble opinion (IMHO, as they say), blogging is not a passing fad, although there are faddish aspects to it that (mercifully) will probably pass quickly out of view with next-generation blogging.

Another reason blogs will embed themselves into our new cultural DNA is that we are living in a unique moment in time when the ancient human urges to converse, communicate, argue publicly, learn collaboratively, share experiences, and archive collective knowledge—urges that are part of the definition of who we are as a species—have suddenly been married with incredibly powerful, fast, ubiquitous technologies. And increasingly, the ordinary mortal doesn't need to know anything about technology to become a blogger or to read blogs or to participate in this new media revolution, because the power of the technology is appropriately baked way down in the deepest regions of software infrastructure. The technologists and the engineers have done their job and given the rest of us a new tool that we do not have to understand in order to use, any more than we have to understand auto mechanics to drive a car.

The results of this unusual moment in time may be nothing short of a new paradigm for modern human communication, conversation, argument, and collaborative knowledge creation. Blogging represents one important wave of innovation that is contributing to restoring the lost voice of the ordinary citizen in our culture. The citizen-expert, the citizen-journalist, and the informed amateur in many realms of knowledge and human endeavor are all gaining prominence as a result of the blogging phenomenon. Yes, crazies and irresponsible people are also gaining access to wide audiences, as are people with evil and even criminal intent. And there is, of course, an overabundance of trivial drivel in blogs. But within all the noise, among the billions of words and pixels of new content being generated every day, lies a very important and steadily rising voice: the ordinary citizenry, on a national and global basis, re-engaging in the lost art of the public conversation.

Despite the oft-heard promises over the past century that each leap forward in technology would democratize communications, the fact is that information, knowledge, and policymaking have gravitated increasingly toward a relatively elite class of experts and professionals. The mainstream media grew to power and influence and, by the late twentieth century, these media had emerged as truly the fourth branch of government, absolutely critical to the function of democracy. In era-shaping controversies such as the Vietnam War and the Watergate scandal, the media frequently established their role as mechanism of last resort for checks and balances on governmental power. But as the press gained this new and important role—even becoming in many situations the check and balance mechanism of *first* resort—it also continued to coalesce into a relatively closed loop of professionals who knew the ropes, understood the systems, and had the credentials. They could make *their* voices heard, but not always *everyone's* voice heard. While niche and micro media have been growing for years (in print, on talk radio, on websites, on cable TV), challenging this mainstream media monopoly, blogging represents a significant qualitative change in the equation. The professionals still have control over the biggest, most powerful, most visible mainstream media (and I believe they will continue to play that dominant role for decades to come, with positive and negative effects), but "everyone" now has a meaningful shot at being heard as well.

A.J. Liebling, the great twentieth-century journalist, once famously said: "Freedom of the press is limited to those who own one." This powerful observation, profoundly true in the last century, is less true in the era of blogs. Today, as a result of the blogging phenomenon, it is not just that anyone has the freedom to speak in the abstract. The growing reality is that anyone can actually turn their words and ideas into published form, that anyone can have at least a small audience, and that anyone who desires a broad hearing can at least be armed to fight for one.

Any student of civilization's pageant knows the powerful changes in every aspect of society wrought by the major developments in communications technology: hieroglyphics, alphabets, papyrus, the Gutenberg press, newspapers, telegraphy, telephony, radio, television, the Internet and the Web. The evolution of blogs and blogging over the last few years—and, more importantly, the next few—may turn out to be a seminal vein in time. It may resemble the period after Gutenberg's printing presses finally started working and churning out print books across Europe. (Incidentally, Gutenberg's influence was felt most strongly a number of years *after* his many years of failures, the big financial losses he incurred for his investors, and several battles between

Gutenberg and his backers over who owned the intellectual property of his inventions.)

We have been talking for more than a generation about the "information age" and the "knowledge society." We have heard for at least two decades about the explosion of data that is leading to information overload and over-choice. We have watched the splintering of mass markets, mass institutions, mass media, and mass culture into thousands of customized, specialized, fragmented mini-markets, new institutions, personalized media, and emerging subcultures. I believe that blogs and blogging represent the missing link—or at least the metaphor and paradigm—for the ultimate software on which the knowledge society will operate. In the blogging phenomenon, we can see at least the software kernels that will be essential to creating structure and architecture (real order would be too much to hope for) out of the chaos of today's torrential information flows. Blogs, in their present form, are primitive tools gesturing in the direction of the new kinds of filtering, contextualization, and information-aggregation utilities that are already desperately needed—and will become even more crucial as billions of global citizens try to wrestle with increasingly complex societies fed by increasingly massive oceans of information.

Ice Age cave painters, Talmudic scholars, revolutionary pamphleteers, and commonplace bookmakers didn't have access to any technological tools to speak of. Equally obviously, much more separates DailyKos and Wonkette from Talmudic scholars and Tom Paine than links them. Nevertheless, as we set out on this journey to understand why the word *blog* was the most looked-up word of 2004, why the number of blogs is increasing by up to forty thousand a day, why tens of millions of people in America and around the world are reading, writing, and posting to blogs, why magazine cover stories are telling us that blogs will change our politics, our businesses, and our lives, we would do well to remember that what we know as a blog today is only the latest, most optimized, most evolved expression of one of the most basic human-felt needs.

Blogs, in the broadest sense, derive from the human urge to give voice to our ideas; to have our ideas understood, acted on, and remembered; and to engage in the quest for knowledge and understanding interactively and collaboratively. Our biological and cultural DNA causes us to want to articulate an idea or a vision and "publish" it, thereby taking ownership of it and credit for it. For most of us, it is very hard to keep our ideas inside our minds. Our biocultural DNA contains instructions that cause us to want to announce our ideas and denounce others, that make us want to interact, comment, converse, communicate, react, respond, elaborate, tweak, inform, refine, argue, criticize—and to do all of this with other members of our tribe across the boundaries of time and space. Blogs today, as well as their forerunner forms over thousands of years, are tools that allow us to engage in these processes. If, as scientists tell us, we are toolmakers, we are also idea generators.

Eventually, of course, quantity can turn into quality, essence can redefine existence. Today, in the middle of the first decade of the twenty-first century, the technologies and social changes that underlie the blogging phenomenon have arrived at their proverbial tipping point. For a brief moment, the medium really is the message (and the massage) and blogs deserve attention in their own right as a special kind of global, instantaneous, mass idea–generation farm; a special volcanic eruption of significant proportions and consequences within the history of the human conversation.

The blogging phenomenon is an exemplar of what James F. Moore of Harvard's Berkman Center for Internet & Society has dubbed "the second superpower." Moore's "second superpower" is not a nation-state but the social force of enlightened citizenry all over the globe, their co-created consciousness, and their collective power to invent, act, and change the world. Bloggers, Moore argues, are among the key citizens of this second superpower. "The current enthusiasm for blogging is changing the way that people relate to publication, as it allows real-time dialogue about world events . . . Meta-blogging sites crawl across thousands of blogs, identifying popular links, noting emergent topics, and providing an instantaneous summary of the global consciousness of the second superpower." Unlike the traditional democracy of the quadrennial voting booth, "participation in the second superpower movement occurs continuously through participation in a variety of web-enabled initiatives." Second superpower citizens are "alive," constantly "touching and being touched by each other, as the community works to create wisdom and to take action." In Moore's visceral descriptive prose, "Like a mind constituted of millions of inter-networked neurons, the social movement is capable of astonishingly rapid and sometimes subtle community consciousness and action."

The political, social, and cultural effects of blogging (and the many blog-like kinds of interactive tools and technologies now proliferating across the electronic cosmos) have analogous trends within the world of business and economics. Business guru C. K. Prahalad talks regularly about leading-edge companies that are "co-creating" their products with their customers. In new media businesses, "customer-created content" (think of Amazon.com reviews, for example, or the protean and constantly growing user-created encyclopedia that is Wikipedia) is suddenly valuable, despite the obvious fact that it costs nothing to generate in the traditional accounting sense of "cost." Visionary tech publisher Tim O'Reilly speaks of the "architecture of participation" in the creation of valuable databases and open source code; author James Surowiecki refers to the "wisdom of crowds"; Yale Law professor Yochai Benkler terms the phenomenon "peer production"; author Howard Rheingold speaks provocatively about "smart mobs"; *BusinessWeek* reports on a theme it calls "mass collaboration" and "the power of us." Pharmaceutical companies, automobile manufacturers, fashion brands, snack foods, and others are tapping the collective wisdom of online communities, as are online focus groups and hundreds of other enterprises. Major daily newspapers have even invited readers to use blogs to become "citizen journalists" and participate in reporting the news.

Blogging is not by any means synonymous with all of the above-referenced phenomena. But it is highly correlated and almost always related in one way or another to the new and rising social software that is at the heart of the new, new economy, the new global culture, and the new way of doing things in our increasingly complex, interactive, electronic world.

Exactly ten years ago, my coauthor, David Kline, and I published our book *Road Warriors: Dreams and Nightmares Along the Information Highway*. That book was one of the first in-depth forecasts to sort out the hype and make a reasonable assessment of the impact that the Web and digital media were likely to have on business and society. We challenged two extreme poles in the debate back then: the neo-Luddites, who somehow hoped that the rise of the new technology could be stopped, and the far more prevalent (and insidious) neo-utopians, who argued that digital technology changed everything, overturned the business cycle, stood the basic laws of value on their head, educated the uneducated, liberated the poor, and democratized society. We coined a term in *Road Warriors* to describe our standpoint in opposition to these extremes: *real-world futurism*. To us, real-world futurism meant being incredibly excited about the potential of digital technology to change our world, yet recognizing that it would take time to suffuse its way into the deep fabric of business, economics, political life, education, and entertainment. It would not happen all at once as many then-experts, drunk on the elixir of the Internet bubble, then thought. It meant understanding that change would come in fits and starts and amid confusion, chaos, and the fog of business warfare. There would be bubbles and burst bubbles to come, as well as policy debates, ethical arguments, government regulations, and much more.

A critical principle of the real-world futurist viewpoint is the understanding that technology *can* be a force for liberation, democratization, and social cohesion, but is not *inherently* so. People and policymakers have to work at making technology a positive force in our lives. Inevitably, all technological change brings with it huge positives and many negatives as well. And, although technological change happens much quicker these days, it still doesn't happen overnight. Even phenomena like cell phones and iPods have been a surprising number of years in arriving at the juncture of critical mass that we see all around us today. The direction of technological change in the future is determined in large part by the political, social, and economic realities of today. Technology's evolution, moreover, is a constantly self-correcting, self-adapting balancing act in the marketplace, overshooting here and there, sowing the seeds of creative destruction, releasing new engines of ingenuity and innovation.

A decade after our prior book, *blog!* is a work of real-world futurism as well. On the one hand, there are the bloggerati, who think mainstream media (MSM) are moribund if not dead already; that bloggers are inherently more authentic and trustworthy than other voices in our culture; and that now everything changes because of blogs. On the other hand, there are the naysayers who think blogs are already overhyped; that most bloggers have nothing to say; and that without traditional editing, rules, filtering, and financial incentives, blogs will soon go the way of CB radios.

The future almost certainly lies in the wide swath between those two polar opposite views. This book is about what's going on in the contemporary world of blogs and blogging and the trends and countertrends that permeate that ugly but ultimately useful word, the *blogosphere*. In the pages of this book, you will meet many of the leading bloggers of our time, while finding yourself engaged in the conversations and debates that are now rampant in the blogosphere. We will discuss what all this twenty-first-century blogging means for the future of big chunks of our global culture.

blog! is divided into three major parts—politics; business; media and culture—and each part includes a thought-leading essay by David Kline, a number of interviews with leading bloggers, and some of the best commentary on the blogging phenomenon that has appeared in traditional media sources. True to our real-world futurism, our book is a hybrid of older and newer media. I believe that print books will be with us for a long time to come, as will all the other media we know and experience today. Print still represents the best way to engage in long-form argument, to collect many ideas and many diverse voices (as we have done in this book) and make this assemblage of ideas available to many different kinds of people in one handy package.

No one knows definitively where the ever-expanding blogosphere is headed. David Kline and I have ideas on that topic—ideas we hope you will find intriguing, provocative, and intellectually stimulating. But we don't presume to have definitive "answers." Somewhat bloglike, this book brings you many different postings from many different leading-edge thinkers. Some of them comment on the general significance of the rise of the blogging phenomenon, some on much more specific aspects of it, but each one has his or her personal take on what's most new, innovative, and interesting in all of this.

Having convened this meeting of writers and readers to discuss the future impact of blogs and blogging, I should probably offer up a few of my own ideas before logging off. So here is my personal list of observations and expectations that come out of the pages of my own "commonplace book," as I have been interviewing bloggers and thinking about the current state and future direction of the blogosphere.

1. **Blogs are the key development at the center of a much wider suite of innovations that, taken together, are beginning to deliver on the promise of the 1990s.** This includes the last decade's promises about the high degrees of interactivity, personalization, and contextualization we would experience on the Web, as well as the promise of ubiquity, centrality, and ease of use of Web-based communications. RSS feeds, wikis, new search tools, new ways to integrate and process images and voice, the movement of music and television content to the Web, podcasting, and mobile blogging are all part of the same phenomenon: We are now getting the multimedia, always-on, highly interactive, highly personalized next-generation Web we imagined a decade ago.

2. **Blogs are particularly interesting because they marry so much personality and attitude with this complex mix of software technologies.** They are the raw, human face of the brave new technological world, showing that we can have more technology without necessarily becoming more depersonalized and alienated as a society. Blogs point the way toward restoring real voice and personality to the citizenry at large—locally, nationally, globally. In an ever-expanding population, with an ever more sophisticated elite set of knowledge workers setting the public agenda, blogs provide counterweight and ballast to the quality of public discussion. The blogging phenomenon may well represent a revitalization of real citizenship in the political and governmental sense, as well as the door-opening tool giving visibility and voice to diverse individuals with diverse ideas that never could have been seen or heard before.

3. **Blogging, in addition to being a huge phenomenon in its own right, is the key metaphor for interactivity, community-building, and genuine conversation: one to one, one to many, many to one, many to many.** Years from now, the kind of blogs we know today may or may not exist in a big way as a discrete genre, but the breakthrough principles of community-building and genuine interactivity they represent will

be incorporated into the way much of our media functions in the future. Blogging is the "killer app" of the current generation of Web innovation, just as email and instant messaging were at the core of the last version.

4. **Blogs will coexist with other media for a long time to come, and there will be continual interactions and cross-fertilizations.** Some of today's top bloggers will become newspaper and magazine columnists and TV news talent; almost all of today's traditional media will develop blogs of one type or another to extend their reach, connect to the younger demographic, be able to expand their coverage and have more advertising product to sell. Many blogs will develop codes of journalistic ethics appropriate to the blogosphere and take other measures to maintain and enhance credibility. These may not be the exact same rules of the road that have guided traditional journalism, but they will be explicit operating precepts just the same. Meanwhile, bloggers will continue to break new ground in covering stories and paying attention to issues the mainstream media tend to ignore, and will continue to gain grudging respect, credibility, and credentials as the creators of one more important type of media.

5. **Blogging is going corporate.** Its repercussions will be felt deep inside the business world, as a number of our interviews in this book point out. Many of the early Web enthusiasts were horrified a decade ago as advertising and e-commerce proliferated in the once pristine Garden of the Internet. If there are any such naïfs left in the age of blogging, they should get ready to see huge impacts on the blogosphere as the impact of the business world is felt in more and more ways. As a May 2005 *BusinessWeek* cover story screamed: "Blogs will change your business . . . Your customers and rivals are figuring blogs out. Our advice: Catch up . . . or catch you later." The first conferences I attended on blogging two or three years ago were populated by academics, literary types, and political pundits. The more recent conferences have had significant turnouts from the likes of General Motors, DaimlerChrysler, Microsoft,

and Procter & Gamble. The interaction of business and blogging will be many-sided and multidimensional. Business is obviously being changed in a number of superficial ways as a result of these trends. But it is also safe to predict that business will be changed in some profound ways as well, just as politics and other aspects of our culture are morphing as a result both of what is said in the blogosphere and the process of saying it.

6. **Blogging is going global.** It is not just us wild 'n crazy, uninhibited, populist Americans who like to rant. The core elements of blogging, as I pointed out at the beginning of this discussion, are connected to some universal human qualities, urges, and needs. There are numerous examples of how blogs are already changing culture and politics around the globe. One good example was the impact of a blog by Etienne Chouard, a schoolteacher from Marseille, widely credited with inspiring the opposition vote against the European constitution in France in May 2005. The rightist government of Jacques Chirac and most of the leftist intellectual establishment were united in their support for the European constitution, but Chouard's and other blogs contributed to a sudden public realization that this movement could be stopped. One could certainly question whether the influence of Chouard's blog was positive for France; nevertheless, the influence was undeniable when the votes were counted and the "no" vote won. When one scans down Technorati's list of the most influential blogs, the names of blogs in Hindi, Urdu, Arabic, Farsi, Japanese, Chinese, and Korean immediately show up. A very knowledgeable Chinese friend recently predicted that blogs would have more impact on revolutionizing China and bringing it fully into the modern world than any other influence. A month after he made these comments to me, the Chinese government seemed to concur with his view of blogs as a forum for revolutionary thought by issuing a series of edicts designed to control and constrain their spread. Blogs are having a powerful impact in all the obvious places where freedom of the press has always been a part of the culture. Blogging software now allows more voices to be heard on more subjects in countries like the UK or Australia or Sweden. But blogs are also proving influential

in places like Iraq, Iran, and elsewhere in the developing world. Just as many developing countries found in the 1990s that cell phone technology could proliferate even without a strong land line infrastructure, many of the same cultures are now discovering that a free, diverse blogosphere can exist even without a free traditional media environment.

7. **Blogs are segmenting.** Personal interactive journals are a huge and growing phenomenon—and interesting to think about. But these personal journals don't have all that much in common with the big political and opinion blogs. They share a style, they share an interface, they are indexed by search engines, they may even share underlying software architecture. But they are their own media form. It is also hard to imagine all the one-man and one-woman bands who are today's top bloggers just continuing forever into the future blogging every day. Some will develop their blogs as real businesses, just as many people have become power sellers on eBay or Amazon. Some will burn out and drop by the wayside, pleased they had their voices heard but exhausted and unhappy that they have not been able to make any money at it. At some point many bloggers will choose to further professionalize, hire small staffs, partner with other bloggers, begin to pool resources and participate in advertising syndicates.

8. **Blogging is not inherently liberal or conservative, Right or Left.** As the events of the American presidential race in 2004 amply demonstrated, blogging can be used by the right as well as the left. Just because some people might assume that liberals would have more affinity for writing personal streams of consciousness late at night in their pajamas, doesn't make it so.

9. **The numbers of bloggers will continue to grow because the numbers of knowledge workers in our societies are continuing to grow.** Our complex, sophisticated, postmodern societies are turning out very large numbers of literate people trained in critical thinking skills and interested in developing new ideas and participating in the discussion of

them. Blogs are being used by people in all sorts of professional niches and subcultures to exercise their intellectual muscles and evince their thought leadership. Indeed, blogs are so low-cost to start, they can exist below the minimum threshold for starting a newsletter, a think tank study, or an academic publication. As a result, blogs are becoming the communications centers for many kinds of new ideas and new thinking. Blogs are a bully pulpit for ideas. Rather than seeing the proliferation of specialty blogs as an indicator of the fragmentation of our society, we should see this trend as providing a way for citizen-experts to emerge and to bring together global constituencies in many disparate fields.

10. **Blogs will engender a variety of successful businesses, but may not create the kind of large new investment category that venture capitalists typically look for as technology paradigms change.** Entrepreneurs will build successful blog-orientated software companies; some will build successful small media companies; some will build valuable aggregation, syndication, and measuring tools. Rupert Murdoch's July 2005 purchase of Myspace.com's parent company for more than $500 million demonstrates that there is, indeed, gold in these hills. But the really big money—the billions, not the millions, as well as the big business battles of the future—will lie in the outcome of the clash of the titans for strategic control of the blogosphere. And the names will be familiar: Google, Microsoft, Yahoo, AOL, for example.

11. **Blogs will continue to be important in politics for a long time to come.** They may turn out in retrospect to have been as important as the advent of televised debates and live coverage during the 1960 presidential campaign. Curiously, if the electorate is not polarized, blogs could actually be less important in the 2008 U.S. presidential election than they were in 2004. They can have their maximum influence in a time of a closely and evenly divided electorate. Like other media, their role is important but actually marginal. It's when marginal matters that blogs can be most influential. If that's the case in 2008, then blogs may make

the difference in who is elected. But if a clear majority opinion develops, blogs will still be an interesting part of the campaign coverage, but less strategically significant.

12. **Blogs (in many cases) may lose their association with a single individual and become aggregation platforms for like-minded or complementary bloggers.** While certain changes are implied in moving from one-person blogs to aggregation platforms, I believe it is possible to retain much of the appeal of today's blogs and, at the same time, leverage the resources of larger platforms.

We can't know in advance all the new forms that will be created, but it is a given that there will be a long period of constant change ahead in how blogs are created and how we experience them. They will change not only our language, but the actual architecture of human knowledge, conversation, and interaction. As today's teenagers and college students grow older, they will remake the form and the genre of blogging they have grown up with. My own view is that the blogs of the future will appear quite different from today's. The word *blog* itself may disappear, along with many of the faddish elements of today's blogging world.

Yet I believe that the global always-on, always-linked, always-archived, always-immediate public conversation of the rest of the twenty-first century will continue to draw on the fundamental ideas and principles that emerged in this decade in what we called the blogosphere. For it was in this decade that we first married the ancient human impulse to publish ideas and converse about them with the powerful new technologies now available to us.

—Dan Burstein
August 2005

PART ONE

POLITICS & POLICY

TOWARD A MORE PARTICIPATORY DEMOCRACY

by David Kline

Our government is being robbed [from us] right before our
eyes, and half the American people are blissfully unaware that it is
happening. They are unaware because the media is owned by the
right wing and is being used to control and manipulate the masses.
It is time to awaken the American people to the horror that will be
their future if the right's vast takeover conspiracy is allowed to
succeed. But since the right wing already controls the media, we
must use other means to educate the American people.

CHRIS M. FICK
Blogger

You people obviously still don't get it, but you will soon. Our
movement is bigger than the left's domination of the universities, the
newspapers, and the film industry; it's bigger than anything that has
occurred since you wormed into power in the 1960s. Now, when a
leftist writes a piece for publication, it will be dragged into the light
by honest people. And it will be flogged to death for every lie, every
misrepresentation, and every exaggeration that it contains. It's over,
you clowns. Now, when you lie, we will report it.

JERRY HURTUBISE
Blogger

Two bloggers. Two fundamentally opposing views of who has power in America. But one shared belief that the threat to American freedoms stems from a vast political conspiracy and that only bloggers can expose the danger and rally the citizenry against it.

What makes these two blog postings especially noteworthy is not their conspiracy-minded sentiments—you can find similar views expressed about virtually any subject in the blogosphere—but rather the way they point to some of the reasons why bloggers have had such a dramatic impact on the American political scene over the past two years, not only in the run up to the 2004 presidential election but afterward as well. Chief among these reasons, of course, is the widespread public dissatisfaction with the mainstream media and the way it has conducted itself as the supposedly neutral arbiter and reporter of political news. Moreover, this widespread discontent with the media—and every poll suggests that it cuts across nearly all political and social lines—is coupled with a general loss of faith in the country's established political institutions, most especially in the ability of the government to act as a force for the public good.

To be sure, not everyone believes that political bloggers have had much of an effect on American political life. "No one reads blogs," claimed Frank Barnako of CBS.MarketWatch.com. Or so he wrote on the morning after the November 2 presidential election when, in his view, the only real clout political bloggers demonstrated on election day was in publishing erroneous exit poll data suggesting Kerry would win, thereby falsely inflating the Democrats' hopes and killing a sixty-point stock market rally.

"At least some [Wall Street] traders read blogs, then, and act on what they read," Barnako observed. "Not so young voters. Advertisers like Nike and Audi think Weblogs are the medium to reach young voters. So where [were] the youth? Not reading political blogs. The percentage of young voters who cast ballots was the same as four years ago."

His conclusion?

"Political blogging is like Ralph Nader. Nobody pays attention."

Perhaps Barnako can be excused for his snarky jab at bloggers' errors in calling the election. After all, the premature triumphalism of some bloggers who claim that they have thoroughly supplanted the mainstream media as the voters' most trusted source of political news is not only infantile, it's downright annoying. Anyone who attempts to inject even a little bit of humility into their ranks, therefore, is to be commended.

But that said, it would be extremely shortsighted to disregard the enormous influence that bloggers are beginning to have upon the American political scene. So far, that influence has largely been felt at the periphery of political life. Nonetheless, despite their often divisive effects upon the electorate, bloggers are transforming the political process itself—and more important, the ordinary citizen's relationship to it—in ways that seem likely to lead to a more representative and participatory American democracy.

Any serious discussion of the impact of political blogging, of course, must begin with an examination of how it has reshaped the way in which Americans get their political news and discuss the political controversies of the day. Because on that score, at least, political blogs really have become, in the words of *Time* magazine, "a genuine alternative to mainstream news outlets, a shadow media empire that is rivaling networks and newspapers in power and influence."

Consider, for example, that during the crucial August period leading up to the 2004 presidential election, the ten most popular political blogs collectively had 28 million visits from readers, which rivaled traffic to the three 24/7 online cable news networks. One of those, the liberal blog DailyKos, drew 7 million reader visits alone that month, which beat Fox News's 5.7 million online visits. And these numbers don't even include the conservative Drudge Report, whose traffic alone often equals that of any of the websites of the major news networks. While still far short of the total viewers of the nightly TV news programs, these numbers suggest that political blogs had more than a little influence on voter opinion (although, as we will demonstrate later, this influence appears to have been wielded primarily among more committed rather than undecided voters).

Since the election, political blogs have continued to demonstrate an extraordinary ability to attract and keep readership. Almost six months after the 2004 presidential election, for example, DailyKos was still attracting

434,132 visits each day, or about 11 million visits per month. The conservative blog Instapundit.com, the second most popular political blog, was drawing 129,289 visits per day, or nearly 4 million visits each month. All told, the combined readership of the top ten political blogs was even higher than it was in August of 2004, with more than 31 million visits from readers. (Please note that it is impossible to determine how many of these visits were from *separate* readers.)

According to a Pew Research Center study, there were over 33 million readers of blogs in November of 2004—at least 11 million of them regular readers of political blogs. These numbers, of course, are only a fraction of the number of regular consumers of political news from traditional mainstream television, radio, and newspaper outlets. But the numbers of people who engage in political discussion or get political news from *all* online sources, including blogs, is skyrocketing and currently numbers over 75 million Americans. And among those who do go online for political news, the influence of bloggers appears to be more substantial than the traffic numbers would at first suggest.

A chart released last year by the blog search engine Technorati showed that, as expected, the top twenty or so mainstream media websites continue to garner the highest visitor traffic from Internet users—no surprise, given their generally superior journalism and incumbency. But it also shows that *collectively*, the influence of *all* political blogs—inbound referrals from other web pages being a good indicator of how much attention is being paid to them—rivals and even exceeds the attention paid to *all* mainstream media websites.

Clearly, political blogs have become a vital source of news and opinion for millions of Americans and an alternative to traditional newspapers and television. But what accounts for the rapid growth in their readership and influence?

First and foremost, of course, is the fact that the media has lost a portion of the respect and trust it once held among the public. A substantial number of Americans, perhaps even a majority, believe that the media is either biased or incompetent or both. And why not? First there was evidence "proving" Iraq had weapons of mass destruction; then . . . oops, suddenly there wasn't. First there were documents "proving" President Bush received favorable treatment during his stint in the Texas Air National Guard, then . . . oops, there weren't. Add to this shameful record a variety of plagiarism and circulation scandals, some even involving the nation's "newspaper of record," the *New York Times*, and you've got all the ingredients of a major meltdown of media credibility.

The truth is that many people don't necessarily trust what they read in the papers or see on television anymore—in fact, according to a Pew Research Center poll taken during the contentious 2004 election, 45 percent of Americans said they believe little or nothing of what they read in their daily newspapers. And they can hardly be blamed, for in many respects mainstream media reportage no longer reflects the interests, attitudes, beliefs, and priorities of the majority of Americans. Consider, for example, the fact that by all measures the United States is far and away the most religiously minded of all the major Western industrial nations. A substantial majority of Americans say that religion is very important in their lives and claim to regularly participate in religious activities. Their religiosity is reflected in the fact that religion is the third most widely syndicated radio format, and religious book publishers continue to set new sales records each year.

And yet, according to a 1997 study of media coverage by Stewart M. Hoover and Douglas K. Wagner, "Religion is remarkable by its absence from [most] mainstream American media." Although most major newspapers have at least one full-time religion writer, the writers' coverage is certainly not daily and in any event rarely finds its way into the front sections of the newspapers unless it involves a major controversy or an event like a papal succession. This contrast between the majority's religious interests and the mainstream media's religion coverage is even more pronounced in the arena of television broadcasting, where until recently there were *no* religion correspondents on network news and only three of the more than six hundred TV stations affiliated with the major networks had any religion reporters at all.

Even some of the media's leading lights concede there is a major contradiction here. As CNN commentator Jeff Greenfield noted, "When it comes to the day-to-day presence of religion in American media, it's a very different story. In fact, usually it's no story at all." Added Dan Rather, who is widely regarded by conservatives as arch-liberal and anti-religion, "Religion [is] consistently underreported. That's especially unfortunate when you remember how many of the worst conflicts today are born of religious misunderstanding. There isn't a news organization that wouldn't benefit from greater attention to the coverage of religion."

Greenfield and Rather made those statements a decade ago. And since then, of course, religious programming on cable and radio has grown dramatically. But traditional mainstream media coverage of religion has changed little, if at all, during this time. And anyone who thinks that the media's neglect of religious issues and themes hasn't had political consequences—most especially in the public's growing disaffection from the media itself—is simply not paying attention.

As a matter of fact, an internal review committee of the *New York Times* announced on May 9, 2005, a number of steps the newspaper should take to restore reader confidence, including "increase our coverage of religion in America" and "cover the country in a fuller way," with more reporting from rural areas and a broader range of lifestyle and cultural stories.

Indeed, the mainstream media's ability to constrict the coverage of political debate to a relatively narrow range of issues and voices has had profound consequences for the shape and character of American democracy. Numerous studies over the last thirty years have demonstrated that the media sets the agenda for political debate—i.e., determines what Americans believe to be the most important issues—by the simple and obvious practice of paying focused attention to some issues and ignoring or minimizing others. In Maxwell McCombs's and Donald Shaw's seminal book, *The Emergence of American Political Issues,* they conclude that "the mass media may not be successful in telling us what to think, but they are stunningly successful in telling us what to think about."

And it is largely in rebellion against this mainstream media "agenda setting" that political bloggers first emerged and attracted large audiences. As Glenn Reynolds, who runs the popular Instapundit.com blog, has noted, "Prior to World War 2, Big Media was countervailed by other institutions:

political parties, churches, labor unions, even widespread political discussion groups. The weblog phenomenon may be viewed as the return of such influences—a broadening of the community of discourse to include, well, the community."

But it is not only by broadening the range of voices and issues for political debate that bloggers, especially political bloggers, have found an audience. The public is also quite clearly fed up with the way that the mainstream media has vulgarized the once-proud traditions of "objectivity" and "balance" in political reporting. Driven by their incessant urge to squeeze some sort of "entertainment" value out of even the most serious news events (the better to compete with "reality TV," or so media executives think), newspapers and television in practice now routinely define objectivity and balance to mean nothing more than allowing two partisan spokespeople from opposite ends of the political spectrum to scream at each other for two minutes or two paragraphs—as if that has anything to do with getting at the truth.

So bastardized has the media's practice of "balance" become, in fact, that the host of the television comedy *The Daily Show*, Jon Stewart—a man who doesn't even claim to uphold the higher principles of journalism—went on CNN's *Crossfire* to blast liberal pundit Paul Begala and conservative critic Tucker Carlson for "hurting America" by constantly hurling unsubstantiated accusations at each other with little real debate. As Stewart and *The Daily Show* team put it in *America: The Book*, "[The press] have violated a trust. Was the president successful in *convincing* the country? Who gives a shit! Why not tell us if what he said was *true*?"

Geneva Overholser, a professor at the University of Missouri School of Journalism and the Pulitzer Prize–winning former editor of the *Des Moines Register* and ombudsman of the *Washington Post*, acknowledged that "this was the year when it finally became unmistakably clear that 'objectivity' has outlived its usefulness as an ethical touchstone for journalism." As she told the *Hartford Courant*: "The way it is currently construed, 'objectivity' . . . produces a rigid orthodoxy. It leads to a false balance of 'on the one hand, on the other hand' stories that make the two 'hands' appear equal even when the factual weight lies 98 percent on one side."

Added Jeffrey Dvorkin, ombudsman for National Public Radio: "The most important change [in the media last year] was the increasingly defensive posture that most journalistic organizations have assumed in order to avoid any charge of media bias. Mainstream media has sought to avoid controversy, even when it goes against their own journalistic values."

And this is what the media's own think about their profession!

No wonder, then, that the public has become thirsty for *real* information—news unfiltered by editors who "know what's best for us," facts boldly stated and supported, and unvarnished opinion openly expressed for all to see and judge. And blogs gave it to them, in spades.

Indeed, readers seem to greatly appreciate the open, honest partisanship and political advocacy exhibited on many blogs and seem undisturbed by their refusal to pose as "objective." The very concept of "objectivity" itself, after all, is only a recent construct in the media—a twentieth-century response to the consolidation of a once diverse and highly partisan media into single-voice monopolies, as well as to the wire services' economic need to distribute news feeds that would be acceptable to newspapers of all political persuasions. For most of our history, in fact—from the time of the Revolution on up to the mid–twentieth century—the American public was gifted with thousands of newspapers and magazines published by political parties, churches and religious organizations, and even labor unions (the latter still published, as late as the early 1950s, over eight hundred pro-labor, anti-business newspapers reaching 30 million people). The Princeton sociologist Paul Starr has estimated that throughout the nineteenth century, some 80 percent of American newspapers were openly partisan in their viewpoint. Even well into the early twentieth century, every large city fielded anywhere from half a dozen to twenty or more daily newspapers—each one expressing and advocating a distinct political viewpoint (not only Democrat and Republican, but socialist, anarchist, protectionist, pro–free trade, etc.).

Thus, in filling the vacuum of political coverage created by a timid mainstream media hobbled by an outmoded definition of pro forma "objectivity," bloggers appear to be leading us "back to the future" to a wildly diverse and openly partisan media environment. They are recreating the nineteenth-century-style era of the political broadside and the "penny press"—only updated, of course, to the online age in which we now live.

This does not, of course, mean that traditional mainstream media is dead—any more than the Reformation of the sixteenth century killed off the reign of the popes. But just as the estimated 6 million pamphlets printed by Protestant reformers did bring an end to the notion of unchallenged papal authority, so, too, are today's political blogs bringing an end to the *unchallenged* authority of the mainstream media to set the political agenda.

This could well have large effects on the character of our democracy. After all, if the mainstream corporate media that cemented itself as the sole "objective" arbiter of political discourse in the last half of the twentieth century helped to produce a sharp decline in political participation and public trust, then the return of a more diverse, partisan, and *engaged* media could well bring with it a resurgence in citizen participation and engagement in the political process.

"What democracy requires is public debate, not information," wrote the media critic Christopher Lasch. "Unless information is [accompanied] by sustained public debate, most of it will be irrelevant at best, misleading and manipulative at worst." Well, if there's one thing that political bloggers do well, it's to combine information with debate. This will inevitably lead to a strengthening of the civic mindedness of the citizenry—a return, at least to some degree, to the extraordinarily high levels of political participation that were present during the nineteenth-century era of partisan media.

To be sure, bloggers offer their readers not just political attitude, but political scoops as well, often in ways that only further dramatize the passivity of the mainstream media. It was not the mainstream media, after all, but Josh Marshall's Talking Points Memo blog and Glenn Reynolds's Instapundit blog that uncovered and reported the speech Senator Trent Lott gave at former Senator Strom Thurmond's one hundredth birthday party on December 5, 2002, praising his segregationist views. The mainstream media ignored the story at first, but as it continued to make the rounds of other blogs and generate public anger, *Meet the Press* finally picked it up. Lott, who was due to become Senate majority leader in 2003, stepped down from his leadership position.

Since that first blow for blogger reporting was struck, there have been many other examples where blogs were the first to provide readers with information they would not otherwise have gotten. It was the TheMemoryHole.com blog that scooped the media by publishing Defense Department photos of the caskets of soldiers who had died in the Iraqi War—photos which (for obvious reasons) the Bush administration preferred to keep from the public. It was the DailyKos blog that first revealed that a Bush campaign ad called "Whatever It Takes" used a photograph of a presidential speech that had been digitally altered to make the crowd seem larger than it actually was (the Bush campaign quickly pulled the ad). It was BlogActive.com that first published audio tapes of Republican congressman Edward L. Schrock, a vocal opponent of gay rights and key supporter of several anti-gay laws, soliciting sex acts from men on a telephone sex line (the congressman quickly resigned). And in the most famous coup of all for political bloggers, it was the conservative Powerline.com blog that first published information exposing as forgeries the documents that Dan Rather used in his *60 Minutes* story on President Bush's service in the National Guard (and yes, Rather soon resigned as *CBS Evening News* anchor as well).

Not bad for some amateur "journalists" with no formal training. But before political bloggers let their newfound success and popular influence go to their heads—on second thought, it's already too late for that—it's worth pointing out that for all their justified critiques of media credibility, at least some of these bloggers have credibility problems of their own.

Take "Mike," who runs the Rathergate.com blog that spearheaded a petition drive demanding the resignation of Dan Rather. According to the *Chicago Tribune*, "Mike" is actually Mike Krempasky, a Republican political operative who serves as the political director for American Target Advertising, a Virginia firm run by Richard Viguerie, the well-known conservative strategist credited with inventing the political direct-mail campaign tactics used to great success by Ronald Reagan and other GOP candidates.

And then there's "Buckhead," the mysterious blogger on FreeRepublic.com who was among the first to raise questions about the documents Dan Rather used in his *60 Minutes* story on Bush's Guard service. According to the *Los Angeles Times*, it turns out that "Buckhead" is actually Harry MacDougald, an Atlanta lawyer closely connected to conservative causes who helped draft a petition urging the Arkansas Supreme Court to disbar President Bill Clinton following the Monica Lewinsky scandal.

Besides the credibility problems of a few bloggers, there is also the well-known truth that it is often easier to criticize the mainstream media for the way it covers the news than it is to actually cover all the news in the way it should be covered. This point was highlighted during a heated conference in Boston in January of 2005 called "Bloggers, Journalism, and Credibility" that was attended by both bloggers and journalists. During the debates, blog evangelist Jeff Jarvis criticized the *New York Times*'s Jill Abramson for the paper's failure to cover an antiterrorism march in Baghdad that an Iraqi blogger had photographed. Abramson replied that given the expense and danger involved in reporting from that city, she justifiably felt the paper was doing a pretty good job covering at least most of the important developments in that country. "Just to sustain a news office in Baghdad," Abramson asked, "does anyone know what that costs?"

A better question would have been, "How many other bloggers covered that demonstration?" The answer, it would appear, was very few if any.

As blogger and journalist Ezra Klein observed in a report on the conference posted on his own eponymous blog, the blogosphere sometimes seems populated with "an endless army of critics well equipped to carp and stab at minute flaws in their betters, but rarely able to excel in the skill they find so easy to judge."

Touché . . . or is it just sour grapes? Regardless of whether you think the mainstream media is hopelessly corrupt or perhaps could merely benefit from some new (blogger) blood, it is clear that the days are over when the mainstream media could exercise a monopoly over what political news and opinion would be delivered to the people. A new breed of citizen journalists has crashed the gates erected by Big Media and succeeded in pushing new voices, new issues, and fresh new opinions into the nation's political discourse—a fact that, to its credit, the mainstream media has widely reported. Bloggers, it would seem, have clearly earned a place at the buffet table of media offerings from which the public now obtains its political news and opinion.

But what have political bloggers accomplished with their newfound influence? Political blogs, after all, are not just political persuaders; they are also (in Lenin's famous description of the political newspaper) "collective organizers." As the rather prescient young communist wrote in 1903, fourteen years before his followers seized state power and founded the Union of Soviet Socialist Republics: " [A political newspaper] may be likened to the scaffolding round a building under construction, which marks the contours of the structure and facilitates communication between the builders, enabling them to distribute the work and to view the common results achieved by their organized labor."

And so it is with political blogs. (In fact, if Lenin were alive today, he would probably be a political blogger, although he would have to lose his pedantic and overlong sentence structure.) For if the short-lived presidential candidacy of Howard Dean proves anything, it's that political bloggers can mobilize and unite large groups of citizens in ways that make insurgent candidates more viable—and that erode Big Money and top-down party control not only of candidate selection but of the issues that drive campaigns.

A fair amount of the credit for Dean's early success—and for the success of other candidates who adopted many of the same online organizing tactics Dean used in his campaign—goes to former campaign manager Joe Trippi. As he told the *New York Times* when he first launched the campaign's blog and started organizing online, "The other campaigns laughed at us. I mean, we were the bar scene out of *Star Wars*—that's what they thought a meetup was," referring to the hundreds of thousands of citizens who attended Internet-organized face-to-face support meetings across the country.

And as he told the authors of this book in an interview, it wasn't just the scorn from more established Democratic candidates that he and his candidate confronted. "Both parties have constructed rules that make it near impossible for an insurgent campaign to get off the ground," he explained. "It's all part of the plan to get a well-known, status quo, establishment candidate on the nomination."

In fact, Trippi goes on to argue, "The Dean campaign would never have gotten off the ground without the Internet. We started with 432 active supporters in the field and that grew to 650,000 in thirteen months. Almost all of it was through the Net. No party insiders would have given us a plug nickel to bet on even getting into contention, let alone getting where we eventually got to."

Central to the Internet-enabled campaign strategy first developed by Trippi (and later copied by all the other candidates) was the unprecedented ability of blogs to serve as fund-raising vehicles, opinion research tools, and grassroots mobilizing engines. With enthusiastic bloggers spreading the Dean message and encouraging their readers to open their wallets, for example, Dean raised over $45 million in online donations that averaged less than $100 per contributor—more than any Democratic candidate in history had ever raised, online or off, including via traditional $1,000-a-plate dinners. The eventual Democratic nominee, John Kerry, would himself raise $60 million online. Nothing like this had ever been done before.

Political blogs also served as sometimes surprisingly effective opinion research tools that helped the various candidates test out ideas and campaign slogans. Indeed, political blogs have in many ways transformed politics from a spectator sport into a participatory one. "Today, it seems that every online political junkie secretly—if not openly—believes he's James Carville, a strategist possessed of such uncontested political genius that a candidate would be crazy not to listen to his advice," observed the *Guardian* newspaper of London. "It's possible to find [bloggers] who'll claim that they could do at least as good a job in winning political races as veteran consultants on the inside."

And in some cases, they're probably right. As the *Guardian* reported: "At least some of them were warning that the Swift Boat Veterans for Truth would be a problem for Kerry and that he should respond hard and fast." Kerry didn't, of course, to his everlasting regret. In a similar vein, DailyKos blogger Markos Moulitsas Zuniga told the authors that Kerry's campaign speech in which he criticized Bush's calls for an "ownership society"—Kerry noted that if Bush were really being honest, he'd also accept "ownership" of the disaster in Iraq and the sluggish economy at home—came from a posting on his blog.

What gives some bloggers their new-found strategic savvy, of course, is their access to information that just four years ago was reserved only for highly placed political consultants. Bloggers can now easily and quickly get their hands on polling data, fund-raising data, media-buy data, every TV ad and press release issued by the candidates—not to mention insider dish on what the media's covering and what it's not covering and why. Building on their access to this once-privileged information, bloggers and their online respondents now don't hesitate to submit their often-dumb, but sometimes quite insightful, ideas to candidates about how they should run their campaigns.

But probably the most powerful role that political blogs played during the recent election cycle was as catalysts for grassroots citizen mobilization. And on this score, the Republicans proved to be at least as adept, if not more so, than the Democrats in using blogs and other online vehicles to rally their base and swing them into action.

Although the official Bush campaign blog did not invite comments from readers and was more top-down in orientation, the party's online efforts nonetheless succeeded in signing up half a million interested volunteers as early as seven months before the election, noted Michelle Levander of Mediachannel .org. In addition, the GOP website's campaign loyalty program called "Team Leader" enabled volunteers to collect points for writing a letter or soliciting a new party member that could then be redeemed for coffee mugs or golf caps emblazoned with the party logo. Using sophisticated web tools, the Bush-Cheney website followed a step-by-step blueprint aimed at converting interested Republicans into committed volunteers. "Within minutes of signing up," Levander reported, "the Web site creates a tailored 'activity center' for each user. It provides contact information for each user's local radio stations and newspaper. There are sample letters they can send on key issues, as well as a tracking system that allows the user—and the Party—to keep score each time someone writes a letter to the editor or encourages a friend to sign up. Regional campaign offices also take advantage of the database."

Not to take anything away from the Republican Web strategists—their man won the election, after all—but Trippi and others maintain that the GOP was not the only party to use the Web to unleash the energy and initiative of millions of citizens and allow them to help shape the course of campaigns.

In the Dean campaign, for example, one blogger's suggestion resulted in 115,632 handwritten letters being sent from the candidate's supporters to eligible voters in the upcoming Iowa caucuses and New Hampshire. Indeed, grassroots activists even helped decide major questions of strategy. In November of 2003, the official Campaign for America blog organized an online vote, asking supporters whether the campaign should opt out of the federal funding system, and 700,000 people voted to have Dean opt out. They trusted that through their efforts, Dean would raise more money than he would receive in federal funds and at the same time be free of the system's restrictions.

"That was an historic vote," Trippi claims. "It happened online. It was the first time in history a Democrat had opted out of the federal funding system and it was only the second time any candidate had ever done it—the first one, of course, being George Bush in 2000. Five days later John Kerry held a press conference and said he was going to opt out as well. If he had not opted out, if that online vote had never occurred, he would have been dead."

Indeed, the impact of political bloggers in reaching out to and mobilizing the grassroots is difficult to overestimate. "It's always been hard to organize the grassroots," notes the activist blogger Jon Lebkowsky. "One problem anyone who wants to do grassroots organizing faces these days is that communities are more atomized, more anonymous. A lot of people are even afraid to open their door to strangers. But they're not afraid to talk to people online."

But even more than their ability to reach large numbers of people, the real influence of political bloggers stems from their ability to reach the *right* people—the so-called influencers among the public—and motivate them to involve their friends, family, and coworkers on behalf of key issues or candidates. Notes DailyKos's Moulitsas: "The marketing industry talks about the 'influentials,' right? I mean, the holy grail of successful marketing is to reach that 10 percent or so of the public who are the most passionate about—or who are experts on—any given topic. When it comes to political influentials," Moulitsas adds, "according to marketing studies, they are even more influential in their sphere than other types of influentials are. And that's who I've got at DailyKos. I don't have many swing voters reading DailyKos, and I don't really want them. I'm preaching to the choir for a reason. It's because we're trying to organize, we're trying to fundraise, we're trying to win elections.

They're the activists. They're incredibly influential. And they can be the key to winning elections."

But alas, as the 2004 election proved, activists alone cannot win elections. And therein lay the weakness of both Trippi's Web-enabled grassroots strategy and of political blogging itself. In the case of the Dean effort, the activist core mobilized so effectively by blogs and other online tools became the primary if not *only* focus of the campaign. As Ezra Klein wrote in an article for the *Washington Monthly*: "The same [web] technologies that enabled Trippi to decentralize [the campaign effort] also shifted its internal balance of power, ceding Dean's identity and message in no small part to the die-hard activists who had made him the frontrunner." The result was that every time Dean tried to shed his firebrand image and reposition himself as a moderate before the larger voting public, the hard-core activists at the heart of the campaign yanked him back into the hot zone. There is no better measure of how ultimately isolating an activist-only strategy is than the fact that seven months after Dean quit the race, his official blog was still getting thirty-three thousand hits a day, almost as much as it was during the height of the campaign. According to Klein, "That's because the Deaniacs long ago stopped coming to talk to Howard Dean [or to potential voters] and began coming to talk to each other."

Preaching to the choir—it was both the greatest strength and the deadliest sin of Democratic political bloggers in the last campaign. And for all the media attention devoted to grassroots Democratic activists, it was ironically the Republican National Committee (RNC) that showed a way around this dilemma during the 2004 campaign. Here's how the *Washington Post* explained the Republican approach:

"They were smart. They came into our neighborhoods. They came into Democratic areas with very specific targeted messages to take Democratic voters away from us,' Democratic National Committee Chairman Terence R. McAuliffe said. 'They were much more sophisticated in their message delivery.' "

But even more important, using nontraditional media, the GOP spent half its money "motivating and mobilizing people already inclined to vote for

Bush, but who were either unregistered or who often failed to vote—'soft' Republicans," noted the *Post*. "Under [pollster Matthew] Dowd's direction, the RNC began investing in extensive voter research. One of the most striking findings, according to Republican consultants, was the ineffectiveness of traditional phone banks and direct mail that targeted voters in overwhelmingly Republican precincts. The problem: Only 15 percent of all GOP voters lived in precincts that voted Republican by 65 percent or more. Worse, an even smaller percentage of 'soft' Republicans, the 2004 target constituency, lived in such precincts."

So what did the GOP do? According to the *Post*, "Republican firms, including TargetPoint Consultants and National Media Inc., delved into commercial databases that pinpointed consumer buying patterns and television-watching habits. Surveys of people on these consumer data lists were then used to determine 'anger points.' Merging this data, in turn, enabled those running direct mail, precinct walking and phone bank programs to target each voter with a tailored message."

Bingo! The above is an embryonic example of a new paradigm in economics and politics that author Chris Anderson famously called the "long tail." In economics, it refers to the observable fact that products that are in low demand or have low sales volume can collectively make up a market share that rivals or even exceeds the relatively few bestseller and blockbuster hit products. In politics, the "long tail" refers to the myriad streams of independent political opinion in America whose collective vote-getting ability, if only harnessed and directed, could potentially rival that of the two main parties. All that's needed to capitalize on the collective market (or political) power of non-hit products (or independent voters) is a low-cost distribution and communication channel that can aggregate and reach those consumers (or voters)—i.e., the Internet.

And herein lies the possibility of bloggers' greatest influence on the American political process. Indeed, political bloggers may over time prove capable of mobilizing large enough sectors of the voting public unsatisfied with the limited choice offered by the two main political parties into a collective voting bloc sizable enough to sustain the launch of a viable third political party.

Still, it's worth remembering that for all their awesome potential to affect the political process in America, blogs are only tools to encourage greater and more diverse political engagement. Absent a compelling vision for a new American consensus, they cannot bring about a radical restructuring of American political life.

As for Joe Trippi, he believes that the Democrats' biggest mistake was in treating their blog-fueled constituency like some giant online ATM machine. "If Kerry had thought about the Internet differently and realized that it could be used for a lot more than just raising money, I think they would have done better. They only asked, what do we do to raise money? They should have asked, what do we do to [mobilize] volunteers?"

There is more than a little truth in what Trippi is saying. According to one study, three out of four Kerry campaign emails between March and November of 2004 made direct appeals for money, compared with fewer than one in five Bush campaign emails. In contrast, 78 percent of Bush campaign emails during that same period urged people to forward the message to a friend, whereas only 5 percent of Kerry emails did so. And 22 percent of Bush campaign emails offered a way to contact an online team of supporters, versus exactly *none* of the millions of Kerry emails sent out during that time.

Like the elephant in the room that no one talks about, however, Trippi's analysis ignores the ultimately fatal effect of Kerry's inability to connect with the majority of heartland voters on issues that most deeply concerned them. Throughout the 1970s and 1980s, Democratic candidates dismissed the public's growing concerns over rising crime rates and a welfare system that seemed to create generations of dependency in its wake as smokescreens for backward voters' racist attitudes. They lost all but one election. In the 1990s, Clinton finally acknowledged that crime and welfare reform were indeed issues that needed to be addressed. And by putting forth a Democratic alternative toward solving these problems, he won. But in the 2004 campaign, facing deep voter concerns over family values and a seeming drift in America's moral footing, Kerry ignored the bitter lesson learned by his Democratic forebears and focused his campaign instead solely on the economy and Iraq. The result should not have been a surprise.

As the Harvard University political theorist Michael J. Sandel put it:

"The Democrats have ceded to Republicans a monopoly on the moral and spiritual sources of American politics. They will not recover as a party until they again have candidates who can speak to those moral and spiritual yearnings" and put forward their own solutions to these concerns.

Still, Joe Trippi is probably right when he says that the role political blogs and online organizing played in the 2004 election will go down in history as being just as transformative as the role television played during the 1960 Nixon-Kennedy debates. For just as the tyranny of the ninety-second TV story format ushered in the era of sound-bite politics, it is likely that blogs will bring about a return to the more substantive issues-oriented campaigning that has been so absent from electoral politics these past fifty years. As a result, victory will go not just to the master of the sound bite but to the candidate best able to mobilize and direct what author Hugh Hewitt called blog-fueled "opinion storms" around key issues.

All one has to do is look at the role bloggers played in rebutting Dan Rather's flawed *60 Minutes* report on President Bush's National Guard service—and the resulting uptick of several points in support for Bush—to get a taste of what is possible here.

Whether or not bloggers can in the long run help build enough of a grassroots opinion storm and unite it behind a single candidate to actually decide an election remains an open question, however. For it is in the realm of consensus building and the healing of divisions that one can see one of blogging's real weaknesses.

As previously noted, political bloggers' principal practical effect lay in mobilizing the base and the activists within each party. They were less effective at reaching across the red state versus blue state divide to bring people together. As activist Jon Lebkowsky pointed out, "You're going to have trouble reaching beyond disagreement unless you listen to other people's views with respect." And—let's be honest here—bloggers are not exactly famous for *listening* to opposing viewpoints with respect.

"Blogs are fun," observed Ezra Klein on his own blog. "I like them. But they're a flawed and problematic medium. They encourage polarization and extremism rather than debate and understanding. They turn on snark and mockery more often than facts and agile argument." In fact, wrote Klein,

"I've not yet—and not for lack of trying—found the blog where smart and engaged partisans are respectfully speaking to each other . . . where the point is to inform and enrich rather than enrage and destroy."

And according to C. W. Nevius of the *San Francisco Chronicle*, "That's what makes those who are going to live in this brave new world of [blog-enhanced] politics a little nervous. [Bloggers are] talk radio without the FCC, opinion columnists without the editors." Adds West Texas A&M University professor Leigh Browning, "Blogs are inevitably going to have more impact on the extreme left and extreme right."

Pay attention to the word "extreme." For although it is certainly true that bloggers did not invent extremist politics—indeed, the deepening divisions within America are the long-simmering outgrowth of myriad and complex forces having to do with the growing sense of alienation and powerlessness in society—there can be no doubt that blogging has given new voice and new reach to the extremist strain in American society.

This extremism has lain at the periphery of American politics throughout our long history. More than forty years ago, in fact, the historian Richard Hofstadter published a famous article in *Harper's Magazine* entitled "The Paranoid Style in American Politics." In it, he described the key features of the extremist conspiracy theories that have played such a dark role in American political life since even before the Revolution. Hofstadter wrote:

> The paranoid [extremist] sees the fate of conspiracy in apocalyptic terms. As a member of the avant-garde who is capable of perceiving the conspiracy before it is fully obvious to an as yet unaroused public, the paranoid is a militant. He does not see social conflict as something to be mediated and compromised, in the manner of the working politician. Since what is at stake is always a conflict between absolute good and absolute evil, what is necessary is not compromise but the will to fight things out to a finish. This demand for total triumph leads to the formulation of hopelessly unrealistic goals, and since these goals are not even remotely attainable, failure constantly heightens the paranoid's sense of frustration. Even partial success leaves him with the same feeling of powerlessness with which he

began, [which] only strengthens his awareness of the vast and terrifying quality of the enemy he opposes.

Doesn't that sound a bit too much like the two bloggers quoted at the beginning of this essay? Multiply them by many thousands more—and instead of an audience of thousands, as such people spoke to in bygone eras, give them now an audience of millions—and you begin to grasp the heightened danger. Right now, today, they are preaching to us that the government is ruled by a conspiracy of the right (or the left), that the 9/11 catastrophe was knowingly aided and abetted by Big Business (or the Jews) anxious to give the American people an external enemy to focus on instead of the disastrous economic situation that has resulted from their own perfidy and greed, that Osama Bin Laden has (depending on their political stance) either already been captured and is waiting to be trotted out at the appropriate time or else *could* have been captured were it not for the machinations of America's hidden traitors. No matter how preposterous the claim, I guarantee that you can find it argued eloquently and vociferously somewhere in the blogosphere, supported by an encyclopedia of "facts."

But lest we all have a good laugh at the absurdities often found on the Internet, we would do well to heed Hofstadter's principal point: "The idea of the paranoid style as a force in politics would have little contemporary relevance if it were applied only to men with profoundly disturbed minds. It is the use of paranoid modes of expression by more or less normal people that makes the phenomenon significant." And what makes it especially *dangerous* today, of course, is that they are attempting to fill the vacuum left by an enfeebled mainstream media.

Still, as a blogger who goes by the name "Scottxyz" noted, "The polarization that blogs have produced is problematic, but the alternative—a homogenized media—is worse." His point is well taken. As William Powers wrote recently in the *Atlantic* magazine, "The fractious, disunited, politically partisan media of the nineteenth century heightened public awareness of politics, and taught the denizens of a new democracy how to be citizens. Maybe [they were] on to something."

Indeed, they *were* on to something. By bringing to life once again the diverse and partisan media that played such a decisive role in shaping our participatory American democracy during its first century and a half, political bloggers have opened up exciting new opportunities for a more engaged citizenry to reshape this country's political future for the better. Whether or not they can help bring about the national unity necessary to realize such political change, however, remains to be seen.

THE SECRET OF DEAN'S SUCCESS
(AND THE DEMOCRATS' FAILURE)

An Interview with Joe Trippi

When Howard Dean announced that he was running for President his mother told New York magazine: "I thought it was preposterous, the silliest thing I'd ever heard." Dean had less than five hundred supporters and $100,000 in the bank. Just over one year later, when his campaign came to a screeching halt (literally) during his Iowa concession speech, he had raised more money than any Democrat in history. Campaign manager Joe Trippi was the man behind the Internet phenomenon that raised the money and galvanized the followers.

Trippi had worked on the presidential campaigns of Edward Kennedy, Walter Mondale, Gary Hart, and Dick Gephardt. But in the 1990s he gave up politics for work as a corporate consultant in Silicon Valley. He joined the Dean campaign in February 2003 and used every resource the Internet had to offer. He rallied grassroots support through Meetup.com, where Dean followers could contact each other and organize fund-raising events—in September 2003 alone, forty thousand people held 664 events across America. Meanwhile, at Dean headquarters, a team of Web-savvy staffers manned computers to allow thousands of people across America to give millions of dollars, mostly in donations of less than $100 each.

But the nerve center of the Dean campaign was Blog for America, the campaign's official weblog, which received hundreds of comments from Dean supporters every day, offering advice and suggestions and discussing the latest news stories. In his book, The Revolution Will Not Be Televised, Trippi

*says: "The blogosphere was where we got ideas, feedback, support, money—
everything a campaign needs to live."*

*Trippi was also instrumental in Dean's decision to forego federal match
funding, which would have limited the amount of money he could raise—
a move that was followed by John Kerry's decision to do the same. Dean
dropped out in February 2004, but the legacy of his online campaign went on
to affect the rest of that year's race. In the run-up to the election, George
Bush was expected to outspend the Democrats by between three and five to
one. In 2000, he spent $125 million to Al Gore's $45 million. But in 2004,
John Kerry raised $182 million—$60 million of which was raised online—to
Bush's $214 million.*

*Although Trippi gives credit to the Net for the financial muscle, he main-
tains the real power of blogging is the power it gives individuals to make a
real change: "It's not about the guy standing on the podium. It's about everybody he's talking to." His blog can be found at joetrippi.com/joesblog.*

Why was the Internet crucial for Howard Dean's presidential campaign?

Both parties have constructed rules that make it near impossible for an
insurgent campaign to get off the ground. It's all part of the plan to get a well-
known, status quo, establishment candidate the nomination.

There's no doubt that the Dean campaign would never have gotten off
the ground without the Internet. We started with 432 active supporters in the
field and that grew to 650,000 in thirteen months. Almost all of it was
through the Net. No party insiders would have given us a plug nickel to bet
on even getting into contention, let alone getting where we eventually got to.

Why were you so successful?

I think the Net finally reached maturity. There have been candidacies and
even campaigns in the past, like Gary Hart's campaign in 1984, that would
have had the ability to galvanize people over the Internet, but the Net wasn't
there. I think even McCain's campaign in 2000 was too early. You still didn't

have enough people who were online, who had used their credit card with Amazon.com or at an auction on eBay, and who understood the power that they had at their terminal. I actually think that four years from now there will be people looking back at the Dean campaign, thinking how primitive it was compared to the tools that will be available for that campaign.

So what did Dean have that previous candidates didn't?

In 2000, the blogosphere had just begun. There were some blogs, but nowhere near the proliferation that we saw in 2003. In three years, it had gone from ten blogs to three million blogs. But you needed a campaign to understand that the Net was out there.

A lot of the people who had been close to Governor Dean during the previous seven years in Vermont thought the same way everybody else thought of the Internet—that it was an interesting waste of time. So battles had to be fought inside the Dean campaign. It's one of the battles that happened inside the Kerry campaign as well.

How did you convince people that online organizing was important?

Dean raised about $59 million. Of that, something like three-quarters was raised in individual contributions of around $77 over the Internet. Before this, no Democrat had ever raised over $45 million. Ever. So the money spoke for itself.

Plus we attracted hundreds of thousands of supporters. You've also got to remember that in November of 2003, the Dean campaign held an Internet vote asking its supporters whether it should opt out of the federal funding system or turn over its continued fund-raising to the grass roots—700,000 people voted to tell Dean to opt out.

That was an historic vote. It happened online. It was the first time in history a Democrat had opted out of the federal funding system and it was only the second time any candidate had ever done it—the first one, of course, being George Bush in 2000.

Five days later John Kerry held a press conference and said he was going to opt out as well. If he had not opted out, if that online vote had never occurred, he would have been dead. After Dean fell out of the race, all the Democrat online support went to Kerry to stop Bush, and that's what made it competitive the rest of the way.

So regardless of whatever problems the Kerry campaign had, the one thing that worked and that kept Democrats competitive was the blogosphere and the effect Internet fund-raising had on leveling the playing field.

Who were the people giving money and volunteering for the Dean campaign?

A lot of them were people who came to distrust the mainstream media. I think it started with the results of the 2000 election, and the final break for many occurred when, during the invasion of Iraq, the mainstream media relied mostly on its embedded reporters for news. Their generally uncritical, gung-ho, and restrictive coverage caused hundreds of thousands or even millions of people to start looking for information somewhere else, and the place they started to find it was in blogs. In a lot of ways the mainstream media helped create the blogosphere because people didn't think they were getting the full story.

At the same time, the Dean campaign was all over the Internet, challenging the Democrat establishment and saying we really need to change things. It was two anti-establishment forces showing up in the same space at the same time.

What did the Democratic Party establishment make of this?

The big funders and the connected power in the Democratic Party establishment—the major donors, for example, and people like former Commerce Secretary Mickey Kantor and former Secretary of State Warren Christopher—are used to every potential nominee going to their door in the early stages of the campaign. He has dinner with them, he tells them he is thinking of running, and he asks for their support.

Then the Dean campaign came along. And he didn't knock on their door, he didn't ask for permission, and he didn't ask for support. At first they thought Dean was rather cute—this little guy who had no chance. And frankly, when we finally did start knocking on a few power brokers' doors, most of them told us they were too busy dealing with the John Kerry and John Edwards people, who they believed at least had some chance of winning the presidency.

What happened was Dean stopped being cute. Suddenly he had 650,000 active supporters out in the field, organizing. And the powers that be realized that if we get Dean elected as president, it would be without their help, and without asking them for permission. If Howard Dean gets elected President of the United States, then they are going to be irrelevant.

So did they kill Dean or did Dean shoot himself?

Well, the establishment raised millions of dollars to try to destroy him, but Howard Dean was also an inexperienced candidate who made some verbal gaffes going down the stretch in Iowa that cost him as well.

Howard Dean was much more middle of the road than the campaign that he waged. I think whenever that happens there is inevitably a disconnect—most of the time he got in trouble was when something he said didn't match up with his campaign. But he understood what was going on. He wasn't just being carried along on a wave.

What's your assessment of the Kerry and Bush Internet campaigns?

The Dean campaign was trying to build a grassroots campaign and we believed that if we built that, the money would follow. I think unfortunately the only lesson the two major parties learned was that the Internet could be a huge money machine. But they never understood fully its ability to bring together and mobilize the grass roots.

The Kerry campaign definitely didn't understand that. On election day, Democrats were actually paying people to go door to door while it was the Republicans who were using volunteers. If the Kerry campaign had thought about the Internet differently and realized that it could be used for a lot more than just raising money, I think they would have done better. In the end, I think they only asked, what do we do to raise money? They should have asked, what do we do to get volunteers?

In other words, Kerry (and Bush, for that matter) used the Internet as essentially a one-way medium. Even his online fund-raising campaigns tended to look like television infomercials, with an 800 number to call and all the rest. There was no real interactivity. It was just sending in money. And if you were a Democrat and hated George Bush enough, you did it. But gosh knows what would have happened if Kerry had actually done something truly big-picture with the Net.

What would you have done differently?

I called the Kerry campaign right before their acceptance speech and I told them that I thought all John Kerry needed to do in his acceptance speech at the Democratic nomination was to give whatever speech he was going to and then at the end say this:

"I want to do something that should have been done a long, long time ago. Tonight, I am going to put the entire future of my campaign in the hands of the American people. I will not accept taxpayer money for my campaign. I will not accept public funding for my campaign. And from this day forward I will never accept a check above $250 from the average American citizen. Tomorrow morning I was going to receive a check for $75 million from the federal government; I'm turning it back. And tomorrow morning I start with nothing but you. It's not what I do now; it's what you do now. If you want health care, if you want campaign finance reform, if you want to change more than presidents, if you want to change the political system itself and kick the lobbyists out I can't do that, but you can. All I can do is give you the opportunity to do it."

You know, I told his campaign people that there's only one medium in the world that would enable millions of people in one day to give a hundred bucks each and thereby change the whole country—and it's not television, and it's not radio. But they didn't think it would work. I still believe, though, that if they had done that they would have had at least $200 million the next day. I mean, people all over the country—particularly the Dean people, the MoveOn.org people, the Kerry people, the DNC email list—would have rallied to him. It would have been average Americans, none of whom would have been allowed to give more than $250, against a bunch of millionaires and multimillionaires—and then we could have had a ruckus about who's going to run this country. But that was not mainstream enough for them, so they went down the other path.

How big a role will blogs and the Internet play in future campaigns?

The Internet is only just starting to flex its muscles. I really think the Dean campaign was nothing more than the Nixon "Checkers" speech—which was the first instance where television said, "I am here."

Nixon was running on Eisenhower's ticket and he had been accused of taking money in paper bags from rich guys and lobbyists. Eisenhower held a press conference in which he insinuated that if Nixon couldn't explain this he was kicking him off the ticket. So Nixon sits in the office and looks dead into a television camera and he says [paraphrasing],

> I want to talk to you about all the stuff that people are saying and I want to talk to you about one gift that a lobbyist from Texas sent me. It came in a crate to our house, and we were curious and we opened the crate up. Inside there was this little puppy—a black and white spotted puppy. And the little girls, well they were just beside themselves. And we named the little puppy Checkers and the girls just love that dog. And I just want to say this to the American people, I don't care what they say about the lobbyists or these gifts, but we're not giving Checkers back.

Well, America got all teared up and damned if Richard Nixon didn't save himself. Letters were coming in with people saying, "Keep the dog! Don't make Richard Nixon give the dog back!" And that was the first time you could see the power of television.

The Dean campaign's use of blogging and the Internet was similar. We're only taking the very first steps in using the Net to empower people, to change governance and to change the media.

Do you think it will change the Republicans more or the Democrats more?

The reality is that both parties have rejected reform from within. John McCain tried to reform the Republicans and he was crushed. Dean tried to reform the Democratic Party and he was crushed. In the past, when this urge for reform was crushed by the establishment there was no place to go. If you went outside of the party how could you raise the money and how could you field hundreds of thousands of volunteers?

Well, that's changed with the Net. Howard Dean proved that you could raise more money than a Democrat had ever raised without any help from the establishment. If both parties continue to crush the reform movement from within themselves that will get pushed outside and now, with the Net, you could have a real third party with $200 million in 2008.

For the Republicans the old way has worked pretty well—they have a majority in the Senate, a majority in the House, and the presidency—so I doubt very much that they will understand the need to reform themselves. But we're now in a very interesting period with the Democrats. If they come out of the ashes saying, we have to change, I think there is an opportunity for them to embrace their grass roots and use the empowerment of the Internet to grow a really vibrant party. If they fail to do that, I think you will see a third party emerge from out of their disaffected grass roots.

Where, precisely, is the power in the blogosphere?

The problem is that we look at the blogosphere the way the mainstream media looks at it: that is, to look at the very top 100 blogs that get a zillion hits. The real power of the blogs is the tail, where millions of blogs exist. Even if the average small-time blog is only getting 10 readers, that's tens of millions of people, and that's an amazing thing.

They offer a different view and it's a powerful view because the people reading it care what the author thinks. For example, if I'm writing a blog and the only people reading it are my family and friends but I say, John Kerry is a great guy and this is why, I'm having a much bigger impact on those people than a TV commercial. If you take that connection across millions of blogs, you're hitting huge numbers—20 million or 40 million—and remember you only need 5 million people to give a hundred bucks to change the entire system.

So I don't buy that this is just a small group. It's a huge group and they're going to have a lot more political impact than most people would ever imagine.

EXTREME DEMOCRACY, BLOG-STYLE

An Interview with Jon Lebkowsky

Jon Lebkowsky is CEO of Polycot (www.polycot.com), an innovative team of Internet technology experts with broad experience creating and managing information systems for businesses and nonprofit organizations. An authority on computer-mediated communications, virtual communities, and online social networks, he has worked as project manager, systems analyst, technology director, and online community developer.

Lebkowsky was cofounder and CEO of one of the first virtual corporations, FringeWare, Inc. He is currently president of the Austin chapter of the Electronic Frontier Foundation, president of the Austin Free-Net Board of Directors, a cofounder of the Open Source Business Alliance, the Austin Wireless City Project, and the national Social Software Alliance, and advisor for the annual South by Southwest Interactive conference. He serves on the Advisory Board for the University of Texas Science, Technology, and Society Program.

A longtime Internet activist, Lebkowsky is also coediting a book on technology, democracy, and advocacy entitled "Extreme Democracy." He recently completed a year-long engagement with the IC^2 Institute at the University of Texas, where he managed Wireless Future, a project that produced a major economic development report on the region's technology future. He has written about technology for publications such as Mondo 2000, Whole Earth Review, FringeWare Review, Wired *magazine,* 21C, *and the* Austin Chronicle. *Lebkowsky also contributes to a number of weblogs, including his own at weblogsky.com.*

What was your personal introduction to the world of blogs and blogging?

Blogging was really just an extension of everything else I'd done online. I never had an interest in stand-alone computers. It was only when I learned that they could connect and communicate that I decided to throw myself into technology. The WELL, one of the earliest and best organized online communities, was my gateway to the Internet. And my first private company, FringeWare, was a "street market in cyberspace" combining commerce and community. All my work from then on was focused on interactive publishing, online community, and virtual collaboration. Internet activism—and eventually activist blogging—is merely an extension of that early work I was involved in.

Interestingly, I wasn't really excited about blogs when they first appeared—at least not until I saw how blogs could really help form and organize online communities. Blogs are conversations; bloggers don't publish in a vacuum. Bloggers are speaking to an audience that talks back—that responds and shares ideas and eventually begins to coalesce into an identifiable group. Even though all my life I had trained to write, the solitary writer thing never appealed to me, I'm too much of a socializer. But doing this sort of collaborative blogging—this "network book" as I think Brewster Kahle called the Internet—is a perfect fit for me.

Describe some of your experiences in grassroots political blogging.

I always avoided candidate politics and strong party affiliation because political parties seemed a bit raw about power, and politics that is more about power than ideas can be nasty, as we all know. However, like so many other people, I felt a growing sense of urgency after the 2000 elections about the direction this country was taking. I wanted to do more. You see, like a lot of Internet professionals, I'd been distracted by work craziness during the big tech boom of the 1990s, and then when the boom went bust, I suddenly had the mental focus to pay attention to what was happening in the Bush versus Gore election battle. And then, of course, 9/11 happened, and after that, the war in Iraq. I knew I wanted to get involved.

Somebody told me about an email list called Discussions of Greater Democracy, and I joined and got into the conversation. We were talking about the need to consider clear alternatives to the extreme right. I'd thought of myself as a centrist, or maybe a left libertarian, but it was time to think about what I really believed in, and that was the kind of discussion I found at Greater Democracy. Most of us in those conversations were hopeful about the impact of technology on society and its political implications. And the statement that I wrote for the group (greaterdemocracy.org/about.html) sort of summed up our mission: "To consider how new communications technologies support democracy, and how we can ensure that the effectiveness of those technologies is not constrained by ill-considered policy or development."

Years before, I had written a piece called "Nodal Politics" that pointed in this direction, but I think some people thought it was crazy idealism. Now I found people who were talking about the same sort of thing, and I had hopes that Greater Democracy would become a platform for more action in this arena. We set up a blog that captured a lot of attention, in fact. But I think we suffered from a lack of consistent leadership within the group. We couldn't quite get it together to be more than a blog. But still, it's a pretty great group blog, and an incubator for democratic thinking.

Meanwhile there were several other platforms emerging, mostly around the Dean campaign. Dean and the guy who became his campaign manager, Joe Trippi, understood that you could have an emergent political force that works from the bottom up. That's what grassroots politics is all about, but it's always been hard to organize the grass roots, hard to find like-minded people and cultivate their understanding of and commitment to common action. Effective organization of that kind had usually been the product of top-down, centralized organizations with strong controls, discipline, and little tolerance for operational diversity.

Of course, the early labor movement was an exception to the rule about top-down organizing. And in the 1960s, there was some successful community organizing around local issues. But one problem anyone who wants to do grassroots organizing faces these days is that communities are more atomized, more anonymous. A lot of people are even afraid to open their door to strangers. But they're not afraid to talk to people online.

So what Dean showed was that you can have at least some success organizing the grass roots with emerging Internet-based technologies. Suddenly that was just so clear to so many people. College students Zack Rosen, Neil Drumm, and Josh Koenig started DeanSpace with that kind of thinking. I joined their meetings and hung out on the edges of the intense collaboration they were into. They were trying to build a software application that would facilitate online community organizing with a political focus. They were influenced by David P. Reed's concept of the power of group-forming (coincidentally, David was part of the Greater Democracy group). In fact, the whole idea for DeanSpace basically mirrored the concept of the Internet itself—build a network of networks, where each instance of DeanSpace would be the platform for a social network, but it would also be a node in a larger network of DeanSpace sites that would share information with each other. Each site would have robust functionality for communication—blogs, forums, group-editable "books," etc. They would be distributed widely and set up by groups defined either by geography or affinity. The more groups that formed, the more powerful the network would become.

I worked with some people in Texas to roll out sites here, but it didn't always work out. In fact, we actually ran into a Dean group in one of the larger metropolitan areas that didn't want any other Dean sites close by. I guess they had some control issues, and man, we had quite a debate about that. But hey, that's what politics is all about.

Anyway, what was clear to everybody, even traditional politicos, was that blogs were a powerful way to launch and spread ideas and news and fundraising clout and organization. Sites like Mitch Kapor's ob4.org (which was probably the first installation to use CivicSpace, which is what DeanSpace became after the Dean campaign ended) and Greater Democracy were set up as "virtual think tanks" with multiple bloggers offering thoughtful critiques of political and other issues. DriveDemocracy was set up as more of a petition-driven activist site, but they added a blog, too, because people want to read and talk and think about politics.

The bottom line, I'd say, is that grassroots activists have begun to discover that blogs and other web tools can really help overcome voter apathy. I don't doubt for a minute that blogs were part of the reason for the higher voter turnout in the 2004 election—blogs and, of course, the fact that people were so polarized.

Didn't DailyKos have a lot of influence among Democratic Party activists even though it was focused primarily on national rather than local politics?

DailyKos covers national issues, and it's a blog with a huge national audience, so it has more of an effect. I know politicos who read Kos first thing every day because that's where progressive news is breaking. It's not a place you'd look for local news, except maybe for news of a hot congressional campaign or something.

So yeah, it's true that you can focus anywhere you want with blog tools—at the local or the national level. We used to say, "Think globally, act locally," but I think most of us would now say, "Think and act globally as well as locally." Whether you have an effect depends on your integrity and the degree of trust you inspire, and whether your blog offers compelling writing that can attract an audience.

If you have a national focus but a local audience, you could still have an effect to the extent that your audience can affect national issues. But for any one city, your effect may be limited. A local focus may have more impact, if only because you might know more and care more about local issues.

What about issues not directly tied to politics and political campaigns? Can blogs be effective organizing vehicles for dealing with local school, transportation, or other community problems?

Blogs may be vehicles for discussion and debate, and in aggregate may be useful in keeping particular issues alive and in helping to organize people, but blogs alone are not going to have an impact on decision making and policy. You have to have people on the ground. Activists still have to go directly to people face-to-face and organize them, and then bring those people to policy makers to confront them. You may get five thousand people to sign a petition online, but if you want five thousand to go down to City Hall and actually get some changes made, you've got to organize people face-to-face. Blogs can help you find those people, but blogs alone can't fight City Hall.

But blogs and political uses of technology are emergent, and we've only just begun to have enough citizens online in the U.S. to have the critical mass we need to use network technology for effective political organizing. And there are projects to extend the technology to underserved populations in the U.S. and to developing nations abroad. While we might not have a lot of examples of blogs used for local organizing at this point, it's only a matter of time, especially as the tools become easier to use and more pervasive. Consider CivicSpace, which is just approaching its version 1.0 release. A couple of years from now, you may see instances of CivicSpace and similar rich interactive tools all across the U.S., with more people trained to understand the nuts and bolts of personal publishing and conversation online. I don't know that we can begin to imagine now what effect that will have socially and politically.

We hear talk about "A-list bloggers" who are at the top of a power-law curve, the few that many read, as opposed to the many bloggers at the bottom of the curve that few read. This misses an important point: that bloggers have impact in aggregate, i.e., many bloggers discussing the same issue or story can have a powerful aggregate effect. It also misses the impact of local bloggers, and the potential effect of networking bloggers so that they share information and influence.

Everyone talks about how blogs can bring together and organize people of like minds and interests. Yet the 2004 election showed, if nothing else, that the biggest users of blogs—Democratic activists—weren't able to reach out to "red state" Americans and try to answer their needs and concerns. Isn't blogging just a good way of "preaching to the choir"?

You have to remember that red states are predominantly rural, where people are less likely to have always-on Internet access and an awareness of blogs and other social software. Adoption is much higher in the blue states.

And rural areas might not have the same access to other information channels. So all the great online work progressives were doing had less impact on red states.

But I agree that the problem the Democrats have is not going to be fixed by blogs or other political technology tools. Trei Brundrett, a bright programmer I know in Austin who worked hard to support Dean and later Kerry, told me how he had visited his dad, a rancher in south Texas. He set up a meeting with several ranchers in the area with beer and barbecue, and talked to them about Dean. They were very smart and very interested, and he realized that they were appreciating that he was listening to them and not talking down to them. To them the Democrats seem elitist and out of touch, unwilling to give them respect and hear their problems. On the other hand the Republicans are listening, and they're working through churches and connecting with values that are more powerful than any of us suspected.

So whether it's through blogs and other media, or face-to-face, you're going to have trouble reaching beyond disagreement unless you listen to other people's views with respect.

BLOGGING THE PRESIDENCY

An Interview with Markos Moulitsas Zuniga

Few individuals have done as much recently to put the citizen back into "citizenship" as Markos Moulitsas Zuniga, a thirty-four-year-old former GI and committed Democrat who writes the political blog DailyKos (dailykos.com). Launched in May of 2002, DailyKos (the name comes from his Army nickname, "Kos") quickly touched a nerve among liberal and Democratic readers, and became a vital source of political news and commentary for tens of millions of Americans. Since then, political bloggers have forced the resignation of Senator Trent Lott, exposed the fraudulent documents at the heart of a CBS 60 Minutes story on President Bush's National Guard career, contributed ideas and slogans to both candidates' campaign speeches, and mobilized millions of party activists to raise money and get people to the polls. As perhaps the most influential of all the political blogs, DailyKos led the way in changing forever the way citizens—and politicians—wage political campaigns today.

Why did you start blogging?

It was in 2002, right after the Afghanistan war. There was this environment in the country where criticizing the president was considered to be some sort of unpatriotic or treasonous act. So I needed an outlet to vent. I mean, I was driving my coworkers and my family and my friends crazy ranting about all the injustices I saw. Anyway, one day I was looking for political information online, and I found this blog called MyDD, written by Jerome Armstrong, who's now my business partner. He was writing about the 2002 elections, and it was the first blog that I really noticed. And I thought, this is really cool. I could do the same kind of thing. So that's when I started DailyKos, as a way to get things off my chest and hopefully not go crazy.

When did you first realize that anyone was paying attention?

Oh, it must have been four or five months into it, but the first time I broke a hundred visitors in a day was kind of a shocking moment for me. I mean, I realized I couldn't fit a hundred people in my living room. And yet all these people are coming to hear me talk? It was ridiculous. But then on the other hand, why not, right?

So anyway, in those days I was basically complementing Jerome's MyDD site—there were way too many races for any one person to cover, so we sort of divided them up—and he started linking to me and I was able to leech off his traffic quite a bit. But then after the 2002 elections, Jerome started consulting for the Dean campaign and he actually shut down his site to work on the campaign full time. So his community ended up migrating over to DailyKos. That was the first big bounce in my audience, which grew to about eight thousand visitors a day by that time.

Still, I'd have to say that it wasn't really until [former Dean campaign manager] Joe Trippi gave me a call that I realized that some important people were paying attention to DailyKos, and that it was having an influence, however small. And it was also right about that time that the media started paying attention to blogging as a political force because of the success the Dean campaign was having in using blogs to organize volunteers and raise money.

Was it the media's attention to blogging in the Dean campaign that really propelled you into the A-list, as it were, of blogging?

Actually, what pushed DailyKos to the next level was the Iraq war. I was the one war critic, left-wing blogger who was an actual veteran, so it was difficult for people to dismiss me as a pacifist or a bleeding heart or whatever. And when *Forbes* magazine did a story rating the top war blogs in March of 2003, I think it was, they put DailyKos in the top five of the best war blogs. The other four were pro-war, conservative bloggers and I was the only liberal anti-war guy on the list.

So DailyKos has really gone through three main growth phases. The 2002 midterm elections were obviously my first big boost. That got me to about 8,000 visitors a day. The Iraq war pushed me to about 30,000. The 2004 Democratic primaries put me at about 100,000 visitors a day. And now I'm at roughly 500,000 visitors a day. [During the weeks before the election, traffic surged to over 625,000 visitors per day.]

That's more than Fox News gets to their site!

Yeah. The traffic now is at the point where, as the site grows, I don't get happy about it anymore. It just means more headaches managing the community. I have to buy more equipment, more servers, and I have more bandwidth costs. I've had to hire somebody to help with customer service, I've had to hire someone to help with the back-end program. So it's just becoming more of a job than it used to be before, when running DailyKos was more of a passion. And like anything else, I think, when what you used to think of as a hobby becomes more like a job, it changes the way you view it. I'm not complaining, because who wouldn't want to have a successful blog with 15 to 16 million visitors a month, but it does change the dynamic.

Is DailyKos earning enough money now from advertising to pay for those staffers you hired and provide you with a living income?

Yes. Right now it's making a lot of money.

Can you quantify that?

I could, but I won't.

As you wish.

It's in the five figures per month. Let's just leave it at that. [According to *Newsday*, DailyKos generates $48,000 per month in ad revenue.]

So it's not just a hobby . . . it's your day job.

It's one of my two day jobs, the other one being my consulting company.

What sort of consulting do you do?

The name of the company is Armstrong Zuniga (armstrongzuniga.com), and Jerome and I do what we call "netroots consulting"—building and leveraging online communities—for political campaigns and interest groups.

Are there synergies between DailyKos and your consulting work?

Absolutely, especially in the issues we address. One problem I write about on the blog, and that we're going to try to address in our consulting work, is the influence that traditional democratic consultants and media firms have over the party. They're not really interested in winning elections. They're only interested in making money.

I mean, there are only eight to ten major Democratic consultancies, and all the candidates want to work with them because they're supposedly "the best." Gotta have the "best," right? It doesn't matter that these consultants keep losing races. It doesn't matter that Bob Shrum, who bled the Kerry campaign out of more than five million dollars, has never run a successful presidential campaign. What matters is that he's supposed to be "the best." And so win or lose, Shrum and the rest of the top consultants are going to get hired on the next election cycle.

Why is that? Wouldn't any candidate want a winning consultant?

We're Democrats. We're not used to winning elections [he laughs].

Maybe that's why the Democratic Party puts up with things that Republicans never would. Like, did you know that Democratic media consultants take a percentage of every media buy they make? That's how they work. Anybody who does television ads for the Democratic Party takes a cut of the media buy. So you can guess where their incentive is, right? It's to book more and more ads, and to hell with paying for more field organizers or doing any of the other important things you need to do to win elections. To me, the only people who are really worth what they charge are the ground people, the actual on-the-ground organizers. But the way things are run in the Democratic Party now, they end up being the bastard stepchild of the campaign.

The Republicans, on the other hand, would never put up with that. Their media consultants charge a flat fee for their services. And since they don't take a cut of the media buys, they have no incentive to keep pushing for more ad spending if it's not really needed. So this means that the Republicans, who already have a big financial advantage over us, are able to put even more of their money into field organizing and other operations than we are. That's really shocking to me. It's just unacceptable.

Do you write about this on your blog?

Yeah, and it's always controversial. I mean, I do get a lot of kudos from some people in the Democratic Party establishment. People say, "We're glad someone is finally telling the truth." But it's all very stealthy, you know, because nobody wants to come out and take on the consultancies publicly.

But I think it's going to be different after the election. I'm hoping the party will be more open to changing the way it operates. Because in terms of our own work, we're in this to win elections and help the Democrats take power. And to do that, we're going to have to basically declare war on the consulting establishment. We're going to take aim at them, and not just with rhetoric, either. We're going to offer actual products and services that are going to hurt their bottom lines.

Such as?

Well, right now, these consultancies are charging obscene amounts of money for things like email spammers [systems for mass emailing campaign messages and requests for donations]. But we've been working with the people behind CivicSpace (civicspacelabs.org), which is a technology platform for grassroots organizing, and we're going to offer an email spammer to campaigns for free. I mean, they'll still probably have to hire one or two guys to implement the system, but they're not going to have to pay $5,000 a month to the email spammer anymore.

So we want to provide essential campaign tools like this for free. That way the money can be put into the stuff that matters most, like developing strategy and key messages, and especially hiring field organizers. I'm obsessed with field organizing. To me that's the holy grail of a winning campaign. And the less that campaigns have to spend on things like technology and media, the more they can spend on putting human beings on the ground, knocking on doors, getting people to the polls. Basically, my goal is just strip as much money from the hands of the consultants as possible and redirect that money into the ground game.

How does DailyKos fit into all this?

Most people agree that the most important thing in political campaigns is to strengthen your connection to the activist base and then mobilize them. And where do you find many of today's political activists? On blogs. On political blogs like mine.

The marketing industry talks about the "influentials," right? I mean, the holy grail of successful marketing is to reach that 10 percent or so of the public who are the most passionate about—who are experts on—any given topic. For example, I have friends I talk to when I want to go see a movie. They see every movie, and I trust their opinions and recommendations. I have another friend I talk to if I want to buy a car. He knows all about cars. And, you know, the movie industry tries to locate these influentials and get them into focus groups or advance screenings. All industries, to one extent or another, try to do the same. These are the people the advertisers try to reach most of all.

When it comes to political influentials, according to marketing studies, they are even more influential in their sphere than other types of influentials are. And that's who I've got at DailyKos. I don't have many swing voters reading DailyKos, and I don't really want them. I'm preaching to the choir for a reason. It's because we're trying to organize, we're trying to fund-raise, we're trying to win elections. They're the activists. They're incredibly influential. And they can be the key to winning elections.

But apparently not, at least this time, for the Democrats.

No, and we've got to look at all the reasons why. Maybe the other side's message was better, maybe their media was better, maybe their turnout was better, maybe they listened better to certain concerns that voters had on their minds. We have to look at all that and learn from our mistakes. But I don't think there's any doubt that blogging changed the political landscape in this country.

There's no way, for example, that John Kerry would have been financially viable, or competitive in the race itself, without the power of the netroots and of blogs and all the online organizing and fund-raising that Democratic activists did from the start of the Dean campaign to election day 2004. And the influence was not just with the Kerry campaign or the Dean and Clark campaigns before that. Across the political landscape, blogs proved to be powerful fund-raising and organizing tools. In my own case, I posted a request for contributions to the congressional campaign of Ginny Schrader in Pennsylvania, and within just a few days, we raised over $20,000. Once word spread to other bloggers, the total raised reached $40,000. By September [of 2004], my blog alone helped raise over $630,000 for various Democratic candidates.

Blogs also serve as a great opposition research center—just ask Trent Lott, or Dan Rather. And they're useful also as large-scale focus groups for testing out ideas and campaign slogans. Kerry's campaign slogan exposing the hypocrisy of Bush's "ownership society" came from our DailyKos blog.

On the other hand, we shouldn't get too carried away with all the hype about blogging. I mean, all I can do, along with other political bloggers, is gather up my readers and talk about the issues, bounce ideas off each other, maybe offer some talking points, and then point them to things that need doing to achieve the political goals we want. But at the end of the day, it's up to each individual to really make that difference at the local level. I mean, it's nothing that I as a blogger can do.

In fact, one of my biggest pet peeves is the way this whole blogging thing is being held up as some sort of end in itself—some sort of magic wand. And it's just not true. Blogs are a tool, an instrument, nothing more. In five years, probably no one will care anymore if you happen to use a blog to communicate to people. There may even be some entirely new communications tool that comes along and is superior to a blog. And when that happens, a blog will seem no more "revolutionary" than a telephone. No one anymore says, "I'm a telephoner." Or if you work on a computer, you don't say, "I'm a computerer." In a few years, probably no one will call themselves a blogger, either.

So what's next for DailyKos?

Let's just say that I'm looking forward to the 2006 cycle.

DOVE BECOMES HAWK IN BLOG TRANSFORMATION

An interview with Roger L. Simon

Roger L. Simon used to be a radical left-wing writer, famed for his novels about the pot-smoking Jewish detective Moses Wine and for a screenwriting career that included an Oscar nomination for his adaptation of the Isaac Bashevis Singer novel Enemies, A Love Story. *Now, Simon is better known as a hawkish neo-conservative Bush-supporter on foreign policy issues (on social issues he is still very liberal) who rails against the Democrats and the* New York Times *in a weblog which has exploded from a daily readership of 2,500 to 20,000 in less than 18 months. Simon's audience is thought to include some of the most powerful people in Hollywood as well as journalists from every major media outlet.*

In October 2003, Simon caused a furor when he attacked Gregg Easterbrook, a senior editor at the New Republic, *who had posted a controversial review of the Quentin Tarantino film* Kill Bill *on the* New Republic *website. Easterbrook had criticized Miramax co-chairman Harvey Weinstein and Disney chairman Michael Eisner as "Jewish executives" who "worship money above all else, by promoting for profit the adulation of viol⋯" Within hours of Simon's blog, Easterbrook was being vilified by the / League and was fired from his job as a freelance contribut / by Disney); both Easterbrook and the magazine were f*

Simon's views have outraged some of his liberal / On rogerlsimon.com he speaks his mind freely, w / successful blog.

You're a successful author and screenwriter. Why did you start blogging?

I started in April 2003 because I had a novel being published in June 2003 called *Director's Cut* and I thought it might be an interesting way to promote my novel. I knew many authors had their own websites but when you go to them it's like static advertisements. So I thought if I did a blog I might attract readers to the book. If I had a book coming out now it would probably be a good help to me but it wasn't that much of a help at that point because my numbers were so low. But then the reverse occurred and the blog itself took off.

Why do you think the blog was so popular?

First of all, I was undergoing a kind of political transformation at the time, so I just was honest about that and I attracted quite a number of people going through similar transformations. When I began I had around 2,500 people visiting my site and it's gone up in almost a straight line, although it has had a few stock market dips. I was quite shocked. I had no idea that it would get this popular because when I started I didn't know that much about blogs.

It's actually a bit scary, to be perfectly candid, because all of this happened by accident. It was not my goal as a college student to be an op-ed writer, but effectively I am a sort of op-ed writer now—an interactive op-ed writer. Of course, I'm still an entertainment writer even when I'm writing my blog in the sense that this kind of writing must be punchy and entertaining. I think one of the reasons I do attract this kind of audience is my attitude and my style of writing.

Do you decide what to write about based on what you think your readers want to talk about, or on what you feel most strongly about?

All of the above actually. Recently, of course, it was the election. It was everybody's mind, including my own. But I've always been very interested tional relations. Some of my novels were set in China, in Japan, in

Israel. You know, I traveled a lot so it's not a new obsession. In the beginning of the blog I wrote about less political issues, of course. I blogged considerably about film and about what it's like to be a screenwriter, for example. I also blogged about the Academy Awards because I am a member of the Academy. My numbers were not as high then as they are now, of course, because the world is at a certain moment in history where everybody is transfixed by Iraq and the election. But after the election I'll return to those issues and others that I'm interested in.

Do you tend to write more about hawkish issues?

Well, I do. Although I have been quite verbose about gay marriage, which I am in favor of. Some of my allies on foreign policy get very outraged by the domestic views I have. But so be it. I mean, this is my blog, and they can get their own. These are my views. And one of the interesting things about blogging is, especially if you allow comments, you are inviting a sort of Socratic discussion with your audience. You are obligated in some sense to respond, otherwise readers will become disinterested. I think one of the unique things about bloggers is that they are a form of participatory journalism. I mean, one of the great lies that we get from the mainstream media is that we are unedited and they are. My God, I have 20,000 people on my site a day, so how quickly do you think that factual inaccuracies (and not just spelling inaccuracies) will be caught? Compare that to the number of editors at the *New York Times*.

Have you ever been wrong?

I've been caught on my grammar and spelling. I have people who enjoy catching me on that. But I have not been caught on tremendous factual error because I realize the medium I am in and I realize that you can't lie in a blog. If you do, you're a horse's ass and you'll be caught out in 10 minutes. So I have refined my arguments and views but I have not committed any major factual errors because I'm very careful.

Who are these people who are scrutinizing you?

On one level, I have no idea. On another level, I have come to know quite a number of them. There are 20,000 visitors on the site on an average day, so it is impossible for me to know all of them. Because I am moving into making blogging remunerative in collaboration with some other bloggers and businessmen, we ran a market research survey on my site about one month ago. The results were that the average person had a post-graduate degree and of course quite a high income—triple digits—and was on the conservative side of the political spectrum.

You have said in one of your blogs that the "real guardian of honesty is diversity." How do you see blogging as fitting into this?

I think every blog is a voice and there is a bit of a meritocracy going on. Every man or woman has one website and there is an audience out there that votes with their mouse. If you believe Technorati there are well over 4 million blogs out there. How many of them are even having 1,000 people a day look at them? It's probably a minute amount. No one is forcing anyone to come to my blog, they are voting voluntarily with their mouse. And just as they are coming to me they are going to Daily Kos—a site with which I disagree completely. Daily Kos is getting more votes than I do by a lot, but nevertheless I applaud the democracy inherent in this.

I really do think that the blogging movement as a forum for political discussion and dialogue is tremendous. Ideas are tested in a public manner in ways that I do not think they have been since ancient Greece. With the size of our global village here, it's hard to test ideas in any way, but thanks to blogs there is now a way. I am always in a discussion with people in Australia or wherever in the world. Online, we are always in the same place.

Your posting about Gregg Easterbrook of the New Republic *certainly had quite an effect.*

The Easterbrook thing was a rude awakening for me because I hadn't realized until that point how many people were actually reading my blog and how influential it was. I think what's interesting about blogs, especially these politically oriented blogs, is that they are read by a very, very politically involved audience. That's why I am aware now that everything that I put online is being read by people at the *Los Angeles Times* and the *New York Times* and the *Post* and the *Wall Street Journal*. They are watching my blog and a few others as well.

When did you first realize that your post about Gregg Easterbrook had made an impact?

I went out for a Saturday morning hike with a friend and when I got back, there was an email from Gregg Easterbrook saying call me. I had never met Gregg Easterbrook in my life. I called him. We talked. I said what was really true: I had no intention of seeing this man lose his job. My criticism was based on what he had said in his piece. I never dreamed that I was going to be responsible for him losing his job. I apologized for that, even though I thought Gregg Easterbrook's piece was terrible. I also think he was tremendously naïve in thinking he could write something like that about someone like Michael Eisner and not suffer the consequences.

Did it occur to you how strange it was that the whole saga was the repercussions of a blog commenting on a blog?

Oh yes, absolutely. It made me realize that blogs, especially when they are written by people who are respected to some degree—which I was early on because I have a reputation from other writing—have an amazing impact. You don't realize it while you type in your room that there really are people out there reading this thing. That's especially so if you have been a writer all your life, where there's usually a big time delay between what you write and when it appears in public. It's a changing experience because you are more engaged with your readers than you ever are as a novelist. So the sense of audience is much more profound. It puts a lot of pressure on you. You can even become a hero to certain people in ways that you don't want to be.

Blogging is also very immediate, so you have to think a little bit before you write. And I learned a lesson from that. Also, I tend now to criticize organizations more than I do individuals. I go after the *New York Times* and CBS. I have gone after Sulzberger but he owns the *New York Times*.

Before blogs, who could take on institutions that large?

It was very difficult. I think that is a tremendously positive thing about blogs because institutions like that should be subject to criticism. The *New York Times* in some ways has more power than the president of the United States and is not subject to being voted out of office, so it's very good that the mass media can be criticized by blogs. It's one of the great things about blogging. I think it can only be positive for democracy in general.

How has blogging changed you as novelist and a screenwriter?

It's been terrible for me as a novelist and a screenwriter. It takes up too much of my time that I could otherwise be writing novels and screenplays. It's as simple as that. But it has attracted a larger audience to my writing. I get anecdotal information on that because people are writing me emails saying, "I never read one of your books before but I love your blog, so I read one of your books and I liked it." I get things like that every other day or so, which is very nice.

What's it like being one of the few baby boomer bloggers?

I think that I may be one of the oldest bloggers. I am always comparing the sixties to what's going on today, and that attracts a lot of readers. I think that in this country there are quite a lot of people who are nearing retirement age who are technologically savvy, which gives them a lot of time to hang out on the Internet. I'm certain that if we aren't finding it now, we will soon be finding retiree blogs.

Like what, "Geezer.com"?

Now that would be fun, wouldn't it?

SEX, LIES, AND POLITICAL SCRAPES

An Interview with Ana Marie Cox

Hers may not exactly be a Cinderella story, but blogger Ana Marie Cox has certainly achieved belle of the ball star status in the blogosphere with Wonkette, a gossipy and quite often funny politico-sex blog aimed at deflating the egos of Washington's incestuous beltway brotherhood of babbling politicians and journalists.

For the thirty-two-year-old Cox, who writes her daily Wonkette postings from the guest bedroom of the Arlington, Virginia, home she shares with her husband, Washington Post *journalist Chris Lehmann, blogging has been something of a dream come true. She gets to write about whatever she finds funny—everything from the sexual preferences and habits of Bush administration officials to, well, the sexual preferences and habits of everyone else in Washington. And she gets to be utterly shameless about it.*

Not bad for a former "failure" of a journalist, as she describes herself. Not bad, either, is the reportedly six-figure book deal she signed recently. In any event, and probably in large part because she may be the only one left in America who does not *take blogging very seriously, she is having a huge amount of fun doing it. She can be found at wonkette.com.*

Okay, here's a question that's not about blogging: What was it like covering the Democratic convention for MTV?

First of all, it was hard work. I mean, do you realize how many sit-ups I had to do? And all because of that unwritten rule that women on MTV have to show their belly buttons. Yeah, it was a real crunch time, as it were.

Did you like being on camera, instead of behind a computer keyboard?

Yeah, I did. I'm comfortable on camera. And it turns out I'm actually pretty good at it. Of course, as my husband put it, finding out that you're good on TV is like discovering you can yodel. It's just a completely useless skill.

Anything else about the experience that was memorable?

Well, someone on MTV actually did say—in this very sort of Lana Turner moment—"Hey, you've got IT!"

So what will you do with your experience as a TV personality?

Oh, probably the same thing that I've done with all my other journalistic experience—waste it.

You're kidding, of course.

Not really. I mean, my position in relation to the journalism profession is something like that of an abused spouse. I've been fired from or left every journalism job I've ever had. *Mother Jones* magazine, the *American Prospect*, the *Chronicle of Higher Education, Suck* magazine. I just never seemed to fit in. One place even chastised me for rolling my eyes and sighing too loudly in meetings.

Well, that sort of behavior doesn't exactly endear you to bosses, does it?

No, it doesn't. But, you know, that's the story of my life. I was even kicked out of "Gifted and Talented" camp for breezing drunk through the girls' bathroom one night. I didn't want to be bad. I wanted to be good. I've always wanted the journalism profession to want me and accept me and like me, but it just never happened. I've always had a very uneasy relationship with journalism as a profession. I couldn't keep a job. I couldn't find work. I was even a lousy freelancer—and how bad do you have to be to be lousy at writing for peanuts for publications that treat you like dirt?

And then Nick Denton came along, right?

And he offered me a job.

That, again, paid peanuts.

Yeah, I make about the same as first-year journalism students. Only I'm about twelve years older than they are. Ah, but the perks! I can write stuff that I think is funny and not have to prove to some editor that it is, in fact, funny. Because how do you prove something is funny if the editor has no sense of humor, which most don't? So I can look good and have fun and not have to work very hard. I can be lazy.

Oh, and I almost forget—I haven't had to buy my own dinner or drinks in a long time. And I'm sort of semi-famous now, at least in DC. It's nice to have people suck up to you. And then, of course, I get to meet all these Washington politicos and talk about who's having sex with whom and stuff like that. That's a lot of fun.

It's easy to see why. But speaking of Washington sex scandals, how'd the whole Jessica Cutler story come about?

She was this girl who worked in the mailroom of a senator from Ohio and she was basically a kept woman. She had something like five different boyfriends, who were all, shall we say, very "generous" with her. One of them even paid in cash. Anyway, she wrote this supposedly anonymous blog that detailed all her sex adventures, and so I linked to it in my blog. Honestly, if

I had known she was as stupid as she was, I probably wouldn't have linked to it.

What do you mean?

Well, she was supposedly anonymous, but she was using people's real initials in her accounts. And she was describing real scenes from her office. So when I linked to her, it turned out that people found it incredibly easy to figure out who she was.

Anyway, the story is that I linked to her blog at eleven thirty in the morning and by the time she got back from lunch, her boss was holding printouts of her so-called "anonymous" writings and she was fired on the spot.

Well, don't feel bad. Word is she's got a photo spread coming up in Playboy.

I guess you're right. Plus it's hard to feel bad for someone who's that dumb.

What else do you like about being this famous blogger called Wonkette?

I like the ability to comment on things and say exactly what I think. I like the feedback, too. You know, it's fascinating how people think they know me because of my blog. They have a relationship with this whole Wonkette persona, only it's all in their fantasies. It's not really me, though. Actually, I should clarify that: Wonkette is me after too many margaritas.

Isn't it true generally, though, that the writing on blogs is much closer to the way people actually talk?

Yeah. When they're drunk.

So what does that indicate about the quality of writing on blogs?

Most of it is not very good, frankly. I mean, that's just the nature of creative output. Most creative output is not good, period. Whether it's music or writing or art or whatever. But to the extent that it's any good at all, it's not because it's blogging as opposed to some other form that makes it good. It is that freedom to do whatever you want, it's that lack of editing, it's that freshness, that immediacy.

Sometimes I compare blogging to the little magazine revolution in the 1930s in New York, where whenever a group of intellectuals would have a fight, they would each start competing magazines. And then they would have another fight, and there would be more competing magazines. Like, there is this desire to get your work, get your ideas, out into the world. Oh and also a desire to use the written word as a medium for settling personal scores. To me that's just like blogging.

I think that good writing is good writing. And I don't think the good writing you find on blogs is any better than good writing you find anywhere else.

But blogs do make it easier for beginning writers with talent to make a go of it, wouldn't you agree?

Definitely. And that actually makes me very happy. Like I said, I do think that most of anything is crap, but there are people out there who are quite good at it. I know someone who had a day job writing ad copy, and he never would have written anything for public consumption had it not been for blogging. He is so good. And now he's started writing for magazines and stuff, and he's become an even better writer through critical exposure. He's got a whole new group of friends and whole new kind of professional opportunity as a result of blogging. It's amazing. I mean, blogging can be a springboard to "real" media—I'm doing air quotes with my fingers but your readers can't see that. But I still think the cases where that will happen will be pretty rare.

Let's get back to your case. What's it like working with Nick Denton?

Umm . . . he's British.

You say that like it explains everything.

I think I'll just agree with you.

Okay, what about your future plans?

My future plans?

Yes.

I would like to do less work for more money.

That's an original thought.

Isn't it? You see, right now I do a lot of work for not very much money. So my goal is to switch that ratio around. That's my goal.

And perhaps write a book?

Maybe [wink, wink].

How long will you continue to write Wonkette?

You know, the whole success of Wonkette is due to this happy confluence of circumstances that has made Wonkette popular. I'm grateful for that, and I'm having so much fun doing it. But I cannot imagine doing Wonkette for many more years. It is a very draining experience.

On the other hand, Wonkette does raise the bar pretty high in terms of how fun my next job has to be. So I could wind up doing this for longer than

I think, simply because I've discovered that I love doing this. And I definitely want to love what I do.

Have you learned anything about yourself since becoming Wonkette?

Yes. I don't want to ruin anyone's life. But I don't mind ruining their day.

FEAR AND LAPTOPS ON THE CAMPAIGN TRAIL

by Matthew Klam*

The 2004 political season became the perfect storm for the blogosphere. The upper-level high of mainstream media—well-coiffed anchormen, seasoned journalists, practiced public intellectuals, and veteran politicians—would collide with a gonzo-like low: disaffected journalists, would-be journalists, would-be muckrakers, political activists, and just plain highly opinionated loudmouths blogging from their kitchen tables while still in their pajamas. Add the general fragmentation of American society into niche groups, a leap in the technology allowing the Web to become a two-way conversation, and a media eager to report on the latest new, new thing (even as it found itself being pilloried) and blogging experienced its own version of the big bang. In 1999 there were fifty blogs; by some estimates, ten million had been created by early 2005.

Matthew Klam, named by the New Yorker *as one of the twenty best fiction writers in America under forty, is also a journalist. Here he paints a vivid and perceptive picture of this storm's havoc in action. Its actors could indeed have stepped out of Hunter S. Thompson's seminal* Fear and Loathing: On

---

*Matthew Klam, a contributing writer for *The New York Times Magazine,* where this article originally appeared, has previously written about Ecstasy and the world of day traders. He also writes fiction and is the author of *Sam the Cat and Other Stories.* Copyright © 2004, by Matthew Klam. Reprinted by permission.

the Campaign Trail, *written about the 1972 presidential campaign. Sage anchormen get to compete with Wonkette—whose online persona, says Klam, is as "a foulmouthed, hard-drinking, sex-obsessed politics junkie."*

Klam concludes his essay with a couple of key questions that continue to haunt the blogosphere a year later: How can the breed survive on traditional media's home turf? What happens when high-flying bloggers come down from nosebleed territory? Will valuable insight and instant fact-checking inevitably give way to fiercely partisan and internecine warfare? Klam's insights are not only worth the ride, but also the read. For more from Klam, turn to his website, matthewklam.com.

Nine blocks north of Madison Square Garden, next door to the Emerging Artists Theater, where posters advertised "The Gay Naked Play" ("Now With More Nudity"), the bloggers were up and running. It was Republican National Convention week in New York City, and they had taken over a performance space called the Tank. A homeless guy sat at the entrance with a bag of cans at his feet, a crocheted cap on his head and his chin in his hand. To reach the Tank, you had to cross a crummy little courtyard with white plastic patio furniture and half a motorcycle strung with lights and strewn with flowers, beneath a plywood sign that said, "Ronald Reagan Memorial Fountain."

The Tank was just one small room, with theater lights on the ceiling and picture windows that looked out on the parking garage across 42nd Street. Free raw carrots and radishes sat in a cardboard box on a table by the door, alongside a pile of glazed doughnuts and all the coffee you could drink. The place was crowded. Everyone was sitting, staring at their laptops, at bridge tables or completely sacked out on couches. Markos Moulitsas, who runs the blog Daily Kos, at dailykos.com, was slouched in the corner of one squashed-down couch in shorts and a T-shirt, his computer on his lap, one of the keys snapped off his keyboard. He's a small guy with short brown hair who could pass for 15. Duncan Black of the blog Eschaton, who goes by the name Atrios, sat at the other end of the couch, staring out the window. On the table set up behind them, Jerome Armstrong of MyDD worked sweatily. Jesse and

Ezra, whose blog is called Pandagon, were lying with two cute women in tank tops—Ezra's girlfriend Kate and Zoë of Gadflyer—on futon beds that had been placed on the tiny stage of the performance space. Their computers and wireless mice and some carrots and radishes and paper plates with Chinese dumplings were scattered between them. A month ago, at the Democratic convention, Zoë had accidentally spilled a big cup of 7-Up on Jesse's computer, killing it. She and Jesse now looked as if they might be dating.

Moulitsas pulled a 149-word story off nytimes.com linking Robert Novak, the conservative columnist, to "Unfit for Command," the book that attacked John Kerry's service in Vietnam; the article revealed that Novak's son is the marketing director for the book's publisher, Regnery. Moulitsas copied and pasted the story, wrote "Novak blows another one" at the top and clicked Submit. A couple of seconds later, the item appeared on Daily Kos, and his hundreds of thousands of readers began to take note, many of them posting their own fevered thoughts in response. Moulitsas read some e-mail messages and surfed around, trying to think of the next rotten thing to say about the right. Beside him, around the same time, Atrios was assembling a few words about Ed Schrock, a conservative Republican congressman vocal in his disavowal of the rights of gays, who had now been accused of soliciting gay love. A Web site dedicated to exposing closeted antigay politicians had posted an audio clip of what they said was Schrock's voice, and he had pulled out of the race. A pizza-stained paper plate sat between Moulitsas and Atrios. Together, they have more readers than The Philadelphia Inquirer.

A year ago, no one other than campaign staffs and chronic insomniacs read political blogs. In the late 90's, about the only places online to write about politics were message boards like Salon's Table Talk or Free Republic, a conservative chat room. Crude looking Web logs, or blogs, cropped up online, and Silicon Valley techies put them to use, discussing arcane software problems with colleagues, tossing in the occasional diaristic riff on the birth of a daughter or a trip to Maui. Then in 1999, Mickey Kaus, a veteran magazine journalist and author of a weighty book on welfare reform, began a political blog on Slate. On kausfiles, as he called it, he wrote differently. There were a thousand small ways his voice changed; in print, he had been a full-paragraph guy who carefully backed up his claims, but on his blog he evolved into an exasperated Larry David basket case of self-doubt and indignation, harassed by a fake "editor" of his own creation who broke in, midsentence, with parenthetical questions and accusations.

All that outrage, hand wringing, writing posts all day long—the care and maintenance of an online writing persona—after five years, it takes its toll. I had talked to Kaus earlier in the summer at a restaurant in Venice, Calif., and he had said he didn't know how much longer he could stand it. After the election, he said, he might just give up. Once, he told me, "I was halfway across the room about to blog a dream I just had, without ever regaining consciousness, before I realized what I was about to do. If the computer hadn't been in the other room, I probably would have."

In a recent national survey, the Pew Internet and American Life Project found that more than two million Americans have their own blog. Most of them, nobody reads. The blogs that succeed, like Kaus's, are written in a strong, distinctive, original voice. In January, a serious-minded former editor at The Chronicle of Higher Education named Ana Marie Cox reinvented herself online as the Wonkette, a foulmouthed, hard-drinking, sex-obsessed politics junkie. Joshua Micah Marshall, in his columns for The Hill and articles for The Washington Monthly, writes like every other overeducated journalist. But on his blog, Talking Points Memo, he has become an irate spitter of well-crafted vitriol aimed at the president, whom he compared, one day, to Tony Soprano torching his friend's sporting-goods store for the sake of a little extra cash. When Marshall's in a bad mood, he portrays mainstream journalists as a bunch of "corrupt," "idiotic" hacks, mired in "cosmopolitan and baby-boomer self-loathing," whose bad habits have become "ingrained and chronic, like a battered dog who cowers and shakes when the abuser gives a passing look." Moulitsas's site, Daily Kos, teems with information—sophisticated analysis of poll numbers, crystal-ball babble, links to Senate, House and governor "outlook charts." But what pulls you in is not the data; it's his voice. He's cruel and superior, and he knows his side is going to win.

Early in 2002, Joe Trippi read on Armstrong's blog, MyDD, that Howard Dean might be running for president, and after Trippi joined the campaign as its manager, he helped bring the Dean movement to life online, in part through the campaign's massive community blog, which connected Deaniacs all over the country, helped them organize and became the access point for the $40 million that fueled Dean's explosive run. The Dean phenomenon drew so many new people to the grass roots (or "netroots," as the Dean bloggers used to call them) of presidential politics that a kind of fragmentation occurred in what had been, until then, a blog culture dominated by credentialed gentlemen like Kaus, Andrew Sullivan and Glenn Reynolds, a conservative law professor whose blog, Instapundit, is read faithfully at the White House.

But just as Fox News has been creaming CNN, the traffic on Kaus's and Sullivan's sites has flat-lined recently, while Atrios's and Moulitsas's are booming. Left-wing politics are thriving on blogs the way Rush Limbaugh has dominated talk radio, and in the last six months, the angrier, nastier partisan blogs have been growing the fastest. Daily Kos has tripled in traffic since June. Josh Marshall's site has quadrupled in the last year. It's almost as though, in a time of great national discord, you don't want to know both sides of an issue. The once-soothing voice of the nonideological press has become, to many readers, a secondary concern, a luxury, even something suspect. It's hard to listen to a calm and rational debate when the building is burning and your pants are smoking.

But at the same time that blogs have moved away from the political center, they have become increasingly influential in the campaigns—James P. Rubin, John Kerry's foreign-policy adviser, told me, "They're the first thing I read when I get up in the morning and the last thing I read at night." Among the Washington press corps, too, their impact is obvious. Back in 2002, Marshall helped stoke the fires licking at Trent Lott's feet, digging up old interviews that suggested his support for Strom Thurmond's racial policies went way back; Marshall's scoops found their way onto The Associated Press wire and the Op-Ed page of The New York Times. Earlier this month, a platoon of right-wing bloggers launched a coordinated assault against CBS News and its memos claiming that President Bush got special treatment in the National Guard; within 24 hours, the bloggers' obsessive study of typefaces in the 1970's migrated onto Drudge, then onto Fox News and then onto the networks and the front pages of the country's leading newspapers.

During the 1972 presidential campaign, Timothy Crouse covered the campaign-trail press corps in Rolling Stone magazine, reporting that he later expanded into his revealing and funny book "The Boys on the Bus." Crouse described the way a few top journalists like R.W. Apple Jr., David S. Broder, Jack Germond and Jules Witcover, through their diligence, ambition and supreme self-confidence, set the agenda for the whole political race. This summer, sitting in the Tank and reading campaign blogs, you could sometimes get a half-giddy, half-sickening feeling that something was shifting, that the news agenda was beginning to be set by this largely unpaid, T-shirt-clad army of bloggers.

A few blocks down Eighth Avenue, thousands of journalists with salaries and health benefits waited for the next speech and the next press release from the Republican campaign. Here in the Tank, Jesse and Ezra sat resting on the futon with some dumplings. Moulitsas was crashing on a friend's floor for the week. Atrios had just quit his job as an economics professor, and Armstrong could fondly look back on stints in his 20's as a traveling Deadhead, a Peace Corps volunteer and a Buddhist monastery dweller.

Like almost everyone in the Tank, Moulitsas started blogging to blow off steam. He seemed as surprised as anyone to find himself on the verge of respectability.

That week, while Moulitsas blogged with gusto—posting a doctored photo of Senator Zell Miller with fangs and bloody eyes and the comment, "Try not to puke," staying late at the Tank to boo during the televised speeches—Wonkette walked through the hall and saw what she described on her site as the "Whitest. Convention. Ever." She wondered on her blog if anyone had seen any photos anywhere of, say, a minority in the house; later, to her relief, someone sent her, and she posted, a few shots of black and Hispanic people, cleaning the floors.

The Wonkette is more fun to read than Daily Kos. She's also more fun to hang out with. Before we went off to the fabulous party that Americans for Tax Reform were throwing at the New York Yacht Club on Monday night, we had time for an expensive dinner at a really nice restaurant in SoHo. Wonkette hadn't been anywhere near the Tank, and when I told her about the scene there, she laughed. "They've got the raw carrots and radishes," she said, "and we've got the raw tuna appetizer." The candlelight reflected off the

Champagne bubbles in her glass. "Other bloggers don't consider me a real blogger," she said. "Kos is the platonic ideal of a blogger: he posts all the time; he interacts with his readers." She swallowed an oyster and smiled. "I hate all that."

Ana Marie Cox has peachy cream skin and eyes of a very bright blue, strawberry blond hair and a filthy mind; she likes to analyze our nation's leaders in their most private, ah, parts. She has been talking this way all her life. Until January, no one listened. She's the daughter of a six-foot-tall blond Scandinavian goddess and one of the bright young men who worked under Robert McNamara in the Pentagon. Her parents split when she was 12, and she was shuttled between them, and like most kids who grow up that way, she made an anthropological study of what's cool. She was a loud, pudgy kid with milk-bottle-thick glasses, and when she finally settled into high school in Nebraska, she immediately ran for class president. She was thrown out of "gifted and talented" camp for weaving, drunk, through the girl's bathroom one night, and when she told me about it, she described it as "the story of my life": the smart girl getting booted out of a place where she belonged. She dropped out of a Ph.D. program in history at the University of California at Berkeley and found happiness for a few years at Suck.com, a snarky social-commentary Web site from the first Internet heyday. She tried freelancing after that, and then spent five frustrating years being fired from or leaving one job after another—such well-meaning, highbrow institutions as Mother Jones, The American Prospect and The Chronicle of Higher Education—plus another place she won't name, where, she says, they chastised her for raising her eyebrows wrong and for sighing too loud in meetings. Finally, last fall, she gave up on journalism. She was filling out applications for a master's in social work when Nick Denton called.

Denton is the world's first blogging entrepreneur. He owns a bunch of these smart-alecky blogs—Wonkette; a New York City gossip site called Gawker; a Hollywood site, Defamer; and Fleshbot, a porn site. Anytime somebody builds a media empire, especially one that includes pornography, you assume the money is good, but in the Wonkette's case, it isn't. Her starting salary was $18,000 a year. (She's getting bonuses now for increased traffic, but not much.) But she likes the fact that Denton hasn't put a lot of restrictions on her. "The only thing he said was that he wanted it to be funnier than Josh Marshall," she told me. "The bar isn't raised too high."

Imagine a fairly drunk housewife stuck in front of CNN, growing hornier as the day wears on. The Wonkette reads like a diary of that day. Cox quickly found her voice—funny, sex-obsessed, self-indulgent. "The Wonkette is like me after a few margaritas," she said. She started with two basic themes: questioning Bush's sexual preference and praising Kerry's anatomical, well, gifts. In March, she discovered a terrific new feature on the Bush-Cheney Web site that let voters generate their own official Bush-Cheney '04 posters with personalized slogans. She dubbed it "The Sloganator," and until the campaign got wind of her project and shut down the Sloganator, Wonkette solicited slogans from readers and printed up very professional-looking Bush-Cheney posters with phrases like "Christians for purification of the Mid East," "Because Satan is coming to eat your kids" and "Crackers Unite" emblazoned across the top. Readers loved it. It took Wonkette just three months to reach the traffic numbers Marshall had been working to build up for three years.

While the Wonkette likes to make fun of Washington's capacity to take itself seriously, sometimes she seems to take it more seriously than anyone. She spent about a month out of her mind with excitement on one totally pointless story, the White House Correspondents' Dinner, wondering online if any of her readers might get her in. A friend finally came through and took her as his date, and the following morning she posted several very keyed-up reports: "Arrive with J. in cab to Hinckley Hilton: Omg. There really is a red carpet. Paparazzi. Sort of junior-varsity feeling, but still. Fumble with wrap, bag, umbrella . . . remember . . . don't show teeth in smile, suck in gut, stick out chest. The paparazzi go nuts! Smile, prepare to wave. . . . Realize that we have entered just behind Jessica Lynch." And then later: "More wine. . . . Keep thinking I see Harvey Weinstein, but it's just random heavy-set mogulish types. . . . Lights flash. Time for mediocre surf-and-turf! . . . waiter passes with tray of Jell-O shots, and for a brief, beautiful moment, it appears that Wolfowitz might take one." She was finally getting paid for being drunk at gifted-and-talented camp.

Not long after Wonkette came to life, Cox's hometown newspaper, The

Lincoln Journal Star, profiled her. Then an online crew from The Washington Post came to videotape her blogging, and then bookers started calling from talk shows. By midsummer, she had been on "Scarborough Country," on MSNBC, which she likes to call "Scar-Co," four times. TV stardom seemed to her to be the ideal next step.

Sure enough, in July, MTV called and asked her to report from the Democratic National Convention. She was thrilled, and she fixed on the idea that this convention gig might turn into a real job at the network. Whatever it is that makes a person want to be famous, need to be famous—and not everything about a ravenous hunger for fame is bad—Cox has that. The carrot of fame now hanging over her was distracting, and I got the sense that certain situations were playing out in her head. "I watched 'Breakfast at Tiffany's' a lot as a kid," she said.

A couple of weeks before the convention, she flew to Los Angeles for a screen test, and when she got back, she told me that she had aced it. "I am very good at this," she said proudly. She was getting a little obsessed. "It's weird," she said. "It's like discovering you can yodel. You know what I mean? I'm good. I really never would've known."

In Boston, at the convention, she hardly blogged at all. MTV had scheduled a single short piece for her to do from the convention floor. "I'm not really doing anything for MTV," she said at the start of the convention. "I'm doing interviews about being hired by MTV." A couple of days later, I ran into her at the FleetCenter. She was in a hurry. "I have to go be interviewed by 'Nightline,' " she said. " 'Oh, and what do you do?' " she went on, pretending to be Ted Koppel. " 'I get interviewed about what it's like to be the MTV special correspondent. I forward media requests. I try to find free food and liquor.' " That evening, from my seat up in the rafters next to Moulitsas, I saw Cox in action down on the floor, holding a microphone, kneeling, interviewing a delegate. It took me a moment to realize that there was no cameraman; it was just Cox, with a microphone and a producer hovering over her shoulder offering little bits of advice.

I couldn't figure it out. Why was she so excited about working for MTV? MTV is for 9-year-olds. It's so 1992. It was as if her sense of what was cool and what was stupid, so unerring on her blog, had abandoned her. How could she think that 18 seconds with those cocky jerks on "Scar-Co" was better than a perfect joke about a president, his dog and a blown kiss? Four months of setting the blog world on fire making dirty political jokes suddenly wasn't enough any more.

But then she wasn't asked to cover the Republican convention for MTV. It would be fair to say that this upset her. Wonkette had seemed like the perfect stepping stone to something big. Now she had to consider, What if Wonkette was as good as it gets?

By the time we sat down to dinner in New York, she was employing that old trick of pretending to be happy with just this. She was focusing on the blog again and its many perks. "I haven't bought my own dinner or drinks in months," she said. She tipped her head to the side and shrugged. "That's the best benefit of being Wonkette. That's the sad truth. They all want something. But that's fine. All I want is dinner and drinks."

In Boston, the day before the convention started and after a long, glittering night following the Wonkette to fancy parties, I came back late and found Josh Marshall in my hotel room, lying sideways on a cot, blogging. He was drinking a Diet Coke, his face illuminated by the glow of his laptop, legs crossed, socked feet hanging off the edge. Earlier in the day, when he mentioned that his hotel reservation didn't start until Monday, I had offered to share my room with him for the night.

The first time I had met him, back in April in Washington, he was drinking a large Coke from Chipotle and a foot-tall iced coffee. He explained that he spent most afternoons at Starbucks, and then he would head back to his apartment to blog all night, drinking coffee, sometimes even editing and revising while lying in bed. "You edit something when you're literally falling asleep," he said. "It can be kind of scary."

In my room in Boston, he had a little hotel ice bucket by his side with two more Diet Cokes in it, and he finished them off before bedtime. It was late, and I was tired and he was disoriented, trying to blog under such circumstances, but before we turned off the lights he wanted to show me his Talking Points Memo ID, which resembled a press badge. He wondered if I thought it looked real. The credentials we would all be receiving the next day didn't require any press badge, but staff reporters of actual news organizations always seem to have separate institutional ID's, thick plastic magnetized deals that can open locked doors. Working off the model of a friend's ID, Marshall had, using his girlfriend's computer and photo printer, made a sober little knock-off, including his picture (in coat and tie), an expiration date and an explanation of company policy: should the company's only employee be terminated, the badge would become the property of Talking Points Memo. He laminated it at Kinko's. He had also brought his own lanyard (each media empire has its own necklace strings) and his own little plastic badge holder. I told him it looked completely legit.

Marshall had been wondering about that for a while. Even before he had finished his Ph.D. in American history at Brown, he was thinking about the impending problem of how to look legit, where to fit in. His father is a professor of marine biology, and Marshall knew, as Cox had known, that academic life wouldn't work. He wanted to be a writer, and he wanted to write about serious stuff, and he wanted to do it with a lot of passion. Marshall's mom had died when he was still in grade school, in a car accident, and he says losing her made it impossible for him to live without believing strongly in something. And he does: he is a guy whose waking state hovers right between irate and incensed, and for him those beliefs require action. Coming out of school, he had a love for history and a handle on American policy issues, and he figured the rest would be simple, job-wise, if only somebody would let him write. Marshall spent three years after his Ph.D. program working as an editor at The American Prospect, the liberal policy journal, and I got the feeling—not so much from him, because he didn't want to talk about it, but from former colleagues—that by the time he quit, he had decided that it would be better to starve than to work for someone else. So for a while he starved.

Marshall started the blog in 2000, during the Florida recount, as a release valve, and it's still working that way; oversimplifying weighty issues, reducing them to their essential skeletons, somehow relaxes him. Since February, with the explosion of blog traffic and the invention of blog ads as a revenue source, a few elite bloggers have found themselves on the receiving end of a Howitzer of money, as much as $10,000 a month. Marshall is one of them, and now that the release valve has become a job, albeit a well-paying one, he has to resist the tendency to ruin it. He wrestles with the question of how many posts are enough, since he's a one-man operation and his advertisers have paid ahead of time, and then there are also those obligations to The Hill, where he writes a low-paying weekly column, and The Washington Monthly, another underpaid gig that harks back to his hungrier days.

When I fell asleep in my hotel room, Marshall was complaining that there are no good books on the Crusades. The next morning, he got back into his clothes from the night before. He looked like a wrinkle bomb had hit him.

The big news, the only piece of news, it seemed, about the Democratic convention was that bloggers had been credentialed as news media, sort of, and after so many months ripping the mainstream press coverage of the campaign, a little tingle hung in the air. How would the new breed thrive on the ancient media's home turf, a news event by and for the big news folks? I spent the day at the FleetCenter, in the terrific accommodations the Democrats had arranged for the bloggers: up in the nosebleed seats, Section 320, where 35 of them, the lucky ones who had been credentialed, could fight for any of the 15 bar stools they had been provided, along with some makeshift plywood desks built along the railing. Whoever got there late sat in the cramped, yellow, steeply banked folding seats, no elbowroom, bad lighting, their power cords snaking down the rows to a couple of surge protectors. Moulitsas was in Section 320, and so was Armstrong from MyDD, Atrios of Eschaton, Zoë from Gadflyer, Jesse and Ezra, Jeralyn of Talkleft, Dave Pell from Electablog, Chris Rabb from Afro-Netizen, Bill Scher from Liberal Oasis and Christian Crumlish of radiofreeblogistan. But no Josh Marshall.

I ran into him later on in the press stands, to the right of the stage, where he had set up shop, squatting at a spot designated for an official news organization in the coveted blue section. He was fiddling with his computer and finishing a cellphone call about what he called "the biggest story of my life," one that would quell any fears about his legitimacy as a real journalist, at least for a while. But right now he was just trying to get online. That damned wireless modem he had spent so much money on really stunk. Verizon was driving him nuts. He had by this point changed into a fresh shirt and different pants from the ones he had been wearing when he left my hotel room, but he appeared, from head to toe, to be entirely wrinkled again, as though his clothing wrinkled at a faster rate than other people's. He gave up on trying to get online, finished his call and sat back. With his arms folded across his chest, in an incensed yet somewhat professorial tone, very up-all-night, very corduroy, he talked on and on about Douglas Feith and Ahmed Chalabi and Karl Rove.

For the entire time we were in Boston, he never seemed curious about where the bloggers were supposed to sit, and whenever I told him I had just come from there—at one point I even called from my cellphone, up in the nosebleeds, and waved—he never went up to visit. He skipped the blogger breakfast that morning, and I had to drag him out to go party-hopping at night—though when he got there, look out! (Just kidding.)

Marshall often seemed stuck between two worlds. In the blogger world, he was a star, author of one of the most popular and most respected sites. But unlike Moulitsas, who consulted on campaigns and helped develop software for political fund-raising and dreamed of marble statues in his image, Marshall seemed unsure of where blogging was leading. In the mainstream media world, he was not a major player, not yet anyway. He published occasional, well-regarded magazine pieces—one in The Atlantic, one in The New Yorker—but nothing earth-shattering. He didn't really seem at home there. Writing for magazines, he said, had become a big pain. Blogging was easier, freer. "In blogging," Marshall said, "there's no lead, no 'What's my point?' " The blog ad money had fallen from the sky, and it had saved him.

"Now I'm not under any financial pressure to write," he said. "What I backed into, in doing this blog, was freedom. And not having to write things I didn't believe and not having to write ways I didn't want to write." It is this unique amount of leeway that has allowed him, over the past two years, to run at his own pace, dig deeper. On his blog, he brings attention to over-looked stories. He wrote about Valerie Plame's cover being blown eight days before The New York Times did. And a paper put out by scholars at the Kennedy School of Government analyzing the fall of Trent Lott singled out Marshall for keeping the focus on a story that had otherwise slipped off the mainstream-media radar.

Like the Wonkette, Marshall loved the idea of being tapped by those who had once ignored him. Over the summer, he paired up with a big network news show on an investigative story, hoping some of its credibility would rub off on him. But then the network bumped the story at the last minute. If only he could turn his back completely on the old way, concentrate on nothing but the blog; but letting go of institutional approval and the security and camaraderie that goes with it is like jumping out a window. He can't decide between loving the big media, linking to it, hoping they'll pick up on stories, and hating it, despising it, insulting it, trying to convince you, or himself, that it's the worst thing in the world and that it's ruining American democracy.

Marshall did a little more heavy sighing and wrinkled himself up some more, rubbing his sour face, and launched into what was really irking him at this moment. "Going it alone is harder than it looks," he said. He had been fairly aggressively attacking the Swift Boat Veterans for Truth and had attracted plenty of fire himself. "I've gotten tons of hate mail over the last few weeks," he said. "You get a very thick skin for it. But it's hard. There's something on the karmic level. You feel the level of hate, and when you get a hundred of those, it's exhausting. Normally I'm oblivious to it, but lately it's getting to me a little." He had blocked mail from certain e-mail accounts, and yet, he said, "even though I haven't answered them—some I haven't answered in a year—they're still writing. This one guy has subject headings like 'Why you're an idiot today.' Certain people read the site to counteract their heart medication."

On April Fools' Day, Moulitsas really blew it. In a swaggering reaction to a Daily Kos reader who wondered in the comment section whether the four American civilian contractors strung up in Falluja deserved the same respect as American soldiers, he wrote, "I feel nothing over the death of mercenaries," and then added, "Screw them." Within hours, he became the focus of an international letter-writing campaign to drive away all of his advertisers. It worked, too. House candidates, Senate candidates, they all pulled their ads. But in a matter of weeks brand-new ads came in to fill the void. "It was a blip!" Moulitsas told me later, a little triumphantly. He had nearly destroyed himself, but not quite.

In the aftermath of what was maybe the worst week of Moulitsas's life, friends asked him if he might not consider choosing between his two roles, as a clearinghouse for activism and an outlet for information. But the site continued to grow, fund-raising chugged along for his candidates, and he wanted me to know that his survival was a big finger in the eye of anyone who said a blogger couldn't be two things at once.

But there was another role Moulitsas hadn't quite mastered yet: his place in the established machinery of the Democratic Party. Moulitsas is a rabid Democrat, devoted to the idea of the party, but he also feels a deep distrust for the party system, and so do many of his readers. Moulitsas has always been an outsider. He was born in Chicago, but moved to his mother's native El Salvador at age 4, and as the civil war there heated up in the 1980's, he remembers stepping over dead bodies. He only returned to Chicago after rebel soldiers passed along photos of Moulitsas and his brother to the family, an invitation to leave or lose their sons. Moulitsas speaks of himself, at the time of his return to Chicago when he was 9, as a tiny geek with a big mouth who couldn't speak English and who quickly learned to say things to bullies, in his heavy Spanish accent, that were just confounding enough for him to make a getaway before the bully realized he had been insulted. In high school, his American experience didn't improve. "I had to eat fast and run to the library to read, because I didn't have any friends," he said. After graduation, at 17, he enlisted in the U.S. Army. He was 5 foot 6 and weighed 110 pounds. Like everyone else, he carried a 65-pound pack on those 15- and 20-mile marches. He had been pushed around all his life, but in basic training, within spitting distance of his drill sergeants, he learned to fight back.

In Boston, I went with Moulitsas to a really swanky party given in honor of the bloggers at a Middle Eastern restaurant on the Charles River. At 2 a.m., as people were filing out to leave, a discussion that had started online spilled onto the middle of the floor. For the last few weeks, Moulitsas had been conversing on at least two different blogs with Jim Bonham, the executive director of the Democratic Congressional Campaign Committee. The D.C.C.C. is the arm of the Democratic Party that provides money, expert advice and technical support to candidates in close House races, and Moulitsas had been complaining that the group was abandoning some viable candidates, especially liberal ones, and leaving them to "flail around." Moulitsas became especially worked up about a Congressional candidate in Pennsylvania named Ginny Schrader. Her race against an incumbent Republican looked unwinnable, until her opponent suddenly dropped out of the race. Moulitsas immediately started soliciting donations for Schrader on Daily Kos, and within a couple of days he had raised $40,000 for her campaign, which the day before had had $7,000 in the bank. The D.C.C.C. was slower to react, and Moulitsas felt outraged and free to take a whack or two at them.

So when Moulitsas and Bonham met by the door at the party, they started screaming at each other. People gathered around to watch, blocking the crowd attempting to leave. Jim Bonham is taller and stouter than Moulitsas, but Jerome Armstrong of MyDD stood behind Moulitsas, kind of grinning and shaking his head. Stirling Newberry, a blogger buddy of Moulitsas's from the Draft Clark movement, tried to act as peacemaker, but it didn't work. Nicco Mele, the official liaison between the D.C.C.C. and the blogosphere, just stood back, horrified.

When I reached the blogger section the next day, Moulitsas was still pumped up. "Did you see my epic battle?" he yelled over to me. Armstrong turned around, grinning his head off. "The D.C.C.C. has never been challenged," Moulitsas said when I got over to his seat. "It was a shot across the bow." Then he re-enacted the fight. "You should've heard him yelling: 'So you can raise $20,000, but I can raise $2 million! You have to understand your role in this!' "

Armstrong said, "I'd have hit him if he said that to me."

Moulitsas said: "I told him: 'Don't yell at me. The rules are changing. You gotta adapt. You gotta wake up and realize your role.' " (I talked to Bonham later, and he said he didn't get why Moulitsas thought the D.C.C.C. was slighting bloggers. After all, Bonham said, the D.C.C.C. had paid for the very top-drawer blogger bash where the fight broke out.)

For Moulitsas and for a lot of other people new to politics in 2004—amateurs who liked the thrill ride Dean had taken them on—the idea that the rules had changed seemed entirely obvious. What was important to these new activists, he told me, was winning—winning the presidency, winning back the Senate, winning as many Congressional seats as possible. Soon after we met, Moulitsas tried to convince me how important it was for the old guard to start seeing politics through the eyes of the bloggers. That meant rapid re-sponse, he said, smart use of technology, constant two-way communication with the voters and grass-roots fund-raising. He told me the story of a flash advertisement that the D.N.C. had posted on its Web site. Moulitsas hated it. "It was horrible, the worst thing I'd ever seen," he said. "So I blogged a post saying, 'That's the biggest piece of garbage I've ever seen in my whole entire life'" (although he used stronger language than that). "What the hell were they thinking?" he asked. "I was embarrassed to be a Democrat. So then I get phone calls and e-mails, 'Well, why didn't you talk to us?' I'm like: 'What's there to talk about? The thing's a piece of garbage.' And then they say: 'It was done by a volunteer. If you attack them, then volunteers aren't going to want to do stuff like that.' I'm like: 'Good! 'Cause it's a piece of garbage.' I'm like, Here's the way it goes. O.K., from now on, keep this in mind: whenever you put up anything on this site, think, How are the blogs going to react?" He was smiling, but all the veins were pulsing in his neck. "You can pout all you want," he said, "but I'm not here to make friends with you guys and go to your little cocktail parties. And that piece of garbage is going to lose us votes."

Although the D.C.C.C. raises a lot more money for congressional candi-dates than Moulitsas does, candidates have caught on to the fact that Moulit-sas's help can be invaluable. While we were sitting up there in the blogger nosebleed section, his phone rang. It was Samara Barend, a young community activist running for Congress in upstate New York. When Moulitsas hung up, he told me she was calling "either to get my endorsement or to get me to write about the race."

Then we headed to the Westin to meet another congressional candidate hoping for some of the same attention from Daily Kos: Diane Farrell, a select-woman from Westport, Conn. We sat down in the hotel's ornate lobby, where delegates and journalists were checking e-mail and chatting. After some friendly introductions, Farrell made her pitch. "The problem is that we don't have a TV station," she said. "We have three daily papers, but direct mail will probably be our biggest expense. Radio costs too much."

Moulitsas said, "Are you doing the heavy ground game?"

"Oh, most definitely."

Moulitsas wondered if the remnants of the Dean movement could help out. "Are there any Dean organizations around you?" he asked.

"Bean?"

Moulitsas cleared his throat. "Dean."

"Oh, yes," she said.

Later, Moulitsas decided to add Barend—but not Farrell—to the short list of candidates he deemed most worth backing and raised more than $10,000 for her campaign.

Moulitsas's "friendly relations" with particular candidates got him into a public fight with Zephyr Teachout, who became briefly famous last winter as the guru of the Dean Internet campaign, which in fact employed Moulitsas for several months. Over the summer, she complained in several online forums, and to Moulitsas directly, that he and other bloggers were blurring the lines between editorial and advertising, lines that had always been sacred in journalism. According to Teachout, they were posting comments in support of candidates for whom they were also working as paid consultants and not explaining that conflict of interest, or at least not fully enough for Teachout. In an online discussion with Jay Rosen, who heads the journalism department at N.Y.U., she wrote, "I think where we essentially disagree is that transparency alone is enough."

"Zephyr can go to hell," Moulitsas said at the Democratic convention. "I'm not about to censor myself on any issue," he later wrote on another Web site. "If I care about something, I'll write about it. It's the essence of blogging. As for the mainstream media, who cares what some joker journalism professor wrote? Just keep blogging, doing your thing, and the blogosphere will continue to do just fine. We should let our accomplishments speak for themselves, and they will."

For Moulitsas, the bigger problem these days is his own success. When we met up again at the Republican convention, we walked around ground zero, and he told me about his rising page views. "I was losing sleep over how I'd survive the traffic," he said. His daily readership had surpassed 350,000, and by most counts he had become the most-read political blogger in the country. He told me he had hired a full-time programmer to take over the technical work of running his site. "I never intended to be here," he said. "Nothing foreshadowed the attention Daily Kos is getting."

Moulitsas said that people had been coming in from Brooklyn and other places just to shake his hand, because they knew he would be at the Tank. "It's weird," he said. "It makes me uncomfortable. People who achieve a certain amount of celebrity plan it. They expect that public attention will be part of the package."

Away from the Tank now, he could relax for a moment and reflect. "I'm really self-conscious of how the blogger community perceives me," he said. "I feel guilty that I don't link to more bloggers, I feel guilty that I'm more successful than other bloggers. I feel guilty that I make as much money as I do now, that I get more traffic. Rather than enjoy it, sometimes I feel really guilty about it. It's silly."

As we neared Wall Street, Moulitsas said: "The other angst I have about blogging is that because I depend on the income, it has become a job. You'd think I'd be happy. I make a living off of blogging! But it's interesting how, once it becomes a job, there's a certain angst that I'm kind of afflicted with. I can't quit."

When the bloggers first arrived in Boston for the Democratic convention, some of them had high hopes for what they would be able to accomplish there—that together they would cough up an astounding Rashomon collective of impressions and insights, interlinked, with empowering conclusions. With their new form of journalism, at once smaller and larger than the mainstream, they planned to bring politics back to the people. But those first few posts, so highly anticipated by their fellow bloggers, the ones who didn't score credentials, were more about the bus ride from the hotel, the heavy security in the parking lot; their seats in the rafters were terrible, they had trouble getting floor passes and, anyway, out on the floor, who would they talk to? Were they supposed to pretend to be regular reporters? Up in the nosebleeds, the delegates overran their special section, and it got so hot at night you could die, especially with a nice warm laptop baking your thighs; the WiFi kept fading, cutting them off from the world, from their Googling and pondering; from up in the cheap seats, the stage was minuscule, the speakers' faces were dots, the sound didn't travel. The only thing the bloggers really had the inside scoop on were the balloons hanging a few feet away from them in the rafters, in huge sacks of netting.

The bloggers had spent this year hammering the mainstream media for failing to tell the "real story" of Howard Dean or John Kerry or George W. Bush. And they hammered at the campaigns, too, for failing to make their message clear, for failing to adapt to surprises on the road, in the glare of all that attention. But now they were finding the campaign trail could be rough. Zephyr Teachout sat down next to me on the night of Kerry's speech and started needling the bloggers. "Look how hard it is to work when the conditions are awful, when you're star struck, when it's hard to find anecdotes that are good," she said.

And as a seasoned reporter myself—after two whole conventions—I can safely say that you get about as many insights into the hearts and souls of the candidates on the campaign trail as you would watching a plastic fern grow. The ever-increasing scrutiny of candidates because of cable and the Internet has only made more evident how impregnable and unfathomable our political machinery has become. Political reporters hanging around drinking and smoking at the conventions said that the bus had changed a lot since 1972. You spend all day watching nothing, fake deli-counter photo ops with six camera crews, and you get yelled at if you walk into the camera shot—that is, if you dare to go near the guy you're covering.

The news media helped create the modern campaign, and now they seem to be stuck in it. The bloggers, by contrast, adapted quickly. By the time the Republican Convention rolled around in August, they had figured something out, staying far, far away from that zoo down at Madison Square Garden. They had begun to work the way news people do at manufactured news events, by sticking together, sharing information, repeating one another's best lines. They were learning their limitations, and at the same time they were digging around and critiquing and fact-checking and raising money. They still liked posting dirty jokes and goofy Photoshopped pictures of politicians, but they had hope, and more than a few new ideas, and they were determined to make themselves heard.

WEB OF INFLUENCE

by Daniel W. Drezner and Henry Farrell*

Unlike the old saw about politics, blogging does not stop at the water's edge. There is the "Baghdad Blogger," an Iraqi blogger writing about the difficulties war imposes on him, his friends, and neighbors. And Juan Cole, a University of Michigan history professor whose Informed Comments informed skepticism about the invasion and occupation of Iraq transformed him from obscure academic to public intellectual.

Add human rights activists in Europe, political activists in Iran, and a Chinese blogger who posts satirical comments about the Communist Party, and it becomes abundantly clear that blogging has become "the fifth estate" all over the world.

This is the world introduced by Daniel Drezner and Henry Farrell. They argue persuasively that despite the fact these bloggers are but a small group of part-time, decentralized, and little funded diarists, they have an outsized impact on what gets covered by the international media.

Daniel W. Drezner is assistant professor of political science at the University of Chicago and keeps a daily weblog at danieldrezner.com. Henry Farrell is assistant professor of political science and international affairs at

*Copyright © 2004 by *Foreign Policy*. Reproduced with permission of *Foreign Policy* (www.foreignpolicy.com) via Copyright Clearance Center.

George Washington University and a member of the group blog at crooked timber.org.

Every day, millions of online diarists, or "bloggers," share their opinions with a global audience. Drawing upon the content of the international media and the World Wide Web, they weave together an elaborate network with agenda-setting power on issues ranging from human rights in China to the U.S. occupation of Iraq. What began as a hobby is evolving into a new medium that is changing the landscape for journalists and policymakers alike.

It was March 21, 2003—two days after the United States began its "shock and awe" campaign against Iraq—and the story dominating TV networks was the rumor (later proven false) that Saddam Hussein's infamous cousin, Ali Hassan al-Majid ("Chemical Ali"), had been killed in an airstrike. But, for thousands of other people around the world who switched on their computers rather than their television sets, the lead story was the sudden and worrisome disappearance of Salam Pax.

Otherwise known as the "Baghdad Blogger," Salam Pax was the pseudonym for a 29-year-old Iraqi architect whose online diary, featuring wry and candid observations about life in wartime, transformed him into a cult figure. It turned out that technical difficulties, not U.S. cruise missiles or Baathist Party thugs, were responsible for the three-day Salam Pax blackout. In the months that followed, his readership grew to millions, as his accounts were quoted in the *New York Times*, BBC, and Britain's *Guardian* newspaper. If the first Gulf War introduced the world to the "CNN effect," then the second Gulf War was blogging's coming-out party. Salam Pax was the most famous blogger during that conflict (he later signed a book and movie deal), but myriad other online diarists, including U.S. military personnel, emerged to offer real-time analysis and commentary.

Blogs (short for "weblogs") are periodically updated journals, providing online commentary with minimal or no external editing. They are usually presented as a set of "posts," individual entries of news or commentary, in reverse chronological order. The posts often include hyperlinks to other sites, enabling commentators to draw upon the content of the entire World Wide

Web. Blogs can function as personal diaries, political analysis, advice columns on romance, computers, money, or all of the above. Their number has grown at an astronomical rate. In 1999, the total number of blogs was estimated to be around 50; five years later, the estimates range from 2.4 million to 4.1 million. The Perseus Development Corporation, a consulting firm that studies Internet trends, estimates that by 2005 more than 10 million blogs will have been created. Media institutions have adopted the form as well, with many television networks, newspapers, and opinion journals now hosting blogs on their Web sites, sometimes featuring dispatches from their own correspondents, other times hiring full-time online columnists.

Blogs are already influencing U.S. politics. The top five political blogs together attract over half a million visitors per day. Jimmy Orr, the White House Internet director, recently characterized the "blogosphere" (the all-encompassing term to describe the universe of weblogs) as instrumental, important, and underestimated in its influence. Nobody knows that better than Trent Lott, who in December 2002 resigned as U.S. Senate majority leader in the wake of inflammatory comments he made at Sen. Strom Thurmond's 100th birthday party. Initially, Lott's remarks received little attention in the mainstream media. But the incident was the subject of intense online commentary, prodding renewed media attention that converted Lott's gaffe into a full-blown scandal.

Political scandals are one thing, but can the blogosphere influence global politics as well? Compared to other actors in world affairs—governments, international organizations, multinational corporations, and even nongovernmental organizations (NGOs)—blogs do not appear to be very powerful or visible. Even the most popular blog garners only a fraction of the Web traffic that major media outlets attract. According to the 2003 Pew Research Center for the People and the Press Internet Survey, only 4 percent of online Americans refer to blogs for information and opinions. The blogosphere has no central organization, and its participants have little ideological consensus. Indeed, an October 2003 survey of the blogosphere conducted by Perseus concluded that "the typical blog is written by a teenage girl who uses it twice a month to update her friends and classmates on happenings in her life." Blogging is almost exclusively a part-time, voluntary activity. The median income

generated by a weblog is zero dollars. How then can a collection of decentralized, contrarian, and nonprofit Web sites possibly influence world politics?

Blogs are becoming more influential because they affect the content of international media coverage. Journalism professor Todd Gitlin once noted that
media frame reality through "principles of selection, emphasis, and presenta-
tion composed of little tacit theories about what exists, what happens, and
what matters." Increasingly, journalists and pundits take their cues about
"what matters" in the world from weblogs. For salient topics in global affairs, the blogosphere functions as a rare combination of distributed expertise, real-time collective response to breaking news, and public-opinion
barometer. What's more, a hierarchical structure has taken shape within the
primordial chaos of cyberspace. A few elite blogs have emerged as aggregators of information and analysis, enabling media commentators to extract
meaningful analysis and rely on blogs to help them interpret and predict political developments.

Under specific circumstances—when key weblogs focus on a new or ne-
glected issue—blogs can act as a focal point for the mainstream media and
exert formidable agenda-setting power. Blogs have ignited national debates
on such topics as racial profiling at airports and have kept the media focused
on scandals as diverse as the exposure of CIA agent Valerie Plame's identity
to bribery allegations at the United Nations. Although the blogosphere remains cluttered with the teenage angst of high school students, blogs increasingly serve as a conduit through which ordinary and not-so-ordinary citizens
express their views on international relations and influence a policymaker's
decision making.

THE TIES THAT BIND

University of Michigan history Professor Juan Cole had a lot to say about
the war on terror and the war in Iraq. Problem was, not many people were
listening. Despite an impressive résumé (he's fluent in three Middle Eastern
languages), Cole had little success publishing opinion pieces in the mainstream media, even after Sept. 11, 2001. His writings on the Muslim world
might have remained confined to academic journals had he not begun a

weblog called "Informed Comment" as a hobby in 2002. Cole's language proficiency allowed him to monitor news reports and editorials throughout the region. "This was something I could not have been able to do in 1990, or even 1995," he told a Detroit newspaper, referring to the surge of Middle Eastern publications on the Internet. "I could get a level of texture and detail that you could never get from the Western press."

Fellow bloggers took an interest in his writings, especially because he expressed a skepticism about the U.S. invasion and occupation of Iraq that stood apart from the often optimistic mainstream media coverage following the successful overthrow of the Baathist regime. Writing in the summer of 2003, Cole noted: "The Sunni Arabs north, east and west of Baghdad from all accounts hate the U.S. and hate U.S. troops being there. This hatred is the key recruiting tool for the resistance, and it is not lessened by U.S. troops storming towns. I wish [the counterinsurgency operation] well; maybe it will work, militarily. Politically, I don't think it addresses the real problems, of winning hearts and minds."

As a prominent expert on the modern history of Shiite Islam, Cole became widely read among bloggers—and ultimately journalists—following the outbreak of Iraqi Shiite unrest in early 2004. With his blog attracting 250,000 readers per month, Cole began appearing on media outlets such as National Public Radio (NPR) and CNN to provide expert commentary. He also testified before the Senate Foreign Relations Committee. "As a result of my weblog, the *Middle East Journal* invited me to contribute for the Fall 2003 issue," he recalls. "When the Senate staff of the Foreign Relations Committee did a literature search on Moktada al-Sadr and his movement, mine was the only article that came up. Senate staff and some of the senators themselves read it and were eager to have my views on the situation."

Cole's transformation into a public intellectual embodies many of the dynamics that have heightened the impact of the blogosphere. He wanted to publicize his expertise, and he did so by attracting attention from elite members of the blogosphere. As Cole made waves within the virtual world, others in the real world began to take notice.

Most bloggers desire a wide readership, and conventional wisdom suggests that the most reliable way to gain Web traffic is through a link on another weblog. A blog that is linked to by multiple other sites will accumulate an ever increasing readership as more bloggers discover the site and create hyperlinks on their respective Web pages. Thus, in the blogosphere, the rich (measured in the number of links) get richer, while the poor remain poor.

This dynamic creates a skewed distribution where there are a very few highly ranked blogs with many incoming links, followed by a steep falloff and a very long list of medium- to low-ranked bloggers with few or no incoming links. One study by Clay Shirky, an associate professor at New York University, found that the Internet's top dozen bloggers (less than 3 percent of the total examined) accounted for approximately 20 percent of the incoming links. Some link-deprived blogs may become rich over time as top bloggers link to them, which helps explain why new bloggers are not discouraged.

Consequently, even as the blogosphere continues to expand, only a few blogs are likely to emerge as focal points. These prominent blogs serve as a mechanism for filtering interesting blog posts from mundane ones. When less renowned bloggers write posts with new information or a new slant, they will contact one or more of the large focal point blogs to publicize their posts. In this manner, poor blogs function as fire alarms for rich blogs, alerting them to new information and links. This self-perpetuating, symbiotic relationship allows interesting arguments and information to make their way to the top of the blogosphere.

The skewed network of the blogosphere makes it less time-consuming for outside observers to acquire information. The media only need to look at elite blogs to obtain a summary of the distribution of opinions on a given political issue. The mainstream political media can therefore act as a conduit between the blogosphere and politically powerful actors. The comparative advantage of blogs in political discourse, as compared to traditional media, is their low cost of real-time publication. Bloggers can post their immediate reactions to important political events before other forms of media can respond. Speed also helps bloggers overcome their own inaccuracies. When confronted with a factual error, they can quickly correct or update their post. Through these interactions, the blogosphere distills complex issues into key themes, providing cues for how the media should frame and report a foreign-policy question.

Small surprise, then, that a growing number of media leaders—editors, publishers, reporters, and columnists—consume political blogs. *New York Times* Executive Editor Bill Keller said in a November 2003 interview, "Sometimes I read something on a blog that makes me feel we screwed up." Howard Kurtz, one of the most prominent media commentators in the United States, regularly quotes elite bloggers in his "Media Notes Extra" feature for the *Washington Post*'s Web site. Many influential foreign affairs columnists, including Paul Krugman and Fareed Zakaria, have said that blogs form a part of their information-gathering activities.

For the mainstream media—which almost by definition suffer a deficit of specialized, detailed knowledge—blogs can also serve as repositories of expertise. And for readers worldwide, blogs can act as the "man on the street," supplying unfiltered eyewitness accounts about foreign countries. This facet is an especially valuable service, given the decline in the number of foreign correspondents since the 1990s. Blogs may even provide expert analysis and summaries of foreign-language texts, such as newspaper articles and government studies, that reporters and pundits would not otherwise access or understand.

Even foreign-policy novices leave their mark on the debate. David Nishimura, an art historian and vintage pen dealer, emerged as an unlikely commentator on the Iraq war through his blog, "Cronaca," which he describes as a "compilation of news concerning art, archaeology, history, and whatever else catches the chronicler's eye, with the odd bit of opinion and commentary thrown in." In the month after the fall of Hussein's regime in April 2003, there was much public hand-wringing about reports that more than 170,000 priceless antiques and treasures had been looted from the Iraqi National Museum in Baghdad. In response to these newspaper accounts, a number of historians and archaeologists scorned the U.S. Defense Department for failing to protect the museum.

Nishimura, however, scrutinized the various media reports and found several inconsistencies. He noted that the 170,000 number was flat-out wrong; that the actual losses, though serious, were much smaller than initial reports suggested; and that museum officials might have been complicit in the looting. "Smart money still seems to be on the involvement of Ba'athists and/or museum employees," he wrote. "The extent to which these categories overlap has been danced around so far, but until everything has been properly sorted out, it might be wise to remember how other totalitarian states have coopted cultural institutions, enlisting the past to remake the future." Prominent right-of-center bloggers, such as Glenn Reynolds, Andrew Sullivan, and Virginia Postrel, cited Nishimura's analysis to focus attention on the issue and correct the original narrative.

As the museum looting controversy reveals, blogs are now a "fifth estate" that keeps watch over the mainstream media. The speed of real-time blogger reactions often compels the media to correct errors in their own reporting before they mushroom. For example, in June 2003, the *Guardian* trumpeted a story in its online edition that misquoted Deputy U.S. Secretary of Defense Paul Wolfowitz as saying that the United States invaded Iraq in order to safeguard its oil supply. The quote began to wend its way through other media outlets worldwide, including Germany's *Die Welt*. In the ensuing hours, numerous bloggers led by Greg Djerejian's "Belgravia Dispatch" linked to the story and highlighted the error, prompting the *Guardian* to retract the story and apologize to its readers before publishing the story in its print version.

Bloggers have become so adept at fact-checking the media that they've spawned many other high-profile retractions and corrections. The most noteworthy was CBS News' acknowledgement that it could not authenticate documents it had used in a story about President George W. Bush's National Guard service that bloggers had identified as forgeries. When such corrections are made, bloggers create the impression at times that contemporary journalism has spun out of control. Glenn Reynolds of "Instapundit" explained to the *Online Journalism Review* that he sees parallels between the impact of the blogosphere and Russia's post-Soviet glasnost. "People are appalled, saying it's the decline of journalism. . . . But it's the same as when Russia started reporting about plane crashes and everyone thought they were just suddenly happening. It was really just the first time people could read about them." Media elites rightly retort that blogs have their own problems. Their often blatant partisanship discredits them in many newsrooms. However, as Yale University law Professor Jack Balkin says, the blogosphere has some built-in correction mechanisms for ideological bias, as "bloggers who write about political subjects cannot avoid addressing (and, more importantly, linking to) arguments made by people with different views. The reason is that much of the blogosphere is devoted to criticizing what other people have to say."

The blogosphere also acts as a barometer for whether a story would or should receive greater coverage by the mainstream media. The more blogs that discuss a particular issue, the more likely that the blogosphere will set the agenda for future news coverage. Consider one recent example with regard to U.S. homeland security. In July 2004, Annie Jacobsen, a writer for WomensWallStreet.com, posted online a first-person account of suspicious activity by Syrian passengers on a domestic U.S. flight: "After seeing 14 Middle Eastern men board separately (six together, eight individually) and then act as a group, watching their unusual glances, observing their bizarre bathroom activities, watching them congregate in small groups, knowing that the flight attendants and the pilots were seriously concerned and now knowing that federal air marshals were on board, I was officially terrified," she wrote. Her account was quickly picked up, linked to, and vigorously debated throughout the blogosphere. Was this the preparation for another September 11–style terrorist attack? Was Jacobsen overreacting, allowing her judgment to be clouded by racial stereotypes? Should the U.S. government end the practice of fining "discriminatory" airlines that disproportionately search Arab passengers? In just one weekend, 2 million people read her article. Reports soon followed in mainstream media outlets such as NPR, MSNBC, *Time*, and the *New York Times*, prompting a broader national debate about the racial profiling of possible terrorists.

Some bloggers purposefully harness the medium to promote wider awareness of their causes. With the assistance of experts including Kenneth Roth, the executive director of Human Rights Watch, and Samantha Power, the Pulitzer Prize–winning author of *"A Problem from Hell": America and the Age of Genocide*, cyberactivist Joanne Cipolla Moore set up a blog and Web site, "Passion of the Present," devoted to collecting news and information about genocide in Sudan. Moore sought out dozens of elite bloggers to link to her site and spread the word about Sudan. The blog of Ethan Zuckerman, a researcher at Harvard Law School's Berkman Center for Internet & Society, not only links to Moore's site but has issued a call to arms to the entire blogosphere:

"Blogs let us tell offline media what we want. When blog readers made it clear we wanted to know more about Trent Lott's racist comments, mainstream media picked up the ball and dug deeper into the story. . . . What sort of effort would it take to choose an important issue—say the Sudanese government's involvement in Darfur—and get enough momentum in the blogosphere that CNN was forced to bring a camera crew to the region?"

In all of these instances, bloggers relied on established media outlets for much of their information. However, blogs also functioned as a feedback mechanism for the mainstream media. In this way, the blogosphere serves both as an amplifier and as a remixer of media coverage. For the traditional media—and ultimately, policymakers—this makes the blogosphere difficult to ignore as a filter through which the public considers foreign-policy questions.

RAGE INSIDE THE MACHINE

Blogs are beginning to emerge in countries where there are few other outlets for political expression. But can blogs affect politics in regimes where there is no thriving independent media sector?

Under certain circumstances, they can. For starters, blogs can become an alternative source of news and commentary in countries where traditional media are under the thumb of the state. Blogs are more difficult to control than television or newspapers, especially under regimes that are tolerant of some degree of free expression. However, they are vulnerable to state censorship. A sufficiently determined government can stop blogs it doesn't like by restricting access to the Internet, or setting an example for others by punishing unauthorized political expression, as is currently the case in Saudi Arabia and China. The government may use filtering technologies to limit access to foreign blogs. And, if there isn't a reliable technological infrastructure, individuals will be shut out from the blogosphere. For instance, chronic power shortages and telecommunications problems make it difficult for Iraqis to write or read blogs.

Faced with various domestic obstacles, bloggers inside these countries (or expatriates) can try to influence foreign blogs and the media through indirect effects at home. Political scientists Margaret Keck of Johns Hopkins University and Kathryn Sikkink of the University of Minnesota note that activists who are unable to change conditions in their own countries can leverage their power by taking their case to transnational networks of advocates, who in turn publicize abuses and lobby their governments. Keck and Sikkink call this a "boomerang effect," because repression at home can lead to international pressure against the regime from abroad. Blogs can potentially play a role in the formation of such transnational networks.

Iran is a good example. The Iranian blogosphere has exploded. According to the National Institute for Technology and Liberal Education's Blog Census, Farsi is the fourth most widely used language among blogs worldwide. One service provider alone ("Persian Blog") hosts some 60,000 active blogs. The weblogs allow young secular and religious Iranians to interact, partially taking the place of reformist newspapers that have been censored or shut down. Government efforts to impose filters on the Internet have been sporadic and only partially successful. Some reformist politicians have embraced blogs, including the president, who celebrated the number of Iranian bloggers at the World Summit on the Information Society, and Vice President Muhammad Ali Abtahi, who is a blogger himself. Elite Iranian blogs such as "Editor: Myself" have established links with the English-speaking blogosphere. When Sina Motallebi, a prominent Iranian blogger, was imprisoned for "undermining national security through 'cultural activity,' " prominent Iranian bloggers were able to join forces with well-known English-language bloggers including Jeff Jarvis ("BuzzMachine"), Dan Gillmor ("Silicon Valley"), and Patrick Belton ("OxBlog") to create an online coalition that attracted media coverage, leading to Motallebi's release.

An international protest campaign also secured the freedom of Chinese blogger Liu Di, a 23-year-old psychology student who offended authorities with her satirical comments about the Communist Party. Yet, even as Di was released, two individuals who had circulated online petitions on her behalf were arrested. Such is life in China, where an estimated 300,000 bloggers (out of 80 million regular Internet users) uneasily coexist with the government. Bloggers in China have perfected the art of self-censorship, because a single offensive post can affect an entire online community—as when Internet censors temporarily shut down leading blog sites such as Blogcn.com in

2003. Frank Yu, a Program Manager at Microsoft Research Asia's Advanced Technology Center in Beijing, described this mind-set as he profiled a day in the life of a fictional Chinese blogger he dubbed "John X": "After reading over his new posting, he checks it for any politically sensitive terms which may cause the government to block his site. . . . Although he is not concerned as much about being shut down, he does not want all the writers that share the host server with him to get locked out as well. Living in China, we learn to pick the battles that we feel strongly about and let the host of other indignities pass through quiet compliance." Text messaging is a much safer medium for the online Chinese community. Some bloggers, however, do manage to push the envelope, as when Shanghai-based Microsoft employee Wang Jianshuo offered candid, firsthand accounts (including photos) of the SARS and Avian Flu outbreaks.

North Korea is perhaps the most blog-unfriendly nation. Only political elites and foreigners are allowed access to the Internet. As might be expected, there are no blogs within North Korea, nor any easy way for ordinary North Koreans to access foreign blogs. However, even in that country, blogs may have an impact. A former CNN journalist, Rebecca MacKinnon, has set up "NKZone," a blog that has rapidly become a focal point for North Korea news and discussion. As MacKinnon notes, this blog can aggregate information in a way that ordinary journalism cannot. North Korea rarely allows journalists to enter the country, and when it does, it assigns government minders to watch them constantly. However, non-journalists can and do enter the country. "NKZone" gathers information from a wide variety of sources, including tourists, diplomats, NGOs, and academics with direct experience of life in North Korea, and the blog organizes it for easy consumption. It has already been cited in such prominent publications as the *Asian Wall Street Journal* and the *Sunday Times* of London as a source for information about North Korea.

BLOGO ERGO SUM

The growing clout of bloggers has transformed some into "blog triumphalists." To hear them tell it, blogging is the single most transformative media technology since the invention of the printing press. Rallying cries, such as "the revolution will be blogged," reflect the belief that blogs might even supplant traditional journalism. But, as the editor of the Washington, D.C.–based blog "Wonkette," Ana Marie Cox, has wryly observed, "A revolution requires that people leave their house."

There remain formidable obstacles to the influence of blogs. All bloggers, even those at the top of the hierarchy, have limited resources at their disposal. For the moment, they are largely dependent upon traditional media for sources of information. Furthermore, bloggers have become victims of their own success: As more mainstream media outlets hire bloggers to provide content, they become more integrated into politics as usual. Inevitably, blogs will lose some of their novelty and immediacy as they start being co-opted by the very institutions they purport to critique, as when both major U.S. political parties decided to credential some bloggers as journalists for their 2004 nominating conventions.

Bloggers, even those in free societies, must confront the same issues of censorship that plague traditional media. South Korea recently blocked access to many foreign blogs, apparently because they had linked to footage of Islamic militants in Iraq beheading a South Korean. In the United States, the Pentagon invoked national security to shut down blogs written by troops stationed in Iraq. Military officials claimed that such blogs might inadvertently reveal sensitive information. But Michael O'Hanlon, a defense specialist at the Brookings Institution, told NPR that he believes "it has much less to do with operational security and classified secrets, and more to do with American politics and how the war is seen by a public that is getting increasingly shaky about the overall venture."

One should also bear in mind that the blogosphere, mirroring global civil society as a whole, remains dominated by the developed world—a fact only heightened by claims of a digital divide. And though elite bloggers are ideologically diverse, they're demographically similar. Middle-class white males are overrepresented in the upper echelons of the blogosphere. Reflecting those demographics, an analysis conducted by Harvard University's Ethan Zuckerman found that the blogosphere, like the mainstream media, tends to ignore large parts of the world.

Nevertheless, as more Web diarists come online, the blogosphere's influence will more likely grow than collapse. Ultimately, the greatest advantage of the blogosphere is its accessibility. A recent poll commissioned by the public relations firm Edelman revealed that Americans and Europeans trust the opinions of "average people" more than most authorities. Most bloggers are ordinary citizens, reading and reacting to those experts, and to the media. As Andrew Sullivan has observed in the online magazine *Slate*, "We're writing for free for anybody just because we love it. . . . That's a refreshing spur to write stuff that actually matters, because you can, and say things you believe in without too many worries."

WEB OF INFLUENCE
Around the World in Blogs

Plenty of bloggers discuss international affairs, but a few, in addition to those mentioned in this article, stand out from the crowd. Jeff Jarvis's BuzzMachine is the single best source for information on the global expansion of the blogosphere. University of California, Berkeley, economist Brad DeLong (Brad DeLong's Semi-Daily Journal) is perhaps the most influential economics blogger, while Tyler Cowen and Alex Tabarrok comment on microeconomic theory and the globalization of culture at Marginal Revolution. The group weblog OxBlog has won serious media attention for its campaign promoting an assertive U.S. foreign policy supporting human rights and democracy.

Blog coverage varies throughout the world. Although Salam Pax paved the way for Iraqi bloggers, he has stopped blogging himself, and only around seventy Iraqi blogs have picked up where he left off. Among the more prominent are Iraq the Model and Baghdad Burning, which respectively support and oppose the U.S. military intervention. Western Europe has a sizeable number of blogs, especially in Britain, with the right-wing Edge of England's Sword and the pro-war leftist Harry's Place. Slugger O'Toole covers the Northern Ireland beat, while A Fistful of Euros seeks to provide an overview of Western European politics. BlogAfrica syndicates blogs from across that continent. Last is the blog of Japanese tech entrepreneur and venture capitalist Joi Ito (Joi Ito's Web). He reportedly visits 190 blogs regularly and averages five hours a day reading and writing blogs.

WEB OF INFLUENCE
Want to Know More?

A lengthier treatment of the effect of blogs on politics can be found in the authors' paper "The Power and Politics of Blogs," presented at the 2004 American Political Science Association (APSA) annual meeting and available at APSA's website. For other studies of blog networks (all available online), see Clay Shirky's "Power Laws, Weblogs, and Inequality"; the Perseus Development Corporation's "Blogging Iceberg"; and Eytan Adar, Li Zhang, Lada A. Adamic, and Rajan M. Lukose's "Implicit Structure and the Dynamics of Blogspace," presented at the 13th International World Wide Web Conference, May 18, 2004.

For general primers on weblogs as a medium, Rebecca Blood's *The Weblog Handbook: Practical Advice on Creating and Maintaining Your Blog* (Cambridge: Perseus, 2002) is a good first start, and Dan Gillmor's *We the Media: Grassroots Journalism by the People, for the People* (Sebastopol: O'Reilly Media Inc., 2004) is a good place to finish. Rebecca MacKinnon's essay "The World-Wide Conversation: Online Participatory Media and International News," available on the website of the Berkman Center for Internet & Society, offers interesting insights about blogs as international information aggregators. Several websites, including Technorati, TTLB Blogosphere Ecosystem, and Blogstreet, are devoted to tracking and ranking blogs.

More broadly, there is significant debate about the Internet's effect on world politics. Ronald J. Deibert argues that the Internet enhances the influence of global civil society in "International Plug 'n Play? Citizen Activism, the Internet, and Global Public Policy" (*International Studies Perspectives*, July 2000). Drezner addresses the limits of the Internet in "The Global Governance of the Internet: Bringing the State Back In" (*Political Science Quarterly*, Fall 2004). Shanti Kalathil examines the impact of the Internet on authoritarian societies in "Dot Com for Dictators" (*Foreign Policy*, March–April 2003).

PART TWO
BUSINESS & ECONOMICS

THE VOICE OF THE CUSTOMER

by David Kline

On May 2, 2005, *BusinessWeek* sent a message to corporate America it could not ignore: a cover story entitled "Blogs Will Change Your Business." Although the magazine focused primarily on the perils and prospects of using blogs as marketing vehicles, the message on the cover could not have been more far-reaching. "Look past the yakkers, hobbyists, and political mobs. Your customers and rivals are figuring blogs out. Our advice: Catch up . . . or catch you later."

Or, as analyst Chuck Richard of the technology market research firm Outsell put it: "Behind the blog sizzle stir the essential ingredients of the next tipping point in the information industry."

All of which calls to mind a similar tipping point in the world of business just a decade ago. When the World Wide Web was first emerging, a fierce debate raged over what role, if any, business would play in this new online medium. Some of the Web's early pioneers, of course, suggested that cyberspace was simply too anarchic, too freewheeling, and too anti-commercial in its essential ethos for corporate America ever to succeed in establishing a major commercial beachhead online. "Information wants to be free!" proclaimed more than a few early Web homesteaders. That may be, replied the realist faction on the Web, but everything else still costs money. And where there's money to be made, they argued, business will always and inevitably follow.

What even the Web's realists failed to grasp, however—indeed, what corporate America itself did not even fully understand—was that while business would certainly transform the Internet into a vast commercial marketplace, it would itself be transformed, reshaped inside and out, by the very medium it set out to dominate. And sure enough, from sales and customer support to supply-chain dynamics and product R&D, the real story of corporate America's embrace of the Internet in the last ten years is not so much a tale of how much money has been made online, although that is considerable, but of how thoroughly almost every facet of global business has been altered by that embrace.

The sensational emergence of blogging as a hugely popular means of individual expression and public discourse over the last few years once again poses a challenge to the world of business. Some insist that because blogs by their nature are resistant to commercial hype, public relations, and message control, business will have a difficult time trying to co-opt the medium for commercial uses. Wiser heads recognize that while blogging certainly poses challenges to traditional marketing approaches, corporate America, as always, will find a way to turn a profit from this new phenomenon, just as it has from every previous new technology and social trend.

Yet here again, most people—or at least most of the media's coverage of business issues in blogging—are missing the fact that the real excitement here is not how much money business can make from blogging, but how dramatically blogging will reshape the world of business from top to bottom and create new sources of competitive advantage for firms that learn how to use this new medium intelligently.

Much is still uncertain about the ways that businesses large and small will embrace blogging. Unlike political bloggers, who had the benefit of a focused electoral campaign in 2004 to help them hone their skills and demonstrate their influence, business-oriented blogging is still in its infancy, with the vast majority of business still grappling with how and to what end to adopt the new medium. But the hesitancy with which most of corporate America viewed blogging during the past year is fast giving way to an almost frenzied rush to capitalize—somehow!—on the phenomenon. As noted earlier, corporate interest in blogging is still primarily focused on its use as a marketing tool, although companies will likely soon realize that a boost in marketing effectiveness may be the least of blogging's benefits to their competitive position in the marketplace. Indeed, if 2003–2004 was the year of the political blog,

2005–2006 seems likely to be the year when business blogging finally proves its value—no, its necessity—to companies large and small.

One thing is certain: blogging will have a large impact upon corporate America, not least because its essential effects run counter to the overall trend of development of large-scale industrial capitalism over the last century. Despite the last decade's efforts by many companies to become more agile, less hierarchical, and closer to their customers, the modern corporation is still largely a faceless monolith, shielded in a variety of ways deliberate and not from direct contact with its customers. Indeed, the only way most companies and their shareholders know if the firm's customers are truly being served with needed products and services is after the fact, when they sum up quarterly and annual sales figures. And until now, the only means that those customers and shareholders have had to influence the quality of those products and services—and to ensure that their manufacturer is responsive to their needs and honest in its financial affairs—has been to rely either on complaint letters or calls to customer service departments, litigation, the investigative diligence of the mainstream media, or the integrity of financial analysts. Unfortunately, as all the recent corporate and Wall Street scandals suggest, these methods are somewhat less than adequate.

Blogging, however, breaks down barriers—between customers and the makers of the products they buy, and between shareholders and those responsible for the financial performance of the firms in which they have invested. Blogging fosters communication, encourages transparency, forces greater responsiveness from once indifferent corporations. It puts a face on "organization man," forces companies to become more accountable, and gives a voice to the anonymous mass we call "the consumer."

But how, precisely, will companies integrate corporate, consumer, and product-oriented blogging into their day-to-day operations? How will blogging in turn reshape these companies and the ways they do business? Will blogging destroy any existing industries? Will it create any new ones? At this stage of the game, it is hard to be certain how these questions will be answered in detail. But by tracing the trajectory of business blogging from it's earliest beginnings and projecting forward, it is possible to contemplate blogging's potential impact on corporate America.

All beginnings are fraught with peril, of course. And so it was with the business world's first major encounter with blogs as marketing vehicles, when the $25 million Kryptonite bicycle lock company was very nearly destroyed during the course of ten blog-inflamed days in September of 2004.

The episode began on September 12, when a blogger by the name of "Unaesthetic" posted a comment on a discussion blog for bicycle enthusiasts informing people of his discovery that the U-shaped Kryptonite locks seen on so many bikes these days could be picked with nothing more than a Bic ballpoint pen. Two days later, the consumer electronics blog Engadget followed up by posting a video demonstrating how the Bic pick is done, along with a comment from editor Phillip Torrone noting, "We're switching to something else ASAP."

Apparently alerted to the rumblings in blogland, Kryptonite attempted to pacify the situation in the usual pre-blog fashion. It issued a non-denial denial asserting that its locks remained a "deterrent to theft." As anyone with even a Bic-sized brain could have predicted, of course, this press release mollified no one. In fact, it only made the firm's customers even angrier. Each day thereafter, more bloggers wrote about the lock problem, and each day thousands more people—soon to become hundreds of thousands more people—read about it. By September 17, the crescendo of complaint caught the attention of the *New York Times* and *Associated Press,* which each ran stories about Kryptonite's problems with its locks and with the blogosphere. These stories further inflamed the controversy. According to *Fortune* magazine, by September 19 over 1.8 million consumers read blog postings about the defective locks.

Having failed to deal with the problem when it was still manageable, Kryptonite executives finally recognized that they were, in essence, committing suicide by blog. On September 22, the company finally announced it would exchange any affected lock for free. That means 100,000 new locks, at least, which along with the associated expenses will cost the company some $10 million, or 40 percent of its annual revenues. As the company's marketing director Karen Rizzo told *Fortune*: "I don't necessarily want to use the word 'devastating,' but [this has] been serious from a business perspective."

Gee, you think?

The lesson, of course, is that in today's world, ignoring what your customers are saying about you, especially in the blogosphere, can be dangerous, indeed. As Jeff Jarvis, the president of media empire Advance Publications' online properties and a well-known blogger himself, put it: "There should be someone at every company whose job is to put into Google and blog search engines the name of the company or brand, followed by the word 'sucks,' just to see what customers are saying."

Other firms have tried to game the blogosphere. In an effort to attract younger car buyers, for example, Mazda created a bogus blog supposedly run by a twenty-two-year-old blogger named "Kid Halloween" to tout its cars. The site featured a link to three videos he claimed were recorded off public-access TV, which depicted a Mazda3 vehicle attempting to do various wild and crazy stunts such as break-dance and skateboard. But other bloggers noticed that the videos seemed far too expensively produced to come from public-access TV, and began spreading the word about Mazda's ploy. "Everything about that 'blog' is insulting," wrote one poster on Autoblog, and his opinion was read and reinforced by literally hundreds of thousands of others. The blog was quickly pulled.

Dr Pepper, too, thought it could pull a fast one on the blogosphere. The company launched a phony blog called Raging Cow to promote its new milk-based soft drinks, and then surreptitiously compensated some young bloggers to fan the hype. But all that did was spark a nationwide "Boycott Raging Cow" campaign among bloggers.

No sane person, of course, would dare to suggest that companies will no longer be able to get away with manipulating or lying to their customers in the era of blogging. But as Steve Hayden, vice president of the giant advertising firm Ogilvy & Mather points out, such behavior—especially on a blog—now carries unprecedented risk.

"If you fudge or lie on a blog, you are biting the karmic weenie," Hayden told *Fortune* magazine. "The negative reaction will be so great that, whatever your intention was, it will be overwhelmed and crushed like a bug. You're fighting with very powerful forces because it's real people's opinions."

And therein lies the fundamental power of blogs that businesses must learn to appreciate and understand: they transform the faceless anonymous mass called "consumers" into flesh-and-blood people who have real opinions and real feelings that can only be ignored or manipulated at the company's peril.

"The consumer is a metaphor," notes Hugh MacLeod, a UK-based marketing and advertising consultant who runs the GapingVoid blog. "The customer is a human being." And in today's new blog-enabled world, he notes, in which the roar of the customer can make or break a product, the future of brands is going to be interaction, not commodity. A brand won't be something you buy so much as something you participate in. A good solid successful brand will, in effect, be a two-way conversation.

To be sure, marketing experts have long appreciated the human element in the creation of successful brands. As the passionate devotion and loyalty shown by millions for Apple's iPod and Harley-Davidson's motorcycles suggest, people develop strong emotional attachments to great brands. What's different is that now, in the age of blogging, these brand attachments have taken on a much more viral quality—they can spread from person to person and multiply in intensity literally overnight—and can more quickly and powerfully determine the success or failure of products and brands.

In part, that's because blogging, like branding, is also about passion. Wherever people are passionate about something—be it knitting, sports, consumer electronics, cars or whatever—that's where you'll find bloggers discussing the ins and outs, their likes and dislikes, of the subject at hand. And they do so oftentimes with almost evangelical fervor, as demonstrated by the adoring iPod fan who took the time and trouble to create his own homemade ad for the product (Mazda should be so lucky).

Bloggers not only tend to be more passionate about their interests and hobbies than other people, they also have marketplace influence far beyond their numbers. As Technorati CEO David Sifry explained to *Business 2.0* magazine, "Bloggers are an incredibly influential consumer segment. These people are huge networkers. They get the word out quickly on products they like—and don't like."

And all that user-generated commentary on blogs gets indexed by search engines, which makes it easily accessible to potential customers doing research on a company or its products. "Even a comment on an obscure blog can generate positive or negative buzz that can impact a company's reputation in unexpected ways," notes Pete Blackshaw, the chief marketing officer at Intelliseek, a research firm that helps companies monitor their presence in the blogosphere. Indeed, an IAB Nielsen/Net Rating study conducted in 2004 clearly linked high search results to better brand recognition and value.

Explains marketing maven Catherine Parker, "If your company is releasing a new product or service, no formal marketing method meant to increase its exposure can match the power of people talking to each other." That's because people are increasingly immune to marketing hype, and as a result, a qualified referral from an influential unbiased blogger can often have more impact than all the advertising in the world.

One example is the hip-hop artist and producer Danger Mouse, who would probably have labored in obscurity in the New York club scene had it not been for blogs. But a handful of hip-hop aficionados discovered his music and began passing it around the blogosphere, where he became a sensation almost overnight. Over a million copies of his *Grey Album,* in fact, were reportedly downloaded in a single week—quite possibly the first example of a smash hit in the music business that had no marketing or other support from any music label at all. Since then, Danger Mouse has been hailed as "the hottest hip-hop producer in the world" by Britain's *New Music Express,* one of the "100 most influential people" by *Q* magazine, one of the top twenty on *Entertainment Weekly*'s "Must List: People and Things We Love," as well as one of *GQ* magazine's "Men of the Year." As blogger entrepreneur John Battelle notes, "None of this would have been possible without blogs and the extraordinarily influential audiences, even if small by traditional standards, that some of them attract."

Still, it will probably be the rare event that a company launching a new product will able to achieve the phenomenal success of a Danger Mouse or iPod music player through independent blogs alone. That's because independent consumer and industry blogs are by their nature resistant to commercial appeals. Most corporate marketers, therefore, will find themselves constrained in the ways they can leverage third-party bloggers, and will have to rely either on pitching their products for review by independent bloggers and hoping for the best, or in some cases, advertising directly on their sites. Such efforts will certainly prove valuable to firms promoting genuinely worthwhile products, but they will not by themselves usually yield blockbuster results.

Instead, smart companies will also want to create their own blogs—blogs of an entirely new type—to capture all the exponential buzz-marketing benefits that blogging makes possible today. This is especially true for firms with "information rich" and "high involvement" products about which consumers typically do significant research or rely on trusted unbiased reviews before making a buying decision.

Online marketing consultant Christian Sarkar calls this new approach *double-loop marketing,* which is based upon the notion that in today's world, marketing must be people- and knowledge-driven rather than product driven. The double-loop approach requires a company to first develop "mind share" by building a company-sponsored blog or bloglike community site that offers genuinely useful information and advice to consumers in the subject-matter areas most relevant to its products. The goal, in this first loop of the firm's interaction with customers, is to achieve thought leadership and credibility on the issues of most concern to potential customers. Only then can the firm, in the second loop of customer interaction, convert that "mind share" into "wallet share." In other words, first community, then commerce.

This approach can yield surprising results—often ten times or greater the number of qualified sales leads as those generated by conventional advertising and marketing approaches, according to Sarkar. He cites the example of one large software company that spent $120,000 on an advertising campaign in independent blogs and other online outlets that in the end generated only 250 qualified leads. But after it sponsored a bloglike community site that captured significant mind share among software engineers, vendors, and users, a mere $20,000 spent on advertising returned 11,000 qualified leads.

Would such an approach work for mass-market consumer products? Imagine, for example, that Procter & Gamble (P&G) wants to launch a new infant car seat to compete against industry leaders Graco and Evenflo. Let's assume also that P&G's new car seat is of excellent quality and offers performance or safety features superior to those of competitors—just for argument's sake, let's say it features a child-safe mini-airbag that inflates in an accident. In addition to all its traditional advertising and promotional efforts, how can P&G use blogs to ensure a more successful product launch?

The first thing P&G should do—and they should do it three to six months before the launch date of its new infant seat—is to map out the online "ecosystem" of parenting and child-rearing blogs. Which have the most traffic and are the most influential in their Google search engine result rankings? Of these "hub" parenting blogs, which appeal most to parents of infants and toddlers rather than older children or teens? What are the most popular keywords used on search engines that drive parents to these sites? Are there any unmet information needs of parents on these blogs?

Without this first critical mapping step, most companies end up flying blind on the periphery of popular attention. But with a clear picture of the competitive landscape in parenting and child-related blogs, P&G can then start to build a company-sponsored community blog of its own that provides genuine thought leadership and information and advice on the parenting issues most relevant to its new product's key selling point—i.e., child safety. Let's call this community blog "KidSafety.com." While it may feature an unintrusive sponsorship logo from P&G, it absolutely must *not* promote its products in the content of the site, either directly or indirectly, or the credibility of the site will be destroyed.

"Many companies don't have the patience to build credibility and 'mind share' before trying to sell products," Sarkar explains. "In their haste to produce results, they often embed commercial messages into the content of the site—thus poisoning the water with PR pollution and destroying the true informational value of the site."

But P&G is known for its patience and long-term vision. Thus "KidSafety .com" will offer the best, most unbiased, and trustworthy information on child safety issues available anywhere—all without any commercial pollution. Although it will be very bloglike in its atmosphere and will even feature blogs authored by noted child-rearing and safety experts, "KidSafety.com" will organize its content around topic areas—"Child-Proofing Your Home," "Safe Toys for Toddlers," "Pool and Backyard Safety," and the like—rather than in reverse chronological order of postings, as most blogs do. (The fact that most blogs are author-driven, rather than reader-driven, will probably be seen in the future as a shortcoming of current blog design.)

If "KidSafety.com" truly offers parents the kind and quality of useful information they can't find anywhere else, it will draw attention from other blogs and the media, and will attract a community of hundreds of thousands of loyal readers. Only when this has been achieved can P&G then begin to convert these readers into customers by placing valuable offers for its new infant car seat—as well as links to reports from unbiased experts such as *Consumer Reports* on the safety and performance of the seat—in a discreet sidebar on the community site. Once readers become customers, P&G can then try to cross-sell Pampers or other P&G baby products as well as provide customer service for these products. Thus, in addition to loyal users of its current product, the company will also have gained a prequalified base of customers for its future products.

Of course, none of this works if the car seat isn't truly a quality product. Most companies with inferior products and services, in fact, will find that the blogosphere is utterly useless to them—or worse—and they will be forced to keep trying to hoodwink customers the old-fashioned way until they are finally driven out of the marketplace.

As noted earlier, most of the business world's attention has been focused on the potential marketing uses of blogs *after* their products have hit the marketplace. But for many companies, the greatest benefits from blogging may well come *before* they even decide what products or services to build. In other words, instead of companies simply trying to tell customers what to buy, why not let customers tell them what to build?

It's not like corporate America couldn't use the advice, after all. Over 40 percent of all newly launched products fail in the marketplace—in some high-tech industries, the failure rate reaches 90 percent! And when executives are surveyed as to the reasons for this high failure rate—as the consulting firm Booz Allen did most recently in October of 2004 when it polled CEOs, chief technology officers, and vice presidents of engineering and product development—across the board they all pin the blame on one thing: an inadequate understanding of consumer wants and needs.

This problem is not new, by any means. It has long been an axiom of business, for example, that successful product development and commercialization requires close communication and idea sharing between engineers, marketers, and customers. And yet as the journal *Strategy+Business* points out, "Few companies are good at managing this exchange—particularly when it comes to capturing and integrating customer insights into product design." Most people, in fact, would be shocked to learn just how many firms regularly undertake multimillion-dollar development initiatives for a new product or service without ever speaking to a single current, former, or prospective customer. Truth be told, this failure to integrate the voice of the customer into the development process for new products has become the dirty little secret of corporate R&D.

Part of the problem, of course, is institutional. In many companies, engineers are treated a bit like the oddball cousins at a family reunion and shunted off to isolated areas of the firm, where they are fed near-lethal amounts of caffeine-rich foods to keep them producing and denied any contact with customers or any voice in the firm's marketing strategy. Such an "engineering-driven" R&D process, as it is euphemistically called, creates what Booz Allen's Kevin Dehoff calls a product development "doom loop" in which satisfying customer needs takes second place to the solving of technical problems.

But another factor contributing to the high failure rate of new products in recent years has been the dramatic shortening of product development times caused by advances in computerized design capability and improved supply-chain dynamics. Faced with ever-increasing pressure to rush new products to market faster and cheaper, many companies simply cut back on their market research functions. Explains Wharton marketing professor Jerry Wind: "When you have such pressures, very often companies skip the marketing research [and] that can be a huge mistake."

Some companies try to get around these problems by taking special steps to ensure that executives maintain close contact with their customers. At Harley-Davidson, for example, many executives are themselves great fans of the legendary "hog," and often attend rallies with other motorcycle enthusiasts. Their involvement creates empathy with customers and provides insight into what sorts of improvements they want to see in the motorcycle. An equally savvy approach is taken by consumer product giant P&G, which conducts

not only focus groups but also anthropological expeditions to see how customers actually use their products in the home.

Still, even when all the tools and techniques available to market re-
searchers are employed effectively—and, again, at most companies they are
not—it must be said that they are still rather blunt instruments for understanding customer wants and needs. That's because even when traditional
market research tells you *what* customers want, it usually doesn't tell you
why they want it. And it is here, in understanding the deeper motivations and
emotional drivers behind people's buying decisions, that the greatest opportunities for building winning products and successful brands are generally
found.

"Great brands are always built on a promise," says Greg Thomas, director of Programs for the Zyman Institute of Brand Science at Emory University's Goizueta Business School. And it's true. A company can promise quality
and dependability, as Lexus does. Or it can promise an enjoyable emotional
experience that people can take wherever they go, as Apple's iPod portable
music player does. Or it can promise a dream of wind-in-your-hair freedom
on the road, as Harley-Davidson does. But unless that promise touches people's deeper motivations, the brand will not succeed.

That's why businesses must use blogs—market researcher Charlotte Li
calls them "the exhaust streams of consumer attention"—to pierce the her-
metically sealed labs of new product engineering with fresh new insights into
customer needs. Instead of asking twenty people in a focus group to pick between various "baskets" of product attributes—a clumsy research technique
hardly improved by the scientific-sounding name "conjoint analysis"—why
not ask them to tell you directly, in their own often-rambling but always revealing words, exactly what they would like your new product to look like
and why? All firms have to do is get their engineers and marketers blogging
with their customers.

To be sure, "product definition" blogging will pose some interesting challenges to R&D managers. New product development plans are usually closely
guarded secrets at most companies, after all, so care will have to be taken
when attempting to use blogs to open up new lines of communication between

firms and their customers. Then, too, although "product definition" blogging can provide companies with better information about customer needs at lower cost, that information will in most cases be available not only to the firms who gather it but to their competitors as well.

"If product definition blogging becomes mainstream and the information about what to build is available to everyone, then the only source of competitive advantage in R&D left to firms is in *how* to build it," explains Brad Goldense of the Goldense Group, one of the country's leading experts in the management of R&D programs and processes. He suggests that to avoid the loss of competitive advantage that might result from publicly available "product definition" blogs, some firms may choose to set up private, members-only blogs with their most loyal customers, compensating them in some fashion.

Ultimately, Goldense argues, "Firms will still invest in trying to discover those unstated, unarticulated, success-determining features of new products that cannot be discovered even through blogs, in order to keep or regain a competitive advantage." In this respect, product-definition blogging may follow a trajectory in business similar to that of other new information technologies: the technology itself gives an advantage to early adopters, but once it becomes widely available to all, then execution becomes key.

Despite the challenges involved, we predict that many large companies—especially consumer product firms with world-class brands such as Apple, Harley-Davidson, and P&G—will begin to integrate product-definition blogs and the customer feedback they provide into the heart of their new product development efforts. This, in turn, will lead to a higher success rate for new products and boost the return on investment from corporate R&D across the board, with all the benefits that brings to the economy.

BrandEverything's Greg Thomas agrees. "There is a wealth of customer insight out there just waiting to be tapped via blogs and integrated into product development planning," he notes. "Smart companies will sooner or later have to recognize that fact."

It is interesting, of course, to speculate on the possibility that product-definition blogging might even morph and migrate to the retail sales channel. The American Customer Satisfaction Index, after all, just recently suffered a one percent drop, its biggest loss in nearly seven years. And this spells trouble not only for the retailing sector—a loss of $100 billion or more in consumer spending—but also for the economy as a whole.

Could not big-box retailers, therefore, use customer feedback blogs to help them customize their shelf space and their customer-support services to suit the varied needs and preferences of customers in different locales? Wal-Mart may not be the best candidate for such an experiment, since it competes solely on price and not on quality. But what about retailers such as Target and Costco, which do compete on the quality and variety of product offerings as well as on service? It's certainly reasonable to expect that as American consumers increasingly demand products and services customized to their individual needs—whether it be on-demand TV programming, tailor-made financial services, built-to-order computers, or simply their own personal favorite concoction of Starbucks coffee—retailing, too, will eventually undergo its own TiVo-ing process.

Back inside the enterprise, meanwhile, employee blogging has exploded into an exciting new means of fostering communication among firms and their customers, suppliers, and partners. Indeed, not since the advent of casual Fridays has a phenomenon caught fire in America's workplaces quite like employee blogging has. Thousands of corporate personnel, from senior executives like General Motors vice chairman Bob Lutz and Sun Microsystems COO Jonathan Schwartz to ordinary employees like Microsoft's Robert Scoble, have been bitten by the blogging bug in recent years. And the stampede has only just begun.

For most companies, the notion of employees speaking directly to customers without a PR flack standing by muzzle at the ready is "akin to putting dynamite in the playpen," notes *BusinessWeek*. But for enlightened firms that actively encourage the practice, such as Scoble's Microsoft and Schwartz's Sun, such blogs have become greatly valued for their ability to lend a human face to "organization man" and, as *BusinessWeek* put it, "transform a [customer's] transaction with a faceless behemoth into a personal relationship with an employee."

Scoble's blog (called the Scobleizer), for instance, gives readers a disarmingly honest look at the daily life of a Microsoft programmer. He listens to complaints about the company's software with an open mind rather than corporate defensiveness. He even praises the software of rival companies when he thinks it's warranted. And as a result, notes *Economist* magazine, "He has made Microsoft, with its history of monopolistic bullying, appear noticeably less evil to the outside world, especially to the independent software developers that are his core audience." Scoble's blog has been so effective in transforming the firm's image, in fact, he is now dubbed its "chief humanizing officer."

The benefits of such humanizing are not simply touchy-feely, but translate into more satisfied and loyal customers, more engaged and contented employees, and more effective collaboration and trust between a firm and its partners and shareholders. But dangers loom on the horizon of employee blogging. Says *BusinessWeek*: "It's only a matter of time before some workplace pundit spills a trade secret, unwittingly leaks a clandestine launch date, or takes a swipe at a CEO that turns into slander."

Already, close to fifty employees have been fired for blogging nationwide, and according to a January 2005 survey by the Society for Human Resource Management, about 3 percent of U.S. companies have disciplined others for blogging. Mostly that's because unenlightened bosses have taken offense when workers have used their blogs to gripe about the company—or about the bosses themselves. But in at least one case—that of Google employee Mark Jen—the reason was that he had blogged about the firm's financial performance and future products. Bloggers would do well to remember that if the law provides few protections for workers who piss off their bosses by making unflattering remarks about them, it provides absolutely none for workers who are simply too dumb to know better than to leak confidential information to outsiders.

Most companies do not yet have official blogging policies, and this only contributes to employee haziness about what is and is not permitted. But even when such policies become widely implemented, employee blogging will still remain a veritable minefield for firms and a potential gold mine for litigators.

What if, for example, some corporate blogger happens to mention that "next quarter's numbers look pretty good"? Has he violated Sarbanes-Oxley rules requiring all disclosures of financial information to be done through the media? If he wants to claim that blogs are, in fact, legitimate media, then is he giving a blogger who leaks trade secrets about future products the same protection that shield laws give to journalists? If trade secrets are leaked by a blogger and he tries to put a positive spin on the incident by posting that "at least now everyone knows that our new product will finally correct that defect in our current line," is he then risking a product liability suit? What if he thinks better of that last post, and the next day blogs that his firm "has already spent more than we probably should have trying to fix that product," has he also now conjured up a potential shareholder lawsuit? And if he finally just throws up his hands in frustration and blogs about "lying scumbag lawyers," has he just bought himself a nice little slander suit besides?

All we can say for sure is that it's probably going to require congressional if not Supreme Court action before all these questions are finally resolved. In the meantime, sensing a problem in need of a (profitable) solution, at least three companies have begun selling software that enables firms to monitor and censor their employee blogs.

However painful the process, though, it is clear that employee blogging will commit companies to a course of increasing openness and responsiveness from which it will be impossible to retreat. The "democratization" of business may be too strong a way of describing it, but we are almost certainly witnessing the death of "organization man."

Although the phenomenon of employee blogging has received considerable attention in the media, its burgeoning effect upon enterprise productivity has been largely ignored. This despite the fact that "industrial strength" or enterprise blogging is already beginning to supplant the traditional systems and methods that managers and employees use to communicate with each other and carry out their daily tasks. That's because blogging software platforms appear to have significant advantages over more costly traditional knowledge management systems designed to enable employees to access, store, forward, and publish everything from departmental reports, sales forecasts, marketing plans, financial analyses, engineering documents, and supplier and vendor contracts to individual to-do lists, appointment calendars, and meeting notes.

For one thing, current knowledge management systems are built upon a veritable Tower of Babel of differing document and data formats as well as application-specific interfaces, protocols, and operating systems. If you don't know what OBDC, SQL, MAPI, or POP3 are, then you're just going to have to trust me that in many firms, trying to access critical information or communicate effectively with colleagues is a bit like talking in tongues—only without all the associated convulsing and dancing about (unless, of course, you happen to be one of the system's harried administrators).

Enterprise blogs, on the other hand, store, publish, and forward everything in the most widely used publishing format on earth: HTML, the language of the Web. And when you add in RSS syndication capabilities—a kind of subscription service that automatically delivers relevant information to those who request it—this means that employees can access all the data and reports they need without having to spend hours hunting for them. (RSS stands for Really Simple Syndication, a web format popular for aggregating updates to blogs and the latest news from websites.)

If, for example, Procter & Gamble CEO A. G. Lafley wants to keep up with the relevant goings on in our hypothetical infant car seat business, he no longer needs to badger his underlings to forward him whatever reports they happen to be able to dig up from their files or from a backup tape in the archive somewhere. Instead, he can simply "subscribe" to the division's most critical information—key departmental reports, sales forecasts, R&D feasibility studies, supplier and distributor communications, product and industry news, market research, and, of course, customer feedback surveys—and have it delivered automatically to his desktop computer to review at his leisure.

As no less an authority than Microsoft chairman Bill Gates pointed out: "If I do a trip report, say, and put that in blog format, then all the employees of Microsoft who really want to look at that can find the information [simply by subscribing]."

Aside from convenience, ease of use, and seamless interoperability, of course, enterprise blogging offers two additional and very powerful advantages over traditional email-based communications systems: persistence and searchability. As David Berlin, the executive editor of industry journal *ZDNet* and one of the most insightful advocates of enterprise blogging, put it: "It's scary [when you realize] that email is not searchable, it's not accessible to anyone else, and most of the time if somebody leaves the company, they just simply wipe it out, even though it [contains] everything that person ever did and everyone they were in contact with. That information is simply lost."

Not so with blogs. For all these reasons, then, a still-small but growing number of firms have begun to use internal blogs as project- or enterprise-wide management systems. Whether blogs will replace current document management systems, or current document management systems will develop blog capabilities, the simplicity and ease of use of this technology virtually guarantees its wider adoption within corporate America.

Will enterprise blogging lead to macroeconomic increases in business productivity and economic growth? Anyone who recalls the "productivity paradox" of the 1980s will certainly be cautious in speculating on that point. During that decade, over 20 million PCs entered the American workplace for the first time, and economists expected a surge in productivity to result. None was detected, however—at least not until the advent of email and networked communications in the early 1990s. Thus the "paradox" was finally understood to mean that automation alone, unless accompanied by improved communications, does not necessarily lead to increased productivity. Or, as the futurist Paul Saffo famously put it, "A computer without a network is nothing more than a paperweight."

Well, if there's one thing we can absolutely and positively say about blogging, it's that it fosters improved communication. It therefore seems likely that just as blogging is finally realizing the Web's original promise as a medium of individual expression and public discourse, so may enterprise blogging bring about some of the larger productivity increases long promised by information technology.

I have focused so far on the ways that blogging may transform the manner in which business does business, along with the larger implications of these changes for companies and for their customers. But is blogging itself a great new business opportunity? Morgan Stanley analyst Mary Meeker certainly thinks so. In her words, "Blogging represents a huge business opportunity."

Blog software and tools companies obviously agree, not least because the bulk of blog-related revenues are currently going to them. But to listen to blog content aggregators such as Jason Calacanis of Weblogs, Inc., and Nick Denton of Gawker Media, the really big blog profits will soon shift to them. For their part, blog advertising networks are also hoping to profit from the phenomenon—just as soon, that is, as blog audiences reach critical mass and they can figure out how to target those audiences effectively for their clients. Meanwhile, BuzzMetrics, Intelliseek, and other research firms have begun selling services that help companies monitor their presence in the blogosphere.

Investors, too, are becoming increasingly excited about some of the business opportunities in blogging. Venture capitalists such as Andreas Stavropoulis of Draper Fisher, for example, invested over $60 million in 2004 in blog-related startups, including in the blog search engine leader Technorati. But as Stavropoulis points out, over the longer term he and other venture capitalists are looking to get in on the ground floor of ventures that can better contextualize search results to more effectively serve consumers' daily life needs.

Not wanting to be left behind, meanwhile, media companies have also begun to invest in blogs and content sources with bloglike capabilities. In the first few months of 2005 alone, Dow Jones acquired CBS.MarketWatch.com; Barry Diller's InterActive Corp. bought the search service AskJeeves.com and its subsidiary Bloglines.com; Yahoo purchased the photo-blogging and sharing site Flickr.com; Knight Ridder, Gannett, and the Tribune Company teamed up to buy a 75 percent stake in Topix.net, and the venerable *New York Times* purchased the blog aggregator About.com for a whopping $410 million. To be sure, the *Times* certainly got a better deal than its seller, Prime Media, got when it paid more than $900 million for About.com during the height of the dot-com bubble. But it still paid the rather extraordinary sum of $830,000 for each of About.com's rather anemic blogs.

Although this price is certainly over-the-top by any current measure of blog profitability, media companies do have some valid reasons to believe that blogs—and especially networks of popular blog content like Calacanis's Weblogs and Denton's Gawker Media, with all their targeted advertising potential—could well become valuable properties. Of course, there also appears to be more than a little desperation behind such moves, given that the mainstream media's own centuries-old business models appear to be eroding right under their feet as the profitable classifieds business moves online and as new online media encroach on their customer base.

How big a business will blogging be? It's simply too soon to tell. But while I have no doubt that investors, content aggregators, advertisers, software and tools companies, and vendors of blog-related services will all make some money—some of them even quite a lot of money—I do not believe that blogging will give rise to any blockbuster companies with Google-sized audiences and valuations.

What is clear, however, is that blogging—or more accurately, the ability to offer consumers the very best blog content as well as the best platform for their own blogging experiences—will decide which of the Web's biggest powerhouse firms will dominate the landscape of competition over the next five years. Will it be Microsoft, with its Spaces blogger services catching hold among MSN users and, in the future, with personal and enterprise blogging and RSS capabilities built into its Office suite and its operating system? Will it be Google, king of the search engines, which is rumored to be planning on melding its popular Blogger publishing software along with Google search, RSS, and Gmail free email into a new Google Web browser? What about Yahoo, the first to integrate RSS blog feeds into the "MyYahoo" home pages of millions of customers, and now moving quickly to provide blog publishing services for its multimillion user base?

Stay tuned.

In the meantime, it's worth speculating about blogging's impact on some existing industries—as well as on whether it might foster new ones. And on this score, it appears that the most likely candidate for the destruction part of what the late economist Joseph Schumpeter called the "creative destruction" effects of new technology is the $2 billion technology research business itself. Research firms such as Gartner, Forrester Research, and the International Data Corporation have been under profit pressure for years, after all, with revenues still down 6 percent from their 2001 peak, even as new technology spending has started to rise again. In response, a flurry of acquisitions have taken place as these companies try to reduce costs and maximize their market share to better compete. Garter recently acquired the Meta Group for $167 million, for example, bringing it's total market share of the research business to 47 percent. And a new wave of consolidations is expected.

But such moves may not be enough to stave off the erosion of their business models. Thanks to the Internet—and to well-connected technology experts who blog—businesses can often find the critical market and technology intelligence they need either for free or at a fraction of the cost of a Gartner or Forrester research report.

As Mark Newman, chief research officer at Informa, told the *International Herald Tribune*: "The costs of entry in this field are very small. A bunch of guys with good contacts in the industry can do an awful lot with very little."

Indeed, with high-quality information and sophisticated research tools now available to practically anyone with a good Rolodex and a sharp intellect, the "blodgening" of information-based industries like the technology research and financial and investment advisory businesses seems likely to continue apace.

This does not mean, of course, that Gartner and Forrester will necessarily go the way of the dodo bird. But it does mean that these companies will have to migrate up the value chain and offer even more exclusive high-value content to their customers, or else expand into new markets such as consulting, conferences, and programs for executives.

Although blogging is beginning to eat away at the foundations of some existing businesses, however, it is also becoming a leading venue for some of the most innovative and exciting research in economics, new technology, the sciences, and management theory and practice. Author Chris Anderson, for example, uses his blog to conduct research and analysis into the new theory of "long tail" economics, which is based on the observable fact that products that are in low demand or have low sales volume can collectively have a greater value than the relatively few blockbuster hit products. This theory holds major implications for businesses, because it suggests that companies can capitalize on the collective market power of these non-hit products by using the Internet as a low-cost distribution and communication channel to aggregate and reach consumers who desire these products, as Amazon.com and DVD rental firm Netflix are now doing.

Meanwhile, ThinkEquity Partners, a boutique investment bank in San Francisco, has launched a blog that attracts analysts, venture capitalists, bankers, and investors to speculate about the new growth areas of tomorrow. According to the *New York Times,* the company "did not see an immediate way to make money from the blog, but viewed it as a way to generate ideas—the lifeblood of research and investment banking."

These and literally hundreds of other blog-mediated research and collaboration efforts suggest that the blogosphere has already become a global incubator of new ideas. Soon it may become the midwife of new industries based on those ideas as well.

We live in exciting times. Blogging is fostering great changes, no less in business than in the world of politics. And one of the most interesting questions arising from the blogging phenomenon is whether the openness and transparency that it fosters might somehow provide us with new insights and better tools for understanding the deep and still largely invisible forces at work in our economy.

The "invisible hand of the market" so famously postulated by economist Adam Smith 250 years ago has, after all, clearly proven itself to be the most remarkable engine of economic growth and social progress ever devised by human beings. And yet still, after all these years, much of its inner workings remain a great mystery.

Which explains, no doubt, the continued popularity of the old joke about how an economist opens a can of soup—i.e., "First, assume a can opener."

Indeed, economics—and especially economic forecasting—is still largely an exercise in making assumptions. Even with all the mountains of quantitative data at their hands, economists still cannot tell us with even a modicum of certainty whether the stock market will rise tomorrow or fall, whether consumer purchasing will be up next month or down, whether employment growth will continue or level off. In part, that's because the so-called science of economics assumes that individuals make rational decisions in the marketplace, and as anyone who has ever observed a parent and child in a toy store can attest, the truth is a rather different matter entirely.

Perhaps what's needed is better *qualitative* data—economics with a human face. Just as "product definition" blogging may tell R&D managers not only what new products their customers want but *why*, maybe "economics blogging"—a statistically valid sampling of consumer and business blogs—could enable economists to get a better handle on the often less-than-rational but always deeply human motivations behind consumer purchasing and business investment and hiring.

Maybe what was invisible in Adam Smith's "invisible hand of the market" was not the hand, but the heart and soul behind it.

BLOGS: HUMANIZING THE FACE OF CORPORATE AMERICA

An Interview with Robert Scoble

The primary rule of corporate blogging is this: humanize it. To succeed, put aside the conventional PR wisdom; failing to do so may turn you into a pariah in the blogosphere—as David Kline's essay at the beginning of this section makes clear.

Ironically, it's a company with a reputation for being impenetrable and for bullying its competition—Microsoft—that has become a leader in creating a human face. That face belongs to Robert Scoble, who started his career selling NEC Tablet PCs. One day, he happened to tell a customer, a Microsoft executive, that he published a weblog. That executive followed Scoble's tech-savvy blog for five months. Scoble impressed him so much that he approached him with an offer to work for the computer giant.

Scoble has since become Microsoft's tech evangelist. Through his Scobleizer weblog (http://radio.weblogs.com/0001011) he communicates with thousands of software developers around the world every day, telling them what's hot and what's not, what Microsoft and its competitors are up to, and what technology trends to watch. An ever-present member of the Technorati Top 100, Scoble has a reputation and a reach that any multinational marketing department would kill for.

The foundation of that reputation is trust. When Microsoft launched a new music player, Scoble didn't just complain about it, he posted that he preferred his iPod. When the company launched its blogging platform MSN Spaces, with content controls that other bloggers greeted with derision, Scoble held up his hands and admitted that Microsoft had made a mistake.

Paying him the ultimate compliment, the Economist *has called him Microsoft's "Chief Humanizing Officer."*

In this interview Scoble lays out the foundation for Microsoft's blogging strategy and explains how companies ranging in size from one plumber to GE's thousands of employees can benefit from the blogosphere. He then makes the case that blogging is here to stay and its future lies in integration with mapping and other forms of content distribution. He also tackles the most frequently asked question about his boss and the blogosphere: will he or won't he?

Robert, you became Microsoft's tech evangelist because they saw your ability at your former employer, NEC, to converse with customers, give tech support, and listen to feedback. Your readership grew because you were always honest about the products. Microsoft has a lot of "tech evangelists." How is your role different? And has working at Miscrosoft forced you to alter your former approach?

Yes, there are other tech evangelists at Microsoft, but they usually work with a specific company—customers like Adobe—encouraging them to build software for Windows. Most of these people are hardcore developers and company-to-company relationship experts. I do the same kind of work, but instead of relating to another company, I serve the technical community as a whole. I work for the average developer out there.

As for the second part of your question, I had, as you suggested, an independent voice before coming into Microsoft. I was on the record as telling Bill Gates to split up the company, for example, and that certainly helps my reputation. When I was hired, Microsoft made it clear that they wanted me to continue talking in the same way.

What makes a good blog, and what can it achieve on behalf of business that other mediums cannot?

To me, a good blog has two things: it's passionate and it's authoritative. Say you're a plumber and you're working here in Seattle. You could use a blog to demonstrate those two things. You could show passion by posting often, by showing up at plumbing events, and by using language that shows you are excited about going to work every day. Then you can show authority by posting pictures and articles showing people how to do their own plumbing, which would demonstrate that you know what you are talking about.

There are very few mechanisms that can scale like a web page for as little effort. Say I spend ten minutes writing a blurb on my blog. It goes out to thousands of people and the tool I use only costs me $40 a year. Other mediums cost far more to reach that many people. A video conference would cost thousands of dollars just to get a few thousand people to join in. Same if I went on TV or did a radio show.

Okay, I've hired the plumber to install a new dishwasher because his blog helped me figure out how to install the new kitchen sink, and he's local. Now it's time to paint the kitchen. There are lots of paint brands out there, and an absolutely bewildering number of color choices. How does a company get my attention, and potential business?

Let's say I'm a paint vendor like Sherwin-Williams. How do you get known on the Internet? How do you beat your competitors? How do you have a better relationship with your customers? How do you find out new kinds of paint trends? Do you hang out with Martha Stewart and see what kind of trends she's going to come up with? Or do you watch what people are saying—and asking—about painting on the blogosphere?

The thing that's really neat now is that I can watch what people are saying in real time. Perhaps they're saying, "I need a quick-drying paint, this is taking too long," or maybe they're saying, "I wish somebody would make a particular color." In the past, you wouldn't know that as a company unless you were paying a lot of money for focus groups or marketing experts. But now you can watch what people are saying about your product category very efficiently. Now, that's not blogging. That's listening to blogs. But it's a good first step.

The second step is to realize that if they are talking about you, wouldn't it be really interesting to talk back? Wouldn't it be interesting to have a

Sherwin-Williams blog where if you saw someone saying, "I'm painting my kids' room this weekend and I'm going to paint it blue," you could link over to that blog and say, "Hey, Joe Smith is painting his room this weekend. How about some techniques he might try to make it go faster." Or, "here's some new paint colors that you might go and check out at your local Sherwin-Williams store." So that would start a conversation.

Companies should also realize bloggers continually look at who is paying attention to them. They might see Sherwin-Williams linking over to their blog and go, "Wow, that's different. I've never seen a big company listen to me before."

That would generate more conversations. And all of a sudden this thing starts snowballing where more people start talking about Sherwin-Williams. Word of mouth gets kicked off and that's really the most important trend businesses should be paying attention to right now.

Word of mouth has always been important. How does a blog improve on that?

Word of mouth has always affected product sales of every kind. A recent survey said 71 percent of car sales are at least influenced by word of mouth. The problem is that until recently, manufacturers never got to see the word of mouth happening, nor got to participate in it. Back in the 1980s, word of mouth was two people talking in a break room or five people talking over dinner on a Friday night. A guy at work would tell you, I bought a Ford Focus last weekend and I really love it, why don't you come check it out? And Ford was never able to be in that conversation when it was happening.

Well, now I have the ability to be part of that conversation. Plus the conversation itself is far more efficient. Now a guy writes on his blog and he can have thousands of people listening. Not only that, but let's say you only have five readers of your blog, but one of them was the Autoblogs guy [autoblog.com]. He would pass that message along, thereby exponentially amplifying this new word of mouth, and very, very quickly. I'm seeing stories go from individual blogs to the front page of the *New York Times* within twenty-four to seventy-two hours. That's a huge shift from even a year ago where it would take a week to five weeks.

From a CEO's point of view, how do you decide which members of a company are going to blog? Should employees be encouraged to blog? Should it be restricted to top executives?

Well, there are very different approaches, and they would be used for different purposes. A colleague and I interviewed Mark Cuban of the Dallas Mavericks for my blog and he said that he won't allow his employees to blog because he believes there should only be one voice for the Dallas Mavericks and that's his voice [blogmaverick.com].

On the other hand, Microsoft hires very smart people across the company and lets them write. It's not just Bill Gates anymore because the company is too big to have just Bill Gates speaking on behalf of the company. I'm seven levels down from Bill Gates and I'm talking about Microsoft strategy and product plans and vision pretty openly.

If I am interested in a company I like knowing the guy who is building the product. Ford let Mustang designers talk about designing the next engine and I really like that. It helps me as an evangelist to talk about a product. And it enables me to tell my friends and to post on my blog about it with more authority. I have some context that isn't just the marketing stuff you see on the Superbowl commercial, which doesn't tell you anything about how the product was designed or built.

It's a two-way conversational ad and there are going to be a lot of different business models for its use in the future. Blogging is certainly the biggest tree in the forest but there's also podcasting, there's drawing with ArtRage [artrage.com], and there's video blogging.

Let's turn to the future. What developments should we be looking for? And will these new developments help companies that facilitate blogging, such as Google and Yahoo, make more money?

Google's new mapping software serves as the metaphor here. (Incidentally, I've already seen MSN's prototypes for this software and they are really exciting.) So, all the various technologies I just mentioned will be coming together around such maps. You're going to see blogs, photo-sharing, and other content mixed in with mapping. So let's say you are coming to Microsoft to visit me and you did a search on "One Microsoft Way." Why shouldn't there be a list of icons there that shows a bunch of different blog posts that people have done? Why can't you mouse over and say, "There's a new sushi restaurant three miles away" and you click on the restaurant and it shows you how to get there. And why can't you have Flickr-style photo-sharing right on the map, so I can take a picture of that sushi restaurant, put it on top of the map and then put a little blog post there about that sushi restaurant. Then, you click on that blog post and now you're over on my blog, looking at my content.

For the big companies it's going to be that integration that really is going to be worth the value because once you build a system like that then you can put advertising into it. Google has been making a lot of money off their text ads search engine and I would expect to see that metaphor expanded to other areas that they're building in content creation and sharing. I'm sure MSN is hard at work trying to figure it all out too.

Google is kicking everybody's butt at the moment. But I think you're seeing Yahoo come on very strongly with their acquisition of Flickr. I also think you're going to see MSN come into the mapping world with a very strong product. Plus MSN has MSN Spaces [spaces.msn.com], with half a million MSN Spaces open in four months. It's a race and it's too early to say that any one company has built the ultimate thing and has grabbed all of the market share.

What about weblogs themselves? How do you think they will change over the coming years?

They're going to be more integrated. That's where you're really going to see the innovation. It's going to be the integration of blogs into other things, like the tagging system that Flickr and Technorati came up with.

All you do is you put one line of code into your blog post in the HTML that tells Technorati that there's a post that's been tagged by the user for a specific page. So now you understand where Sherwin-Williams can come in and have a blog that's tagged with the word *paint*. Then anybody that comes to the Technorati page and searches on the word *paint* would find the Sherwin-Williams blog or photos.

It's not just a blog world anymore. When you want to share yourself on the Internet, you can share video, audio, drawings, pictures. Soon with maps you're going to be able to tell people where you are from your cellphone. There's already prototypes out there where people are carrying around cellphones with GPS devices that tell everybody where they are.

"RSS" seem to be the acronym du jour, popping up even in the mass media. Why is it important, and how will it help the evolution of blogging?

RSS is the technology that corporations should pay more attention to than even blogging. [The initials stand for "really simple syndication," which is a techie's way of saying it allows a blogger to offer his Weblog for people to subscribe to, as well as to integrate links and news from other websites.]

Remember that five things made blogging hot. I call them the five pillars of conversational software. The first was "ease of publishing." The second was "discoverability," with tags and pings that let services like PubSub [pubsub.com] and Feedster [feedster.com] and Technorati [technorati.com] get on top of the blogosphere. The third was "cross-site conversations," where I could see who was linking to me with trackbacks. The fourth was "permalinking," where I can isolate a URL that will take me directly to a post. And the fifth was "syndication," the last "S" of RSS.

Syndication started in the late 1990s but it wasn't important back then because I wasn't watching ten or fifteen websites a day. But once the blogosphere started expanding I found it impossible to keep up. That's when I got into RSS and understood why it was so important. Because it meant I could see a large number of sites, and not only that, but I got them on my terms. I never had to give any marketing information or my email address and it just organized itself.

There is another term often mentioned in the same breath as blogs: wikis. What is the relationship between these two? Have they added to the value of blogs?

Wikis are really important but they are completely separate from blogs. It's a great technology for getting groups of people to work on a project [in that it allows a team to keep adding new data to advance a specific task]. It's certainly been interesting on Microsoft's Channel 9 [channel9.msdn.com] site because people went up there and created a spec list for the next version of Internet Explorer. The team watched and considered the list very closely, plus it kept getting better and better all the time.

A blog is great at posting new stuff. But it's not great for factoring in and working together with people on a single idea or project. I see wikis as complementary to blogs.

A question about the future closer to home. There has been a lot of talk since early 2004 that Bill Gates may join the blogosphere personally. Will he?

He was working on one but he just doesn't have the time to do it continuously and he doesn't want to put up five blog posts and then disappear for five months. He wants to make sure he can expend the commitment on it and I understand that. His life is just so mad.

I met with him a year ago and he's very passionate about blogging and is watching the space very closely. Clearly Microsoft has made an investment in MSN Spaces and is putting RSS all over the place. So I think you're going to see a lot of things coming out of that.

So do you believe the blogging phenomenon is here to stay? That blogs are not simply one more soon-to-disappear fad?

People keep calling them fads but they've been calling them fads for five years. The reason that they're not a fad is that people keep blogging. Why, you ask?

Go back to the plumber again. Let's say you live here in Seattle. Say I go home tonight and my basement pipes are leaking and I need a plumber. Where do I go? I can go to my Yellow Pages or I can go to the Web and search MSN, Google, or Yahoo for a plumber in Seattle. Now, if I search on-line, research shows that the top ten listings on Google or MSN are a lot more likely to get my business.

If you search for me, I'm the number one Robert in the world. Why am I higher than Robert Redford? More people in the world know Robert Redford than know me. It's because I have more inbound links than him. And the reason I have more inbound links is because I write on the Web.

The more you blog, the greater chance you have of being recognized—and listened to. So Google is paying back the blogosphere for adding content to it. It's a virtuous circle.

THE CORPORATE WEBLOG MANIFESTO

The rules of engagement for the blogosphere do not require a serious management tome or the writings of Sun-tzu. Indeed, they would be counterproductive in the new medium. Still, a handful of fundamentals are key. Here they are, courtesy of Robert Scoble, who wrote this "manifesto" around the time he started at Microsoft. He continues to preach—and live by—this gospel.

Thinking of doing a weblog about your product or your company? Here's my ideas of things to consider before you start.

1. Tell the truth. The whole truth. Nothing but the truth. If your competitor has a product that's better than yours, link to it. You might as well. We'll find it anyway.

2. Post fast on good news or bad. Someone says something bad about your product? Link to it—before the second or third site does—and answer its claims as best you can. Same if something good comes out about you. It's all about building long-term trust. The trick to building trust is to show up! If people are saying things about your product and you don't answer them, that builds distrust. Plus, if people are saying good things about your product, why not help Google find those pages as well?

3. Use a human voice. Don't get corporate lawyers and PR professionals to cleanse your speech. We can tell, believe me. Plus, you'll be too slow. If you're the last one to post, the joke is on you!

4. Make sure you support the latest software/web/human standards. If you don't know what the W3C is, find out. If you don't know what RSS feeds are, find out. If you don't know what weblogs.com is, find out. If you don't know how Google works, find out.

5. Have a thick skin. Even if you have Bill Gates' favorite product <http://radio.weblogs.com/0001011/2003/02/26.html#a2351> people will say bad things about it. That's part of the process. Don't try to write a corporate weblog unless you can answer all questions—good and bad—professionally, quickly, and nicely.

6. Don't ignore Slashdot. [Slashdot (slashdot.org) is a popular website, updated many times daily with articles that are short summaries of stories on other websites with links to those stories, and provisions for readers to comment on the story. It is often criticized for posting inaccurate, highly biased, and/or inflammatory story summaries among its news and commentary.]

7. Talk to the grassroots first. Why? Because the main-stream press is cruising weblogs looking for stories and looking for people to use in quotes. If a mainstream reporter can't find anyone who knows anything about a story, he/she will write a story that looks like a press release instead of something trustworthy. People trust stories that have quotes from many sources. They don't trust press releases.

8. If you screw up, acknowledge it. Fast. And give us a plan for how you'll unscrew things. Then deliver on your promises.

9. Underpromise and over deliver. If you're going to ship on March 1, say you won't ship until March 15. Folks will start to trust you if you behave this way. Look at Disneyland. When you're standing in line you trust their signs. Why? Because the line always goes faster than it says it will (their signs are engineered to say that a line will take about 15% longer than it really will).

10. If Doc Searls says it or writes it, believe it. Live it. Enough said. [Doc Searls, who runs Doc Searls Weblog (doc.weblogs.com), is a senior editor for *Linux Journal* and owns and manages Doc Searls' IT Garage (garage.docsearls.com), a group journal launched by the publisher of the *Linux Journal*.]

11. Know the information gatekeepers. If you don't realize that Sue Mosher reaches more Outlook users than nearly everyone else, you shouldn't be on the PR team for Outlook. If you don't know all of her phone numbers and IM

addresses, you should be fired. If you can't call on the gatekeepers during a crisis, you shouldn't try to keep a corporate weblog (oh, and they better know how to get ahold of you since they know when you're under attack before you do—for instance, why hasn't anyone from the Hotmail team called me yet to tell me what's going on with Hotmail and why it's unreachable as I write this?).

12. Never change the URL of your weblog. I've done it once and I lost much of my readership and it took several months to build up the same reader patterns and trust.

13. If your life is in turmoil and/or you're unhappy, don't write. When I was going through my divorce, it affected my writing in subtle ways. Lately I've been feeling a lot better, and I notice my writing and readership quality has been going up too.

14. If you don't have the answers, say so. Not having the answers is human. But, get them and exceed expectations. If you say you'll know by tomorrow afternoon, make sure you know in the morning.

15. Never lie. You'll get caught and you'll lose credibility that you'll never get back.

16. Never hide information. Just like the space shuttle engineers, your information will get out and then you'll lose credibility.

17. If you have information that might get you in a lawsuit, see a lawyer before posting, but do it fast. Speed is key here. If it takes you two weeks to answer what's going on in the marketplace because you're scared of what your legal hit will be, then you're screwed anyway. Your competitors will figure it out and outmaneuver you.

18. Link to your competitors and say nice things about them. Remember, you're part of an industry and if the entire industry gets bigger, you'll probably win more than your fair share of business and you'll get bigger too. Be better than your competitors—people remember that. I remember sending lots of customers over to the camera shop that competed with me and many of those folks came back to me and said "I'd rather buy it from you, can you get me that?" Remember how Bill Gates got DOS? He sent IBM to get it from DRI Research. They weren't all that helpful, so IBM said "hey, why don't you get us an OS?"

19. BOGU. This means "Bend Over and Grease Up." I believe the term originated at Microsoft. It means that when a big fish comes over (like IBM, or Bill Gates) you do whatever you have to do to keep him happy. Personally, I believe in BOGU'ing for EVERYONE, not just the big fish. You never know when the

janitor will go to school, get an MBA, and start a company. I've seen it happen. Translation for weblog world: treat Gnome-Girl as good as you'd treat Dave Winer or Glenn Reynolds. You never know who'll get promoted. I've learned this lesson the hard way over the years.

20. Be the authority on your product/company. You should know more about your product than anyone else alive, if you're writing a weblog about it. If there's someone alive who knows more, you damn well better have links to them (and you should send some goodies to them to thank them for being such great advocates).

Any others? Disagree with any of these? Sorry my comments are down. Now Hotmail is down too. Grr. Where's the "Hotmail weblog" where I can read about what's going on at Hotmail? So, write about this and link to it from your weblog. I watch my referer links like a hawk. Oh, is that #21? Yes it is. Know who is talking about you.

Source: http://radio.weblogs.com/0001011/2003/02/26.html of Wednesday, February 26, 2003. Used with permission from the author.

THE WHOLE BECOMES HUGELY GREATER

An Interview with Nick Gall

Nick Gall is the kind of guy whom the Apple advertising people must have had in mind when they came up with the slogan: "think different." Formally, he is Vice President and Distinguished Analyst at Gartner, Inc., and a founding member of Gartner's Enterprise Planning and Applications Strategy practice. He is also a former intellectual property litigation attorney as well as a leading authority on middleware, infrastructure planning, technical architecture, and XML Web services. Turn to his blog, however, and he describes himself simply as "an ironist currently employed as an IT Industry Analyst" (http://radio.weblogs.com/0126951/).

And what does he mean by ironist? Quoting from the American philosopher Richard Rorty's book, Contingency, Irony, and Solidarity, *"The ironist . . . is a nominalist and a historicist. She thinks nothing has an intrinsic nature, a real essence. So she thinks that the occurrence of a term like "just" or "scientific" or "rational" will [not] take one much beyond the language games of one's time."*

To innovate, Gall is saying, don't follow common sense (irony's opposite). Ah, the perfect credo for a blogger. And the perfect reason why, as he explains below, colleagues used to belittle his weblog. Nowadays, of course, his colleagues and clients are just as bitten by the weblog bug as he is.

In this interview, Gall explains how companies are employing weblog technology to improve their business and how the world's largest corporations are finding ways to make money out of the open-source revolution.

Can you explain what provoked your interest in blogging?

Well, I had been exploring the medium since I started covering emerging technology for META Group. [META Group was acquired by Gartner, Inc., in April 2005.] But I started my blog in June 2003 because I didn't have a channel for some of my thoughts. There's a certain form and a certain type of information that our clients are seeking that really didn't fit all of my areas of interest so I thought blogging might be a good way to express myself.

At META Group the initial reaction was one of skepticism and derision. Blogs were considered the domain of teenagers. No one really considered them to be a medium worthy of corporate interest. The fact that I thought blogs were going to be a really big deal at the time, even in the corporate world, was met with a lot of skepticism because it wasn't mission critical and didn't have all the normal attributes of high-end corporate software. But META Group had a very laissez-faire environment and nobody questioned what I was doing because I was doing it in my own time.

When I moved to Gartner there was some concern about my blog, but surprisingly enough it didn't come down to the content issue. The real concern was brand management. They wanted to make sure that the Gartner brand wasn't adversely affected by my blog. So we came up with a very simple ground rule, which I agreed to work with: I simply wouldn't mention Gartner or my work at Gartner in any way, shape, or form.

It sounds like there were some issues surrounding your blog. Why even continue if it meant risking your career?

When I first heard that Gartner might have a concern with my blog even I was surprised by my reaction. I basically told everyone concerned, and I warned my wife, that this was a nonnegotiable issue and that if Gartner wouldn't allow me to continue my blog I wouldn't accept the offer of a job. I had found that the ability to express myself and to know that people were reacting to it and connecting to it was very empowering. I had never really connected directly with people like that on a broad basis before and I wasn't going to give it up now.

What about the companies you deal with at Gartner. What kind of interest have they shown in blogging?

By and large the subject of blogging will come up because I might name drop that I have a blog or that I read something on blogs, then the client would mention that they had a personal blog or that they too found reading blogs to be a great source of information—more the latter than the former. Certainly, in the IT sector those on the leading edge are interested in the power of what is published on blogs. It is often of a very high quality and is full of insightful information about leading trends in technology.

The majority of clients I talk to begin exploring the blogosphere for information that's emerging from the leading edge. I have done my own informal research on corporate blogging and a number of major organizations have been quite public about their blogging, wiki, and other social software experiences. Capital City/ABC Disney uses a variety of blogs across the corporation for sharing information, primarily internally. It's a very inexpensive, lightweight, easy to navigate, easy to train way of sharing information. I have yet to talk to or run across any organization that has tried it and didn't embrace it.

Can you explain what makes blogging such a powerful tool for businesses?

Many of the aspects of blogging are really just a result of the notion of the Internet as a "spanning layer." David Clark, who was the chairperson of the Internet Engineering Task Force, coined the term "spanning layer" to explain what it was that made the Internet so explosively successful. He did this using the concept of an hourglass.

The notion of the hourglass is a standard or a system that overlays a wide and diverse set of technologies at the bottom. The wider the hourglass at the bottom the better, because the more it overlays and integrates the more powerful it will be.

Equally in accordance, but even more difficult to achieve, is a wide top to the hourglass. The wide top is a technology that enables a diverse set of uses, the more diverse the better. So any *specific* application technology is weaker under this model than anything that's general purpose.

So, very broad at the top in terms of what it can be used for and very broad at the bottom in terms of what it can be deployed on top of. Then you have the narrow waist—this is the tricky part. A narrow waist is a minimal set of standard specifications that enables all of this powerful open-endedness from the top to the bottom. That is the spanning layer. And that's the design shape of the Internet itself, the IP protocol. It's the design shape of the Web and it's the design shape of Web services.

It's the same for blogs. If you look fundamentally at what enables blogs you see two sets of protocols, the good old traditional HTML, HTP, URL, which is the Web. But as we all know, the other magic ingredient of blogging is the variety of RSS protocols that make it possible to subscribe to various blogs and, with trackback technology, to see who's talking about whom. So if you look at basic blogging architecture, and the array of incremental services on top of that, like Flickr.com and Furl.net and Del.icio.us, they are all protocol-based technologies that enhance and extend the interactiveness of what we call blogging.

What do you envision the benefits of these combined technologies to be?

The obvious first benefit is a more direct channel of corporate communications, both business to business and business to consumer. I think everyone is looking for better ways for corporations to humanize and personalize their interactions with consumers and other businesses. And I think blogs have done that in the IT environment very well. There's no question that the IT intelligentsia pays a lot of attention these days to what bloggers at Microsoft or IBM or Sun or BEA are saying. And there's no question that has an influence on thinking about technology in a pretty profound way. It's the developers themselves who are having this extended dialogue and debate about the pros and cons of the Web services approach to integration.

Have you noticed any pattern among these companies towards making the best use of weblogs?

Well, the building of blogging capabilities into products is fairly minimal. Probably the closest version I can think of is Microsoft's new blogging platform,

MSN Spaces, but other than that I haven't seen RSS or blogging capabilities built directly into any of their shrink-wrapped products. Obviously there are small vendors that are direct players in the blogging arena but major corporate IT vendors, by and large, have not yet built their technology or their architectures around blog protocols. I think that will happen once it matures but right now they are using it as a tool for communication as opposed to a part of their system architecture.

The obvious play for blog technology is really in the collaboration space, but anyone doing this must deal with Microsoft's dominance on the desktop and in "office" applications. No one has yet made a major effort to derail Microsoft's expansion from desktop "office" dominance to office-server-based information-sharing dominance. Lotus has a huge legacy-installed footprint but they seem to be retreating towards embedding collaboration into line-of-business applications. This is a great way to generate service revenue but not a great way to foster the growth of collaboration and free-form activities like blogging or wikis. Novell has tried to make a dent in collaboration for a long, long time and nothing they did was ever successful. It's the same for Oracle and for Sun.

Although application architecture is hugely popular among IBM and the others, most of them aren't investing tons of money in collaboration architecture. There are huge profits to be made there but it's hard to take away business from Microsoft. Perhaps Google will take up the gauntlet.

What about Google? How are they challenging their competitors?

Google is probably the best example of somebody that is showing there are vast opportunities in what were once considered played-out markets. They did it first in search. All of the conventional wisdom was that search is totally played out. Now Google is branching out into other services and everybody is very expectant that they will get into all forms of collaboration.

Google's biggest play so far is Gmail; that's a key collaboration tool. Now that they have picked up Blogger we'll see what they do with that. The other example of where they have done rethinking of what was considered to be a played-out technology was mapping software. Google Maps has astonished a lot of people with its usability and some of the open-endedness of what you can do with it.

Can you explain how RSS and wiki technologies fit into this?

The magic word that we haven't mentioned nearly enough in this conversation is this wonderful notion of peer to peer. That's a big part of the cultural design principle that underlies blogs and wikis. It's this notion of bottom-up innovation. It's got a lot of different names including the term "mass amateurization." Clay Shirky originated the term, and it has been picked up and discussed by lots of people, myself included. It's also been referred to as "pro-am."

"Mass amateurization" is the notion that people have an avocation that is so intense they will spend hours, days, weeks, years working on it. It's like a hobby, but because of the power the Internet gives hobbyists to connect you get this emergent effect, where many hobbyists reinforce each other's efforts. Sometimes it results in things you could never imagine a volunteer effort doing. Probably the best example is Linux. But if you look at open content you get the same thing. Wikipedia is a bunch of volunteers who spend hours, days, weeks of intense effort to contribute their intellectual property for free into this emergent encyclopedia and the results are just astonishing.

How do your Fortune 500 clients feel about trends in which people provide services for free?

It scares those who haven't been focusing on this phenomenon but those who have been tracking open source for a while get that ethos. They try to look ahead and understand how to make a lot of money out of what looks like free content. They understand how to strategically play the open-source game because they can make even more money than they did in a closed-source economy. They do it with services.

My favorite example is IBM. The content that gets generated on open source is pretty good. It's 80 percent there but that last 20 percent is where you can make some money by offering for those Fortune 500 organizations the extra 20 percent that they need. They can't get by with just "off the Web" software. They need indemnification or they need higher availability, and IBM will add that extra layer.

Have you noticed any companies maneuvering in this way with blogging trends?

Well, blogs may run their course for whatever reason. I'm not going to vouch for the specific format that we now know as blogging. But what is a bigger trend is this notion that information is being shared in ways that were considered anathema to major corporations. They are now playing around with forms of intellectual property sharing inspired, in part, by blogs. And it all has to do with this notion of *open*—open content, open source, open intellectual property.

As an example, here's IBM, the largest holder of patents on the planet, probably with the least incentive according to conventional wisdom to ever forego their right to their patents. But instead they are foregoing those patents aggressively because they see that in a world in which the whole is much greater than the sum of the parts the pie gets dramatically bigger for everyone if you give up your proprietary rights, if you let the information be shared and combined in ways outside of your control.

When people post on a blog, they are putting something outside of their control, People can take the information that I put on my blog, talk about it discuss it, link to it, copy it. But in return I get interaction and feedback. My information becomes part of the larger integrated information space, where the whole becomes hugely greater then the sum of the parts. But it only works if everybody throws their information into the pot.

JAPANESE BLOGGER CHAMPIONS INTERNET DEMOCRACY

An Interview with Joi Ito

Cookery tips, political discussions, bizarre news stories, and absurd photographs: Joi Ito's website is a daily mishmash of news, views, and communal chitchat. The king of Japanese blogging is just as likely to host discussions on the merits of Paris's Charles de Gaulle Airport as he is to debate the war in Iraq. His weblog (joi.ito.com) has become a meeting place and a talking shop for people from all over the world, and it attracts more than 125,000 unique visits every month.

Ito has always been a leading player in the Internet industry. Based in Tokyo, he is the founder of the venture capital firm Neoteny. He helped create Infoseek Japan, the nation's second-largest Internet search site after Yahoo Japan, as well as PSINet Japan, the first commercial ISP in Japan. He also leads the international and mobile operations of Technorati, a real-time search engine tracking and indexing a wide range of blogs.

As if not busy enough, Ito is also involved in helping to shape global public policy when it comes to web-related issues. He is a board member of Creative Commons, a nonprofit venture that is trying to create a flexible copyright system for Internet users. He is also a board member of the Internet Corporation for Assigned Names and Numbers (ICANN), which manages and coordinates the domain name system worldwide.

Ito started his first website in 1994, but since switching to blogging software Movable Type in 2002, he hasn't looked back. In fact, he liked it so much that his firm Neoteny recently invested in Six Apart Ltd., the California company behind Movable Type and TypePad.

What motivates you to find the time and energy to blog these days, having done it as long as almost anyone and having so many business and public policy interests competing for your attention?

My blog serves a couple of different functions. I write about anything of interest and as a result of having written about it, I will get comments that enhance and deepen my knowledge. So the first order value to me is that I get an enormous amount of feedback, and the feedback increases my ability to learn and helps me find other people with similar interests. My blog has become a place and it supports a community. Many of my posts are really questions that start a dialogue. I am just a facilitator of the community.

The community aspect of my blog is much more central to me and the people who read my blog. You can see it in the format, where the comments are all just as important as the post, everything from font size to the way that comments are displayed and tracked. Many blogs do not allow comments or have less focus on the community.

So how do you put your persona on this community?

I've had several online communities in the past, and I've usually named them something functional. The first mailing list that I ran featured cool websites and was called NetSurf Japan. But inevitably the community of users starts getting in fights over every little thing, so this time I just decided to call my website Joi Ito's Web. It's not necessarily a vanity thing, but more so I can say, "You can do what you want but you're in my living room, so be respectful because I have to take care of this place." I feel like I am a custodian of a community. I am happy to have people come but it really is kind of like a party in my living room.

If you were trying to express in a nutshell the role of the blogging phenomenon circa 2005, what would you say?

It used to require a significant investment to become a creator or a publisher: you had to learn an instrument, you had to go to school, you had to buy a video camera. But for a whole bunch of different kinds of content now, the tools used to create and publish and circulate content have become very affordable. There is still a digital divide, but if you have a day job at a 7-Eleven, you can still be a musician or a blogger or an amateur creator. This opens up a completely different type of business model.

For instance, many bloggers spend money to operate their blogs and yet many of them don't get paid money when people read their blogs. This is the opposite of the traditional content business model, which is that people get paid to create and people pay to consume.

I think the key here is, once you enable people to have a voice, most people are more interested in talking to each other than they are blindly consuming something that is created by a machine. I think in all its forms, creativity is going to become much more driven by the people. The consumer is now becoming the producer, and I think that this is going to have an across-the-board change in everything from music to media.

What kind of change?

Basically, it's going to become more expensive to become popular, and it's going to become less expensive to distribute the stuff. I think you are going to see a rebirth in folk art and folk music. I think that now we are in a period where we are in a very constrained, narrow, mass communication method—television, radio, newspapers—where you try to tune the whole world into a very narrow band, where you have big stars like Michael Jackson, where the definition of a bestseller or a big hit is that it's not very good. I mean, how can a hundred million people like the same song? It's very difficult if you think about the fact that we are quite culturally diverse.

Chris Anderson of *Wired* magazine wrote recently about something called the *"long tail."* He shows that the average bookstore like a Barnes & Noble can only stock about 130,000 books, but the fact is that Amazon.com sells more of the books that aren't in the top 130,000 than those that are in the top 130,000. I think what blogs and all these other alternatives to mass media allow is an emergence of the non-mainstream.

It allows people to find each other, find niches, and find communities. I think these communities of interest look a lot like how folk art and folk music were before we had television and radio. The utopian inside me wants to believe that blogging and other technologies like this are going to help people participate in culture, participate in politics, and will increase in diversity and locality and maybe offset some of the negative effects of globalization.

What is Creative Commons all about and what's your involvement in it?

Right now every time you create something, it is automatically copyrighted and if somebody wants to use some content on the Internet you can't tell for sure whether they would care if you used it or not. Creative Commons lets you select a certain kind of copyright license. We have a bunch of questions like, Would you mind if someone created a derivative work? Would you mind if people used it for commercial use? Or do you want it only noncommercial use? We even have a new license where you can copy something freely in developing nations.

What's important here is that you are making clear your intention. MIT licensed courseware using a Creative Commons license, so now a school in Vietnam is using that courseware to teach classes. The key here is that the Vietnamese didn't have to ask permission because permission was already granted. If you have Creative Commons licenses attached to your work then that information moves much more freely.

We are not against copyright. We are just saying that copyright is not either on or off. There is a spectrum of rights that you have as a copyright owner and, if you feel like it, you should be allowed to give certain ones up. We are trying to help artists to decide what rights they would like to reserve and what rights they would like to give away and then make it clear.

Is there any other challenge for creativity on the Internet?

Up to now, the Internet has been kind of a free-for-all, loosely organized, working anarchy of geeks and libertarians. The U.S. government was quite good at allowing a kind of bottom-up governance approach, but as more and more of the world economy starts to rely on the Internet for basic infrastructure, people are hoping and trying to regulate its use in increasing ways. Hollywood is trying to make it difficult for you to send files, the telephone companies and other guys are going to make it more and more difficult for people to set up their own networks. There is going to be a struggle to keep the Internet as open.

On the one hand, there will be people who say that we must keep it open, but I can easily imagine that there will be arguments soon, if there aren't already, that the Internet assists terrorism and assists pirates and is just a bad thing. So there is a risk that ten years from now the Internet is going to look a lot like cable TV or commercial radio and not the kind of emergent democratic system that it I hope it will be.

How might that happen?

What Microsoft or anybody could do is create a system where if you access a website that isn't authenticated with the proper cryptographic certificate you will get a warning that says, "This site may contain a virus. Downloading any content from this site voids your Microsoft warranty. Continue: yes/no?" And if it's a weblog that's been set up by somebody independent of Microsoft you may say "no."

Of course, I shouldn't just pick on Microsoft, but this whole Trusted Computing Initiative and Microsoft, which are to try to get rid of spam and viruses is also saying, "Let's make the Internet so that you can only connect to computers that are authorized and authenticated and secure." And it's saying that the data shouldn't actually live on your computer but on the server, with all computers just hanging off of this big network. Part of the dot-net vision of Microsoft is really that—that everything is on the network and your computer is just a stupid terminal and not in your control.

In this world it would be very difficult for you to set up a computer and have people access it. You might have to register at "AOL Blogs" or "Microsoft Blogs" and they may have a bunch of terms-of-use policies that prohibit a bunch of things, like saying "fuck." There are many technical ways that freedom of speech can be suppressed and I don't think we can take it for granted. [Since this interview, Microsoft has launched their version of blogs called MSN Spaces which DOES forbid profanity.]

My hope and my intuition is that blogging will prevail. In a funny way I think the fact that George Bush won the 2004 election in the United States is going to push people towards trying to protect their freedom of speech. Now that freedom of speech is being challenged, people aren't going to take it for granted.

Okay, for now anyway, bloggers are being heard without much difficulty. But they are not being paid. Do you see that as a problem?

I don't think that's necessarily going to be the point. Because I don't get paid I have a different level of legitimacy on my blog. I'm not influenced by my advertisers, I can say what I want, I can tell people this is my damn living room and I can do whatever I want here. That's the freedom that makes blogging fun. If I had an editor and if I had advertisers then I would have to be accountable to something other than what I am aspiring to, which is really to communicate how I feel.

I don't think professional journalism is going away, but I think that the excitement and the fun that you get out of actually participating is a huge incentive to bloggers. This "amateur revolution" thing is a real phenomenon.

Open source proves that too. Linux is made by a community of people who aren't getting paid by Linux to do the work. Yochai Benkler, who is a Yale law professor, wrote this great paper called "Coase's Penguin," which talks about a new mode of production called commons-based peer production.

[Benkler's paper built on the work of Ronald Coase. In the 1930s, Coase defined two modes of production: the first was based on employees working within a firm, and the second was based on individuals working in a free market. In 2002, Benkler added a third mode of production, commons-based peer production, in which groups of individuals linked by a computer network collaborate on a project without financial compensation. He named his paper "Coase's Penguin" after Linux's penguin logo.—Ed.]

It's the mode of production in which people are collaborating outside of a company without individual ownership of copyright. He defines different reasons people do that: one is for reputation, another is for the fun of learning, another is the joy that you have when you collaborate with other people.

A lot of us would like to have more money but there are a lot of things in life that you can't buy and some of those things are friendship, reputation, and community. I would much rather keep a healthy community and my network of friends than make a little extra money here and there. If it means that I have to have a day job to keep my blog the way I want it, then that's the way I'll do it.

What is your favorite blog that would not be obvious to people who visit all the well-known blogs regularly?

My favorite is Reverend Akma's blog [akma.disseminary.org]. He's a reverend from Chicago and he's a really wonderful person. Once, I wrote a very flippant post about God, about how "it's all you religions that believe in one god that are doing all the fighting, not like Shinto where we have multiple gods." He was offended and he wrote this on his blog. So I called him and I said, "So, explain this God thing to me. I don't really get how you can act the way you do." And he sat with me for over an hour explaining God to me.

I would never have had the opportunity to call up a reverend and have them explain God to me, and he would probably never have gotten a call from somebody in Japan asking to explain God to him, if it weren't for the fact that we stumbled upon each other on blogs. Now, if he shows up in my chat channel sometimes and people are talking and the chat becomes too rude, Reverend Akma will cough. He's like the chaplain in M*A*S*H.

In this discussion, you have emphasized the positive powers of blogging. Are there any negative side effects?

One risk for many of us is to delude ourselves into thinking that we are more inclusive than we are. In the lead-up to the 2004 presidential election, there was a kind of a tendency to hang out with people who have similar tastes, similar interests. So there is a risk of starting to think you are listening to everyone, even though those involved in your community actually represent only a certain part of the spectrum.

But I also think that having a lot of voices is one of the best things about the way that blogs work. Not only that, but blogs have a good filtering mechanism for noise and a good amplification system for signal. If somebody blogs about something, it is very easy to ignore it, but if somebody writes something interesting, it's very easy to find it.

Giving people a voice may be more important than giving people the vote. The issues that face us are so complex and the mass media, particularly television, is just unable to convey enough information or range of thought.

Because Technorati indexes every five minutes you can see the links coming in and it creates a continuous conversation throughout the day. The speed and the barrier of committing to text all these thoughts has gone down significantly. A lot of the media are thinking about blogs as a new form of publishing but it's really a new form of conversation and a new form of community.

TAKE AN OBSESSION, THEN FEED IT!

An Interview with Nick Denton

If any one name is associated with blogging as a business, it would have to be Nick Denton. Indeed, the thirty-six-year-old British expatriate and for-mer Financial Times *reporter has founded what* Fortune *magazine called the first "empire of the fledgling weblog industry"—an empire that includes such hot name-brand blogs as Wonkette (for lovers of Washington politico-sex scandals), Gawker (a must-read for the New York chattering classes), De-famer (for those who can't get enough Hollywood celebrity dirt), Gizmodo (appealing to high-tech gadget lovers), Fleshbot (for . . . well, we all know what that site is all about), and a number of other gossipy high-concept blogs operating under Denton's Gawker Media umbrella.*

The formula, Denton explains, is actually quite simple: "Take an obsession—say, a gadget obsession—and feed it." And feed it he does, with more content than eighteen- to thirty-four-year-old Internet surfers could ever find anywhere else. And the more wickedly irreverent the content, the better. "As with addicts," notes Denton, "the more you give them, the more they want." Anyway, once the audience is suitably hooked and fattened up, then Denton sells this deliciously sweet demographic to advertisers.

Although in the interview that follows Denton tries to downplay the hype over blogging in general—and the prospects for success for his Gawker Media empire in particular—there are indications that the Gawker formula may be gaining some traction, revenue-wise. His Jalopnik blog for car afi-cionados recently signed an exclusive sponsorship deal with Audi, and some *"associates" claim the various Gawker sites are now bringing an average of $5,000 each in ad revenue monthly.*

Compared to the ad revenues of traditional media outlets, of course, those numbers (even if true) still make Denton's Gawker Media company look more like a lemonade stand than a new media empire.

But then the same was said of Yahoo and eBay less than a decade ago. Denton does not maintain a blog but keeps his fan base informed about Gawker projects at nickdenton.org.

Why do you prefer to hire unknown writers for your blog sites rather than writers with track records in the media?

Because the unknowns are hungrier, and because often a track record in print journalism is no advantage in writing a weblog. We've got actually a rather poor experience with established journalists, trying to convert them into bloggers. It's sort of like trying to turn journalists into screenwriters. It's a whole different format, and it's not easy for most people to make the switch.

Besides, the fact of the matter is that the market for writing talent in the United States is extremely inefficient, and there are mediocre people who end up getting jobs and there are talented people who don't. In fact, if you look at the way people get jobs in the New York media world, you see that a lot of it seems to be about who you know and how well you schmooze at parties. Weblogs are more meritocratic, in my opinion.

So when looking for new writers, we don't look for résumés, and we don't look for great clips, which are often less a guide to somebody's writing ability than they are a guide to the editorial ability of the person who's been line-editing them.

Of course, it works the other way too. Writers who are good webloggers often don't do that well when they try to make the transition to magazine journalism or newspaper journalism. But if I was actually looking at hire people from traditional media organizations, I wouldn't necessarily look at the writers. I'd look at the editors.

Why is that?

Because I'd want someone who is used to taking garbage from reporters and making it funny. I mean, look, I think we're beginning to learn what works and what doesn't in this medium. Brevity is important in blogs. So is personality. And certain topics—things that people are passionate about, like politics, sex, gadgets, cars—work very well in blogs, whereas others don't. That's why we look at weblogs as the purest way to judge somebody's writing talent as applied to our needs. So I see us continuing to look for younger, fresher talent—people who would have a hard job getting anywhere in mainstream journalism.

You've made some comments in the press lately that suggest you're not really sure there's a real business in blogging—or at least you're not sure how big a business it will be—and yet you're a blog entrepreneur?

I don't see why that's controversial.

No one is saying it's controversial. But it is interesting to see someone in your position trying to damp down some of the hype around blogging.

Well, the hype has been pretty impossible lately. There has been far more attention paid to the weblogs than is actually healthy. I mean, people need to remember that none of today's weblogs approach the audience that Matt Drudge has. And even Matt Drudge himself, although he has a substantial audience, it's still a relatively modest business. It's just him and one other person. It gives him a good living and that one other person probably a decent salary.

But aren't the advertising possibilities with weblogs pretty lucrative, especially the possibility of targeting the "influencers" in society?

In theory, yes. But a lot of people who theorize about marketing don't have much contact with the way that media buyers actually work. And most media buyers, at least for the larger advertisers, aren't even going to look at any site unless it's got five million unique visitors a month, regardless of how "influential" its audience is.

I mean, we're the closest to being an advertiser-ready form of blog media today, and we're only now starting to get the RFPs [request for proposals] from the bigger agencies. So while I think it's interesting to speculate about larger CPM [cost per thousand] rates for the more influential readers that blogs tend to attract, I think what will end up being more significant—or what will be more significant sooner—is the movement of a certain demographic away from television to online and, within online in particular, to blogs. I think the real opportunity lies in pitching the eighteen- to thirty-four-year-old demographic, at least the eighteen- to thirty-four-year-old male demographic, to advertising. That's certainly been our focus, anyway—building up our audience among eighteen- to thirty-four-year-olds so we can deliver a critical mass of them through one of our sites or a collection of our sites to big media buyers.

Do you think you'll be successful in this effort?

Obviously, I believe that weblogs can be a good business or I wouldn't be doing this. Our sites are growing at about 20 percent a month. And that sort of growth rate is mirrored elsewhere, throughout the miracle of compound growth. Over the next five years weblogs will aggregate much bigger audiences and have a larger impact on society and politics and culture and business as a result.

But people talk about weblogs as if they're this totally revolutionary new phenomenon. And the biggest thing they get wrong is they look at weblogs in isolation, as being entirely new and springing up suddenly in the last couple years, when in fact we've already had some extremely successful independent media sites that have a lot of the attributes of weblogs. Sites like Suck or Drudge or Smoking Gun, sites that are much, much larger than even the largest weblogs.

The truth is, weblogs are merely the latest iteration of independent Web media, and they're not rocket science. People want to complicate blogs more than is warranted. But there's nothing revolutionary about weblog publishing or the magic of RSS and newsreaders or of weblog advertising.

Even the reverse chronological order of weblog postings isn't new, either. The news wires, for example, have used reverse chronological order forever. And when you're looking at something on a computer screen, that's a logical way to read things. That's what your email inbox looks like, right? You start at the top and you read down until you get to an item you've already dealt with and you know you can stop. That's been an established computer screen metaphor for years.

You know, I really hate to be boring, but I don't think that any of this is all that new. Everything that is, and that will be, has been before.

So blogs represent more of an evolution than a revolution?

Yeah, but sometimes an evolutionary process can be dramatic enough that it has the effect of a revolution. It can destroy whole industries. For example, at some point, music compression and digital music files and the Internet and file sharing all came together—the price was right and the connectivity was right—and they first damaged and then transformed the music industry. I can certainly see the same thing happening to the news business. But I don't think it's going to happen overnight and it's not going to happen because of any one single development. What'll happen is, as the audiences grow, so will the advertising potential. And as publishing software improves and its costs decline and Internet technology overall matures, then at some point the revenue potential of blogging will outweigh the costs and blogs will really begin to transform the news business in much bigger ways than it already has. I think it's reasonably obvious that weblogs are going to unbundle the existing newspaper publishing business.

What do you mean by "unbundle"?

I mean that people won't necessarily go to the front page of the *New York Times* or *Fortune* as much as they do now. They won't be loyal to any particular newspaper or TV news channel. Just as TiVo allows television watchers to make their own channel, so will weblogs allow individual users to make their own "newspaper"—a newspaper that will be put together from hundreds or even thousands of different news and information sources, some of them traditional publications and some of them weblogs. I mean, already thanks to weblogs more than half the people coming to the *New York Times* website come in through a link in a blog or other publication they're reading rather than through the front page. And that trend is only going to increase as readers rely less and less exclusively on traditional media sources and more and more on nontraditional ones. That's what I meant about newspapers becoming disassembled.

But that said, I don't think anyone's going to replace, anytime soon, the role of the *New York Times* in providing, for example, reporting from Baghdad. Weblogs don't have the resources to do that. So while I don't think blogs are going to change the structure of original reporting, they are going to supplant in some ways the editorial layer of the news—and by that I mean the role of *the New York Times* in deciding what's important and what goes on the front page. The *New York Times* will no longer have as much of a trump edge in determining the national agenda. Instead, I think increasingly it's going to be weblogs that will collectively decide what's important. They will pick out some story embedded deep within the *Times,* on some inside page, and promote that story's importance over perhaps what's on the front page. And that process will, in turn, influence how the *Times* decides what to put on the front page. So I think it'll be the editorial selection of the news business that weblogs will influence more than the story writing itself.

What about the question of legitimacy? People still rely on the New York Times, *for example, to determine what's really true and not true on a whole host of controversial issues, from whether or not there were weapons of mass destruction in Iraq to whether an alien spaceship really landed in New Mexico fifty years ago. Do you think weblogs can replace traditional media's role as neutral arbiter of truth?*

I don't think there's a simple answer to that, because blogs can be better but are often worse than the established media in their reporting. Take reporting in Iraq, for instance. The *New York Times* has made some mistakes, but it's been generally authoritative in its reporting on the search for weapons of mass destruction. On the other hand, a blog like Salaam Pax's provides a kind of insight, a human voice from within Iraq, that the *Times* simply cannot.

But of course it all depends on each individual blog whether or not, and on what sorts of issues, it can earn readers' trust as an authoritative news source. A lot of bloggers don't have any special expertise in any subject, or any special access to newsmakers, nor are they close to the "street" of any situation or conflict. They just sit in their armchairs pontificating on their political views of things. Which is fine, there's nothing wrong with that. But I don't think most of them are going to earn readers' trust as being more authoritative than the *New York Times*. I just don't see it.

IS IT THE TORTOISE AGAINST THE HARE?

An Interview with Jason Calacanis

If Nick Denton's Gawker Media company epitomizes the "People maga-zine" mass-market approach to the blogging business—lots of gossipy sites built on salacious consumer obsessions such as celebrity and sex—Jason Calacanis's Weblogs, Inc. aims for the vertical niches where industry and trade journals thrive. His blogs cover everything from the inside-outs of wireless technology and magazine design to playing digital music and raising babies. Where Denton aims to lure common denominator consumers, Calacanis sees gold in information and service blogs for both businesses and consumers with highly specialized interests.

There are other differences as well. Denton's Gawker Media hires writers for a small salary. Calacanis's enterprise partners with bloggers for 50 percent of the advertising revenues. Of course, 50 percent of not-a-lot is even less, say critics of the Calacanis approach. But then since Denton isn't exactly raking in the dough, either, the debate seems rather snarkily academic.

Suffice it to say that at this point in the emergent blogging business, there is more than enough room for multiple approaches to blog profits (or lack thereof). In the meantime, Calacanis, the former publisher of the popular print magazine Silicon Alley Reporter *during the dot-com heyday in New York, keeps plugging away in his tortoise race against Denton's hare. Calaca-nis can be found at calacanis.weblogsinc.com.*

What first attracted you to blogging?

I always loved the "unplugged" acoustics and live sets at rock shows. Like going to Carnegie Hall. You know, you can see an orchestra, or you can see Bob Dylan on the stage with just a guitar, harmonica, and his soul—no major production, you just focus on the music. To me blogs are like that, less produced, more soulful—more real.

I love building editorial brands, and I did it on the Web, in email, in-person-events, and in print. This makes me a little different from a lot of the bloggers out there who have not started a print magazine. When you compare the amount of work and expense that goes into a print magazine—think millions of dollars a year—to blogs, it is truly inspiring.

You can start a blog for next to nothing, and in six months it can reach 500,000 to 10 million page views, or thousands to millions of readers. You can't really do that in print. Of course, because it is so easy to start, you really need to put your focus on finishing.

I have a sign in my office that says "Starting Is Easy, Finishing Is Hard." That's the truth about blogs as a business.

What's the current scale and scope of your blog-related ventures?

We have about sixty-five blogs, we will have a couple of hundred.

We started by doing lots of micro-niche blogs, now we are doing some broad categories like gadgets at engadget.com, travel at gadling.com, parenting at bloggingbaby.com, and video games at joystiq.com. We could split each of those blogs into at least ten nano-blogs each. But the broad blog seems to enable you to have more to write about, and it lets you gain a larger audience. We are still doing highly niche stuff as well.

We make money by advertising. We have a lot of big advertisers like HP, Google, Audible, Suzuki, etc. The early deals were three- or four-figure deals, now they are five-figure deals. End of this year, early next year they will hit six figures, I'm sure. We have a huge advantage because we can offer an advertiser a menu of sixty-five blogs, of which they might advertise on ten to sixty-five of them. So, one of our ad sales is like ten to sixty-five times that of a single blog. That is key to the model.

What's the business case for your blogs? Can these be profitable businesses?

They can be profitable, and many of ours are profitable. However, having one be profitable is hard, though, because if you're not careful the second you put salaries on them the model breaks.

I think each blog is a tiny business—say, a $10,000 to $500,000 business each. So, running one can make a individual enough money to quit their job and you see that all over the place. However, it's very hard to hire people to work for you and make the business sustainable without investment or having many blogs.

In terms of the similarity of blogs to other media businesses, I'd say they are just like other media businesses in the sense that they are advertising based. But they are much different from other media businesses in that the scale is usually smaller and the content is unfiltered. No one edits the writers! That is a huge difference, and that is the core of blogging.

How are your blogs supplementing traditional media offerings?

I think cable is the best analog to look at. Before cable you had food shows on PBS, now you have a food channel. Before cable you had *Friday Night Videos*, now you have MTV plus five others. Before blogs you had niche magazines, now you have a car blog [autoblog.com] that is updated 20 to 30 times a day. You couldn't do that blog on TV or in print. The audience is too small to make enough money from them to justify the production costs.

Are blogs a "technology" investment as well as a media investment?

There are no media or technology investments anymore. There are technology companies that leverage media, and media companies that leverage technology. It's all coming together, smart VCs are getting that. Media wasn't a big investment before, and the portals stayed away from it. But now media is starting to come up on everyone's radar because it is more efficient, more predictable, and more scalable.

What revenue streams from blogging will end up being the most significant—advertising, subscriptions, or share of blog-mediated transactions?

Advertising. Advertising. Advertising

How do blogs fit into other trends that entrepreneurs and venture capitalists have been interested in, such as social networking and search technology?

Social networks are a feature, not a business. Just like you can send email from within applications and web pages now, you'll have a list of related friends connected to applications and web pages. Blogs help search a whole lot because they are so frequently updated, and they cover so many things that have not been covered before. Google finds more stuff, and more relevant stuff, because of blogs.

Can blogs be useful to companies?

Blogs are good for companies that are good, and bad for companies that are bad. TiVo and JetBlue can and should write blogs all day long because people love those services. Verizon, with all their customer support issues, shouldn't do a blog until they first make a commitment to treat their customers better! You have to be honest on a blog and let the users give feedback; if your users hate you then your blog will be like a drunk going to group therapy when they are half in the bag—it's ugly.

How is Silicon Valley in general looking at the blog phenomenon—does it have a big impact? Is it seen as any kind of killer app?

My personal theory is that if we're doing our job right we should have at least three killer apps every two years or so, and those killer apps should take five years to play out. So, at any given time there are five or six killer apps floating around. Blogs, RSS, social software, search—these are killer apps all, but many killer apps are not businesses in and of themselves. They are platforms on which to build a business. For example, email and instant messenger are killer apps, but what are the big businesses that represent them? Hotmail? The list gets really short after that, but then try and list businesses that don't use them and you get an even shorter list!

THE BLOG BUSINESS: IT'S MORE LIKE MUSIC THAN PUBLISHING

An Interview with John Battelle

There are not a lot of people who have John Battelle's entrepreneurial experience in new media. One of the cofounders of Wired *magazine (and its various online spin-offs) and the founder and former chair of Standard Media International (publisher of the former* Industry Standard *magazine and TheStandard.com), Battelle has been responsible for or involved in the launch of more than thirty magazines and websites both here in the United States and internationally. He was named a "Young Global Leader" by the World Economic Forum, as well as a finalist for Ernst & Young's Entrepreneur of the Year Award in 2001. A founding executive producer of the Foursquare Conference on intellectual-property-leveraged industries and the Web 2.0 Conference on the Internet industry, Battelle is also a columnist for* Business 2.0 *magazine and a visiting professor (on leave) at the University of California Graduate School of Journalism. He is the author of an upcoming book from Penguin Portfolio entitled* The Search.*

Currently, he is chairman and publisher of Federated Media Publishing, a new blog-related business launched in 2005. Having spent most of his career defying conventional wisdom in the media business, it is hardly surprising that Battelle takes a different approach to building a blogging business than most of his industry colleagues. His own Searchblog can be found at battellemedia.com.*

You've been critical of the approach taken so far to building a business out of blogging. Would you explain why?

The approach many entrepreneurs have taken to monetizing the blogging phenomenon has generally made the same mistake that we all make when we're confronted with something new that has words in it—that is, we look at it as if it's part of the print business, the magazine publishing business. We apply print publishing mentality to this space and try to monetize it like print, and we try to market, distribute, and promote it like print, and we try to relate to the audience the same way we do in the print business. And that may well prove to be a mistake.

In trying to tackle the business-to-business side of blogging, for example, some are trying to be the Primedia of blogs—you know, a blog for every key word, a blog for every potential niche. And others are going for something of a Condé Nast of blogs approach, starting with sites that make sense from that point of view, and then identifying a list of other markets they want to march through, hiring writers against those markets. I think both those models may misconstrue the fundamental nature of what blogging is really all about. It's not that they won't succeed, there's room for all types of models. But I hope to adopt a model that feels more native to the form.

What do you mean "more native to the form"?

I believe blogging is all about personal voice, and because of that, it is much more akin to music or book publishing than it is to the newspaper or magazine business. Blogging is highly personal, just like the music and book business, and it's personal on both sides of the equation. It's personal because it's the individual voice of the blogger that attracts the audience, just like a band does. And it's personal in that the audience reacts to the voice of the blogger much like it reacts to that of a musician. They're fans. They're critics. They love you, they hate you, but they pay attention to you because of your individual voice. The print business isn't quite like that.

But isn't "voice" also a factor in the magazine business?

For the good publications, yes. *Martha Stewart Living*, for example. For readers who respond to her voice and her sense of style as expressed in that magazine, they do so passionately. But you don't get that sense of personal voice—or such a passionate bond with the audience—with most other magazines or print media.

Why is that audience bond so important?

The core thing to understand about blogs, at least from a business or marketing point of view, is they develop these extraordinarily valuable and compact set of influencers who pay attention to them. Talking Points Memo [talkingpointsmemo.com] may have a million readers, but even more important is the fact that this million-plus audience includes ten thousand of the most important people in the country who read that blog every day. And when you get that phenomenon going, that's powerful stuff.

I mean, the bloggers that have the most respect are the ones that actually listen to their community and respond to it. They understand the demands and informational flow of their community, and that's in large part the source of their credibility. And there's a scarcity of people who can do that. You know, one of the myths of blogging is that since anybody can have a voice, then anybody can get an audience.

There's a takeoff on the old Andy Warhol maxim that says everybody is famous to fifteen people.

Right. But it's just not true that anybody can gather an influential audience, any more than it's true that any band can generate a following influential enough to move music in a particular direction. But what is true is that credibility and influence—things that are critical to motion in a society, to action in a society—are no longer restricted to institutional arbiters like newspapers and television or politicians. Thanks to blogging and other forces in society, credibility and influence are now also in the hands of ordinary people. The economy of credibility has flattened.

So, from a marketing point of view, the goal is to get not just the respect of the blogger, but the inferred respect of the influential community that the blogger has a relationship with. But up until now, the instruments for expressing that influence, or for targeting those influencers and decision makers, have been far more blunt. Blogging makes it easier to coalesce and identify influencers, just like it makes it easier to identify and promote new talent. It's not like blogging is enabling all these new Shakespeares to emerge from the hinterland. There are only so many Shakespeares out there; there are only so many people with talent. But the delta between how many there are and *how many there are that you know about* is actually quite significant. That's because the publishing business is ill-equipped to handle all the talent that does exist out there.

So while there may not be any more talent in absolute numbers, blogging narrows the distance between that talent and its discovery.

Exactly. Blogging makes it easier for smaller audiences to find their bliss. Take a hip-hop producer like Danger Mouse, for example. He does a lot of remix productions, and he would have probably labored in obscurity most of his career, doing the New York club scene, had he not found an audience through blogs that recognized the artistry of his *Grey Album*, which is a mashup of the *White Album* by the Beatles and the *Black Album* by Jay-Z. And as soon as that was discovered and passed around the blogosphere, he got huge overnight. He had something like a million downloads of his album in a week! It was really, I think, the first example of a smash hit in the music business that had nothing to do with a music label at all. None of this would have been possible without blogs and the extraordinarily influential audiences, even if small by traditional standards, that some of them attract.

[*Since then, Danger Mouse has been hailed as "the hottest hip-hop producer in the world" by Britain's* New Music Express, *one of the "100 most influential people"* by Q *magazine, one of the top twenty on* Entertainment Weekly's *"Must List: People and Things We Love," as well as one of* GQ *magazine's "Men of the Year."—Ed.]*

The problem with the traditional print business is they just see the one million readers, and they charge advertisers on a CPM, or cost-per-thousand, basis for access to them. But they don't know how to mine the real value of this compact set of ten thousand very powerful and influential people who are the *real* source of that blog's influence.

So if "voices"—and the passionate audiences that gravitate around them—are what distinguish blogs from the traditional print media, how do you build an effective business around that?

By creating a service platform for high-quality voices. Like a music label. That's a metaphor that seems to make people understand what I'm talking about.

How would it be different than the traditional print-publishing model?

There are two answers to that. One, if you're reasonably connected to the space right now, you already know who the good voices are. So you sign them to your "label." And you provide them with things that a music label typically provides a musician, or a publishing house provides an author. Like revenue. I could name half a dozen bloggers I know personally who have great voices and have very influential audiences who have no idea how to monetize that audience in a fashion that respects the audience. That's really important. You know, they could throw up AdSense or some Ads That Work bullshit, they could get sponsorships, but these guys are artists. You might as well ask Jerry Garcia to sell tickets to shows. It's not what Jerry Garcia did, right?

But we're still not talking about serious revenues yet, are we?

No, not yet. But that's where it gets interesting. Here's the beauty of it—a little micro example, which is my own personal proof point on my journey to thinking about starting this business. Take the collective blog Boing Boing [boingboing.net]. They've built up a sizable audience—it depends on the month, but somewhere between a million to two million people come to Boing Boing every month. Now if you're an online publisher—let's use Info-World, because they cover technology and Boing Boing focuses on technology, too—if you're InfoWorld and you have a million people coming to your site every month, that's a multimillion-dollar business in advertising revenues. Now, they can cross-sell against their print and they have a lot of advantages that a little five-person outfit like Boing Boing with the same audience size does not have.

But okay, we've got four authors, right? These guys are all freelance journalists, authors, event planners, right? They each need a modest amount a month to live. The overhead of that site is about $1,500 a month. So with their input, we agreed to put up three sponsorship ads as an experiment. Now, knowing how well respected Boing Boing is, we went to a certain group of people who run companies. We asked them if they'd like to sponsor Boing Boing. And here's what it looks like: you can have a million people see your ad every month for $3,000. Now, that's a good deal, by any CPM metric, and it's a particularly good deal because they know that they're buying Boing Boing and they get to be an exclusive sponsor, right? So we sold those three in a matter of about a week. And now the people at Boing Boing are getting $9,000 coming in a month. Whereas before that, they had zero. Take out the overhead, split it four ways, and all of a sudden they can spend a good amount of their time on Boing Boing. Before that, Boing Boing was just a hobby. Now they've got the luxury of actually spending more time with the blog, making it better, listening to their audience, and perhaps developing other things within the site that might be interesting to their audience.

But how is that different from what a print publisher would do by getting ads or sponsorships for the site?

On the skin of it, it's not different at all. But the core difference here is you've got an endemic audience and endemic voice that exists already. You're not saying to them that you as a publisher have a vision of the market you want to go into. You're not saying let's go make a list of all the markets we want to march through and we're simply going to hire a writer against those markets. That is a very print approach to the world.

A music approach to the world asks, What are the bands that seem to be really happening in the clubs in Seattle? And then let's go sign those bands that have an endemic audience, that already have a voice. That's a whole different approach than saying you want to get angry fifteen- to eighteen-year-old boys whose family has an income of forty to sixty thousand dollars a year. That's the wrong approach. You say, how come all these kids are listening to that band? Who cares? They just are. I'm going to sign 'em. You're starting with the editorial as opposed to starting with the market opportunity.

And then what? Aggregate them into labels and deliver them to both their audiences and to the advertisers?

No, in fact, the opposite. I think the key is to let each individual gem of a blog be an individual gem. You don't see music labels trying to cross-promote one band against the others, or saying, "Hey, become a Sony music consumer or an Arista consumer." People don't care about Sony or Arista, what they care about is the band. So you don't ever market your label, you market the band—or in this case, the blog—and let the blog do its work in building its endemic audience. Where the brand matters is with the marketer; FM Publishing will be known by advertisers, I hope, as a place where advertisers can have valuable, well-considered conversations with high-quality blogs.

What's in it for the band—or rather, the blog—with your approach?

We're solving two sets of problems with this approach—one set of problems for the marketer, and one set of problems for the author of the blog.

For the author, you're solving both the revenue problem and what you might call the studio problem. Again, using the example of a band, most can't afford to own or rent a studio, nor do they even have the skills and resources to use one effectively. It's the same with bloggers. Sure, anybody can put up a basic blog with off-the-shelf technology, but it's not so easy to create blog sites that look good, that work right, and that have all the little bells and whistles like tagging and referral analysis and comment moderation. But if there was a service that provided it for them at no cost, that created high-quality sites for them, you'd really be providing a service.

And for the marketers and advertisers, you're solving the problem of having to plow through 150 blogs and try to figure out their demographics and attitudes and then guess as to whether or not they make sense for you as a marketing vehicle. It's just too much work, too much friction, to do all of that. Hell, it might make more sense just to go to AdSense, right, and specify the key words you want to target and then insert ads wherever those words pop up in a search at a blog site. Well, the problem with that, of course, is AdSense isn't buying individual sites. AdSense is buying key words. So your message might end up on the liberal blog DailyKos and it might also end up on the site of the conservative *Washington Times*. You're not really buying the audience you truly want, which violates a basic principal of marketing which is to create and solidify a strong relationship between the advertiser and the consumer.

Why waste money trying to sell guns to advocates of gun control?

Exactly. So from the marketer's point of view, the business approach I am describing will be a brand or a label that they can come to and say, "I want to buy a million unique users during the week of May ninth and I want to focus on people who love cars and technology." And my marketing team would say, "Okay, we'll build you a plan that focuses only on the five specific blogs that have that audience, and we'll do it in a way that respects their sensibilities because they don't like to be yelled at or hustled, and here's what it's going to cost you." In other words, we'll be the marketers' bridge to the audience, which the marketers don't really understand or know how to even find. We'll bring them just the audience they want to reach, an endemic cohesive audience, and they don't have to worry about anything. And we do it for a cut of the ad revenue spent.

Do you think it'll work?

We'll know soon enough. It's certainly worth a try.

GOING OUT ON A LIMB, WHERE THE FRUIT IS

An Interview with Andreas Stavropoulis

"Risk takers by definition often fail," the workplace philosopher Scott Adams once observed. "So too morons, and in practice it is hard to tell the difference."

Andreas Stavropoulos has no doubt heard that biting aphorism a few hundred times by now. But as a managing director at the high-profile venture capital firm Draper Fisher Jurvetson, where he leads the firm's investments in blogging and social networking ventures, it's Stavropoulis's job to turn risk into reward against all odds.

This is not as easy as outsiders might imagine, for the venture capital business demands an extraordinarily fine calibration of the contradictory talents for visionary imagination on the one hand, and hard-nosed dollars and sense on the other (not to mention, say some critics, an instinct for the jugular). But it is especially difficult in new industries—or rather, potential industries—for which viable markets do not yet exist.

Is the blogging phenomenon going to lead to profitable businesses? Although a summa cum laude and Phi Beta Kappa graduate of Harvard College as well as a Baker Scholar at Harvard Business School, where he graduated first in his class, Stavropoulis will freely admit that he simply does not know for certain. But he says that without any particular concern in his voice, as if he knows something that we don't.

Perhaps he is simply a practitioner of that sage old maxim that "the best way to predict the future is to invent it." Stavropoulis does not write a blog but he can be found at dfj.com.

What sort of investments has Draper Fisher Jurvetson made in blog-related businesses so far?

Our most recent investment was in Technorati, which is a real-time search engine that keeps track of what is going on in the blogosphere. Another investment I'm involved with is a company called WaveMarket that's enabling mobile blogging via cellphone. And we're looking at, but still haven't really pulled the trigger yet on, a number of photo-blogging companies.

But let me expand the definition of "blog-related" businesses a bit to include a range of technologies and services that enable blogging, social networking, and other forms of self-publishing and community conversation online. If we look at it from that broader perspective, then I should also mention our investment in Meetup.com, an online facilitator of face-to-face meetings between people sharing similar interests.

To my mind, anything that's got to do with treating the Web not as a static space like a shopping mall but rather as a real-time enabler of conversations is going to be something that we're interested in. Some people call it the "social web," others call it the "semantic web"—the ability to apply meaning and context to online interactions—but whatever label you choose, we're looking at ways that we can invest in this arena.

Why do you think that blogging and related ventures aimed at building the "semantic web" can become profitable businesses?

Well, I'd be lying to you if I were to tell you here's exactly how it's going to work and here's how it's going to make a billion dollars. But I can lay out the set of assumptions upon which we base our investments.

But first, let's look at the three basic ways of making money. The first way is give people something valuable that they're willing to pay for. Selling software or tools to consumers or to businesses, selling subscriptions for premium services, that sort of thing. The second way to make money is to generate traffic, readership, viewership, an audience that advertisers are willing to pay to promote their products and services to. This second form, advertising, is the oldest way of making money on the Web, of course. And then there's the third way of making money—by facilitating transactions online and then taking a piece or a cut of those transactions. That's what eBay does.

I think all three are valid potential revenue models for the Technoratis of the world and for many of these emerging social-networking and blog ventures.

Which is the most developed revenue stream right now?

Advertising. Although even here, the numbers are not large, and I don't think they will be for a little while yet. The traffic still needs to scale, and we also need to figure out how to monetize the added value of the influencers who read blogs. You know, in advertising, an eyeball is usually just an eyeball. For every thousand eyeballs you can deliver to the advertiser, they'll pay you so much money. That's CPM, cost per thousand. But with blogs, some eyeballs are "more equal" than other eyeballs, to borrow an old phrase. If I'm in the PC business and I can reach the top one hundred influencers of PC buying habits, what's that worth? A lot. A whole lot.

What's likely to be the biggest source of revenues?

Well, over the real long term, I'd say it's the transaction model. We're not there yet, but it'll come. There's just no way that the blogging phenomenon and the whole notion of the semantic web can come into its own without transaction aggregation. I don't know if it'll be Technorati or another company that'll do it, but someone will figure out how to move beyond the static, inefficient, domain-based, and venue-specific "virtual marketplace" approach to transactions that we've got now.

Can you give an example of how blogs could facilitate transactions that are more real-time and less venue-constrained than what we have now?

Okay, let's say you've got tickets to some event. A Madonna concert. Now, you can go to eBay and hope that, amongst all the people looking for Pez dispensers and cars and antiques, there might also be some who are looking for Madonna tickets in a timely enough fashion that you can hold an auction and unload your tickets. Or you can go searching around trying to find an online secondary marketplace for event tickets. But that's a lot of work, and you might not be successful.

But what if you have a way of putting, say, the equivalent of a blog post out there in the cyberspace ether—a post that contains the semistructured data describing the type of event, the performer, the date, the location, the price—and have that post immediately parsed and syndicated through RSS [really simple syndication] all around the country? And what if someone else has previously put out a post requesting Madonna tickets or even just tickets for any concert taking place within a specified period of time and distance from his location? Neither of you has to be checking eBay every five minutes. Neither of you has to stumble upon the same specific Internet site where such tickets could possibly be sold, like Craig's List. And yet you find each other easily and efficiently, and a transaction occurs.

Or imagine that you're in the market for a particular type of used car within a particular radius. You're a student, and you don't really care about colors or options that much. You just want a decent car at a cheap price and you want it quickly. But you don't want to always have to be checking edmunds.com or eBay or Craig's List or any of the other specific Internet sites where cars are sold. You just want to be hanging out with your friends, and whenever a car-for-sale notice that matches your request hits the blogosphere, you want to be the first to know about it. You want to get a ping on your cellphone that gives you a short description of the car and the phone number of the guy selling it. And you don't want to wait until you get back home to your computer so you can start searching each of those car trader sites hoping that you haven't already missed out on the sale. You want the information immediately, and you want it to come to you rather than you having to go out and browse through fifteen sites to find it.

But can't people do this already? Can't someone go to Google, for example, and search for cars for sale regardless of whether those for-sale notices are posted on eBay, Edmunds.com, or someone's classic car blog?

No. There's no way they're going to be covered effectively by Google. First of all, they don't exist long enough to justify being listed by Google. And even if they did, the Google spider [searching technology] only looks for and indexes things that are in the top 10 percent or so of Web traffic once every couple of weeks at most. I mean, there are over four million blogs that Technorati covers right now, and if Google indexed ten thousand of them once every couple of weeks, I'd be surprised. What's more, even if Google did track these blogs—or other timely information like cars-for-sale notices—many would already be stale by the time Google listed them in their search results. Great, here's your car-for-sale listing, but sorry, the car has already been sold.

Look, I don't want to be negative about Google. What they're doing is great. It's just that Google's technology is not well attuned to the rapid real-time demands of collecting and propagating timely information, be it blogs or other timely information.

You're saying we need a more sophisticated technological approach?

That's right.

Which, I suppose, brings us to Technorati.

That's right. Technorati calls itself the "real time web" for a reason. You can't search for this kind of information properly by using a spider and going around and classifying and indexing stuff. You have to do it real time, which means you have to do it very differently, which means you have to get the information sources—the blogs, or the sellers of used cars or concert tickets—to be pinging you rather than waiting around for some search engine spider to crawl on over to them. If you want to be a search engine for this new, quick, and nimble semantic Web, you can't be laboriously asking millions of

Internet sites, "Did you change?" You have to get them to tell you, "I just changed and here's the change." Boom, right?

But ultimately, aren't you talking about more than simply the ability to find more timely information?

Yes, absolutely. I'm talking about lending more context and more meaning to the information we seek and to the interactions and transactions we have online.

Imagine how interesting it would be if you could go on to Yahoo and say, "Point me to any messages or any news or any activities that have anything to do with my Harvard Business School section mates." Right now, there's no way you could ever find that, and in fact, the reason why I mentioned this is because just yesterday it so happened I got the Harvard Business School bulletin and was catching up with all my classmates and holy cow! I didn't realize that guy is at Yahoo now! I should make a note of that. So wouldn't it be great when I'm actually looking at some Yahoo page if I got a little pop-up that said, "There are three people in your network with recent activity here"? Maybe someone has posted to a Yahoo Finance site, someone else has gotten a job at the company, and this third person was mentioned in a Yahoo business news article.

Now, there's an obvious utility to being able to do this sort of thing on a dating site, because the closer someone is to you, the easier it is to get a date with them because you have people who can refer you to that person. You can also see what your friends or friends of friends have to say about that person, so you get a better sense of what they're like before you go out with them. And, all things being equal, having social connections in common means that you'll probably have more to talk about when you do go out.

But the practical value of being able to see and leverage social context online extends far beyond dating to many fields of business, professional, and social life. Take that used car we talked about buying. Since I'm less likely to get screwed if I buy a car from people who have some connection to me, however vague, what if I could do a search for car-for-sale postings that only showed me the cars being sold by people no more than two degrees of separation from me—people who know people who know me? I don't want to see cars for sale from Edmunds.com.

The same goes for simply going to Google and doing a blog search. Since I'm more likely to have some shared attitudes and life experiences with people who know people who know me, what if I could apply a filter to the search results that will show me only those blog postings written by people who are not more than two degrees of separation from me?

Is it even possible technologically to identify who on the Web might be two to three degrees of separation from you?

Well, it doesn't exist yet. Social networking sites are just starting to do some of this within the confines of their own sites, although it's still rather limited. But work is under way to develop standards for capturing this social network information—for recognizing the relationships between these data objects called "people descriptions"—and making it available on a real-time distributed basis in a variety of contexts. And there's no reason why this emerging ability to track social context needs to live in any particular site. It should be with you wherever you are on the Web.

For a venture capitalist, you certainly seem to take what some might call a "visionary" approach to the hard-nosed challenge of making money, don't you?

Absolutely, and in some ways that defines Draper Fisher Jurvetson. We are early-stage investors, and we like to lead packs instead of follow them. This is more risky in some ways, because you never can be sure in the early beginnings of a phenomenon such as blogging where it's ultimately going to go and how successful it's going to be. But we try to mitigate the risk of investing early by investing more modestly, in terms of the amounts of funding we provide. And so far, this approach has been mostly successful—we made money on every single one of our email-based communications investments in 1994 and 1995, at a time other VCs still thought the Internet was for cowboys.

So hopefully you're not crazy to invest in blogging, is that it?

No risk, no glory.

MARKETERS MUST LEARN TO RESPECT THEIR CUSTOMERS

An Interview with Christian Sarkar

Christian Sarkar (christiansarkar.com) is a Web marketing and design consultant who coined the term "double-loop marketing" to describe the need for blog marketers to develop trust and reliability in a community of customers before trying to pitch their products and services. Sarkar's motto is "First mind share, then wallet share." In his view, most corporate blogs are doomed to fail because they neglect the needs of their customers for reliable and useful information, instead offering only hype and PR—which blog readers will usually avoid at all costs. Sarkar has worked on Internet-based projects for the likes of Bechtel, Mobil, Exxon, Oracle, and Sun Microsystems. He is also affiliated with the Goizueta Business School at Emory University.

Is blogging really ushering in a new paradigm for corporate marketers? If so, why?

Blogging is a symptom of a movement toward transparency in all aspects of life—from families to business to politics and policy. People have always talked to their neighbors. But now with the Internet, your neighborhood is not restricted by physical space. Blogs are the voices of people—real people talking to each other about things they care about deeply, passionately, and even heroically. They're authentic.

And it's not driven by communication committees and PR professionals, but rather by amateurs—individuals with a point of view. Fresh air that somehow escaped from the trenches and made it all the way to the oxygen-less boardroom. And unlike journalists, bloggers don't pretend to be objective.

Blogging also builds community. At the very least, a "true" blog allows comments and feedback. Readers are invited to post their own opinions, share stories and insights. Some even become real-life collaborators and friends. And it's not just the visitors on your site; blogrolling, the practice of naming the other blogs your read or like—builds an ecosystem of like-minded bloggers across the Web.

Blogs usher in a new paradigm of transparency. It's about information, interaction, discussion. And a search for something the traditional media forgot about—the truth. Blogs deliver information and ideas quickly, but the conversation doesn't just end with the first post. Conversations gets linked, cross-referenced, and an idea builds its own web of voices across the blogosphere—for and against.

Now businesses come into this new world and think, "Hmm . . . how can I be a part of this conversation?" Or even, "How can I control this conversation to sell more products?"

And so the CEO orders the communications team to start blogging, or worse—blog *for* him. These are the blogs that no one reads. Blogs that get polluted by press releases. One-way blogs that tell what the company wants you to believe.

Marketers must learn to respect their customers. And most importantly, listen.

Does your company listen to what your customers are saying?

Does your company's blog allow comments, including critical ones—without editing?

Do you respond to these comments without becoming defensive?

If you allow your lawyers to review your blog postings for potential legal problems, do you at least make sure that they don't add their own kiss-of-death legalese to them?

If you answered no to any of the above, you are probably going down the wrong road. Don't waste your time splashing about in the blogosphere if you can't swim.

Can you cite some examples of bad corporate blogs, or of a self-defeating corporate use of independent blogs as marketing vehicles?

The list of corporate blogs is growing rapidly—not quite so rapidly as the list of individual bloggers, but it shows that companies are paying attention. But many of these have serious deficiencies.

When Dr Pepper created RagingCow.com, for example, the intent was to get some viral buzz about their new flavored-milk product. They recruited teen bloggers to blog about the product, but apparently urged them to hide the fact they had been recruited. The only people ending up raving about the site were hard-core bloggers who started a "Boycott Raging Cow" movement and put the site out of its misery. It is now defunct.

The "Boycott Raging Cow" initiative is an example of what happens when companies try to co-opt the blogosphere. Bloggers are not so easily fooled or muzzled.

But there is a *right* way to blog, in the business-to-business world, at least. A few companies like Microsoft and Sun, where blogs are considered the work of individual employees, have made great gains in forging closer and more trusting ties with developers, partners, and users. They prove the wisdom of getting the PR people to stay out of your blogging efforts, and instead letting your employees do what they do best—i.e., talk with passion and honesty about their work, and listen open-mindedly to the needs of their customers. An example—the Scobleizer [radio.weblogs.com/0001011/]. The blog says it all: "Robert Scoble works at Microsoft (title: technical evangelist). Everything here, though, is his personal opinion and is not read or approved before it is posted. No warranties or other guarantees will be offered as to the quality of the opinions or anything else offered here." Scoble takes on everything and everyone—even Microsoft CEO Steve Ballmer. And Microsoft is stronger because of it.

In the consumer world, blogging gets harder. You have, for example, a corporate blog at ka-thunk.com brought to you by that friendly appliance maker Maytag. The site's okay, it does have an individual voice, but the content itself is boring. Their site statistics speak for themselves: 209 visitors a day, average visit 59 seconds. This is a waste of time, both for Maytag and its consumers. The question I have is, Why doesn't Maytag put up a blog or sponsor one that offers truly useful information to its customers?

That's the approach taken by Sony and their sponsorship of Gawker Media's lifehacker.com. This is a site about computers, and the content is relevant to the consumers interested in the subject. And Sony scores with every eyeball visiting the site.

But even this sponsorship approach can be risky. CheapTickets.com cancelled their sponsorship of Gridskipper.com (another Gawker property) after only a week because of the blog's supposedly "racy tone." Blogging is not safe, but it does get attention. Companies like CheapTickets.com need to decide who their audience really is or stick to conventional advertising.

Geico's "gecko" blog is another example of faux-blogging. It's a safe PR read, but is anybody listening? This is another worst practice in business blogging because it gives the reader absolutely nothing useful. Sure, it tells me where to buy a bobble-head gecko doll or which NASCAR races Geico is sponsoring or which jingles they used in which commercial. But, really, does anyone really care? This is an example of a hyper PR team blogging because they can. I predict this will end soon. Why? Because they don't have anything to say.

A far better example of corporate blogging is the GM FastLane blog (fastlane.gmblogs.com). What started out as a corporate communications stunt has become a real blog, thanks for the most part to one crucial point: FastLane allows user comments—and actually responds to them. Now they've added podcasts—and not just from Bob Lutz, but the actual thoughts of Johnny O'Connell, a factory driver in General Motors' Corvette Racing program. That's the best way to be authentic in a corporate blog: let the people who do the working do the talking as well.

Yet another angle on business blogging is "enterprise blogging." This is blogging within the company to exchange knowledge, communicate, share lessons learned, even motivate employees. It's the two-way Intranet! IBM, for example, has over 2,800 internal blogs—at least that's what I heard recently. The challenge for internal blogging is knowledge harvesting: how do you capture ideas and turn them into a product or service? Of course this is a challenge that predates blogging!

The enterprise blog can extend outside the company as well. Interested in improving communications with your channel partners? A small business can build a partners-only blog with updates on ideas that sell, promotions, offers, etc. What's important is that it is interactive—that partners add their own experience and suggestions.

Are there any ways that blogging can help small businesses in particular, as distinct from large corporations?

This is probably the most fertile ground for business blogging. Let's say you're the owner of a small bookstore and you happen to be passionate about books. Why not blog about books, new authors, the classics, or book-signing events? You'll build a loyal following, locally and beyond. In fact, a number of leading independent bookstore owners are doing exactly that.

John Hagel and John Seely Brown (well-known management consultants) just wrote a new book. More importantly, they also published a site *and* a blog that goes with the book [edgeperspectives.com]. They've built an audience of over five thousand executives *before* the book was even published.

Even tailors have blogs. How many tailors are there anyway? Thomas Mahon has over twenty years' experience of hand tailoring in Savile Row, with clients like Prince Charles. His site [englishcut.com] is an example of the right mix of professionalism, humor, and personal history. I'm sure his blog helps his business.

Want to learn about the food service industry in Australia? Check out Vic Cherikoff's Blog [cherikoff.blogspot.com]. Again, an authentic, individual voice with a distinctive point of view.

The point I'm trying to make here is that small business blogs have the liberty that the large companies do not—the bloggers can be themselves: opinionated, but infinitely more enjoyable and attention getting than the safe PR blogs of corporatedom.

Another real-life example, jeffburrows.com is a small business coaching company which teaches owners how to grow and optimize their businesses using proprietary improvement processes. The company created a blog at emythblog.com to build an audience around the key concepts it teaches.

What's absolutely critical here is the blogger's ability to post useful content for the target audience. It works—the Emythblog.com grew an audience of three thousand members in a little over a month. That may not seem like much, but for a small business, it's a marketing coup.

I need to end this by reminding people that, for the most part, blogging was invented (no, not by Al Gore) by Dave Winer [www.scripting.com], who is largely to blame for blogging, RSS, and now even podcasting. We all owe him for bringing the voice of the individual back into the public realm. Dave still blogs daily on everything under the sun. Perhaps the very first authentic voice in the blogosphere.

BUILDING A MORE POWERFUL NETWORK WITH BLOGGING

An Interview with David Teten and Scott Allen

David Teten and Scott Allen are co-authors of The Virtual Handshake: Opening Doors and Closing Deals Online *and both blog at thevirtual handshake.com.*

David Teten is CEO of Nitron Advisors, a research firm that provides venture capitalists, hedge funds, and other investors with direct access to frontline industry experts. He is also chairman of Teten Recruiting, a recruiting firm specializing in the institutional investor, investment banking, and strategy consulting industries. Both of his companies leverage blogs and other social software to help clients recruit and partner with the best possible people. His personal blog is Brain Food (teten.com/blog). He runs thevirtualhandshake.com, a free resource site for the social software industry.

Scott Allen is a leading expert on building quality business relationships online, offering consulting services and public educational programs on leveraging online communities and blogs, and social software for marketing, sales, and business development. A twenty-year veteran entrepreneur and IT executive, Allen has implemented solutions for clients such as IBM and Amazon.com. Allen is also a paid professional blogger for About.com (entrepreneurs.about.com).

They carried out their interview with us via email, yielding a more crafted set of answers, but, at the same time, allowing them the advantage of speaking in one voice.

What is "social networking," and how can bloggers use it to become more successful in their business and professional life?

"Social networking" means leveraging your network of personal and business friends to help you achieve your goals. In our book, *The Virtual Handshake: Opening Doors and Closing Deals Online,* we discuss how people can become more productive and successful by using new tools such as blogs to create a dramatically more powerful network.

However, this is not a book about "networking" in itself: how to win friends and influence people. We're not interested in socializing. Instead, we're interested in the *results* of your relationships: opening doors, closing deals, and your professional success. Whether your goal is a client, a new business partner, or a new job, you will achieve that goal through your network. We want to make sure that you achieve your goal.

There's no doubt that learning how to use blogs can significantly accelerate your career success. In the first place, they make it possible to keep up with your friends, family, coworkers, and clients, without everyone having to be in the same place either physically or virtually. But more importantly, blogs can help you establish a credible, high-profile presence for yourself in the business and professional community and highlight your credentials in the job market or the products or services you offer.

As Usman Latif noted, "A blog with tutorials on 3-D graphics might not get much traffic, but it might still land the blogger a job with a 3-D game developer." And it's certainly true that there are any number of people—from technology professionals to political consultants—who have developed lucrative careers because of the attention and respect their blogs have attracted within their respective industries.

Building and leveraging a social network is just as important, if not more important, for career success as it is for personal happiness. More people, for example, find jobs through personal contacts than by any other means. People with extensive social networks are paid better and promoted faster than those without. And some 75 percent of start-up companies secure venture capital funding through the informal grapevine of business colleagues and contacts.

What does blogging have to do with the social networking websites such as Friendster.com, Meetup.com, and Tribe.net that have sprung up in recent years?

As Mark Pincus, CEO of Tribe Networks, put it, "All the social network sites are dumbed-down versions of what's going on in the blog world."

The major difference between blogs and social networking sites is that, while still social in nature, blogs are far more individualistic. You don't need to join a particular online site to participate in a discussion around, say, new technology trends. And in terms of the discussion itself, the communication is centered around the personal voice or views of the blogger rather than on the group, as it is in discussion forums on networking sites.

Sometimes there can be great synergies between blogs and social networking sites. During last year's Democratic primaries, for example, Howard Dean's campaign blog used the social networking site Meetup.com to organize meetings of Dean activists around the country. But linkages such as these between blogs and social networking sites are still fairly rare, particularly outside the political arena.

Ultimately, blogs represent a free (or near-free), standardized, and completely open way in which to demarcate and build your own individual social network. Unlike most of the current social network systems, with a blog your network data is not owned or controlled by any one company. Your inbound and outbound links to and from other bloggers are readily accessible to you for use in expanding and leveraging your social network. And your blog can also reach the whole world, not just those who have decided to join a particular online community.

This openness has led many people to use their blogs as their primary online social networking tool. For those who have something to say—especially those with a strong personal voice—blogging is a great networking tool, because with it they can easily connect with their circle of colleagues and business and professional contacts using the blog technology of their choice and in exactly the style and manner they wish.

What can you do with a blog that you couldn't do with a more traditional website or online newsletter?

Blogs are simply a better mousetrap. Let's say that you just read a great article that you want to comment on and share with your friends and business contacts. We analyzed how long this would take via either traditional Web publishing or email versus how long it would take via a blog. In the traditional website or email approach, there were over forty steps involved to do this. With a properly configured blog, it's only four or five steps. The end result may look exactly the same, but when the effort is an order of magnitude easier, as it is with a blog, it changes the dynamic completely.

By way of analogy, email and regular postal mail accomplish precisely the same results: to send a message from one person to one or more people. But the tremendous ease of use and low cost of email has completely changed how people communicate.

Clearly, blogging has enabled a tipping point for personal publishing on the Web. Although people have had the ability to create personal web pages for years, even without any technical expertise, ongoing maintenance has always been burdensome. Blogging technology puts the ability to publish directly into the context of your Internet experience, rather than it being some disconnected external task. That fundamentally changes the way people write, just as cell phones changed the way people communicate. Your blog is with you everywhere you go online, just as your cell phone is with you everywhere you go.

Are the social networks built around blogs empowering new voices to be heard? Could they actually change power relationships in society?

Certainly new voices are being heard. Television, radio, and the major print media have always exercised tight control over citizen access, and have not been very open to nonmainstream voices or even the voices of ordinary citizens. On the rare occasion when the media does provide a forum for ordinary people or those with nonmainstream views, they usually try to marginalize those voices.

Even the way that the mainstream media frames the debates over crucial public issues tends to silence most ordinary voices. CNN, for example, thinks it has analyzed the abortion debate properly when it picks an intransigent pro-lifer and a dogmatic pro-choicer and lets them shout at each other for ten minutes. This is not balanced journalism, and it's certainly not allowing the voices of most people—whose views on abortion, according to most polls, lie somewhere between the two extremes—to be heard. But with blogs, everyone can have their say. And that's why you tend to see a far greater diversity of views being presented on blogs than you see in the mainstream media.

So yes, blogging will tend to enable the "rise of the citizen voice" as more people realize how *simple* blogging can be. But let's not forget that, at the same time, blogging may also tend to increase the influence of corporate and establishment voices as more companies and government officials realize how *effective* blogging can be.

How will this shake out in terms of power relationships in society? It's impossible to predict. But given the number of strongly anti-commercial voices in the blog world, it's unlikely that corporate voices will ever completely dominate. For one thing, people who blog with a hidden agenda [e.g., blogging on a corporation's behalf] are rapidly found out and discredited. And for another, blogs do give a voice to citizens who never had one before. As Benjamin Franklin once said, "Never argue with a man who buys his ink by the barrel." So since blogs give more ink to many more people, perhaps the best answer is that they're bound to spread out power relationships in society to some degree.

Can you cite any examples of blog-enabled social networks effecting change?

Blogs were instrumental, as we know, in helping to create a potent network of grassroots organizers for the Howard Dean campaign for the 2004 Democratic nomination. Although Dean ultimately lost the nomination, blogs are continuing to change they way that political campaigns organize and activate a network of supporters. The DailyKos blog, for example, used its social network of liberal blog readers to raise over $630,000 for Democratic candidates nationwide.

Beyond the world of politics, there are many examples of blogs making a difference socially, sometimes in the strangest ways. For example, Boobiethon.com has raised over $10,000 for various charities—mostly breast cancer charities—by the posting of racy photos of people's chests [mostly female]. In another case, hundreds of bloggers worked together to knock the anti-Semitic JewWatch.com's "definition" of the word *Jew* out of the top results people get when they look up that word. The blogging community did this by first choosing a neutral definition of *Jew*, from Wikipedia [http:// en.wikipedia.org/wiki/Wikipedia]. Then they created thousands of new links to that definition, thereby boosting it to the number one spot in the search results for the word *Jew* on Google, the most popular search engine.

But don't blog-enabled social networks tend to be narrowly special-interest in character, thereby increasing the fragmentation and polarization of society?

It's true that blogging helps people with special interests group together. As C. S. Lewis once said, "Friendship is born at that moment when one person says to another, 'What! You too? I thought I was the only one!' " The Internet allows you to find others who share your interests, and blogs make this process even easier by enabling you to meet with others to discuss those interests without having to create a real-world or online clubhouse to do it in. And because blogs help people form niche interest groups rather than remain in larger organizations that don't really meet their needs, perhaps there is the risk that bloggers may find themselves spending most of their time in an "echo chamber" of people who think and feel exactly the way they do. Talking with people who think just like you do is no way to grow intellectually.

But that risk is mitigated by the fact that bloggers are so heavily dependent on linking—to objective news sources, for example, or to other blogs— because this helps to keep their minds open and the dialogue healthy. In fact, recent studies [such as the Pew Research report available at pewinternet.org/ pdfs/PIP_Political_Info_Report.pdf show that liberal bloggers often link to sources with which they disagree. The same goes for conservative bloggers. This is a healthy trend that augurs well for blogging—and for the country as a whole.

The flip side of this question is that blogs can also be a powerful social unifying force when an idea—a *meme*—captures the public imagination. Look at the response last year to the call for Gmail addresses to be donated to soldiers stationed in Iraq. The word spread through blogs so quickly that within a matter of days there were more Gmail donations than needed.

Can these types of blog-centered social networks help small businesses become more successful?

Blogs are extremely useful for small business, particularly for revitalizing the small business website. Many small business sites are nothing more than an online business card or brochureware. Many more started out with the intentions of providing up-to-date information on a regular basis, but fizzled out over time because of the difficulty of keeping the site current. Blogs can offer a real solution to these problems and, if done right, can create a vital, energetic social network around the business that materially enhances the company's success.

Imagine, for example, a local restaurant posting weekly events and specials and inviting feedback and menu suggestions from its customers. Or a specialty movie theater with a blog reviewing its current attractions and inviting reader reviews of recent movies, suggestions for films they want the theater to run, and even critiques of the quality of the popcorn. These possibilities are now cost-effective in terms of both money and time. And all that fresh content additionally attracts search engines and other bloggers, making blogs a highly effective marketing tool for small business and the self-employed.

Are there any examples of large corporations doing this as well?

One of the most interesting uses of a blog by a business is the way Dallas Mavericks owner and serial high-tech entrepreneur Mark Cuban uses blogmaverick.com. Professional sports club owners are typically rarely heard from after the post-game press conference. Cuban, on the other hand, uses his blog as a way to publicly respond to local and national sportswriters (of whom he has been very critical) as well as to fans, for whom he has been a very vocal advocate. His openness is extremely refreshing, and has not only endeared him to fans, but has probably helped ticket sales as well.

Microsoft has been very innovative in their use of blogs. Robert Scoble, who provides an inside look at Microsoft, is the world's most famous corporate blogger. Microsoft's other particularly noteworthy use of blogs is Channel 9—the name comes from the audio channel on United Airlines flights that lets passengers hear what's going on in the cockpit—which is a collection of blogs by internal Microsoft developers that has created an unprecedented level of open, public communication between product developers and users [channel9.msdn.com]. In our opinion, Microsoft has demonstrated an amazing level of both trust and openness with their bloggers. The posts aren't all run through the PR and legal departments as one might expect in a company the size of Microsoft. They provide some general guidelines and then put faith in blog readers' and posters' judgment.

Then there's Japanese venture capitalist Joichi Ito, who has been one of the most influential and innovative bloggers for several years. He has been a great advocate of the technology, and has even invested in Six Apart, creators of blog software Movable Type, and Technorati, a popular blog search engine and analytical tool. He has built his own integrated real-time community with the popular #joiito IRC [Internet Relay Chat] channel. He has also been one of the early adopters of photoblogging [posting photos to your blog] and moblogging [mobile blogging]. And he has been a leading advocate for e-democracy, the use of blogs and other technology to promote democracy worldwide.

It's worth noting that, especially for large firms, blogging can really address the public's desire for more openness and transparency from corporations. It has not yet had significant market impact, but over time it probably will. Companies that provide open communication channels will foster greater loyalty than those that don't, and over time that will pay off in higher customer retention and higher earnings.

THE NEW MEANING OF
"GOING TO LUNCH WITH YOUR PUBLISHER"

An Interview with Michael Cader

For an industry that only recently (and grudgingly) adopted email as an accepted form of communication—and that still takes an average of twelve to eighteen months to bring out products that consist, after all, merely of words on paper—book publishing is hardly what one would call on the cutting edge of innovation. Which makes it all the more surprising that a lone-wolf book packager with an entrepreneurial bent like Michael Cader could have had such a transformative impact on the industry.

In less than four years, Cader's upstart industry blog, Publishers Lunch (publishersmarketplace.com), has become as vital an industry resource as the venerable one-hundred-fifty-year-old trade magazine Publishers Weekly. *It has more readers, offers more information and services that book industry professionals need to do their jobs, and it may even have more influence on publishing trends and directions. "People care about what Cader says . . . and react to it," argues Stuart Applebaum, a senior vice president at Random House.*

In short, Michael Cader's blog has fundamentally transformed the way authors, agents, editors, and publishers conduct their daily business in the book publishing trade. Here's how he did it.

How did you get started with Publishers Lunch?

At the very beginning, Publishers Lunch was primarily an aggregation of stories that I found on the Web that related to my business, which is book publishing. A lot of it was focused on electronic publishing possibilities and how traditional publishing might try to relate to that, which was a big tension point in our industry at the time. It was the early days of traditional book publishing's efforts to reckon with the electronic world, and I discovered that I seemed to understand the place where these two worlds might intersect in a different way than some of my colleagues did.

Why was that?

It may have been because as an independent book packager and producer I had come to embrace technology in my own business. But I was also spending more and more time on the Web because I did a lot of reference and popular reference books then, and it was only just around that moment in time, in fact, that you began to find solid, reliable information on the Internet. So I was finding a lot of information online about the publishing business that I was not seeing in the traditional sources of information for our business, such as the *New York Times* and *Publishers Weekly*. And some of the information I found was on these things called blogs—this was maybe five years ago—and I thought some of them were really good.

Why did you decide to not simply read blogs, but to write one as well?

Well, as I mentioned, I was experimenting in my head with new models for publishing that would embrace the Internet and get publishers closer to readers. I was accumulating links lists that I was visiting for book research, and along the way I was also accumulating links lists of places that had information about my business or about electronic publishing, etc. So I was slowly building my Yahoo pop-up links list. I would work my way down my list of sites each day to see what was interesting—it would pretty much take up my whole morning, particularly if I was looking to procrastinate—and like many book people I'd have this little internal dialogue going on in my head about whether I thought this or that item was interesting and did I want to save the article, or did I think the author was dead wrong and didn't understand anything about book publishing. And I guess at some point I got the idea that this internal dialogue of mine might be interesting to others.

So I basically took this internal dialogue and decided that that should be the website that I played around with. And I think I became aware of blogs as I was doing this and thought, yeah, what I'd like to do is sort of like what those guys do but different, because to me, part of what kept it interesting for me was not just the links, but the internal dialogue brought to life. The wisecrack, or the observation, or, I mean, I'm an editor by trade, so I like working with other people's material. I like going through a two-thousand-word article and pulling out the great quote and leaving behind the dull stuff, or taking the things the person's done wrong and fixing them, or taking the stuff that's good and knitting together the larger thesis or conclusion that perhaps the reporter didn't see because they were in the middle of a story, or relating that story to three other stories and building a larger arc out of it. That's what I'd been doing as a book packager for twenty years already, so it was a natural process for me to do it in the form of a blog.

Did you know that there would be an audience for Publishers Lunch?

I think it was one of those paradoxical things in which you simultaneously think that no one would be interested in it, but then again maybe a lot of people would be. But I finally decided that, you know, all this great stuff I'm finding about the publishing industry is certainly keeping me interested every day—and at that point I'd already created and produced a couple hundred books, so I can't be a complete idiot, right?—so chances are it's going to be interesting to others in the industry.

So I threw this up as a blog, I told a maximum of twenty-five colleagues, and they all thought it was kind of cool. But anyway, there I was busy updating the site every day and these colleagues would come back a month later and say, "Oh, you updated the site." Yeah, I updated it sixteen times since you last visited! Where were you? Which quickly made me realize if I was going to keep doing this, it probably needed to be in the form of emailed information rather than a pure website, because back then book publishing people were barely even getting email and most still weren't on the Web.

Most of them were not on the Internet?

No. Book publishers are very slow adopters. Anyway, I kept building up my email list and adding to the kinds of information and commentary that I was sending out. And the feedback was that this was good stuff, you should keep doing this. And since I was having fun doing it, I decided to keep going and keep expanding its offerings.

So over the next six months or so, I kept plugging away at it without being able to explain to anyone, my wife and myself included, why I was doing this rather than playing golf or doing my job as a book packager or whatever else I could have been doing with my time. But I'm an entrepreneurial person, and I believed that there had to be *something* to this notion of taking interesting work by other people, aggregating it, giving it my own special spin and focus, and directing it toward a very particular audience in a very focused manner.

In retrospect, of course, my audience was tiny at first. But it seemed like right away, people who mattered in the book publishing business were looking at it and talking about it. And so eventually there came a point where I had to figure out, Am I trying to turn this into a business, or do I just love doing this so I'm going to do it anyway?

And that's when I had a kind of epiphany—that this wasn't just a newsletter, it wasn't just a blog. What I was actually doing was capturing the attention of some of the most influential people in the book publishing business and bringing them together. And once I understood that, I knew that Publishers Lunch was just the beginning. There were dozens of other things I could be doing with all that attention—practical information and services I could offer, other means by which I could help people do business with each other more effectively and efficiently, and additional ways that I could create a sort of electronic home base for people in the publishing business.

Once I grasped all that, then I realized—or maybe I should say I trusted—that somewhere in all this I'd find a business model that worked. If you can get the attention of the most influential people in an industry and then do something useful and productive for them, then you've got the makings of a business. Or so I hoped.

Have the results met your expectations?

Publishers Lunch is now the largest circulation publication in the book business worldwide, by far. I have twice as many trade subscribers as *Publishers Weekly*, the 150-year-old former pillar of the industry. I email Publishers Lunch to 30,000 people every day, whereas the trade circulation of *Publishers Weekly* is about 15,000 and the *Bookseller* in the UK has about 10,000. So after only a few years, Publishers Lunch is bigger—and I'd say more influential, too—than any other trade media in the book publishing industry. And our emailed circulation continues to grow by about 100, 150 names a week. What's more, my "open rates" [the percentage of emails sent that are actually read by the recipients] continue to be in excess of 100 percent, so the mail doesn't just get sent. It gets opened, it gets looked at, it gets reopened, forwarded, reread, etc.

I soon realized, of course, that delivering email was a great way of pushing news to subscribers. But to offer all the other services I thought the industry wanted and needed, we would have to create an electronic home for the book industry. So now, in addition to our email subscribers, we're generating about 30,000 page views a day on our website, Publishers Marketplace, and that continues to scale very quickly as well.

What sorts of services do you provide there?

Our idea has always been that Publishers Marketplace would be a kind of ancient Greek agora updated to the electronic age. It would drive the attention of our book publishing industry and let publishers, agents, authors, and everyone else in the business set up electronic stalls—or, in our case, member pages. So you could search for and find, let's say, a freelance editor who specialized in cookbooks and had worked on Indian, Middle Eastern, and Turkish cookbooks.

Anyway, the job board was the first service we offered, and it has grown steadily ever since it was launched. And we've just kept adding features ever since. We now have a daily deal page and an archive of recent publishing deal information that's searchable. We have a rights board, where foreign, TV, film, or other rights are offered on over five hundred book titles. The job board and the rights and proposals board both help writers connect with agents and publishers. And of course we have an archive of every day's emailed Publishers Lunch postings that's also searchable.

All these features enable book industry professionals to do their jobs better. For example, over two hundred agents host their own Web pages on Publishers Marketplace, which makes it the most popular source in the industry for information about top literary agencies. The deals database and daily updates give agents essential negotiating information, which they can search to reveal editors' buying patterns. And the book tracker and book review index lets them follow books for their agencies and clients.

Editors can also post their own web pages, though most currently rely on the live daily deal information to check proposals they're considering against recent sales, find and follow agents, watch the competition, and figure out who represents whom. The book review index is a massive time-saver for pulling jacket quotes, checking critical opinion, and identifying small press books worth a look.

We're also going to large companies and asking them to take out site licenses. We can show them stats on how many of their employees are already visiting and how many are signing up on their own to pay us $20 a month. And we tell them, "Why not find a high-value way of serving all your employees instead of just a small segment?" That's becoming a serious revenue stream for us.

Plus, we're publishing our own books—reference books for the trade. The first book takes deal information from a particular period in time and resorts it so it's very easy to look at: cross-index versions of every deal an editor or an agent or a house has made and then analyze it by genre, by price range, etc. It's stuff that's all in our database but is not necessarily easy to get at and analyze quickly if you're doing electronic searches. And again, for an industry made up of people who are still print-driven in their hearts and souls, this may be a better way to package it.

And we're probably also going to do other books in the future that make use of the enormous wealth of proprietary information we have in our databases. For example, we have our representation database of fifteen thousand authors and their agents which, if you were to reverse engineer it and break it down in all sorts of ways, would be of enormous value not only to writers but also to editors who are looking for agents with whom they can develop relationships with or buy books from. We also have information on about 1,500 agents, which is the best database of agent information in the industry.

Bottom line, there's a lot of people in the industry interested in the kind of information we have to offer. The deal book will be the first, but there's certainly enough high-value content to drive all kinds of profitable print products.

Is it these services that explain why Publishers Lunch has more readers—and in many ways more influence—than the 150-year-old Publishers Weekly?

Well, I'm probably the wrong guy to answer that objectively. But here's what I would say. I think my vision of what I'm doing has always been completely different from what *Publishers Weekly* does—completely different from what most traditional trade media do. I'm not here as a dispassionate, objective outsider trying to tell insiders about their business. Rather, my belief is that the sole purpose of trade media is to help people do business better. To provoke them and lead them and guide them and help them into thinking about how to conduct their business faster, better, and with more transparency and success. So what I offer is a personal, insider perspective filled with concrete information that is useful and can help book people conduct their business.

The deal reports are one part of what drives Publishers Lunch, because at the end of the day you can have all the news stories you want, but the heart and soul of the publishing business is authors and editors buying books and selling them to bookstores and then selling rights to other territories and so on and so on. That's the publishing business, and people involved in this business need actionable information—*inside* information—in order to succeed. And that's what Publishers Lunch gives them.

As a result, Publishers Lunch has become an essential part of how people do business in the publishing field today. It's what they talk about at lunch. It's where they expect to get their news. It's where they look for titles to acquire. It's where they announce that they've acquired something, so that they'll get more submissions, so that they'll sell rights, so that they'll interest TV or film producers. It's part of the fabric, the lifeblood, of the publishing business today.

In short, Publishers Lunch is becoming a model for what trade media should be in the twenty-first century.

What insights have you gleaned about the future of blogging from your experience putting out Publishers Lunch?

Well, it turns out there are great similarities between blog publishing and book publishing. Most of book publishing is not a mass medium. It's a niche medium. We already have too many books; the challenge lies in matching up writers with readers, in creating these circles of passion around an author and his or her voice.

Similarly, blogs are all about allowing individuals with a strong voice to find their audience and gain influence very quickly—without needing any of the traditional trappings of brands, capital, or scale of enterprise. Really, the Web is great for tiny enterprises—and more than that, for enabling tiny enterprises to gain enormous influence—and I think that this is a very hard thing for traditional large enterprises to get their hands around, or accept.

Now, maybe that speaks to why many traditional magazines and companies haven't been able to achieve the same success online that they enjoyed in the real world, operating under the old mass-market paradigm. But in any event, it seems clear to me that the best role for blogs is as niche media. They achieve outsized influence and success by being "unscaled." They are not meant to be "just like other media enterprises only smaller."

OUR CUSTOMERS WANT AUTHENTICITY

An Interview with Jonathan Schwartz

Jonathan Schwartz, president and chief operating officer of Sun Micro-systems, is one of America's highest-ranking executive bloggers. Within months of entering the blogosphere in June 2004, he made an impact with his out-spoken postings attacking rivals, speculating about competitors, and com-plaining about unfair media reporting.

More than 175,000 people visit Schwartz's blog every month to read about the company's latest competitive moves or Schwartz's personal opin-ions on industry controversies. Occasionally, they will be treated to the more trivial delights of business trips to faraway places and his experiences with foreign cuisine. Staff, journalists, analysts, and rivals read Schwartz's weblog [blogs.sun.com/jonathan]. Crucially, it is also visited by potential Sun cus-tomers, many of whom now use rival operating systems.

Schwartz says the advantages of blogging are immense. He envisages a day when many if not all executives will maintain a blog. Meanwhile, com-pany bosses who once jealously guarded access to Internet and email are en-couraging their employees to blog. By the end of 2004, more than a thousand Microsoft staff were blogging, as were workers at Yahoo, Google, Intuit, and Monster.com. But now, in the first-ever such move by any American com-pany, Sun has officially encouraged all 32,000 of its employees to start their own blogs.

You are president of a multibillion-dollar company. Why did you feel the need to start a weblog?

At a fundamental level the job of any leader, whether they are in the public sector or the private sector, is to communicate. And the real challenge in communications, especially in leadership roles, is really twofold. The first problem is reach: can you reach a cross section of the demographic that you care about? And the second is authenticity: does your message sound authentic? In a corporation, there is an enormous sea of people employed to interpret your perspective and to convey that interpretation to the marketplace but there is no voice that is more authentic than my own.

Beginning the blog was a way of reaching the broadest cross section of people. It allows me to communicate not simply with customers but also with my own employees. Because I am using my own voice I can create a compelling and interesting place, and entice people back to get updates and revisions.

What about HP [Hewlett-Packard]? They weren't too happy with your blog.

Well, it does really frustrate our competitors. We carried out a full analysis of HP's operating system strategy that announced the demise of HP-UX—so I published it on my blog. They had their lawyers send a cease and desist letter, which we turned around and published. That drove a huge number of readers from the HP-installed base and further destabilized the tenuous grasp they had on their customers.

It really showed that authenticity is fundamentally what customers want. They don't want mindless marketing and interpretation. If you read my blog you will see no one else writes it. It comes straight from me. It takes up a fair amount of time but on the other hand leadership is all about communication. If there is any one thing I am going to spend my time doing it is communicating. A blog is one of the most efficient means of getting the message out and making sure it is heard with integrity and fidelity.

How is blogging better than more traditional means of communication like emails and press releases?

Think of your daily life today. If I were to send you an email I would be competing with about 450 people who want to sell you everything from a new vacation home to a new online webinar for making money on the Web. Email has become so dysfunctional that it is no longer a useful tool for communicating with people, at least with fidelity.

People choose to visit my blog, which means that I do not have to intrude by sending out an email. But my blog is also the one place where I can rely on no one interpreting or reformatting whatever I say. It is something that is really, truly from the source. In some sense it is the ultimate in transparency.

Is there a danger that you weblog is too transparent and that you could overstep the mark? Are there any issues with confidentiality?

Sun has a tremendously progressive legal community, partially because we have been living on the Internet for twenty years. But it was really interesting to watch the tension between the old school at Sun, which is traditionally based on a network-culture school of thought, and the new school, which is a bunch of newly minted lawyers wandering around trying to protect Sun in the new era of Sarbanes-Oxley corporate openness. [Sarbanes-Oxley is a law mandating greater corporate transparency and honesty in the wake of the Enron scandal].

The old school said the Internet is a good thing. Blogging is simply another form of communication and there's nothing we need to change about our policies or practices. If anything, blogging simply makes what is being communicated to the world more transparent.

The new school included lawyers who had recently joined us who weren't familiar with a network culture. They said we needed to shut down blogging because it is going to be a risk for confidentiality. They said there was a risk some engineer in the organization could leak a trade secret. Of course, the old school won.

So how does blogging fit into this new era of openness?

Blogging and online communication is a means of achieving a much greater sense of transparency. It enables things like Sarbanes-Oxley compliance because it puts everything out in the open. You can find errors and issues much more rapidly. I think the legal community is going to have to wrap its head around the fact that blogging is completely consistent with Reg. FD [Regulation Fair Disclosure].

Reg. FD produces a lot of anxiety in large-scale enterprises: What are we disclosing? When are we disclosing? How are we disclosing it?

There is a very interesting little irony being set up in the world right now, which is that if Sun wants to make a statement about its business and if I want to be compliant with Reg. FD, I have to make a statement through an accredited news organization like Reuters. I cannot simply do it through my blog, even though my blog is free and is available to a broader cross section of the world than Reuters news. Isn't that ironic, if what the SEC is trying to do is to ensure information is given out on a timely and equal basis to all investors?

So do you think blogging will change the way companies release information?

I think it has to. Let's face it, Sun issuing a press release through conventional wire communications to a news agency and waiting for them to write a story and put it into the mainstream media is ridiculously inefficient. Sun issuing a statement about its business through a blog or website is a much more efficient means of propagating news when it is available.

The fundamental issue behind blogs is that readers are now in control of when and if they choose to get updates and revisions. I think it has to change because the industry is just being turned on its head.

But more people will read the Reuters report than your blog won't they?

I don't believe that for a second. Let me turn that around. More people *could* read my blog than *could* read Reuters. If I make an announcement to the *Wall Street Journal*, that is considered consistent with meeting my Reg. FD obligations, but the *Wall Street Journal* is paid content online, not free. That seems like a regressive piece of legislation doesn't it? If only the investors who can afford the *Wall Street Journal* are allowed to get updates on business news, then they're going to be better informed than the proletariat reading Slashdot [slashdot.org, a technology weblog].

Have there been any other benefits from your weblog?

Huge benefits. I can communicate with a very relevant demographic nearly instantaneously and, more importantly, nearly simultaneously. It saves me time and effort.

I don't have to fly to Topeka, Kansas, to have a meeting with an IT department, because they have all read my blog. Or I fly around the world, I show up in some location and twelve people walk up to me and say, "I read your blog last week, loved what you had to say."

Thousands of people every day read exactly what we want them to read. For us to get that rich a demographic to digest such targeted content would cost tens of millions of dollars a year, so communication savings alone, much less the time savings, are immeasurable.

What is the value to Sun of being able to communicate instantaneously to all of HP's installed base about the uncertainty of HP's operating system? How much would that cost me otherwise? That would probably cost me tens of millions of dollars but I can do that over a weekend. And I will then be aided and abetted by *Computer World*, which covers what I have written, which puts it out to an even broader marketplace.

If it is so good, why are so few executives doing it?

I think there are a couple of reasons. Firstly, there is a generational issue. Most traditional executives aren't really steeped in a network culture. I meet a lot of senior executives who still don't even get email. It's also a little terrifying to look over the precipice and think that what you write will be read by potentially hundreds of thousands if not millions of people. I think for people who don't have an authentic voice or who are worried about the authenticity of what they are saying, that's probably pretty frightening. But if executives just get the marketing department to write their blog, they won't get any readership because it won't be authentic.

What about employees blogging?

Well, by the time your book goes to print I will have sent a message to all 32,000 employees at Sun recommending that they blog. And why? Because they can all speak with a level of authenticity to a potentially very unique audience. And where will we draw the line? Well, all we will do is point them towards the employment agreement they signed when they joined Sun.

There's really no difference between a blog and a website and a mobile-phone call. It's all just communication. We all have to be responsible, but I think we also need to be authentic. And authenticity, I think, is a really competitive weapon for Sun because we actually believe in what we talk about. It is the DNA of the company. It's the fact that all of Sun is about the network culture. It preceded me at Sun. I became a part of it; it didn't become a part of me.

So, as president of a technology firm, how do you think blogging will affect technology of the future?

I think we are at the very beginning of a major change but I am hesitant to attribute all this to blogging. We are still at the beginning of the Internet and the rise of two-way communication.

If you take podcasting as an example, podcasting is to blogging what TiVo is to a TV set. You can basically store up time-based media, like a news broadcast online, store it on your iPod and then listen at your own leisure. So it's a means of building caches on the Internet for content that you think is interesting.

The whole notion of scheduled programming is something that will be completely anachronistic three or four years from now. The notion that *Friends* is on TV at 8:00 p.m. on Thursday night is just going to completely go by the wayside, because you're going to either have TiVoed it or cached the content. I think you will see a cacophony of authors contributing their content to the Web.

Many of them will be senior executives in companies and those that rise to the top will be those that have authentic voices. I think we are going to see a lot more personalities, whether it's John Markoff or Dan Gillmor or people of that stature. They will build a brand for themselves that escapes the traditional confines of traditional publishing and media. I don't think blogging makes you famous, but I do think that personalities will have a vehicle for establishing their relevance in different markets.

Are there any areas where you see dangers for the Internet and blogging?

I am still struggling to see why there is a downside to free speech or a free market. I'm sure there are some who would like to believe that having a planned economy would be easier to understand, but I think at the end of the day those that are the best at what they do—the most talented, the most competitive—will rise to the top. I think the same is true with online communications as it is with media formats or automobiles.

Of course free speech and free markets are risky. But I think the trade-off will make it all worthwhile. The real challenge for executives in the network world is that the network follows you wherever you go. Given how porous the boundaries are between personal life and professional life, those boundaries are disappearing more every day.

Those of us who are committed to what we do, try to set up boundaries that allow you to not do it twenty-four hours a day. But the Internet by definition is always on and that can be enormously distracting. I think it's a real challenge not to be controlled by that glowing monitor in the corner.

So what changes are we likely to see in the next few years?

I think there are two things. Firstly, bandwidth will grow. What today is a relatively static communication, largely based on text with a little bit of audio, will be supplanted by more and more video communication which will largely be a result of more pervasive and ubiquitous adoption of bandwidth. Secondly, I think we will begin to see a set of cultural changes wash over the way that people communicate, which is what's happening with me at Sun or others in the industry. But ultimately most of the shift in the IT community is a cultural shift, not a technical one, and this is something the media has not yet grasped.

For example, NBC paid I think $6 billion or $8 billion for the rights to broadcast the Beijing Olympics in 2008. By the time that rolls around, you are going to have college kids in the stands with mobile handsets that are broadcasting video at the same quality as most commercial cameras today. So NBC paid $8 billion for the rights to what they thought were exclusive to NBC—only there are going to be thirty thousand college kids in the audience with a different perspective on the world. Plus, there's going to be a certain set of those kids who are particularly good at or interested in, say, track and field or javelin throwing. So what did NBC pay $8 billion for?

That's the kind of cultural adaptation that I think news organizations specifically are going to have to grapple with. But I think it also represents an immense social opportunity to further connect the world together, and I think the net of all this is there will be enormous economic opportunities for those who figure out how to take advantage of technologies that connect people. Google and eBay are perfect examples of immense value that can be created when you figure out how to get in front of social tides. I think blogging is just another instantiation of a social tide and there will be people who do quite well figuring out how to navigate those waters.

I don't have any prescription and if I did I would be investing a lot of money in private companies right now. All I know is that at the end of the day you are going to need computing infrastructure to make this stuff work. And that is Sun's business. And that's partially why we are so fixated on building our infrastructure to scale to the planet's appetite.

WHY THERE'S NO ESCAPING THE BLOG

by David Kirkpatrick and Daniel Roth*

The teaser Fortune *put under the headline of this story says it all: "Freewheeling bloggers can boost your product—or destroy it. Either way, they've become a force business can't afford to ignore." It's all here: the case studies of blogs that turned into highly successful business tools—Scoble's blog "humanizing" Microsoft, GM's information on its engines for techies, a hiker's invention of a solar-powered backpack—and what blogs became dogs: Kryptonite's (after failing to acknowledge its locks were easy to pick), and Mazda (for turning their blog into a thinly disguised ad).*

Along the way, the story also provides some of the keys needed to be successful in the "ultimate word-of-mouth marketing channel," as one entrepreneur puts it. It's a conversation, not a sales pitch; it needs candor, not denial; and it needs to be perceived as a resource and not a marketing campaign.

The most important key of all is honesty. In a quote we vote to the top of our "the best things ever said about blogs" list, the vice chairman of the advertising giant Ogilvy & Mather says, "If you fudge or lie on a blog, you are biting the karmic weenie."

Kirkpatrick and Roth wind up the story with an insightful look at the companies and technologies that will keep the trend booming.

*This essay originally appeared in *Fortune* on December 27, 2004. ©2005 Time Inc. All rights reserved. Reprinted by permission.

Early in the evening of Dec. 1, Microsoft revealed that it planned to take over the world of blogs—the five-million-plus web journals that have exploded on the Internet in the past few years. The company's weapon would be a new service called MSN Spaces, online software that allows people to easily create and maintain blogs. It didn't take long for the blogging world to do what it does best: swarm around a new piece of information; push, prod, and poke at it; and leave it either stronger or a bloody mess. The next day, at the widely read Boing Boing blog, co-editor Xeni Jardin opted to do the latter.

She titled her critique of MSN Spaces "7 Dirty Blogs" and hilariously sent up the fickle censoring filters Microsoft appeared to have built in. MSN Spaces prohibited her from starting a blog called Pornography and the Law or another entitled Corporate Whore Chronicles; yet World of Poop passed, as did the educational Smoking Crack: A How-To Guide for Teens. Within the first hour of Jardin's post, five blogs had linked to it, including the site of widely read San Jose Mercury News columnist Dan Gillmor. By the end of the day there were dozens of blogs pointing readers to "7 Dirty Blogs," a proliferation of links that over the next few weeks topped 300. There were Italian blogs and Chinese blogs and blogs in Greek, German, and Portuguese. There were blogs with names like Tie-Dyed Brain Waves, Stubborn Like a Mule, and LibertyBlog. Each added its own tweak. "Ooooh, that's what I want: a blog that doesn't allow me to speak my mind," wrote a blogger called Kung Pow Pig. The conversation had clearly gotten out of Microsoft's hands.

Typically Microsoft would have taken the hits and kept powering forward. That is the Microsoft way. For years such behavior has done little but make people feel defenseless against the company. But this time Microsoft deployed one of its most important voices to talk back: not Bill Gates or Steve Ballmer, but Robert Scoble.

Scoble has been at Microsoft only 19 months and has neither a high-ranking title (he's a "software evangelist" who works with outside programmers) nor such corporate perks as a window in his office. What Scoble does have is a blog of his own, Scobleizer, on which he weighs in daily with opinions about happenings in the tech world—especially the inner world of Microsoft. On a recent day he posted nine remarks, each averaging a paragraph, on topics ranging from how a company programmer had fixed a security bug to the fact that his wife is becoming a U.S. citizen. Nothing too profound or insightful, yet Scobleizer has given the Microsoft monolith something it has long lacked: an approachable human face.

When it came to the criticism emanating from Boing Boing, Scoble simply . . . agreed. "MSN Spaces isn't the blogging service for me," he wrote. Nobody at Microsoft asked Scoble to comment; he just did it on his own, adding that he would make sure that the team working on Spaces was aware of the complaints. And he kept revisiting the issue on his blog. As the anti-Microsoft crowd cried censorship, the nearly 4,000 blogs linking to Scoble were able to see his running commentary on how Microsoft was reacting. "I get comments on my blog saying, 'I didn't like Microsoft before, but at least they're listening to us,' " says Scoble. "The blog is the best relationship generator you've ever seen." His famous boss agrees. "It's all about openness," says chairman Bill Gates of Microsoft's public blogs like Scobleizer. "People see them as a reflection of an open, communicative culture that isn't afraid to be self-critical."

The blog—short for weblog—can indeed be, as Scoble and Gates say, fabulous for relationships. But it can also be much more: a company's worst PR nightmare, its best chance to talk with new and old customers, an ideal way to send out information, and the hardest way to control it. Blogs are challenging the media and changing how people in advertising, marketing, and public relations do their jobs. A few companies like Microsoft are finding ways to work with the blogging world—even as they're getting hammered by it. So far, most others are simply ignoring it.

That will get harder: According to blog search-engine and measurement firm Technorati, 23,000 new weblogs are created every day—or about one every three seconds. Each blog adds to an inescapable trend fueled by the Internet: the democratization of power and opinion. Blogs are just the latest tool that makes it harder for corporations and other institutions to control and dictate their message. An amateur media is springing up, and the smart are adapting. Says Richard Edelman, CEO of Edelman Public Relations: "Now you've got to pitch the bloggers too. You can't just pitch to conventional media."

Of course, it's difficult to take the phenomenon seriously when most blogs involve kids talking about their dates, people posting pictures of their cats, or lefties raging about the right (and vice versa). But whatever the topic, the discussion of business isn't usually too far behind: from bad experiences with a product to good customer service somewhere else. Suddenly everyone's a publisher and everyone's a critic. Says Jeff Jarvis, author of the blog Buzz Machine, and president and creative director of newspaper publisher Advance Publications' Internet division: "There should be someone at every company whose job is to put into Google and blog search engines the name of the company or the brand, followed by the word 'sucks,' just to see what customers are saying."

It all used to be so easy; the adage went "never pick a fight with anyone who buys ink by the barrel." But now everyone can get ink for free, launch a diatribe, and—if what they have to say is interesting to enough people—expect web-enabled word of mouth to carry it around the world. Unlike earlier promises of self-publishing revolutions, the blog movement seems to be the real thing. A big reason for that is a tiny innovation called the permalink: a unique web address for each posting on every blog. Instead of linking to web pages, which can change, bloggers link to one another's posts, which typically remain accessible indefinitely. This style of linking also gives blogs a viral quality, so a pertinent post can gain broad attention amazingly fast—and reputations can get taken down just as quickly.

No one knows that better than Dan Rather. In a now infamous episode, the anchor fell like Goliath to the political bloggers during the presidential campaign. From the start, it was clear that these nobodies with laptops were going to have an impact. Conservative blogs, like the hugely popular InstaPundit, run by Glenn Reynolds, a University of Tennessee law professor, and Little Green Footballs, written by web designer Charles Johnson, or left-leaning sites like Markos Moulitsas's DailyKos, were rallying their hundreds of thousands of daily readers to whatever cause they alighted on. Then, in mid-September, came what the blogosphere—the term used in the blogging world for the blogging world—calls Rathergate. On 60 Minutes, Rather scooped rivals with memos that offered proof of George W. Bush's dereliction of duty while in the Texas National Guard—or that seemed to. Within a half hour of the broadcast, bloggers started questioning the authenticity of the memos. Others picked up on the suspicions and added their own thoughts and findings. After denying it at first, CBS later admitted it could "no longer vouch" for the memos. Soon after the election, Rather announced his retirement and the blogosphere declared victory—to the chagrin of the mainstream press. "We used to think that the news was finished when we printed it," says Jarvis. "But that's when the news now begins."

Just as Rathergate was breaking, corporate America got its clearest sign of blogger muscle—in this case, brought on not by memos but by a Bic pen. On Sept. 12 someone with the moniker "unaesthetic" posted in a group discussion site for bicycle enthusiasts a strange thing he or she had noticed: that the ubiquitous, U-shaped Kryptonite lock could be easily picked with a Bic ballpoint pen. Two days later a number of blogs, including the consumer electronics site Engadget, posted a video demonstrating the trick. "We're switching to something else ASAP," wrote Engadget editor Phillip Torrone. On Sept. 16, Kryptonite issued a bland statement saying the locks remained a "deterrent to theft" and promising that a new line would be "tougher." That wasn't enough. ("Trivial empty answer," wrote someone in the Engadget comments section.) Every day new bloggers began writing about the issue and talking about their experiences, and hundreds of thousands were reading about it. Prompted by the blogs, the New York Times and the Associated Press on Sept. 17 published stories about the problem—articles that set off a new chain of blogging. On Sept. 19, estimates Technorati, about 1.8 million people saw postings about Kryptonite. . . .

Finally, on Sept. 22, Kryptonite announced it would exchange any affected lock free. The company now expects to send out over 100,000 new locks. "It's been—I don't necessarily want to use the word 'devastating'— but it's been serious from a business perspective," says marketing director Karen Rizzo. Kryptonite's parent, Ingersoll-Rand, said it expects the fiasco to cost $10 million, a big chunk of Kryptonite's estimated $25 million in revenues. Ten days, $10 million. "Had they responded earlier, they might have stopped the anger before it hit the papers and became widespread," says Andrew Bernstein, CEO of Cymfony, a data-analysis company that watches the web for corporate customers and provides warning of such impending catastrophes.

Those who have tried to game the blogosphere haven't done much better. Mazda, hoping to reach its Gen Y buyers, crafted a blog supposedly run by someone named Kid Halloween, a 22-year-old hipster who posted things like: "Tonight I am going to see Ministry and My Life With the Thrill Kill Cult. . . . This will be a retro industrial flashback." He also posted a link to three videos he said a friend recorded off public-access TV. One showed a Mazda3 attempting to break dance, and another had it driving off a ramp like a skateboard, leading in both cases to frightening crashes. Other bloggers sensed a phony in their midst—the expensively produced videos were tip-offs—and began talking about it. Suddenly Mazda wasn't being hailed; it was being reviled on widely read blogs. "Everything about that 'blog' is insulting," wrote a poster on Autoblog. Mazda pulled the site after three days and now says it never intended it to have a long run. "It was a learning experience," says a spokesman. Tig Tillinghast, who runs the respected advertising industry blog Marketingvox.com, calls Mazda's blogging clumsiness "the moral equivalent of doing an English-language print ad that was written by a native French speaker."

"If you fudge or lie on a blog, you are biting the karmic weenie," says Steve Hayden, vice chairman of advertising giant Ogilvy & Mather, which creates blogs for clients. "The negative reaction will be so great that, whatever your intention was, it will be overwhelmed and crushed like a bug. You're fighting with very powerful forces because it's real people's opinions."

It all sounds like so much insanity: a worldwide cabal ready to pounce on and publicize any error a company makes. Yet it's not as if corporations are just sitting ducks. For one thing, not every negative voice is that influential. For every Rathergate or Kryptonite, there are thousands of other posts that disappear into the ether. Simply railing against Wal-Mart or repeating the latest conspiracy theory about Halliburton doesn't guarantee that the blogosphere will take notice.

More important, obsessive blogs can mean obsessive customers. The witty blogger behind Manolo's Shoe Blog may bash Birkenstocks and Uggs, but he drools over Coach, Prada, and, of course, Manolo Blahniks. Before blogs, finding someone like him—a person who probably helps others make buying decisions—would have been difficult and costly. Now it's just a matter of Googling or searching on any of the blog-specific search engines like Technorati or Feedster. For those who want to go deeper, firms like Intelliseek and BuzzMetrics use sophisticated software to analyze the blog universe for corporate clients. They use this growing online database of constantly updated consumer opinion for marketing and product-development ideas.

But how to speak directly to this swarm? Wary of a Mazda-like fiasco, most companies that want to blog try to walk a fine line: telling employee bloggers to be honest but also encouraging evangelism. Corporate propaganda almost always drives readers away; real people with real opinions keep them coming back. At the GM Smallblock Engine Blog, employees and customers rhapsodize about Corvettes and other GM cars. Stoneyfield Farm has several blogs about yogurt. Not surprisingly, the earliest adopters have been tech firms. The biggest chunk of the 5,000 or so corporate bloggers comes from Microsoft, but others work at Monster.com, Intuit, and Sun Microsystems—where even the company's acerbic No. 2, Jonathan Schwartz, gets in on the action. (A recent Schwartz post openly criticizes competitor Hewlett-Packard: "Yet another series of disappointing announcements.")

At best, these blogs can act like tranquilizers in an elephant: slowing a maddened charge against a company but not stopping it. Macromedia three years ago set up a few employee blogs to give customers a one-stop place for info and tech support. The blogs, and the employees running them, quickly became an important resource to customers—as well as to the company. When Macromedia in 2003 released software that was maddeningly slow, the company bloggers quickly acknowledged the need for fixes, helping ease some of the tension. "It was a great early-warning system and helped us frame the situation," says senior vice president Tom Hale. "It accrued a huge benefit to us."

"I need to be credible," says Microsoft's Scoble. "If I'm only saying, 'Use Microsoft products, rah rah rah,' it sounds like a press release, and I lose all ability to have a conversation with the world at large."

Unfiltered conversations aren't exactly the kind of things in-house counsel encourage, though. And employees have been fired at Starbucks, Harvard University, Delta, and social-networking software company Friendster for blogs the organizations apparently deemed offensive, though none will comment. Even blogging boosters Microsoft and Sun have hit bumps. Microsoft fired a temp who posted photos of Apple computers sitting on a company loading dock. Sun CEO Scott McNealy was urged not to blog after he showed trial posts to company lawyers and colleagues. "I've got too many constituents that I have to pretend to be nice to," he says.

As big companies try to maintain a delicate balance, it's often the smaller players who are nimbly working blogs to their advantage. Entrepreneurs like Shayne McQuade have learned that bloggers can be an easy—and free—marketing arm, if used right. McQuade, a onetime McKinsey consultant, in 2002 invented a backpack with built-in solar panels that enables hikers and Eurotrippers to keep their gadgets charged. He spent $15,000 getting the company up and running, outsourcing design and manufacturing to jobbers in Asia and warehousing and shipping to a company in New Jersey. The only thing left for him was getting the word out: He ended up outsourcing that to bloggers.

In late September, just after McQuade received an early sample of the Voltaic Backpack, he asked a friend, Graham Hill—who runs a "green design" weblog called Treehugger—if he'd mention the product. Start up the swarm! Within a few hours of Voltaic's hitting Treehugger, the popular Cool-Hunting blog mentioned McQuade's product, which got it seen by Joel Johnson, editor of Engadget competitor Gizmodo. Each step up in the blogging ecosystem brought Voltaic to a broader audience. (Yes, for all its democratic trappings, there are hierarchies of influence in the blogging world.)

In came a flurry of orders. Ironically, McQuade—who had helped research Net Gain, a seminal book on how the Internet would change business—was unprepared. "Overnight what was supposed to be laying a little groundwork became my launch," he says. "This is the ultimate word-of-mouth marketing channel."

These are still the early days of blogging, and the form is still morphing.

Blogs that host music and video are popping up, people are starting to blog text and photos from their phones, and sites like NewsGator, using a technology called RSS, allow people to subscribe to blogs. Plus, an arms race is building behind the scenes. Venture capitalists last year invested a still tiny $33 million into blog-related companies, but that was up from $8 million the year before, according to research firm VentureOne. Blog ad companies, which place ads and pay per response, are enabling bloggers to earn money from their sites. And blogging publishers have emerged. Two of the most prominent, Jason Calacanis and Nick Denton, are going head-to-head with stables of popular blogs (Engadget and Autoblog vs. Gizmodo, Gawker, and Wonkette, among others). More important, some of the most competitive companies in tech are throwing their weight behind blogging.

The newest kid on the blog block, Microsoft, has already seen what the sites can do for it. Now it thinks it has a chance to grab the youth market. Blake Irving, the VP who oversees Hotmail, the e-mail service, with 187 million users, and MSN Messenger, with 145 million IM accounts, views MSN Spaces as "the third leg of the communications stool," one that Microsoft hopes to turn into an advertising-fueled business. MSN is already selling ads on some Spaces for things like Lacoste shirts at Neiman Marcus online. E-mail is for old people, says Irving; kids prefer to communicate by phone and IM, and, now, by keeping blogs. So Spaces is tightly integrated with the latest version of MSN Messenger. Says Bill Gates, who claims he'd like to start a blog but doesn't have the time: "As blogging software gets easier to use, the boundaries between, say, writing e-mail and writing a blog will start to blur. This will fundamentally change how we document our lives."

Google, the company that Microsoft is playing catchup with (its Blogger.com division is the largest blogging service right now), also expects blogs to become as important as e-mail and IM. Right now, it's working on ways to better help people find content they want in blogs, says Jason Goldman, Blogger's product manager. But if Google's internal use of Blogger is any indication, it also sees it as an essential business tool. Since 2003, when it bought Pyra Labs, the company that launched Blogger.com, Google's employees have created several hundred internal blogs. They are used for collaborating on projects as well as selling extra concert tickets and finding Rollerblading partners. Google's public relations, quality control, and advertising departments all have blogs, some of them public. When Google redesigned its search home page, a staffer blogged notes from every brainstorm session. "With a company like Google that's growing this fast, the verbal history can't be passed along fast enough," says Marissa Mayer, who oversees the search site and all of Google's consumer web products. "Our legal department loves the blogs, because it basically is a written-down, backed-up, permanent time-stamped version of the scientist's notebook. When you want to file a patent, you can now show in blogs where this idea happened."

But when you live by the blog, you die by the blog (or at least feel serious pain). Perhaps the best example comes from Mena and Ben Trott, the husband and wife team who founded Six Apart, creator of Movable Type, the blogging software that now runs some of the most prominent blogs on the web, including InstaPundit and Jarvis's BuzzMachine. The Trotts, both 27, started the company after the success of Mena's blog, Dollarshort.org. ("A day late and a dollar short," she says. "A lot of my stories were about people picking on me and being a dork.") Unhappy with the software she was using, Mena enlisted programmer Ben to design their own blog software. They announced the product in October 2001 with just a post on Mena's blog, and had 100 downloads the first hour. Companies paid a flat rate of $150 and individuals were invited to pay what they thought the product was worth. "If we got $50 or $60, that was nice," says Mena.

The Trotts soon started a hosting service for blogs, called TypePad, and lured $11.5 million in venture financing—along with some big customers, including Disney, the U.S. Air Force, Fujitsu, and Nokia. Yet until May, Six Apart was relying on its original pricing scheme. The Trotts decided to upgrade. Mena posted a long message describing the new fee structure on her company blog, Mena's Corner. Less than three hours later, the first comments started rolling in. "Looks like I'll be dumping Movable Type soon" was the first. Many others echoed that outrage in what became a total of 849 customer comments in about ten languages.

Six Apart didn't erase any of the comments, even the most negative ones. Mena read every comment in full, then kept posting notes explaining why the company had changed the pricing structure and that it was still working on revising it. Looking back now, she says, "We made people feel heard." And she knows that sooner or later, the process will start all over again. Says CEO Barak Berkowitz: "When everybody has a tool for talking to the rest of the world, you can't hide from your mistakes. You have to face them. Once you commit to an open dialogue, you can't stop. And it's painful." As the impact of blogs spreads through global business, that pain—and promise—will be something companies will have to deal with. And if they don't? You're bound to read about it in a blog.

BLOGS WILL CHANGE YOUR BUSINESS

by Stephen Baker and Heather Green*

Five months after Fortune *ran their cover story on blogging,* Business-Week *followed suit. BW's teaser carried the same message, but in more colorful terms: "Look past the yakkers, hobbyists, and political mobs. Your customers and rivals are figuring blogs out. Our advice: Catch up . . . or catch you later."*

In an effort to show the magazine au courant and able to counter the moniker "MSM" (mainstream media), writers Stephen Baker and Heather Green one-upped the competition and wrote their story in the style of a blog—informal (at least for BusinessWeek*), a bit breathless, and instead of the traditional subheads, letting the story evolve as if it were written as day-by-day postings. (We can't help but wonder if grassroots bloggers wouldn't have considered this to be one more outrageous example of LSM—lame mainstream media.) The article certainly made the case that if anyone thought blogs had only to do with media or politics or personal issues, they were missing one of the biggest elephants in the room: big business.*

Among other interesting topics, the BusinessWeek *authors tackle an important question: "Any chance that a blog bubble could pop?" The answer comes quickly: "No." Baker and Green say it's true the statistics keep floating upward à la the dot-com bubble (Technorati says 23,000 blogs are being built*

---

*This article appeared in *Business Week* on May 2, 2005. Copyright © 2000–2005, by The McGraw-Hill Companies Inc. All rights reserved.

every day; the BusinessWeek *story ups that to 40,000). And yes, venture capital is jumping in with both feet. All-too-familiar terms are also reappearing:* scaling, aggregation, eyeballs. *But wait, argue Baker and Green, venture capitalists have poured in only three percent of what they poured into dot-coms in 1999. And the blogging trend is powered by "normal folks," while the dot-com era was powered by companies.*

The story was accompanied by some case studies and a list of tips, all of which can be found on BusinessWeek's *website (businessweek.com). And to show that the magazine practiced what it was preaching, it also announced it had joined the blogging revolution, launching their blog, Blogspotting.net.*

<u>Monday 9:30 a.m.</u> It's time for a frank talk. And no, it can't wait. We know, we know: Most of you are sick to death of blogs. Don't even want to hear about these millions of online journals that link together into a vast network. And yes, there's plenty out there not to like. Self-obsession, politics of hate, and the same hunger for fame that has people lining up to trade punches on *The Jerry Springer Show*. Name just about anything that's sick in our society today, and it's on parade in the blogs. On lots of them, even the writing stinks.

Go ahead and bellyache about blogs. But you cannot afford to close your eyes to them, because they're simply the most explosive outbreak in the information world since the Internet itself. And they're going to shake up just about every business—including yours. It doesn't matter whether you're shipping paper clips, pork bellies, or videos of Britney in a bikini, blogs are a phenomenon that you cannot ignore, postpone, or delegate. Given the changes barreling down upon us, blogs are not a business elective. They're a prerequisite. (And yes, that goes for us, too.)

There's a little problem, though. Many of you don't visit blogs—or haven't since blogs became a sensation in last year's Presidential race. According to a *Pew Research Center Survey,* only 27% of Internet users in America now bother to read them. So we're going to take you into the world of blogs by delivering this story—call it Blogs 101 for businesses—in the style of a blog. We're even sprinkling it with links. These are underlined words that, when clicked, carry readers of this story's online version to another Web page. This all may make for a strange experience, but it's the closest we can come to reaching out from the page, grabbing you by the collar, and shaking you into action.

First, a few numbers. *There are some 9 million blogs out there,* with 40,000 new ones popping up each day. Some discuss poetry, others constitutional law. And, yes, many are plain silly. "Mommy tells me it may rain today. Oh Yucky Dee Doo," reads *one April Posting.* Let's assume that 99.9% are equally off point. So what? That leaves some 40 new ones every day that could be talking about your business, engaging your employees, or leaking those merger discussions you thought were hush-hush.

Give the paranoids their due. The overwhelming majority of the information the world spews out every day is digital—photos from camera phones, PowerPoint presentations, government filings, billions and billions of e-mails, even digital phone messages. With a couple of clicks, every one of these items can be broadcast into the blogosphere by anyone with an Internet hookup— or even a cell phone. If it's scandalous, a poisonous e-mail from a CEO, for example, or torture pictures from a prison camp, others link to it in a flash. And here's the killer: Blog posts linger on the Web forever.

Yet not all the news is scary. Ideas circulate as fast as scandal. Potential customers are out there, sniffing around for deals and partners. While you may be putting it off, you can bet that your competitors are exploring ways to harvest new ideas from blogs, sprinkle ads into them, and yes, find out what you and other competitors are up to. More tomorrow.

<u>Tuesday 6:35 a.m.</u> How big are blogs? Try *Johannes Gutenberg* out for size. His printing press, unveiled in 1440, sparked a publishing boom and an information revolution. Some say it led to the Protestant Reformation and Western democracy. Along the way, societies established the rights and rules of the game for the privileged few who could afford to buy printing presses and grind forests into paper.

The printing press set the model for mass media. A lucky handful owns the publishing machinery and controls the information. Whether at newspapers or global manufacturing giants, they decide what the masses will learn. This elite still holds sway at most companies. You know them. They generally park in sheltered spaces, have longer rides on elevators, and avoid the cafeteria. They keep the secrets safe and coif the company's message. Then they distribute it—usually on a need-to-know basis—to customers, employees, investors, and the press.

That's the world of mass media, and the blogs are turning it on its head. Set up a free account at *Blogger* or other blog services, and you see right away that the cost of publishing has fallen practically to zero. Any dolt with a working computer and an Internet connection can become a blog publisher in the 10 minutes it takes to sign up.

Sure, most blogs are painfully primitive. That's not the point. They represent power. Look at it this way: In the age of mass media, publications like ours print the news. Sources try to get quoted, but the decision is ours. Ditto with letters to the editor. Now instead of just speaking through us, they can blog. And if they master the ins and outs of this new art—like how to get other bloggers to link to them—they reach a huge audience.

This is just the beginning. Many of the same folks who developed blogs are busy adding features so that bloggers can start up music and video channels and team up on editorial projects. The divide between the publishers and the public is collapsing. This turns mass media upside down. It creates media of the masses.

How does business change when everyone is a potential publisher? A vast new stretch of the information world opens up. For now, it's a digital hinterland. The laws and norms covering fairness, advertising, and libel? They don't exist, not yet anyway. But one thing is clear: Companies over the past few centuries have gotten used to shaping their message. Now they're losing control of it.

Want to get it back? You never will, not entirely. But for a look at what you're facing, come along for a tour of the blogosphere.

Wednesday 7:38 a.m. Hmm. How to start this post? Idle talk about the weather, or maybe that red wine with dinner last night? No. Let's dive right in: One misstep and the blog world can have its way with you—even when the coolest, most tech-savvy companies are involved.

Google is regarded as a secretive company. So in January, when a young programmer named Mark Jen started blogging about his first days in the

Googleplex, folks in the 'sphere instantly linked to him. Jen certainly wasn't dealing out inside dirt. But he griped that Google's health plan was less generous than his former employer's—Microsoft—and he argued, indignantly, that Google's free food was an enticement for employees to work past dinner.

Two weeks later, Google fired Jen. And that's when the 22-year-old became a big story. Google was blogbusted for overreacting and for sending an all-too-clear warning to the dozens of bloggers still at the company. A Google official says the company has lots of bloggers and just expects them to use common sense. For example, if it's something you wouldn't e-mail to a long list of strangers, don't blog it.

Jen clearly flunked that test. "As the media got hold of it, I was quickly educated," he says. He says he should have understood the company's goals and concerns better and been more sensitive to them. Still, his adventure turned him into an overnight celebrity. He was wooed by recruiters at Amazon.com, Microsoft, and Yahoo! A month later, Jen landed a job at Plaxo, an Internet contact-management company. A key part of his job, says a company spokesperson, is to help coordinate *Plaxo's blogging efforts*—a pillar of Plaxo's promotional strategy. So what got him fired turned out to be his trump card. Plaxo, like many other companies, is now drawing up norms for blogging behavior, so that employees know what's in bounds, and what's not.

2:22 p.m. It sounds like the joke answer on a multiple-choice exam. Name a leading company in blog communications: General Motors?

That's right. For a company that's slipping in the auto biz, GM is showing a surprisingly nimble touch with blogs. GM uses them on occasion to steer past its own PR department and the mainstream press.

In January, Vice-Chairman *Bob Lutz* launched his own *FastLane Blog*. Bloggers applauded, and car buffs flooded Lutz with suggestions and complaints. Lutz posted lots of barbs from outsiders and won points for balanced responses. Like his answer to criticisms of new Pontiacs: "Did you take a look at seat tailoring? Carpet fits? . . . hood gaps, hem flanges? We used to be bad at those, too."

But Lutz is only part of GM's blog strategy. In April the company yanked $10 million in advertising from the *Los Angeles Times* and demanded that the *Times* make retractions. Journalists asked GM for specific complaints, and the car company held off. It said it wanted to work quietly with the *Times* and not battle it out in the press.

How to get the word out through a back channel? GM directed journalists to a blog, *AutomoBear.com,* that detailed GM's beef. (It had to do with a comparison between two cars, which GM thought was unfair.) Both GM and Miro Pacic, the blogger at AutomoBear, say that GM provided Pacic with information but that no money passed hands.

Fair enough. But even if GM doesn't pay for positive coverage in blogs, just consider the possibilities in this new footloose media world. There's little to stop companies from quietly buying bloggers' support, or even starting unbranded blogs of their own to promote their products—or to tar the competition. This raises all kinds of questions about the ever-shrinking wall between advertising and editorial. We'll cover that later, when we get to the blogs' impact on our own business—the media.

Thursday 8:56 a.m. It's the latest wrinkle on Descartes. I blog therefore I . . . consult. An entire industry is rising up to guide companies into this frightening new realm. And the consultants establish their brands and reps with their blogs.

Perhaps the biggest is *Steve Rubel.* A year ago, the exec at the PR firm CooperKatz & Co. started his blog, *Micro Persuasion.* He was already pushing such clients as WeatherBug and the Association of National Advertisers into the blog world. Then early one Sunday morning, as he recalls it, "my wife was sleeping, and I was sitting in the living room, laptop on my lap, and thinking if I am talking to clients and reading these blogs, I should jump in." When launching his site, he had the smarts to contact big shots such as Dan Gillmor, who was a leading blogger and tech reporter with the *San Jose Mercury News.* Gillmor linked to Rubel's site, and his traffic took off. It was great for his brand, and it also gave Rubel a blogger's education. "I became a living guinea pig for what I preach," he says.

Now Rubel is positioned as an all-knowing Thumper in a forest of clueless Bambis. The first job, he says, is to monitor the blogs to see what people are saying about your company. (An entire industry is growing to sell that service. Even IBM's banging at the door.) Next step: Damage-control strategies.

How to respond when blogs attack. He says companies have to learn to track what blogs are talking about, pinpoint influential bloggers, and figure out how to buttonhole them, privately and publicly.

He gives the example of Netflix. When a fan blog called *Hacking Netflix* asked the company for info and interviews last year, Netflix turned it down. How could they make time for all the bloggers? Predictably, the blogger, Mike Kaltschnee, aired the exchange, and Netflix faced a storm of public criticism. Now Netflix feeds info to Kaltschnee, and he passes along what he's hearing from the fans. Sounds like he's half journalist, half consultant—though he insists Netflix doesn't pay him.

Friday 10:46 a.m. The question came up at a panel discussion last week: Any chance that a blog bubble could pop? The answer is really easy: no.

At least not an investment bubble. Venture firms financed only $60 million in blog startups last year, according to industry tracker VentureOne. Chump change compared to the $19.9 billion that poured into dot-coms in 1999. The difference is that while dot-coms promised to make loads of money, blogs flex their power mostly by disrupting the status quo.

The bigger point, which is blindingly obvious when you think about it, is that the dot-com era was powered by companies—complete with programmers, marketing budgets, Aeron chairs, and burn rates. The masses of bloggers, by contrast, are normal folks with computers: no budget, no business plan, no burn rate, and—that's right—no bubble.

The role of the blog startups is to build tools for this grassroots uprising. Six Apart, a four-year-old San Francisco company, leads in blog software. Technorati and PubSub Concepts are battling it out in blog search. The founders all insist that they plan to remain independent. But if recent history is any guide, most of them will wind up in the bellies of the blog-minded Internet giants—led by Google, Yahoo, and Microsoft. The latest to disappear was *Flickr*. A photo-sharing service that spread madly across the blog world, 13-month-old Flickr was still running its software in its beta, or testing, phase when it was acquired by Yahoo in March for an undisclosed sum. *Caterina Fake*, Flickr's co-founder, wrote about the deal in her blog the day it happened: "Don't forget to breathe. It's not the end, it's the beginning."

Monday 10:23 a.m. If this were a true blog, that last post would have generated a mountain of comments over the weekend, most of them with the same question: If there's no clear business model, why are the Internet giants so bent on getting a foothold in blogs? Look at it from their point of view. A vibrant community that has doubled in size in the past eight months is teeming with potential customers and has a mother lode of data to mine. "Blogs are what's causing the Web to grow," says Jason Goldman. He's project manager at Google's Blogger, the world's biggest service to set people up as bloggers.

David Sifry looks at it a bit differently. He's a serial entrepreneur and founder of Technorati, the blog search engine.

For Sifry, it's not the growth of the same Web, but an entirely new one. It's wrapped up far more in people's day-to-day lives. It's connected to time. The way he describes it, the Web we've come to know is mostly a collection of documents. A library. These documents don't change much. Try Googling Donald Trump, and you're more likely to find his Web page than a discussion of his appearance last night on *The Apprentice*. Blogs are different. They evolve with every posting, each one tied to a moment. So if a company can track millions of blogs simultaneously, it gets a heat map of what a growing part of the world is thinking about, minute by minute. E-mail has carried on billions of conversations over the past decade. But those exchanges were private. Most blogs are open to the world. As the bloggers read each other, comment, and link from one page to the next, they create a global conversation.

Picture the blog world as the biggest coffeehouse on Earth. Hunched over their laptops at one table sit six or seven experts in nanotechnology. Right across from them are teenage goths dressed in black and thoroughly pierced. Not too many links between those two tables. But the café goes on and on. Saudi women here, Labradoodle lovers there, a huge table of people fooling around with cell phones. Those are the mobile-photo crowd, busily sending camera-phone pictures up to their blogs.

The racket is deafening. But there's loads of valuable information floating around this café. *Technorati, PubSub,* and others provide the tools to listen. While the traditional Web catalogs what we have learned, the blogs track what's on our minds.

Why does this matter? Think of the implications for businesses of getting an up-to-the-minute read on what the world is thinking. Already, studios are using blogs to see which movies are generating buzz. Advertisers are tracking responses to their campaigns. "I'm amazed people don't get it yet," says Jeff Weiner, Yahoo's senior vice-president who heads up search. "Never in the history of market research has there been a tool like this."

Tuesday 9:12 p.m. Back to that coffeehouse. Sitting at one large table is a collection of some of the most gifted geeks you can imagine. These folks built the blogosphere. And they're using it to link with each other. They share ideas, test them, and get them up and running in a hurry. Many of them transform the network itself, making it more muscular—and disruptive.

The innovation that sends blogs zinging into the mainstream is *RSS*, or Really Simple Syndication. Five years ago, a blogger named Dave Winer, working with software originally developed by Netscape, created an easy-to-use system to turn blogs, or even specific postings, into Web feeds. With this system, a user could subscribe to certain blogs, or to key words, and then have all the relevant items land at a single destination. These personalized Web pages bring together the music and video the user signs up for, in addition to news. They're called "aggregators." For now, only about 5% of Internet users have set them up. But that number's sure to rise as Yahoo and Microsoft plug them.

In time, aggregators could turn the Web on its head. Why? They discourage surfing as users increasingly just wait for interesting items to drop onto their page or e-mailbox. Internet advertising, which traditionally counts on page views and clicks, could be thrown for a loop. Already Yahoo is packaging ads on the feeds. Google is testing the waters.

But here's the really insidious part. If you set up your own aggregator page, such as *my.yahoo.com,* and subscribe to feeds, you soon discover that blog and mainstream postings mingle side by side. Feeds zip through the walls between blogs and the rest of the information world. Blog posts are becoming just part of the mix, swimming on the same page with the Associated Press, and yes, *BusinessWeek*.

Winer also ushered in a second tech breakthrough, *podcasting*. A back-and-forth between Winer and Adam Curry, a blogger and former MTV host, led last year to a system that easily distributes audio files. Looking for National

Public Radio's On the Media or the latest ska compilations from a disk jockey in Trinidad? Sign up on a Web page, and the program gets automatically delivered to you—as an audio feed. Last summer, Curry created software called *iPodder* so these MP3s could hitch a ride on an iPod. That was the birth of podcasting: radio programming whenever and wherever you want it. Since then, some 5,000 podcasting shows have sprouted up. They cover everything from yoga to the blues.

It's an overnight sensation. Before podcasting, only about 150 people a month bothered to download the audio files of *Morning Stories,* a show on Boston's public station WGBH. After the station switched to podcasting in October? Eighty thousand. Chalk it up to the bloggers. They pushed podcasting to their own circles, and it grew from there.

11:48 p.m. One more idea. Think of TiVo, think of the iPod. When you're using one of them, do you consider the company that provides the programming? CBS, for example? Not much. You're putting together your own package. The pieces come from lots of companies and artists. Often you don't even know where.

Aggregators do the same job for the Net. So, just like the record companies, which have figured out how to market bits and pieces of their albums as standalone songs and ringtones, the rest of the media and entertainment world is going to have to think small. Content, whether it's news or a Hollywood movie, is going to travel in bite-size nuggets. The challenge, for bloggers and giants alike, is to brand those nuggets and devise ways to sell them or wrap them in advertising.

Wednesday 6:31 a.m. A prediction: Mainstream media companies will master blogs as an advertising tool and take over vast commercial stretches of the blogosphere. Over the next five years, this could well divide winners and losers in media. And in the process, mainstream media will start to look more and more like—you guessed it—blogs. Clay Shirky, a Web expert at New York University, calls it "an absorption process where the thing doing the absorbing changes."

Take a look at blog advertising today, and it's hard to see a glittering future. Sure, enterprising bloggers make room on their pages for Google-generated ads, known as AdSense, and earn some pocket change. Some blog entrepreneurs, such as Nick Denton, publisher of New York's *Gawker Media*, sell ads for everything from Nike to Absolut Vodka. Popular blogs can land sponsorship deals for as much as $25,000 per month, say consultants. O.K. money for an entrepreneur, but a rounding error in the ad industry.

Blog power simply doesn't translate yet into big bucks. For now, it's running mostly on people's passion to communicate—especially in developing markets. Consider *Hossein Derakhshan*. He's a 28-year-old Iranian blogger based in Toronto. He has thousands of readers, and politicians respond to his postings—even as the Iranian government frantically tries to shut down the servers hosting *his blog*. Yet Derakhshan can't yet cash on his fame. "Google doesn't have AdSense service in Persian yet," he says.

Still, blogs could end up providing the perfect response to mass media's core concern: the splintering of its audience. Advertisers desperate to reach us need to tap niches (because we get together only once a year to watch the Super Bowl). By piggybacking on blogs, they can start working that vast blogocafé, table by table. Smart ones will get feedback, links to individuals—and their friends. That's every marketer's dream. The big companies have what the bloggers lack. Scale, relations with advertisers, and large sales forces. They can use these forces to sell across all media, from general audience to bloggy niches. Already, Yahoo and Microsoft have been investing heavily to position themselves for niche advertising. And in February, the *New York Times* laid down $410 million for About Inc., a collection of 500 specialized Web sites that smell strongly of blogs. "What's to stop them from turning those 500 sites into 5,000?" says Dave Morgan, founder of TACODA Systems, an Internet advertising company.

Thursday 9 a.m. Hate to get wiggy here. But if the blogs eventually swallow up ad revenue, what's going to happen to us?

Yes, we, too, are under the gun. MSM, the bloggers call us. Mainstream media. And many of them delight in uncovering our errors, knocking us off that big pedestal we've occupied since the the first broadsheets started circulating.

We have to master the world of blogs, too. This isn't because they're taking away ad revenue, at least not yet, but because they represent millions of eye-witnesses armed with computers spread around the world. They are potential competitors—or editorial resources.

Blog reporters showed their value following the Asian tsunami in December. Thousands of them posted pictures, video footage, and articles about the disaster long before the first accredited journalists showed up. MSNBC, which ran hours of tsunami footage on its Web site, has since opened an *entire page* devoted to citizens' journalism.

Dan Gillmor, who quit his San Jose newspaper job, is lining up investors for a new type of media company, Grassroots Media. He's interested in elements of an online journalism business in Korea, called OhmyNews. It mingles articles from 50 staff journalists with reports e-mailed and text-messaged in from thousands of citizen reporters. OhmyNews says it has been profitable for a year and a half and expects revenue this year of $10 million. "I keep hoping that all of the new conversational forms will augment the existing one," Gillmor says.

11:57 p.m. Thinking out of the box here for a minute. What would this article look like if it were a real blog, and not just this glossy simulacrum?

Think of the way we produce stories here. It's a closed process. We come up with an idea. We read, we discuss in-house, and then we interview all sorts of experts and take their pictures. We urge them not to spill the beans about what we're working on. It's a secret. Finally, we write. Then the story goes through lots and lots of editing. And when the proofreaders have had their last look, someone presses the button and we launch a finished product on the world.

If this were a real blog, we probably would have posted our story pitch on Day One, before we did any reporting. In the blog world, a host of experts (including many of the same ones we called for this story) would weigh in, telling us what's wrong, what we're overlooking. In many ways, it's a similar editorial process. But it takes place in the open. It's a discussion.

Why draw this comparison? In a world chock-full of citizen publishers, we mainstream types control an ever-smaller chunk of human knowledge. Some of us will work to draw in more of what the bloggers know, vetting it, editing it, and packaging it into our closed productions. But here's betting that we also forge ahead in the open world. The measure of success in that world is not a finished product. The winners will be those who host the very best conversations.

Friday 11 a.m. So why not start here? We've done our research on blogs, made our dire pronouncements. Pretty soon, someone in production will press the button. But this story should go on, as a conversation. And it will, starting on Apr. 22. We're launching our own blog to cover the business drama ahead, as blogging spreads into companies and redefines media. The blog's name? *Blogspotting.net.* See you there.

PART THREE

MEDIA & CULTURE

I BLOG, THEREFORE I AM

by David Kline

On March 23, 2005, cartoonist Stephan Pastis published an installment of his *Pearls Before Swine* comic entitled "Rat's Book Signing" that seems especially relevant to the current debate over the impact of blogging on American media consumption habits.

In it, the humble Pig asks a passerby if he would be interested in buying his friend Rat's new book of comic strips.

"Comic strip? What's a comic strip?" asks the passerby.

Rat, ever the know-it-all, is ready with an answer: "It was a once thriving medium killed by decades of mediocrity, fueled by the insidious tradition of older strips never going away, resulting in an apathetic generation of younger readers who no longer have reason to even open their newspaper."

The passerby looks confused: "Newspaper?" he asks.

Pastis thus took an ironic and well-timed poke at the current notion, popular in some blogging circles and even among a few establishment pundits, that the nation's established print and television media are going the way of the dinosaur as growing numbers of young people turn to blogs, podcasts, Google search, text messaging, niche TV programming, and other new and customized media.

Oh, to live in revolutionary times! It would all be so exciting if we hadn't heard it all before. For as anyone old enough to have a driver's license may recall, it was barely a decade ago that the evangelists of the early World Wide Web, online commerce, electronic publishing, and new interactive media claimed that "old media" was dead, the shopping mall was doomed, print-on-paper books would soon disappear—and that all the frantic efforts of traditional media and publishing companies to adapt to new media's insurgent threat would prove as useless as "rearranging the deck chairs on the Titanic."

One of the most widely quoted proponents of this view was the conservative social critic and technophile George Gilder (a man who, unsurprisingly, is rarely quoted anymore). "Over the next decade," he claimed in 1994, "TV will expire and transpire into a new cornucopia of choice and empowerment . . . Hollywood and Wall Street will totter and diffuse to all points of the nation and the globe. . . . [and] the most deprived ghetto child in the most blighted project will gain educational opportunities exceeding those of today's suburban preppie."

Well, actually more than a decade has passed now, and unfortunately for those who believe that new technology can rewrite existing social and economic reality as if it were a blank slate, things did not exactly turn out the way that Gilder expected. Yes, thanks to cable's growth and the emergence of on-demand programming opportunities, TV offers many new choices (although one would be hard pressed to call *The Apprentice* or *Showdog Moms and Dads* exactly "empowering"). Nonetheless, the most popular and critically acclaimed shows still emanate by and large from the traditional networks. Hollywood and Wall Street, meanwhile, have despite their many challenges just experienced their most profitable decade in history. And as for our nation's ghetto children, it should be obvious to even the most utopian-minded among us that it will take a lot more than Internet access to overcome the institutionalized forces of deprivation that continue to cripple their educational and work opportunities.

Today, once again, we confront the possibility that a new communications and publishing technology—in this case blogging—will engender massive change in our society, most especially in the role and power of the traditional mainstream media. But in trying to assess the likely shape and scope of those changes, we would do well to remember that tomorrow's possibilities are always forged upon the anvil of today's social and economic realities. Change, in other words, comes to the world on the world's terms, constrained by the limits of our political economy and human nature.

So, will blogging mean the death of Big Media? Quite a few bloggers have predicted that outcome. Even some in the mainstream media believe the MSM to be hopelessly moribund. Notes Harold R. Gold, editor of Barron's Online, "It has become fashionable these days for many in the media to indulge in self-flagellation, hail the emergence of 'citizen journalists' and applaud the death of dinosaurs who 'don't get it.' "

And, indeed, at first glance, the numbers certainly do not look good for traditional media. Newspaper circulation, for example, has fallen 11 percent since 1990, and continues to decline at a steady rate of 1–3 percent annually. Today only 54 percent of American households read a newspaper, down from 80 percent in 1964, and the readership that remains is concentrated disproportionately among people forty-five and older.

Even more alarming for newspaper executives is the dramatic drop in newspaper reading among young people. According to a recent Gallup poll of teenagers, only 28 percent said they had read a newspaper the previous day— even less than the percentage (33 percent) who claimed to have read a book.

"That young people aren't reading newspapers is a pretty fatal formula," Colby Atwood, a media analyst for Borrell Associates, told the *New York Times*. "If all your customers are dying off, you've got to be concerned."

And concerned is exactly what newspaper executives are. The only bright spot in that Gallup poll of teens was the fact that 60 percent said they use the Internet daily. Web usage trends are especially important because, unlike the case with other media, users of the Internet tend to take time away from other media to do so. In addition to reading fewer print newspapers, for example, Web users generally watch less TV and listen to fewer minutes of radio. The flip side of the Web's cannibalistic effect on other media, however, is that it is rapidly becoming a primary source of news for people—not to mention the fastest-growing sector by far of the advertising business. Seventy-five percent of Americans now use the Web either at work or at home, with the average user devoting three hours a day to communicating, shopping, or reading news and other information sources. According to *Advertising Age*, the combined Web-based advertising revenue of Google and Yahoo will rival that of the big three television networks at some point in 2005, constituting a "watershed moment" in media history and in the evolution of the Internet.

Though some may have to be dragged kicking and screaming, few newspaper executives doubt that their biggest growth opportunities—if they have any—lie on the Internet.

To be sure, mainstream media's challenges do not lie solely in the circulation trend lines. Sixty-two percent of the public now believes that the press is biased in its political reporting (up from only 42 percent as recently as 1988), according to a Pew Research Center survey. And according to a recent Gallup poll, only 44 percent trust the established media even to report the news accurately. That's a whopping 10 percent drop from the percentage who said so just one year ago—and an equal 10 percent below the historical norm.

"[One] reason [blogging] is so compelling is that we're all a little angry at the power holders," explained Molly Wood, a senior editor at the online news site CNET.com. "Big media has been laying down the rules for a long time, and there's no doubt they've abused their power, lost our respect, and alienated an increasingly tech-savvy generation."

What's so fascinating about this issue is that while Big Media's perceived biases have contributed to its loss of trust, similar biases on the part of bloggers have had the opposite effect: they have actually inspired trust among readers. One reason may be that Big Media's biases are often covert, hidden by a screen of presumed "objectivity," whereas bloggers' biases are usually openly and proudly stated—indeed, shouted from the desktops. Bloggers are also far more transparent than the mainstream media about the process used in writing their articles, providing readers with links to documents and other information sources. By contrast, most readers often don't have a clue what sources (other than those quoted) a traditional reporter may have relied upon, or why. Finally, many bloggers are far more open and forthright about their mistakes—their sharp-eyed readers make sure of that—than is the mainstream media. In fact, despite the addition of ombudsmen and public editors, most major newspapers continue to bury reports of error in a small corrections box on an inside page.

[In a report recommending ways to restore reader confidence that was released as this book went to press, an internal review committee at the *New York Times* suggested that editors write more regularly about the inner workings of the paper, limit the use of anonymous sources, and provide readers with the complete transcripts of interviews and other documents used in stories.]

The good news for the mainstream media, of course, is that despite its declining circulation and trust levels, it still remains far and away the dominant and most credible source of news among the American public. This is true even on the Internet, where the websites of established news organizations consistently draw readership numbers that bloggers can only dream of matching. *CNN*'s website draws more than 22 million users a month and MSNBC 20 million—more than double the number of even the most popular political blog. The *New York Times*, *USA Today*, and *Knight Ridder*, meanwhile, each draw 10 million users monthly, far more than 99.99 percent of all blogs.

"It is the large branded providers that people are going to [online]," says Charles Buckwalter, vice president for client analytics at Nielsen/NetRatings. Thus although the mainstream media may no longer enjoy the high levels of trust and public support it once held, the silent majority of news consumers still rely on it overwhelmingly to keep them informed about critical news happenings in the world.

As for those who cite blogs as their primary news source, they, too, are usually relying on the mainstream media, albeit indirectly. Few bloggers, after all, actually gather and report the news. Instead, they utilize the news gathering resources of traditional media and then apply ideas, opinions, ironies, links, and other kinds of context to the work originally done by the reporter. The readers of blogs may or may not be aware of this distinction, but it illustrates that a new kind of symbiosis between traditional media and new media is evolving—at least in terms of the division of labor between original reporting and context provisioning.

Even in the world of print-on-paper newspapers and magazines, the malaise of declining circulation does not necessarily translate into a terminal condition. More than 352 *million* magazines were sold in the United States last year, a number that ought to make even the most die-hard blogger contemptuous of "dead tree" media green with envy. And for an industry supposedly in its death throes, the magazine business continues to demonstrate surprising vitality, launching seventy-six new titles in the first quarter of 2005 alone.

Even with declining circulation and viewership, in fact, mainstream media have been able to *increase* what they charge for advertising space and time, thereby scoring revenue gains in spite of reaching fewer eyeballs. While paid advertising on blogs (now in its infancy) will no doubt grow rapidly, the hard-working blogger can still only dream about getting the comparatively sky-high CPM (cost per thousand, the basic unit of paid advertising metrics) charged by the traditional media to traditional advertising clients.

The point being that it would be a mistake to write off the mainstream media just yet. They still enjoy massive revenues. They own comprehensive global communications networks. They have institutional force and incumbency. And although they may not always be able to compete with today's new breed of bloggers in freshness of content and diversity of opinion, they alone have the resources, professional skills, access to power and insider sources, and, ultimately, the credibility necessary to reliably carry out the key functions of the Fourth Estate in a democratic society—namely, to keep the public informed about critical news of the day, investigate and expose abuses of power, and serve as the informal fourth branch of government. It is still primarily the traditional media that gives the citizenry at large the information and the tools they need to participate in contemporary political and cultural life in America.

The mainstream media has also demonstrated an unrivaled ability throughout history to adapt to new media and its challenges. When radio first came into its own as a commercial medium in the 1920s, for example, newspapers unbundled their serialized fiction sections—radio's broadcast dramas were clearly superior—from its core news coverage. They also capitalized on the new medium's popularity by running comprehensive listings and reviews of radio shows. Similarly, when television took off in the 1950s, newspapers wisely chose to avoid duplicating what readers already saw on their TVs, focusing instead on explaining the larger meaning of news events. In this, newspapers were no different than other incumbent media in demonstrating a Darwinian ability to adapt and survive—as AM radio did when it reinvented itself as a talk and news medium after FM radio became the preferred music channel in the early 1970s.

By continuing to adapt, mainstream media will in all likelihood not only survive its encounter with blogging, but will actually profit from it. Most of the nation's leading newspapers, after all, are already launching blogs or bloglike content features alongside their regular reporting to give a greater voice to their readers and solicit their reportorial contributions. And television is doing something similar: witness CNN and other news networks that have regular inside-the-blogs segments in which TV reporters share with TV newswatchers interesting things they have found on blogs. At the same time, the established media are reexamining long-standing reportorial standards in order to better distinguish between genuine fairness in reporting and the sometimes false "objectivity" that in recent years has accomplished little except to obfuscate the truth and prevent journalists from expressing meaningful opinions or innovative ideas.

Indeed, the media appears to be shaking off the self-doubt that has afflicted it in recent months and has begun to take the offensive to restore public trust and advertiser confidence. The magazine and newspaper industries have both launched multimillion-dollar image advertising campaigns of late. One ad depicts a *Newsweek* cover one hundred years in the future that features an aerial view of the United States with the state of California split off from the mainland. The headline is "California Island: More Popular Than Ever 62 Years After the Big Quake." The point, of course, is to show that the print media, even after its 250-year-long run at the head of the buffet table of media offerings, believes it will continue for at least another century.

Of course, whether or not print media will survive in anything like its present form for 250 more years is anyone's guess. But for the next 25 years at least, one can safely bet that the mainstream media, reinvigorated by blogging and by a closer and more transparent relationship to readers and viewers, will not only survive but will maintain the upper hand over what is now thought of as the emerging blogging media, when measured in terms of power, influence, and revenues.

Still, it's not really an either-or choice between blogging and the mainstream media. Indeed, blogging and the mainstream media will probably continue to deepen the symbiotic relationship already established by reporters sourcing story ideas from bloggers and bloggers in turn referencing and linking to the news stories reporters write. As illustrated by the thousands of firsthand accounts they posted from the December 2004 tsunami disaster, bloggers have an unmatched ability to lend an immediate and vivid human scale to the great news events of the day. But as the *Guardian*'s Simon Waldman correctly notes, "[Their] great weakness, though, is the lack of shape, structure and ultimately meaning [of what] all this amounts to. It is one thing to read hundreds of people's stories. It is another to work out what the story actually is."

In fact, Waldman argues, "The disciplines of traditional media—space, deadlines, the need to have a headline and a cohesive story rather than random paragraphs, the use of layout or running order to give some sense of shape and priority to the news—aren't just awkward restrictions. They add meaning. They help understanding. Without them, it's much, much harder to make sense of what's happening in the world."

So, no, "old" media is not dead—not by a long shot. But that said, it can surely kiss goodbye the unchallenged *monopoly* of influence that it once enjoyed.

"The Roman Empire that was mass media is breaking up," argues Orville Schell, dean of the University of California at Berkeley's journalism school. "We are entering an almost-feudal period where there will be many more centers of power and influence."

This fragmentation process is being driven, of course, by changes in the nature of the media market. Indeed, much like the ancient unitary global land mass of Pangaea, the mass media market is today splintering into discrete continents of consumer taste, each with its own ecology of political, cultural, and economic interests. And to avoid extinction in this new environment of niches, established media are being forced to adapt and respond to a whole new set of challenges—not the least of which comes from a wholly unprecedented source: the audience.

"Journalism finds itself at a rare moment in history where its hegemony is threatened not just by new technology and competitors but by the audience it serves," noted a 2003 report New Directions for News. "Armed with easy-to-use Web publishing tools, always-on connections, and increasingly powerful mobile devices, the online audience has the means to become an active participant in the creation and dissemination of news."

Or as Tom Curley, the head of the Associated Press, put it: "[There is] a huge shift in the balance of power, from the content providers to the content consumers."

Citizen-created media is exploding. Blogs, video blogs, podcasts (or audio blogs), and customized on-demand television, radio, and online newspaper content are beginning to populate a richly diverse landscape of citizen-created media. As a sign of their belief in the potential for citizen-generated media, Mark Potts, a cofounder of Washingtonpost.com, and partner Susan DeFife recently launched Backfence.com, a network of local news sites relying entirely on reader-contributed content. Similar ventures are launching with regularity.

This is not the first time that citizens have created their own media, of course. During the Renaissance, for example, "commonplace books" helped educated citizens cope with the information overload of the then newly emerged printing era. In these self-published books, people wrote down their favorite sayings, poems, or speeches in order to help them organize and classify information as well as remember key moral precepts. Much like blogs today, commonplace books reflected the personal experience and conscience of their authors. As Rachel Toor noted in an article for the *Chronicle of Higher Education*, "Reading the commonplace books of historical figures like George Washington, Thomas Jefferson, or any number of antebellum Southern ladies gives us an interior view of each person's self-image and the words that motivated him or her."

Citizens continued the practice of chronicling and making sense of their lives through self-created media throughout the nineteenth and twentieth centuries, observes the futurist Paul Saffo. "In the late 1900s," he explains, "[people] invented these little letterpress printing systems, and you could buy one cheaply and print up whatever you wanted. It was a big phenomenon, very exciting at the time. But it eventually disappeared."

Other citizen-created media followed. During World War II, people cut their own records on Victrola-type machines to send to troops stationed overseas, with everyone in the family's voices on it. Mimeograph machines were big during the 1960s, as were cassette tapes in the 1970s, when people sent audio letters to each other.

"Each one of these media phenomenon was a big deal in its time," Saffo notes. "But then it settled down and some of them transformed into something even bigger, like the Internet, and some of them just plain disappeared from the face of the earth."

In one sense, then, blogs are simply a continuation of a phenomenon that, at least in the form of oral storytelling, reaches back to antiquity. But in terms of its enormous scale, scope, and cultural impact, nothing in history compares to today's explosion of citizen-created media. Tens of millions of people around the world are now documenting their lives, exploring their religious and political beliefs, and engaging in public conversations on everything from poetry to classic cars to the latest advances in nanotechnology. And they do so not only through blogs, but also through virtually every digital communications tool they can get their hands on. They create and distribute their own movies, record and narrate their own audio and video podcasts, send text messages to their friends' handheld devices, and share photos via their camera phones.

Analyzing this explosion of amateur content, a fascinating new study entitled "The Pro-Am Revolution" by the British think tank Demos notes that "the twentieth century was shaped by the rise of professionals in most walks of life. From education, science and medicine, to banking, business and sports, formerly amateur activities became more organized, and knowledge and procedures were codified and regulated. As professionalism grew, often with hierarchical organizations and formal systems for accrediting knowledge, so amateurs came to be seen as second rate. Amateurism came to be a term of derision. Professionalism was a mark of seriousness and high standards."

Journalism was also affected by this process. The streetwise men and women immortalized in Ben Hecht's *The Front Page*, who had mastered the craft of reporting from the ground up, were pushed aside during the latter half of the twentieth century. Journalism schools were founded, professional societies formed, codes of ethics written. And thus was the professional journalist born.

"But in the last two decades," the Demos report continues, "a new breed of amateur has emerged: the Pro-Am, amateurs who work to professional standards. The Pro-Ams are knowledgeable, educated, committed and networked by new technology. The twentieth century was shaped by large hierarchical organizations with professionals at the top. Pro-Ams are creating new, distributed organizational models that will be innovative, adaptive and low-cost." As a result, the study argues, "Knowledge, once held tightly in the hands of professionals and their institutions, will flow into networks of dedicated amateurs."

And therein lies a perfect description of the blogging phenomenon.

What accounts for this unprecedented new surge of citizen media? Certainly the fact that the tools for creating and publishing citizen-generated media are much more affordable and easier to use than ever before in history is part of the answer. Then, too, access to useful information—whether it be polling data used by political bloggers or photography tips and tricks for video-bloggers—is so much simpler and instantaneous than ever before. Finally, thanks to the Internet, the distribution of this amateur content to a worldwide yet targeted audience is now made possible by the costless click of the mouse.

But the fact that millions of people now have the means and opportunity to be publishers and broadcasters does not tell us *why* they wish to be. For that we need to look to the alienation, powerlessness, and crushing anonymity that seem to be such overpowering features of modern life.

As a response to these forces, then, blogs and other citizen-created media should properly be seen as the revolt of the voiceless against the heedless.

Indeed, it is telling that in a recent survey of people's favorite movie quotes on Terry Teachout's cultural blog, About Last Night, the most popular quote of all came from the movie *Network*: "I'm mad as hell and I'm not going to take this anymore."

Blogs help break through the anonymity and isolation of modern life. They give people a voice and a forum with which to speak truth to power—

or at least to reach out and touch someone. And although blogs certainly won't give rise to a million new citizen-Shakespeares, they do enable talented but heretofore unacknowledged people with something to say to find an audience—and thereby pluck from the indifference of daily life a bit of validation for themselves, their ideas, and their creative abilities.

In other words, blogging's ultimate product is empowerment. A weblog "creates a fluid and living form of self-representation, like an avatar in cyberspace that we wear like a skin," says the Web producer Tom Coates. "Through it we articulate ourselves."

Or, to put it another way, "I blog, therefore I am."

And if you think this process can't have life-changing consequences for people, consider the case of former child star Wil Wheaton (*Stand by Me* and *Star Trek: The Next Generation*), who used his blog about his trials and tribulations as a struggling actor to reinvent himself into a successful writer read by millions of people. Or the case of ex-soldier Colby Buzzell, whose blog about the mindless boredom, terror, and blood he witnessed in Iraq not only helped him stay sane, but landed him a book deal as well.

Even when blogging doesn't spark a career change, it can certainly produce a new and powerful sense of meaning in a blogger's life. Tens of thousands of women, for example, are now documenting their rites of passage as new mothers or in new careers through blogs—and, just as important, sharing those experiences with others and receiving support and counsel in the process. In a similar vein, many others are writing a daily record of their battles against cancer and other deadly illnesses, sharing their strength, hopes, and fears with friends and supporters they never knew they had.

Not everyone is pleased, of course, that the untrained rabble now dares to speak in public. "One wonders for whom these hapless souls blog," snipes Indiana University dean Blaise Cronin. "Why do they choose to expose their unremarkable opinions, sententious drivel, and unedifying private lives to the potential gaze of total strangers?"

Leave aside for a moment the pinched-nose snobbery that underlies Dean Cronin's question. Ignore also the fact that far more sententious drivel has been produced in the hallowed halls of academia than will ever emanate from workaday America. Does the good professor really need to be reminded that while 90 percent of blog writing may, indeed, be "unedifying," so is 90 percent of all professional writing (and probably 95 percent of all academic writing)?

The truth is that these are not just the tiresome ramblings of the boring written to the bored. Though for the most part not professional writers, bloggers are often eloquent in the way that those who are not self-consciously polished often are—raw, uncensored, and energized by the sound of their newly awakened voices. And by keeping a daily record of their rites of passage, bloggers often give a shape and meaning to the stages and cycles of their lives that would otherwise be missed in the helter-skelter of modern existence.

Sages and psychotherapists, after all, always advise us to view the struggles of our lives as journeys—as pilgrimages, if you will—so that we might gain from them not just the memory of difficulties endured but the wisdom of lessons learned and challenges met. Finally this advice is being put into practice on a massive scale, by millions of ordinary people through their blogs. And while it is impossible to divine the end result of this epic social experiment on either the individual lives of the bloggers themselves or on society as a whole—other than, perhaps, to predict a decline in the numbers of people who visit therapists just to have someone to talk with about their lives—one must assume that the more deliberatively people appraise and document their lives, the more purposefully those lives will be lived.

All of which raises some interesting questions about where our culture might be headed. As the personal and intimate becomes increasingly fit for public discussion thanks to blogging, are we in danger of even further eroding the privacy rights that are so basic to our civil liberties? As our 24/7 online news culture focuses ever more strongly on its ability to constantly update information in real time, are we squeezing out the time needed for reflection and synthesis—the hallmarks of genuine knowledge and wisdom as opposed to mere data? And because the empowering voice that blogging gives to people is still so heavily concentrated among the young, the educated, the relatively affluent, and the white, are we in danger of replacing one narrow coterie of opinions and interests in the national discourse (i.e., the establishment's) with an admittedly broader but still dangerously unrepresentative one?

One thing seems clear: the once impermeable boundaries between creator and consumer, between viewer and participant, are now blurring if not disappearing entirely. Whenever boundaries become unclear, of course, there's a greater likelihood that people will step over the line—do we really want to read bad poetry from frustrated office workers when we already get plenty of it from actual poets? But perhaps this is not too high a price to pay for all the benefits a society gets from boundary removal, including a stronger exploratory vigor among its citizens and a greater likelihood of new discoveries.

Moreover, in a blog-enabled society in which citizens are increasingly actors as well as reactors, creators as well as consumers, traditional elites inevitably lose some of their privilege and power. We are already witnessing this effect in media and in politics thanks to the high-profile role played by political bloggers in recent years. And the same is also now beginning to happen in the realm of culture and the arts.

Popular literary blogs such as Beatrice.com, BookBlog.net, and BookSlut.com, for example, are already drawing thousands of readers each day to their book reviews and discussion of publishing news. Although they certainly haven't supplanted the *New York Times Book Review*—at least not yet—they are providing book lovers with a compelling grassroots alternative to the often stodgy guardians of literary criticism. Moreover, TV's Oprah and radio's Don Imus are no longer the only ones whose word can spell success or doom for an author's new book.

Blogging's "democratizing" effects on culture can also be seen in the arena of poetry and other "obscure" arts, for which there is already more vital original work and criticism appearing in blogs than in the traditional publishing venues. Certainly that's the case with Foetry.com, a website dedicated to "exposing the fraudulent 'contests' " and "tracking the sycophants" it says are destroying this art form. And as art critic Terry Teachout points out in his interview, blogs are today reviewing off-Broadway shows and performances that would otherwise never get covered by the press.

But what about *standards*, traditionalists ask? What worries them is not just that blogs are enabling (admittedly smart) amateurs to encroach on the privileged domains of literary critics and other professional elites. They also fear that the abbreviated format and language of blogs and other digital media tools may be undermining literacy itself.

It's called Netspeak. Originally developed by users of instant messaging (IM) and other brief text-based communications tools, it's a method of conveying text, thoughts, and even emotions in the shortest form possible. Exploring Netspeak's implications in an article on the E-Media Tidbits blog, Larry Larsen showed how the phrase "By the way, let's get together for lunch, do not be late" would be rendered in Netspeak as "BTW, lets F2F 4 lunch, DN b 18" (where F2F means "face-to-face"). While obviously helpful in speeding the communication of information between people online, will the growing use of Netspeak mean that our grandchildren will read Shakespeare as "2b or Ø 2b"?

Fear not, said a panel of experts at a recent Washington symposium on language on the Internet. Netspeak, they said, was probably doing more good than harm because, if nothing else, it serves as an incentive to get young people to write more. And as any school teacher can attest, the more kids write—even if they write badly at first—the more educated and successful they will surely be in later life.

All the fears people have about blogging—from the language used to the fact that millions of nonprofessionals are speaking out about matters that they (according to their betters) know little about—there is just such a déjà vu quality about them. Weren't similar fears about the vulgarization of language and the decline of civilized discourse expressed a hundred years ago when the telegraph and telephone first appeared?

Of course they were. Ah, but this time it's different, say the worrywarts. When some guy sitting in his pajamas in front of a computer thinks he can tell Congress and the president how to save social security—or tell the *New York Times* that its articles about Saddam Hussein's supposed stockpiles of weapons of mass destruction are just a lot of hooey—and do so in language that any teenager with a Net hookup can understand and appreciate, well, gosh!, what's this world coming to?

What the world is coming to, of course, is what we were always taught it was supposed to be in the first place—a democratic society in which *everyone* has a voice and the change to get a hearing for his or her views. Not that every voice would be smart, or right, or even polite. Not that every voice would be truthful or used for positive purposes. Just that we would all have a voice.

The only difference now is that everyone has finally gotten one.

And you can thank blogging for that.

CHILD STAR–TURNED-BLOGGER DISCOVERS LIFE'S SECOND ACT

An Interview with Wil Wheaton

The second act of child star Wil Wheaton's life got painfully under way one day in June of 2000, when he and his best friend, Darin, walked into a Hooters restaurant in Pasadena, California, for lunch. After taking their order, a waitress (portentously named Destiny) paused at the table, as if slightly embarrassed, and leaned in close to Wheaton with a question on her lips: "Didn't you used to be an actor?"

And thus it was that Wil Wheaton realized he had become what he'd always feared most: a has-been. The acclaimed star (with River Phoenix, Corey Feldman, and Jerry O'Connell) of Rob Reiner's hit movie, Stand by Me, Wheaton had been acting since the age of twelve. He literally grew up on screen, in fact, as the teenage space-going cadet Wesley Crusher in the TV series Star Trek: The Next Generation. But childhood success as an actor, it turned out, had not translated very well into an adult acting career. Casting directors couldn't get past his squeaky-clean looks to see the experienced talent underneath, and as roles that had been promised him disappeared one after another and his family's bills piled up, Wheaton came face-to-face with the old maxim that "Hollywood is the only place in the world you can die of encouragement."

Then came blogging, which provided Wheaton with the vehicle and the venue for rediscovering himself and coming to terms with what it means to be famous—or more precisely, famous for having once been famous. The result is nothing short of astonishing: a million visitors a month to his blog at wilwheaton.net, two nonfiction books to his credit (Dancing Barefoot and, more recently, Just a Geek), and a new identity as a writer (who just happened to have once been an actor).

Are you still acting?

A little bit. I still do some stage work, and of course there's my improv comedy. But while I certainly haven't lost my ability as an actor, the number of people who are willing to hire me is rapidly approaching zero. Even my agent, who I'd been with for years, recently dropped me. He said he wanted to put his energy into more edgy actors. He actually used the word "edgy," which is like a knife in my gut.

Yes, in your book you talk a lot about that word edgy—and about what Hollywood producers and casting directors may have meant by the term.

Yeah, I finally figured it out. It means "not Wil Wheaton." "Edgy" means not that working-class actor in his late twenties who still looks like a wholesome teenager.

But looking too young could be a good thing, right? A smart casting director could cast you against type—as a drug addict, for example.

Duh, you think?

Well, in your blog and your book you certainly do reveal the indignities that many actors have to endure during the audition process. It's painful stuff.

That's the way it really is. Years ago, for example, I went in to read for one of the *Lonesome Dove* movies, I forget which one. And the writer, Larry McMurtry, was sitting in the room. So I walked in, and I said, it's really nice to meet you, I really admire your work, etc. And he was like, yeah, whatever. So I begin to read. And in the middle of my reading, he turns—I can see him because he's standing behind the person I'm reading with—he turns to someone, I don't know if it's one of the producers or someone else, and he starts talking. I mean, talking in a voice loud enough I can hear. And he's not talking about me, he's talking about something they were going to do when the casting session is over, and he's pointing to things on a piece of paper and going on like I wasn't even there in the room. Another time I went in to read for Oliver Stone, and the entire time I was reading he sat five feet from me— reading a newspaper!

This happens all the time. And it just blows my mind that these people can get away with treating actors this way. But they get away with it because we actors are so terrified of making a casting director angry with us, or putting off a producer or a studio, that we just sit there and take it. If you complain—even if you just ask politely for their attention since *they're* the ones that asked you in to audition—then you're blackballed. And our silence only encourages this kind of behavior.

Now, I have a lifetime of dealing with this sort of thing as an actor, so my coping mechanism is securely in place. And I have always tried very hard to keep my chin up, even as the rejections piled up. But the truth is that it's very disappointing, very painful. It feels like such a huge rejection. How could it not, when you've worked so hard to develop your talents and create something that you feel is worthy of attention?

Many of your readers say that it's precisely this honesty in talking about all the rejections and humiliations you've suffered that attracts them to your blog.

Yeah, a lot of people were surprised that I was willing to speak so honestly about what it's been like for me in Hollywood. I hear from people who say, "I can't believe how honest you are about your story." But I really wanted to write something that didn't suck. I had a story to tell that I thought was interesting, and I learned a lot about myself through these experiences. So I thought that maybe what I wrote might be enlightening or inspiring to others.

But why a blog? What led you to even think of doing one?

Part of it was chance. If I had not stumbled upon this collection of blogs called the Open Diary [opendiary.com] one night while surfing the Web—and if I had not then been completely consumed with this one girl's, this one diarist's life—it might not have happened. Anyway, through Open Diary I followed something like five years of this girl's life as she changed from a teenager to a college student. And it was fascinating to watch her as she dealt with growing up and with relationships—I mean, every guy she met was the guy she was *definitely* going to marry—and to see how she evolved.

That experience really stayed in my head. And I realized that I wanted to do that, I wanted to keep a blog. I wanted to write about my experiences and try to make sense of them. And my friend Loren said to give it a try. So I did.

Was it technically difficult to get started with your blog?

No, not with today's blogging software. It makes it ridiculously easy to take what's in my head and put it on the Web. It makes it ridiculously easy for me to share my ideas and have it look cool. Really, even a lame-ass like me can do it! And believe me, when I started this, I was not technologically savvy at all. Go look at my original website at Geocities and you'll see just how lame-ass I really was.

It sounds like it wasn't the typical Hollywood fan site, right?

No, that angle didn't interest me. I don't respect it, it's not worth my time. In fact, when I was designing wilwheaton.net, I worked very hard to emulate the sites that I liked, which were all personal websites written by real people. I was not interested in Hollywood publicity sites, and I've been told by people that this is something that really sets my site apart from other so-called celebrity sites. I don't think of my site as a celebrity site, which tend to be very disingenuous and are usually trying to sell something. Reading them is more like watching *Entertainment Tonight* rather than actually getting to know someone.

But at one point you did use your blog to market something, didn't you?

Yeah, but it was hardly an example of marketing my success. The thing was, I was having extreme financial difficulties at the time, and as usual, I wasn't getting any acting work. So I auctioned off this Wesley Crusher action figure I'd kept from my *Star Trek* days, and it brought in $300. Which enabled me to pay the water bill and a few other bills. You know, I had a real hard time doing that; it just didn't feel right to me. But I had a family to care for, and my pride was just not as important. So in a sense, my blog really saved me in more ways than one.

As for the writing itself, at first I was basically just taking the conversations I had with my friends and family or with other actors and putting them out there for the reader. Like, I'd write about how I called my friend Travis and said, "Do you believe this idiot casting director looked right through me like I wasn't even there?" Or I'd describe how when my wife called and asked how the audition went, I told her, "Great, if you ignore the fact that no one laughed and it's supposed to be a comedy!"

And from the very beginning, writing the blog was very liberating for me. I mean, it may sound dumb, but I had always assumed that my failures were unique to me because I had made bad choices, or because it was my fate or something. But by writing about this stuff in my weblog and getting feedback from all those readers, I realized that I wasn't alone in the struggles I was going through.

Later, of course, I realized that I wasn't being fully honest with my readers. You see, I still wanted to have a successful film career. I wanted to prove to everybody that *Stand by Me* wasn't a fluke. I wanted to prove to everyone that *Star Trek* wasn't a mistake. And I wanted to prove to myself that I deserved the success that I'd had as a kid. So even when I wrote about not getting some part in a movie, my blog entries would often end with this little pep talk about how my career was "just about" to take off again, or about how getting that big role in so-and-so's new movie was a "sure thing."

It's interesting, you know, one of my good friends once said that creativity is the absence of fear. When you're not afraid, you're totally free to be creative. And it's true. Once I stopped being afraid of not getting work—once

I stopped being afraid that what I wrote on my blog might come back to hurt me in the industry—my writing got a lot better. Once I figured out that I spent an entire lifetime sitting on my fears and it hadn't gotten me anywhere, I decided that I was going to write the truth.

But I have to tell you, I found it really, really hard to admit that I was approaching thirty years of age and my acting career was going nowhere. It was like I was on some sort of speeding freight train, and I was doing everything I could to make the train go this way or that way in order to get me where I thought I wanted to go. But what I really needed to do was just step off that train and let it go on over the cliff without me. That's what my story is really about.

Reader reaction has been positive?

Overwhelmingly so. It's hard to believe, but my weblog is read by almost a million visitors each month. That's between twenty thousand and fifty thousand a day, which ranks my blog among some of the highest-trafficked sites. I've also got a huge number of people who read my blog through syndication—they read it either through the RSS syndication feed or through a news aggregator or they read it syndicated through LiveJournal or AOL. It's all over the place.

But some would say your blog is famous only because you're famous—or as you put it in your book, only because you once were famous.

I really disagree with that argument. Because what I keep hearing from people who read my blog is that they can personally relate to the kinds of things I write about. Failure. Disappointment. Being honest with yourself—and then using that honesty to rebuild your life on a stronger footing. That's what I write about, and more than anything else, that's what my readers say they like about the blog.

I'll give you an example. In one of my blog entries, I wrote about how the organizers of an upcoming *Star Trek* convention decided not to invite me to speak, even though I had been a member of the cast for all those years. I guess

I had become too minor a celebrity. Anyway, I was really hurt; I felt completely rejected. But my readers were outraged, and they swamped the organizers with email and phone calls and faxes until they changed their minds and invited me after all. And from what readers told me, it wasn't because they liked my work on some TV show I did years ago. They stood up for me because, as one of them put it, "You're one of us. I'm tired of getting kicked when I'm down, and now I see that you're getting kicked when you're down, too." People stood up for me not because I was famous, not because I was different from them, but because I was just like them—I was just a geek like them.

That's quite a testament to the power of blogging! Do you think you would have gotten that reaction if you'd simply written an article about the incident?

No. You see, a good weblog creates a conversation between the author and the reader, regardless of the subject matter of the blog. And the relationship between the author and readers grows over time, as each takes part in the ongoing conversation that makes up the core of the blog experience. That's what makes blogging such a powerful new medium. We may forget this nowadays, but the original purpose of the Internet wasn't to sell things, it wasn't to watch movies, and it wasn't to download pornography. The original purpose of the Internet was to allow people separated by culture and by virtually every kind of demographic imaginable to exchange ideas and information, and to communicate and converse with each other on an equal footing.

Blogging finally achieves this goal. And it does so in a very egalitarian way. It gives anyone, regardless of how rich or famous or well connected they are, the same level of volume in the debate. I don't have to be someone special to write a blog, and I don't need anyone's permission. All I have to do is be a good writer. . . .

Define "good."

Right, I should rephrase that. All a person really needs is a unique voice and something interesting to say to attract an audience. It doesn't matter how much money someone throws at a blog, and how much promotion he does, or how much hype he puts behind it. If the content isn't there, if it's not interesting and doesn't have a unique voice and personality, then the audience moves on very quickly.

One of my friends runs a weblog called Fark [fark.com], which gets a huge amount of traffic. And we were talking the other day about how people are always asking him for links—you know, asking him to mention them in his blog and drive more visitors to their sites. And he tells them that, sure, he can throw links to their blogs all day long, but if the content isn't intrinsically interesting to people, they're just going to leave. It doesn't matter how much traffic he sends there, nobody's going to come back. The other side of that, of course, is that if you build it, they truly will come—"it" being a blog that really has something interesting to say and is written from the heart, written with some passion for the subject. So blogging offers more opportunity than any other media I know of for unique voices to be heard.

It sounds like writing is more satisfying to you now than acting.

Yeah, I'd say so. What I love about both acting and writing is the opportunity each offers to be creative. I also really enjoy the collaboration—with other actors and the director, in the case of acting, or with readers in the case of writing my weblog.

Still, with acting, I'd have to say that I have much less control over the finished creative product than I do with writing. I can work very hard to create a character, for example, and then deliver an honest and strong performance, and yet I still have no control over what ends up on the screen. I've done movies in which my performance on the set was really strong, and yet by the time that particular performance was edited, music was added, and commercials were put in, it didn't resemble at all what I had done on the set. Or there have been times when I worked very hard on a movie, when I felt like the script was really good and I had a solid take on a character. But I was working with other actors who just wanted to cash their checks, or the director was way over his head, or maybe the studio wasn't really committed to promoting the film. In other words, there were all these things standing between my creative work and the audience that could go wrong—and often did go wrong. That was very frustrating for me.

When writing my blog, however, there's nothing standing between my creativity and the audience. The only gatekeeper I have to get past is my own internal critic.

Still, you did get to kiss Ashley Judd in an episode of Star Trek: The Next Generation, *did you not?*

Yes, I did.

Perhaps that's one argument for acting over blogging.

Good point.

In any event, when did you first realize that you might not be an actor who happens to write a weblog, but a writer who happens to have been an actor?

I don't know if there was a single moment in time when all of a sudden it hit me. But a couple of things stand out as really influencing how I saw myself and my career.

One big turning point, of course, was when Tim O'Reilly [founder and CEO of O'Reilly Media] asked me to write a book for them. As I found out later, one of O'Reilly's editors was pitching a book on website design and he kept referring to my blog as an example of good design. So finally Tim went and read my blog and told that editor, "Wil's writing is not bad; why don't we ask him to write a book for us?"

Now, I had already self-published a little book called *Dancing Barefoot*. So Tim came up to hear me do a reading from that book at Powell's bookstore in Portland [Oregon]. And he was just blown away by the size of the crowd there. So was I, to tell you the truth. And that's when he offered to become my publisher.

Wasn't O'Reilly still mainly a technical publisher of computing books?

Yeah, but Tim said they wanted to publish me because they were interested in exploring new territory in terms of the content of their books, and perhaps even start an imprint for more general-interest narrative nonfiction. So they hoped to use my book and the audience I would bring to them to help start that endeavor. I felt it was quite an honor to be given such opportunity.

As far as O'Reilly wanting to explore new territory with my book, I could really relate to that. Because from the time I sat down and wrote my first weblog entry four years ago to today, everything that I've done has been new territory. So it's really exciting for me to be trusted with this kind of opportunity to explore new ground for O'Reilly Media. None of it would have happened had I not created my weblog.

There's a nice little vignette in Just a Geek *when you describe how your mother tried to tell you it was time to think seriously about switching careers.*

Yes, she reminded me that when I'm trying to be an actor, I'm battling against this huge head wind. But when I'm writing, she said, I've got the wind at my back.

How'd you respond?

I hemmed and hawed, and mumbled something like, "Oh, I don't know, Mom."

What'd she say?

She said, "I do. You're supposed to be a writer, Wil."

So . . . is she right?

You know, the first half of my life I worked real hard to be an actor. I had success early on, but then everything started to go sour. I had a hard time accepting the fact that I was failing—that I was famous only for having once been famous.

Instead of just struggling over it all with my wife and friends, I decided that since I'd always been a bit of a technology geek, I'd start a little blog and struggle over it with anyone who'd listen. Now, blogging is a hot topic these days, but back then it was way under most people's radar screens. So I'm not sure if I thought anyone would really read my stuff, or even if they did, if it'd be worth reading at all. But I thought I'd give it a try. And what do you know, it turns out that blogging has helped me rediscover myself and rebuild my entire career.

Who says there are no second acts in life, right?

Yeah, who says?

A GI BLOGS THE WAR IN IRAQ

An Interview with Colby Buzzell

When former U.S. Army specialist Colby Buzzell, a Stryker Brigade gunner then based in Mosul, Iraq, started writing a blog, it wasn't to achieve fame or fortune. Nor was it to pontificate on the deeper political meaning of the war in Iraq. His blog, he says, was simply a means for him to ease the boredom and monotony that constitutes 99 percent of a soldier's life in a war zone (the other 1 percent consisting of sheer crap-your-pants terror). And in the finest tradition of GI griping that has characterized the American Army in battle from the Falaise Gap sixty years ago to Falluja today, he named his blog Colby Buzzell F*** This War, or CBFTW for short (cbftw.blogspot.com).

In his blog, Spc. Buzzell vividly described the day-to-day experiences of an American soldier at war abroad: the monotony of standing on parade in the burning sun, what it felt like to come under fire, and how U.S. troops were received by the Iraqi population. Even with his spelling errors and obscenities, the Wall Street Journal *noted, his writing "conveys the sort of raw honesty that prompts military mothers to write weepy e-mails by the score."*

But it was Spc. Buzzell's dramatic account of an insurgent ambush on his patrol that catapulted him to celebrity status in the blogosphere—and signaled the beginning of the end for CBFTW. The posting, entitled "Men in Black," gave a riveting account of a bloody firefight between his unit and scores of black-clad insurgents, beginning with an enemy mortar attack that sent him and his comrades scrambling into action. "People were hooting and hollering, yelling their war cries and doing the Indian yell thing as they drove off and locked and loaded their weapons. Bullets were pinging off our armor, and you could hear multiple RPGs [rocket-propelled grenades] being fired and flying through the air and impacting all around us. I never felt fear like this. I was like, this is it, I'm going to die."

Spc. Buzzell's account of the battle caught the attention of the News Tribune *in Tacoma, Washington, which covers Buzzell's home base at Fort Lewis. It also reverberated through the blogosphere, generating some ten thousand hits a day from readers around the world. But it also got noticed by the Pentagon's in-house clipping service and soon thereafter landed on the desk of the battalion commander, Lt. Col. Buck James, who ordered Spc. Buzzell to his office.*

Spc. Buzzell arrived to find Col. James reading a large printout of all his blog postings, which someone (probably in military intelligence) had helpfully marked up with a yellow pen. The colonel, who according to Spc. Buzzell looks like a cross between George Patton and Vince Lombardi, peered up from the printouts of Spc. Buzzell's blog and said, "You're a big Hunter S. Thompson fan, aren't you?"

Then Col. James got to the point: Although Buzzell, he said, had "performed gallantly" as a soldier, he had also come dangerously close to violating operational security by mentioning that his unit had run low on water during the hours-long firefight and describing some of the steps he took to get more ammunition as the battle raged on. From now on, said the colonel, Spc. Buzzell would have to clear his blog postings with his platoon sergeant.

Even though he didn't like being edited, Spc. Buzzell posted a few more times. But when he included in one of those posts a mocking dig at the military intelligence officers he now knew were reading his blog, he was confined to camp.

Colby Buzzell left the army in early 2005 and is currently a part-time cab driver in New York City. His book, My War: Killing Time in Iraq, *will be published in the Fall of 2005.*

Why did you decide to blog and who did you think would read it?

I was at the point in my deployment where the letters from friends and family were getting few and far between, and I needed something to combat all the extra time and loneliness of being on deployment for a long time. So I thought doing a blog might be a fun thing to do and help kill some time. And it worked. Time started flying by once I started the blog. I had no idea how to write or form a sentence—I still don't—but I figured, what the hell, just do it.

The response I received was pretty overwhelming. I received a lot of emails from people all over the world and also from older veterans, like from the first Gulf War and Vietnam. People were also going to my site to find out what their sons and daughters were experiencing in Iraq.

Almost all of the responses I have gotten have been positive. People liked my blog because they all wanted to know what it was like in Iraq, and my blog as well as other milblogs were a nice alternative from the usual media reporting. That my blog become so popular was never my intention at all, but it just worked out that way. I had no idea that it was going to get as big as it did.

What do you think of the media's coverage of the Iraq war?

I try not to think about the media's coverage of the war because it makes me sick. I had no idea how the media was reporting the war to people back home, but every now and then I would get a glimpse of the news coverage on the TV at the fitness center and the chow hall and I'd just shake my head and say, "That's just not what it's like here." The reporter would be reporting something and it would be clear he didn't really know what he was talking about.

When I started doing the blog, I had no idea there were so many people who were angry at the media and the reporting that they were getting. In the comments people sent me about my blog, many said, "This is what we need to hear. This is the stuff the news ain't reporting." I don't know how the media does their reporting, but it's my impression that a lot of it is probably just press releases from the Army.

A big thing for me was that a lot of important stories never got any coverage whatsoever. We were in the northern theater of Iraq and my whole time there I never saw an embedded reporter. I have gotten emails from other soldiers in different theaters of Iraq that were also emailing me saying the same thing: "We got no media here and a lot of stuff that happens here never even gets mentioned back home."

How long did it take you to write your postings? Did you ever feel concerned writing about your comrades or your feelings about the war?

I wrote almost all my postings on my blog in one take. At the end of every day I would just turn on my laptop and write about what happened that day, save it, and go outside and smoke a cigarette or two. Then I'd go back and reread what I just wrote, add and subtract stuff, save it on a diskette, and then go over to the Internet café and paste it up on my blog. My friends in my platoon never tripped out about me writing about them. I thought they would but they were all extremely cool about it.

How did you decide what you could and could not include in your blog?

I just used common sense. Like, I would never discuss weapon system capabilities, weaknesses in our equipment, go in-depth on our tactics, or talk about upcoming missions. I never talked shit about my chain of command, and I never gave out grid coordinates and specific locations, that sort of stuff.

I also left out a lot of the negative stuff because I knew from the get-go that it could be monitored. I thought as soon as they found out about it that they were gonna totally pull the plug, but that didn't happen.

And yet after you wrote your "Men in Black" post, your blog was censored, right?

After I wrote "Men in Black," all of a sudden, like overnight, it was linked to every single blog and everyone was emailing everyone about it. So they had a problem. Here's this soldier whose blog is being quoted in newspapers back home and who's doing all these interviews and stuff, and they didn't know how to handle that.

Anyway, my battalion commander called me in his room and said, "Look, you're walking a thin line here on OPSEC [operational security] with this stuff about running low on water and needing more ammo." But he said I never really blatantly crossed the line. So he told me to continue blogging as long as I don't violate operational security. I would have to send in my stuff to my platoon sergeant first and have him read it over, and then to the CO so he could read it over. They could make sure nothing's wrong with it, and then I could post it on the Web.

So I put up a couple of postings under those rules, including one called the "Mad Mortar-Man Goose Chase," where I talked about how we chased some mortar-men around, and the next thing I know I was told that I could continue to write but I couldn't go on any missions anymore.

That was the worst thing they could possibly do to me—being stuck on base while the rest of the platoon went on missions every day. You know, I love the guys in my platoon. You form this bond with them, and then when they go out on missions without you, you feel like you're letting them down, and you get angry and upset. To me, that was worse than any Article 15 [non-judicial punishment] or any other punishment they could give me. If they'd just told me to stop writing I would have stopped writing. But I couldn't take being separated from my platoon.

Did you ever think about becoming a writer?

I never wanted to be a writer, nor did I ever take any creative writing or English classes. But I've always been an avid reader. I've always enjoyed writers like Bukowski, Hunter S. Thompson, Kerouac, Hemmingway, Vonnegut, and a lot of the San Francisco Beat writers, but I never tried to become a writer. I never thought I was good enough, and besides, I didn't think I really had anything to write about. The blog was never meant to become a creative work, it was just something to help break up the monotony of a combat deployment.

And yet your battalion commander was quoted in the Wall Street Journal *saying this about you: "Personally, I think he is a talented writer and a gifted storyteller and should pursue his talent."*

Well, I think the experience of doing the blog made me realize that maybe I can write. So I am currently working on a book about my whole experience in Iraq *[My War: Killing Time in Iraq]*. The book will discuss everything that I was unable to talk about on my blog, and I think people will be pretty shocked when they read what I have to say. I won't be in the Army then so I'll be able to write about what it's really like over there without fear of reprimand. It's going to be a lot more graphic than anything I wrote on the blog— which only told about half of the stuff I saw over there—because I want this book to be a true document of my experience over there.

What do you hope your blog achieved? Do you think future wars will be blogged?

My blog achieved what I set out for it to do, and that was to help speed up the time and make things a little bit more tolerable for me. Over there you get a lot of time sitting around doing absolutely nothing and I was getting sick of reading the same books over and over again. I thought a blog would be something constructive to do. I didn't go over there to be this huge mil-blogger, or to tell the true story of the Iraq war. I just wanted to do it for fun.

As far as future wars being blogged, I highly doubt it. It wouldn't surprise me at all if one day the military banned blogs from soldiers in combat zones.

A MAYHEM OF MEDIA POSSIBILITIES

An Interview with Adam Curry

Actor, entrepreneur, television personality, MTV anchor, and radio host Adam Curry has been at the forefront of new media experiments for nearly twenty years. While living in Amsterdam, the Netherlands, in the 1980s, Curry was the host of the hit music television show CountDown, *which was broadcast in twenty-two European countries, and was named the most popular TV and radio personality show in Europe for three years running.*

He later returned to the United States where he served as veejay host of MTV's highest rated music television program, The Top 20 Countdown, *as well as several top-rated radio shows in the U.S.*

As a technology entrepreneur, Curry founded the Web-based production company OnRamp in 1994, which was later acquired and went public on the NASDAQ stock exchange. Indeed, few individuals have crashed through as many media barriers as Adam Curry, nor done it as successfully. Perhaps that has something to do with Curry's motto, emblazoned on the top of his daily blog (live.curry.com): "There are no secrets, only information you don't yet have."

Curry's latest foray into the intersection of technology and media is podcasting—an audio blog (much like a radio show) that people can subscribe and listen to on their computers or iPods and other portable music players. Newsweek *magazine called the technology "TiVo for your MP3 player." This new citizen-created radio format has already been embraced by such established media outlets as BBC radio, Air America, and Public Radio International. On May 13, 2005, in fact, the Sirius Satellite Radio network launched a new four-hour daily podcast hosted by Curry him-self.*

Let's cut to the chase—What do you think blogging ultimately represents for the role of media in our lives?

I think it's all about the liberation of the news and information we read, watch, or hear from the constraints of Big Media control.

You can see this process clearly in the ways that television is already changing, and it's exactly what I predicted several years ago, not that that matters. The first thing that's changing is the shape of the television. The flat screen is now a reality. And that's because we really want our TV screens on the wall, and we want it to have surround sound, because that way it feels more like a movie theater. We also expect more from television now. We want it to be a customized experience: we want it to record all the shows we're interested in and none of the other garbage, and we want to watch it when it's most convenient for us and not just when the networks choose to broadcast it. And we want to watch it without commercials. TiVo is doing that for us. It's creating a customized television experience for us.

In short, we're taking control of our televisions. And it's not going to be all that important anymore where the programming on our TV is coming from, whether from broadcast or cable or the Internet. Forget about all the talk a few years ago about five hundred channels. Television is becoming just one channel—*our* own personal channel of just the programming we want, commercial-free—and it's really the center of our media watching experience for home theater, cinema-style programming and live events.

Then you have radio, which is this totally wireless technology that's everywhere. Radio has big advantages over other media because it's available right where you spend a lot of your time, which is in your car. And that's be-coming customized, too, with satellite radio and even blog radio, which I've been doing a lot of lately.

Finally, thanks to the power of computers and the Internet, most espe-cially blogging, we're gaining control of our print media, too. You can now link to hundreds of different news sources, and you can even create your own news and information for others to read. It gives you the ability to triangulate—to read the *New York Times* version of some bombing in Baghdad, for example, while at the same time reading the weblog reports of people on the ground there who witnessed the explosion, complete with maybe a fifteen-second video clip of the incident.

I mean, look what happened with September eleventh. That was a major, major moment in the history of media and in the rise of weblogs. It was humongous. We didn't just see what CNN and the other networks showed us. People were out on the street with digital cameras, with video cameras, with their laptops—all reporting on the events as they happened and linking to each other's stories. And the feedback loop that you got, especially from all the blogs that started during that time, was extraordinary. So however tragic the events were, from a media standpoint—from the standpoint of new citizen-created and -controlled media being born—it was a wonderful thing to see happening.

So we're talking about immediacy, many voices, many perspectives . . .

It's mayhem. Total mayhem!

And you're saying no one can control it anymore?

Well, you know, the media business has always operated with the goal of trying to get people hooked on their brand—whether it's the *New York Times* or CBS. Same with the computer business . . . they try to get users trapped into their format or their operating systems. But now you have the boundaries between the media business and the computer business blurring. And people are figuring out that they have these really powerful computers hooked up to this incredible worldwide information and communications network that enables them to do a whole lot of things with media that they never thought possible before. So the users and consumers of computers and media are off and running. They don't particularly care what Microsoft or Apple or CBS or the *Times* thinks they should be doing. They're doing whatever they want. Jeez, they're building their own operating systems. Look at Linux.

You've probably heard of Doc Searls, right? He's one of the authors of the Cluetrain Manifesto [a call-to-arms against corporate control of the new Internet-connected world—Ed.]. He talks about something he calls the "DIY IT" garage, meaning do-it-yourself information technology. What he says is that software and media are basically now just like construction. There's always some wood laying around somewhere. There's always some nails and stuff. And if you don't feel like hiring a contractor or going to the hardware store anymore—and here he's talking about the software companies and the traditional media outlets—you don't have to. You can pick up your software and your news for free and put it together any way you want.

But do you really think that the average citizen is able to—or even wants to— ditch his daily newspaper and CNN and create his own daily news show?

No, of course not. But certainly a large number of citizens—including the five million people who write blogs and the tens of millions who read them— don't want to be limited to what CNN broadcasts and when they choose to broadcast it anymore.

Look, this process of escaping the limits of traditional media is going to take a long time. I'm just finally catching on, and I've been doing it for many years. You know, it took us almost ten years to figure out how to use the Internet as a personal printing press. And we're just now starting to appreciate the great things we can do with media.

Like what?

Well, with blogging in particular, we can influence the kinds of stories that the major organizations run. We can push undercovered stories to the forefront, and we can force the media to correct their mistakes in reporting much more easily than we ever could in the days of letters to the editor.

For example, in my own case, I was able to influence the tone of the *New York Times* regarding Pim Fortuyn, a politician who was assassinated in the Netherlands a couple years ago. Like many other media outlets, the *Times* referred to Fortuyn as a right-wing, anti-immigrant racist—a Dutch version of France's racist Jean-Marie Le Pen.

But see, I was living there at the time. I was very involved with Fortuyn and people around him. Friends of mine were hosting the show where he was killed—they were standing right next to him when he was shot—so I was very close to all of this. I also knew where Fortuyn had come from, had read several of his books, had followed his campaign, and knew why he was so popular in the Netherlands. And one thing I knew for sure was that the way the *Times* described him was completely wrong.

So I wrote a piece for my blog called "The Big Lie" that talked about who he really was and why the media kept repeating these lies about him. I'm not a great writer, but I put a lot of passion into it and just tried to write it as well as I could. And that's one thing about bloggers who have had some influence—they may not have the grammar, style, or spelling down, but they're passionate. And that's what leads to results.

Anyway, about forty-eight hours after I wrote that post, the follow-up stories in the media started to change. The *Times* followed with a story that noted that the "racism" and "anti-immigrant" charges against Fortuyn were really just based on one interview which he did once where he said it was shameful for foreign Muslim clerics to come to the Netherlands and condemn Dutch homosexuals—this from a culture where men often imposed medieval restrictions on their women. He was defending the Dutch tradition of tolerance, not espousing racist or anti-immigrant ideas.

It was interesting to see how I and other bloggers were able to influence the media and the public debate. We did it by keeping the conversation going— making trackbacks and comments, responding to other people who are posting about it, writing new posts and generally just keeping the issue alive. And with every new comment, with every new link to my "Big Lie" piece, the story kept moving up towards the top of Google's search results for "Pim Fortuyn." And as a result, reporters who were doing follow-ups on the story couldn't help but come across the evidence we put forward that the charges against Fortuyn were false.

So that's how we did it, and I'm proud to say I played some role in setting the story straight about Fortuyn. As a blogger, you've got to work at it, but if you do, you can really make a lot happen.

Has your blogging ever had an unforeseen negative consequence?

Unfortunately, yeah. I was on the computer one weekend around Christmas of 2003 and I got an instant message from Lex Harding, who was my old boss at Radio Veronica. And he asked if I had heard that Rob Out, who was his partner at Radio Veronica, had just died. Anyway, it was just a short conversation on instant message, but then mindlessly, I guess, I made a post to my blog about his death and offered condolences to his family. Only thing is, I didn't know that the family had not yet announced his death, and they weren't planning to for another day or two. But it was too late: all of a sudden I was being quoted as a source by every newswire, and that really sucked. And the worst part of it was that people accused me of doing it for egotistical reasons, to try and have some kind of scoop. Which really sucked, because I was just passing along a message to my friends on my weblog. But I didn't think through the implications of announcing his death without checking with the family first.

Anyway, that really made me think twice about the stuff I put on my weblog.

How many people have wished that they had used the delete key before sending an email?

Of course, of course. And I guess that's one of the things we'll all have to learn with this new medium of blogging. If we're going to be citizen journalists, then we'll have to learn that there are responsibilities that go along with that.

It's interesting, you know. I have a site called schoolblogs.com, which offers free weblogs for schools and kids and teachers. I set it up with my daughter's third-grade teacher a couple of years ago. He's actually gone off and made a formal business about it in the UK. But that's the sort of thing we should be teaching in schools. You kids want to learn how to read and write? Here—write a weblog. Read your friends' weblogs, put together project weblogs, let your parents look at them, let people comment on them. Make your own news, and learn the responsibilities that go with it.

What do you think our kids will do with blogging and other forms of citizen-controlled media?

I don't think we'll have to wait for our kids to take over to see really dramatic changes in what we do with media. Even today, for example, RSS [really simple syndication, a technology that enables people to subscribe to and receive various information sources right on their PCs] enables us to add functionality and make our computers do more than Apple or Microsoft ever intended us to do with them. It gives us a way of retrieving information published anywhere in the world without having to go out and search for it, and then very easily transferring that information from one place to another. And we can plug it together in ways we never could before, and this is where I think the magic is going to come from.

For example, there are millions of iPods out there. This is potentially a huge, totally compatible network, but nothing's really connecting these iPods yet. But it's certainly possible to have a little application running on your computer that goes out and records every song mix you like, every radio show, every new audio book. And then every time you dock your iPod to your Mac or PC, it automatically downloads this stuff to your iPod and you can take it with you wherever you go.

How all that stuff that gets to your computer is something that we as users can completely control. We don't need some big music company or radio station to make that happen. It could just be some blogger posting a review of the song mix, say, and then attaching an MP3 audio file as an enclosure to it that then, thanks to RSS, is sent and downloaded right into your computer and then to your iPod. There are no subscription fees, no registration, and it's as easy as turning on your radio.

You're already seeing some of this sort of thing with television. BitTorrent, for example, is a peer-to-peer file-sharing protocol that's become really popular among people who record and watch television shows. There are people who meticulously collect and record TV shows and edit out all the commercials and make sure it's all clean and really high quality. We're talking about hundreds of megabytes of TV programming. And they share these shows with others, including those who also record other TV shows to share. It's a Napster-type technology.

Okay, now I live in the Netherlands. And I really like American TV, but I can't get such great pleasures as *The Simple Life with Paris Hilton* over here. But with these BitTorrent files, which is a really efficient way of distributing large media files, I can get the show from any number of other people who watch and record it. Now, though, some people are enclosing these BitTorrent files in RSS feeds and aggregators, which means that every time a new episode of *The Simple Life* is put out on the Net, it is automatically sent and downloaded to me. It puts it right onto my machine and I can watch it whenever I want.

This sort of technology is getting more powerful all the time. Soon, you'll be able to subscribe to a collection of TV shows or even just a friend's home movie feed just by dropping an icon into a folder on your computer's desktop. And you'll also be able to distribute TV shows that you've recorded, or any home movies you've shot, to anyone else in the same way—just by dragging an icon into a folder on your computer desktop.

And that's more or less possible now. By the time our kids take over, the sky will be the limit. Already today kids have this huge distribution network of tapes and CDs all being shared over the Net. And they're saying things and doing things that neither you nor I could probably understand half of. They're using digital cameras, iPods, email, instant messaging, and talking on the phone simultaneously while SMSing [text messaging] to a television program they're watching. I don't know if so much media is totally good, but one thing you can say about these kids is, they're connected!

And they are already using technology in ways that we never intended them to.

Darn it! Those freaky kids.

Yeah, they're not like we were, right?

No, they were supposed to follow the game plan so that Nike or whomever could get $6.95 out of everything they do. But they just won't follow the plan.

BIG MEDIA GUY LEARNS TO "TRUST THE READERS"

An Interview with Jeff Jarvis

If anyone could be called a Big Media guy, Jeff Jarvis is the man. The for-mer TV critic for TV Guide *and* People, *creator and founding editor of* Enter-tainment Weekly, *Sunday editor of the* NY Daily News, *and a columnist for the* San Francisco Examiner, *Jarvis is today the president and creative direc-tor of Advance.net, which oversees the Internet vision and strategy for Ad-vance Publications, one of the world's great media empires. Along with such valuable magazine brands as the* New Yorker, Vanity Fair, Allure, Glamour, *and* Architectural Digest, *Advance Publications also owns thirty daily news-papers (including the* Star-Ledger, Cleveland's *Plain Dealer, and Portland's* Oregonian), *forty city business newspapers, and the* Parade *magazine Sunday insert. Jarvis's job is to translate some of these media brands into high-value online franchises. Toward this end he has helped concierge.com, epicurious.com, and style.com, as well as local online destination sites such as Oregonlive.com, Cleveland.com, and NJ.com become popular consumer sites. He also led the creation and syndication across all Advance.net media sites of a number of local, political, sports, and cultural blogs.*

Jarvis started blogging after witnessing and surviving the September 11, 2001, terrorist attacks in New York, and has been an evangelist to the cause of grassroots media ever since. Asked recently by an interviewer whether he didn't think enabling ordinary citizens to write their own news via blogs wasn't the antithesis of traditional media, Jarvis had this to say: "It's not the antithesis. It's the future." He still finds time to write his own blog, buzzmachine.com.

How does a Big Media guy such as yourself end up such an advocate for the grassroots blogging phenomenon?

It's not in every lifetime that you get to see a whole new medium being created. Blogs are an entirely new medium—the first that allows ordinary people to publish whatever they want. It's really citizens' media, and that's what is so exciting about it.

Think about it: we in the so-called cathedral of journalism have owned the printing press (and later also the broadcast tower) for centuries. Now the people own the printing press with all its power, and that's unleashing this huge creation of content and conversation and a whole new view of the media.

For me, this is all extremely exciting. I love seeing new things start. I've been lucky enough in my career to be able to start a magazine [*Entertainment Weekly*], but this is even more exciting. It's just so completely new.

Why is this phenomenon happening now? People have been able to put up Web pages or write online articles for years now.

First of all, the publishing tools are so much easier now. Yeah, you could put up a Web page, but it wasn't easy. And changing it was even harder. So the fact that blogging tools allow you to say something and publish it to the world immediately, and then easily update it on a daily basis, that's important. Secondly, the ubiquity of connectivity and higher bandwidth makes it easy for tens of millions of people to log on and take part in the worldwide conversation and exchange of ideas we call blogging.

So what you're really talking about is the rise of the citizen voice?

And a means for it to be heard. It's history's easiest publishing tool tied to history's best distribution network. Now, everybody can publish. And blogs have a couple of very unique features as a publishing medium. First, there's a sense of proprietorship—it's the blog writer's own personal voice that drives his or her writing—and I think this improves the quality of the content. Secondly, the fact that bloggers link to and reference the work of other bloggers means that, generally speaking, the most intriguing stuff—the best stuff, if you trust the audience, and I do—filters to the top. In short, the cream rises. So it's not just that you can publish to the world, blogging has a built-in meritocracy and culture of transparency that promotes the best writing.

What do you mean by a "built-in meritocracy and culture of transparency"?

The meritocracy is built right into the fact that in blogging, as opposed to traditional news, the audience mediates and influences directly what sort of content is most visible and widely read. Out of all the millions of blogs out there, after all, why do some get noticed and referenced and linked to by other blogs and by readers of blogs, thus increasing their audiences? If you trust the audience—if you believe in the "wisdom of crowds," as James Surowiecki puts it in the title of his new book—then for the most part it's because these blogs offer the most informative, passionate, and best-written content. Even before you venture online to read blogs, the audience has already judged which are the best. You can see it in the frequency of links that drive them to the top of the Technorati lists or Google search results, and this points you toward those blogs that probably have the best content. This audience mediation adds real value by helping you sift through the garbage and find the stuff online that's most worth reading.

Why do you assume that the audience pushes the best blogs to the forefront? Reality TV shows have large audiences, for example, but you wouldn't necessarily call these the best shows on television, right?

TV is a very different kind of media, a mass-market media, in which the lowest common denominator still drives programming. In the blogosphere, however, we see a medium composed of thousands of niches—political blogs, cultural blogs, sports blogs, music blogs, food blogs—each of which is driven mainly by the audience's search for quality and usefulness. All the people who read food blogs, for instance, know which food blogs are the best, and they reference them and link to them. There's a meritocracy at work here that you don't often see in television, and this drives the best of the blogs in each category to the top and makes them the most popular.

In what way does blogging promote media transparency?

In the world of blogs, as the blogger Ken Layne [kenlayne.com] famously put it, "We can fact check your ass!" And it's true.

When something is published on a blog and distributed over the Internet, it's not finished. That's just the beginning of the process. When I write something on my blog, oftentimes somebody will come after me and say, "No, you've got it wrong." And maybe they're right that I do have it wrong, or they copy edit me, which I well need.

Then there's the Dan Rather *60 Minutes* case. Only minutes after Dan Rather aired a *60 Minutes II* report with documents from the 1970s allegedly revealing news about President Bush's military service, bloggers retyped those documents in Microsoft Word and proved them to be clumsy forgeries. What Dan Rather should have said to those bloggers was, "Thank you. Thank you for helping us all get to the truth." Instead, he stupidly attacked them as partisans (aka voters) and refused for more than a week to even admit that he could have made a mistake. That reveals everything that is wrong about haughty, self-important, pompous, isolated big media and everything that's valuable about citizens' media.

So the blogosphere offers a much speedier cycle of correction than traditional media do. That happens because the audience is so much more involved in creating, fact-checking, and improving the content than they are with newspapers. When people read something on a blog, they often ask more questions or offer more facts of their own or give more perspective to it. If people feel they're not being listened to or their concerns are not being addressed, as they often do with traditional media, now they have an opportunity thanks to blogging to do something about it.

Like the radio host Scoop Nisker says, "If you don't like the news, go out and make your own."

Absolutely. The news is transformed from a lecture into a conversation.

News as a "conversation among citizens" sounds good, but as you know, rumor, myth, and fantasy thrive on the Internet. Don't we still need professional media to do things that "citizen journalists" can't—to conduct the complex and costly investigative reporting that exposed Watergate, for example, or to serve as arbiters and "newspapers of record" in verifying what is true and not true?

Well, I'm certainly not suggesting that this new blogging medium will replace traditional media. I see it as a complement to traditional news publishing. But we in Big Media have got to be smart enough to see it that way. We've got to learn how to listen better to our readers, and use their collective wisdom to improve the news.

Unfortunately, traditional media has a history of being dismissive of its audience. When I was at TV Guide, I literally received letters written in crayon and no way was I going to respond to them. Working journalists have always hated having to deal with readers they saw as cranks.

The problem with that attitude is that most readers are obviously not cranks. So when Big Media has this attitude that says, "Look, we're the professionals, we know better than you what's news, so we'll tell you what you need to know," people are right to say, "No, you don't necessarily know better than us. Why don't you listen to what we care about, listen to what we want to know before you tell us what we need to know?"

Of course, in a world where there's only one printing plant in town and ordinary people can't use it except to get an occasional letter to the editor printed, there's not a lot of listening going on. But now that blogging enables everybody to own their own printing plant—and enables readers to be writers as well (in the words of NYU journalism professor Jay Rosen)—it changes the media's fundamental relationship with its audience. Instead of acting like a priesthood guarding the gates of the news business from the uninitiated masses, reporters and editors should start treating their readers as partners in the search for truth.

Will this new blog-enabled culture of transparency, as you call it, change the way that the New York Times, *for example, writes its stories?*

It already has in some respects. Bloggers have already had an impact on the *Times'* fact-checking and corrections policies, and of course its editors and reporters have already started to use blogs as good sources for stories.

Probably the last thing to change, though, will be this never-never land of so-called objective journalism that the *Times* and other traditional media still live in. The truth is, this media neutrality is often just a pretense, as *New York Times'* public editor Dan Okrent noted in a piece recently, in which he conceded that, in all sorts of ways, the *Times* really is a liberal newspaper. Besides, neutrality just leads to boring he said–she said articles filled with the obligatory quotes from "both sides" that neither get at the actual truth behind the issues nor even really advance the debate around them.

Isn't this "neutrality" essential if the media wants to serve all its readers—the whole mass-market audience—no matter what their political persuasion?

Why? We can see that readers are increasingly gravitating towards media that openly reveal their underlying political perspective. You can see that in the popularity of Rush Limbaugh on the one side of the radio dial and Al Franken on the other, or of Fox News on the one hand and the *Guardian* newspaper on the other. And of course you can see it clearly in the huge popularity of blogs, where viewpoints are loud and clear.

Anyway, it's a moot point. Mass market media is dead. Welcome to the world of niche media!

Well, is that a good thing? Isn't there a danger that if each of us only reads those newspapers and blogs that adhere, say, to our own particular political views, then we'll lose the shared national experience that comes from reading media and watching TV news shows that at least attempt to serve the whole citizenry?

This view of our national shared experience through mass media is a thing of the past. It pretty much died with "Who Shot JR?" [on the 1980s TV show *Dallas*]. I watched it die while I was at *People* magazine. It used to be you could put a top TV show on the cover and it would always sell. Then by the late 1980s, those covers stopped selling. Why? Because with the rise of cable TV, we were all now watching different things.

What's interesting is that if you look back, you'll see that this national shared experience through media lasted only about three decades, from the late 1950s to the mid-1980s. That was the era of three TV networks and one-newspaper towns, and pretty much nowhere else to go to get your news. But prior to that time, you had multiple voices and newspapers in each city. You had papers on the right and papers on the left and local voices of all sorts. And people read the paper they wanted to read. It was actually a world of niche media.

What happened? TV happened. And as we know, network TV is what helped to drive the niche voices out and create these one-newspaper towns. It's ironic that for all the hoohah about media concentration today, in some ways the media was far more concentrated during the heyday of the mass market than it is now. So yes, during that time, you could have a Walter Cronkite, the "nation's anchorman," turn against the Vietnam War and move the whole country as a result. Maybe that did create more of a shared national experience through the media. But that shared experience also meant more control—control of the message by the media. And you also had the *Beverly Hillbillies*. Now we have HBO, the *Sopranos*, and much less control. Which is better?

I think niches are good. Niches are fun. There's nothing wrong with niches. The bottom line is, you've got to have trust in the people. That's what blogging has taught me. It's made me much more of a populist.

BLOGS AS BOTTOM-UP INNOVATION

An Interview with Clay Shirky

Clay Shirky is a producer, programmer, professor, designer, author, and consultant who has tackled a variety of technological subjects from the philosophical characteristics of WAP to the effects of the British Empire on the use of English on the Net. All of this from an arts major from Yale who started out as a theater director in New York before "falling in love with the Internet."

Shirky says that the Internet bug that he was bitten by in the early 1990s was the idea of a medium that enabled group communication. But in the years that followed he became disillusioned as the Web turned into a one-way tube along which companies broadcast their products to a receptive audience. Now, to Shirky's delight, weblogs and wikis are turning things around again, reimagining the Web as an environment for communication.

It's a subject Shirky's clients and students know well. As well as running a consulting practice focused on the rise of decentralized technologies, Shirky also teaches how networks and culture influence each other, as an adjunct professor at New York University. His writing has appeared in a raft of newspapers and magazines, including the New York Times, Wired, *the* Wall Street Journal, *and* Business 2.0. *To describe the grassroots nature (and importance) of blogging, he coined the phrase "mass amateurization."*

In this interview, Shirky discusses the rise of the weblog, how it is threatening the established media industry, and how businesses are using it as a tool. He does not write a blog, but links to his many writings can be found at shirky.com.

Can you share with us your thoughts on how blogging began?

Well, there are two critical characteristics of weblogs.

The first distinction is between readers and writers. For the first three years, 1998 to 2001, most of the weblog readers were also weblog writers. It was very much a community of practitioners. At some point in that middle period of 2001 to 2002, the number of people reading weblogs began to grow faster than the number of people writing a weblog, and the readers tended to cluster around a small number of highly trafficked weblogs as they do to this day.

The second split is whether you are talking about conversation or publication. LiveJournal is an enormous platform with a huge number of users but very often when people are talking about weblogs they will suggest that LiveJournal doesn't count. LiveJournal violates their sense of weblogs as publication.

When you look at LiveJournal, it's quite obvious that people are using the weblog as a way of staying in touch with a group of friends. It's a conversation. You will see somebody post something like, "Me and Sandy went to Melissa's house and we spent the whole afternoon in the pool." That's the entire post, and you think, why on earth would someone publish that? and the answer is, they're not really publishing it, they're having a conversation with their friends and you're listening in.

Then there are the people who consciously think of themselves as writers and publishers who are putting material out in the public domain. Those groups regard weblogging as an act of public disclosure.

The word "weblog" has stretched to mean everything included in those two axes: the reader-writer split and the publication-conversation split. And as a result the word itself is becoming less useful.

So, is there a way of defining what a weblog is?

It's a lightweight publishing platform that's so simple an individual can do it. It orders things from now back into the past and it is post oriented—it uses the web page as a way to display web posts but the posts are a discrete unit. Those technological facts say nothing about the uses to which weblogs will be put.

People are starting weblogs internally for corporate dissemination and conversation, there are system administrators using weblogs to report on the status of their machines where what's going into the content of the system administrator's weblog aren't even written by humans. There are group weblogs that are thematically oriented, there are official weblogs from institutions, there are political weblogs. The very flexibility and value of the weblogging platform means that in the future the word "weblog" is going to less and less conjure up an image of a particular kind of user and a particular kind of behavior.

Could you explain why four of the weblogs in the Technorati top ten are in the political blog category?

That is the rise of the readerly weblog. Certainly, weblogs privilege opinion and editorial comment over any other form of expression. In the aftermath of September 11, the run-up to the Iraq war, and a fantastically contentious election in the U.S., there was a huge spike in framing political opinion around what became suddenly incredibly momentous matters. The tradition of the op-ed page was already there thanks to newspapers, so there was a model for the kind of thing DailyKos [dailykos.com] and Glenn Reynolds [instapundit. com] do.

It's very difficult to remember now, but the Clinton administration coincided almost perfectly with an eight-year economic boom to the point that politics was regarded as a kind of unimportant, almost caretaker function. I think people's discovery that politics was vitally important coincided and helped support the rise of the politically opinionated webloggers, particularly around the red state–blue state split in the U.S. I think that was the moment people were looking for some kind of expression outside the bounds of network television.

So, if the U.S. entered a similar phase of economic stability in the future, would we see a decline in those kinds of blogs?

I think that political weblogs are here to stay. And the reason is that the Web follows a fairly predictable pattern, which is disaggregation of the old model. In this case, since we have a relatively print and photo driven weblog world right now, what's being disaggregated is largely the newspapers.

In the newspaper what went together were ads from your local pizza place, ads from your local shoe store, national news from some syndicate, school lunches, and sports scores. There's no particular reason that those things belong in any kind of coherent bundle, except that the cost of printing meant that once you could do one of those things you could reach relatively easily into any of the others.

Weblogs come along and suddenly we say, "My God, the op-ed page has broken off and floated out into the ether." And then a bit at a time we started to get examples of real honest-to-God reporting. The first photos that came in from the tsunami were largely taken with digital cameras and were completely outside the tradition of traditional photo journalism. The tsunami tag on Flickr was a big source of people being able to grasp the enormity of the catastrophe.

With all these sections of the newspaper floating around in the blogosphere, how are we going to know where to look for what we want?

Well, I only have so many hours in the day. So at the point where some people want to read some number of weblogs, and I'll say it's a dozen or so, what tends to get privilege is weblogs that offer a higher breadth of vision and a moderate but focused diversity of choices. So I think that Boing Boing [boingboing.net] is number one for inbound links, because it's the avatar of what's coming, which is a number of people getting together to syndicate what could otherwise be individual weblogs.

You can readily imagine Cory Doctorow and Xeni Jardin (Boing Boing coeditors) having their own weblogs. But the argument they are making is that it is better for them to pool their efforts than to do things separately. Certainly both the success of Boing Boing as a business and the success of Boing Boing as a target of reader affection bear that out. I think it's no accident that the people occupying the number one spot on the Technorati Top 100 are also paid. Weblogs succeeded because of the deprofessionalization of publishing, but Boing Boing now points out an environment where we are seeing the professionalization of opinion making and filtering.

The old syndication models are driven around supply-side constraints—newspapers are expensive. The new syndication is going to be driven around demand-side constraints, which is that reader time is scarce. What readers of Slashdot (slashdot.org) and Boing Boing are saying is that once there are more interesting weblogs to read than we can follow, we're going to start to privilege ones that act as tastemakers and filters. The group weblog is going to arise around the economics of demand.

So where does that leave newspapers?

The media in general and newspapers in particular are correct to regard any increase in the supply of interest in reading materials as a threat to them because the law of supply and demand suggests that if you increase supply without increasing demand—price falls. They're doubly right to be worried when you increase supply of something that happens at zero cost, because that increases the competitive edge of the weblog.

The defensive hysteria on the part of the mainstream media appeared at exactly the moment that weblogs started to take advertising revenue. It was the moment at which the Google AdWords phenomenon reignited the advertising industry and people discovered the long advertising drought from 2000 to 2003 was over.

This is really the conundrum of newspapers, which are first in the line of fire. Newspaper editors point out rightly that weblogs are not paying people to go into war zones to do live reporting, but if newspapers fail it will be because their ad revenues decline, not because they are not performing a function that can't be done elsewhere.

The media that relies on direct-user fees, principally newspapers and magazines, are going to suffer most. They can see in weblogs the harbinger of their own doom. I think the thing that worries the newspapers, especially the smart ones, is the recognition that an increasing amount of traffic to newspapers' online sites comes from the weblog world.

If you look at the front page of news and weblog aggregators like Daypop [daypop.com], you'll see that a huge number of pointers are to the *Washington Post* or the *New York Times*. If these newspapers are increasingly relying on weblogs to drive traffic to certain of their articles, then the plans to set up those articles behind gateways and then charge fees for them are actually going to reduce the traffic by even more than they had feared.

But there are already rumors that the New York Times *is maneuvering towards a paid-for online service. Going by what you have just said, will that be the death of the* New York Times*?*

It may be the death of the *Times* online. There was a fascinating article in the *Times* itself about this. Everyone who said they were erecting a pay wall around newspapers said the reason was not to make money but to stop losing money. So everyone admits that the moving to "for fee" is a defensive move against inevitable erosion.

If the *Times* starts charging for daily content, it will be two catastrophes for them. One, readership will plummet as pointers into those stories will plummet. The second thing it will do is it will destroy their syndication business. They will either have to hack down their syndication business or only syndicate things to newspapers that also charge.

What will happen to these big newspapers in the next five or ten years?

They will try all kinds of things but nothing will stop the flow of readers to the Web over the long haul. It's really interesting to see the *Times* wrestling with this. They launched the mutual fund listings with great fanfare during the boom years as an alternative to stock listings because there were so many mutual funds. It was an entire separate section of the paper in which there were also little articles. About six months ago they said, you know nobody is looking at these in the paper anymore, everybody looks online, we're just going to stop publishing this. And that's really the thin end of the wedge, that is, when the *Times* says more people look at this online than on paper so we're going to stop publishing it in print. Over time that's going to come to refer to the entire newspaper.

You really think online news will kill off the newspaper?

I think so, though it will take years. To get a new reader a newspaper has to have a place it can take the satellite signal, run it off a printing press, and hand it off to a distribution network: that includes fees for everybody from the ink manufacturer down to the paperboy. To get a new reader online all you have to do is distribute the URL. The growth of the readers of the paper is largely constrained by economics but the growth of readers online is not.

It's not so much that people will turn away from getting the paper as that all the growth opportunities are moving away from physical distribution. I get the *Times* every morning. I like it on paper because you can tuck it under your arm, you can read it on the subway. But if I couldn't get the paper, which is true of most English speakers in the world, I would be happy to read it online.

The medium of storage and transport of anything on paper is stupid—it takes a long time, it's heavy. Those rolls of newsprint that go into the print room of the *Times* could crush you in a heartbeat. It's a lot of work just in terms of physical labor. And really the principal value of a paper is a means of display: it's high contrast, it's lightweight, you can scribble on it, you can fold it, you can read it in low light. The display characteristics are still superior to the screens we use. So if you could find a way to store and transport the words electronically but to display them on paper, that hybrid is better than either of the extremes. And printers are getting good enough and cheap enough that people no longer have to choose between getting it online and reading it on the subway.

What about people who say that corporations and blogging do not go together?

I've seen this movie five times. I didn't like it the first time I saw it and I don't like it any better now. Something comes along, it's picked up by early adopters, and everybody says, "This is going to stick it to business." Then they're always shocked when business gets around to adopting it. There's nothing in weblogs that prevents businesses from doing it. The fact that a significant number of blogs at the top of the Technorati list take advertisements indicates that there's no barrier to business adopting this.

The change is that you don't *have* to have a profit motive to publish—it's not that you *can't* have a profit motive to publish. The change here is the spread of the publishing model from "profit only" to "profit or nonprofit." And that's a huge change.

In the history of publication there has really only been three ways to publish anything in any kind of large scale. You do it for the money. You do it because the government has decided it's a good idea and they support it with tax dollars. Or you get bankrolled by a wealthy group of individuals who believe that the message is so important that it's worth getting out from under the profit motive.

We have never in history had a publishing medium that says, "If you want to publish something and make it globally accessible you can, no matter what your motivation." That's a huge change but it's an additional type of publishing. It doesn't threaten the other three types. And I think that the people who look at the world in the beginning with a kind of keeping-it-real thing misunderstood that the creation of a medium that doesn't require a profit motive is not the same as the creation of a medium that doesn't allow for a profit motive.

Can you explain how this change is benefiting businesses?

All kinds of ways. First of all, it's a lightweight publishing platform so it's a way for a lot of people to get the word out about things they are doing, particularly small companies. It benefits small companies with good products because people are talking about them online and you can point to them. Weblogs represent a shift in power from producer to consumer, so a lot of the effort requires that the company has a good product or service and a relatively open communications policy.

A lot of companies are also using weblogs as a way of publishing things internally. The principal design strategy of the corporate intranet was to not let anybody publish anything they weren't supposed to. As a result no one ever published anything. A weblog allows people to say, "Hey guys, look at this." In fact, Blogger [blogger.com] started as a project management tool for Evan [Williams] and Meg's [Hourihan] company. It wasn't their project. They were doing something else and they made a way of keeping track of things like a kind of bulletin board. So there are a number of companies adopting weblogs as a way of internal tracking and conversational tools.

Could we look at some of those companies in particular? Has Apple benefited from weblogs?

Apple has benefited enormously because there is a very loyal and very vociferous but very thinly spread Apple community. They can now find another and essentially interamplify in the same way that Slashdot has benefited the Linux community enormously by providing a place where advocates can congregate.

The overall benefit to Apple has been huge. However it's been a tremendous challenge in terms of secrecy because they make a lot of money on unveiling a new surprise every year. It affects both the stock price and the desire of people to purchase the products. The problem is the classic Machiavellian one of, how much loyalty are you able to command at the edges of your empire? For rank-and-file employees it's possible to get more street cred among people who don't work for the company by blogging this stuff than it is continuing to do a good job for your superiors. It is going to be a long-term problem for Apple, as it is for any company that relies on secrecy as a way of creating value or surprise.

What about Robert Scoble at Microsoft? He isn't afraid of criticizing his company, in fact he even seems to be rewarded for doing so.

That's different because he's not violating a nondisclosure. There are certainly plenty of people who have taken Apple to task for power supply problems in their laptops and so forth. If you bought bad product it's now possible for it to turn into a class action without a class action lawsuit. Every company is going to have to deal with that pressure. But Scoble doesn't reveal details of future Microsoft products.

Blogs like these probably help groom future executives because, in a way, what you want in an executive is someone who can simultaneously question and be loyal to a company. So it may be that those people who are able to maintain an active, engaged stance of "I love this company but also this product we make sucks," that may in fact turn out to be a good way to find people you want to promote.

Are there any companies at the moment that you could single out as doing particularly well or particularly badly?

In terms of the public stuff, I think the real test case is Apple, which is doing both. Apple has an incredible amount of value being created around its products because it's switched to a platform that's open enough. Also, the invention of podcasting and this method of using a weblog-inspired infrastructure to distribute audio content for your iPod, that's just a huge chain of value that mostly benefits Apple.

But at the same time Apple has a terrible time because its culture of secrecy and surprise requires behavior from the staff that many of them are no longer willing to engage in. And it's much the same story with Apple around the open-source movement. They've both embraced it and been wary of it.

Microsoft has done remarkably well given their previous culture of secrecy, but I think they recognize that Slashdot created a wave of attention for Linux and they realized that the only way they were going to get that was to stop speaking in a corporate voice and to start speaking in a personal voice. Hiring Scoble was a brilliant move for them.

WILL BLOG FOR BOOK DEALS

An Interview with Kate Lee

There are not many twenty-seven-year-old assistants at literary agencies who get a profile written about them in the New Yorker. *But then not many of them—probably not any of them—had the vision and go-getter attitude of Kate Lee, who saw in the blogging phenomenon a potentially rich source of talented new book authors.*

Lee, who works at International Creative Management and is now twenty-eight, has developed quite a roster of name-brand bloggers to represent since the New Yorker *profiled her in a "Talk of the Town" piece in May of 2004. Will books by bloggers soon become "a trend, a cultural phenomenon," in the words of the* New Yorker? *If so, you'll in large part have to thank—or blame—Kate Lee for that.*

How did you happen to focus on bloggers as potential clients?

First of all, I should say that I'm a voracious reader of magazines and media of all types. Not just the *Times* and the *New Yorker*, but really everything—especially if it covers the New York media world or the LA celebrity world. That's my own background, by the way: celebrity and entertainment reporting. Well, it happens that a good many bloggers focus on these same topics, so I naturally started reading their work. At first, I just thought their blogs were fun. But later I realized that some of these bloggers were actually really good writers.

You know, I'm a younger person in this industry, and the reality of my position here was that I didn't have an established list of best-selling novelists I was representing, so I had to find other ways to find writers to represent. That's the way the business works—you're always encouraged to find new talent any way that you can. And bloggers just seemed to me to be an untapped market. I mean, I could see that younger people were reading blogs, and that the form was beginning to gain some traction culturally. And yet no other agents were looking at bloggers. So I thought I'd take a chance and try to work with some. It just seemed like a natural and logical place to look for undiscovered writers. And I've found some really talented people, funny people, who I might not have found before.

What do you like about blog writing?

I think some of it's very fresh, very spontaneous. You can see the lack of an editor, which I think can make the material much stronger in terms of voice. The flip side, of course, is that there are good reasons why we have traditionally had editors. But I like the unique ways that many bloggers express themselves, and when it comes time for them to write books, well, we can get the editors involved then.

Another thing about bloggers is that they are often great examples of the old maxim about "writing from your own experience." Of course, a lot of times you'll see bloggers taking that too literally—you know, writing about how they picked up the dry cleaning today or whatever. But the better bloggers, like all writers, I suppose, are taking their personal experiences and transforming it into something larger, more universal.

I also think blogging is enabling very talented people who would never have been discovered before to develop their talent and find an audience. And I would like to see the publishing industry take note of these people and nurture them.

What's been the response so far of your colleagues in publishing?

Well, most people heard about my work representing bloggers from that little profile of me in the *New Yorker*. On the publishing house side of the business, the main thing I heard from people was, "Wow, what a great way to find new people . . . we'd like to see some of these people you're finding." And in terms of other agents, the response has also been very supportive. Mostly, they think it's great. Among the older generation of agents, of course, some of them aren't really interesting in blogging. As a matter of fact, some don't even know what blogging is.

So what sort of deals have you gotten for bloggers?

The first book I sold was *Bar Mitzvah Disco* by Roger Bennett, Nick Kroll, and Jules Shell, based on the website of the same name. It's sort of a nostalgia book of bar mitzvah culture that has all these wild and wacky and tragic bar mitzvah stories and photographs. It's actually an anthology, with about thirty luminaries contributing to it. Anyway, I contacted these people and we worked on a proposal for about six months and then sold it to Crown.

The second book I sold is *The Tinkerbell Hilton Diaries* by Phillip Brooke, who writes Gawker Media's Screenhead [screenhead.com] blog under the pseudonym Dong Resin. It's a takeoff on—a parody of—Paris Hilton. The blogger had written this really funny post making fun of Paris Hilton from the point of view of her dog. It's basically her dog talking. Anyway, an editor saw the blog, contacted the writer, the writer contacted me, and we put together a deal with Warner Books.

I've also gotten a deal for Will Leitch, author of the "Life as a Loser" series of web columns, for a young adult novel entitled *Playing Catch*. We also got a deal for him to do the *Anti-Valentine's Book*—a novelty book about disliking Valentine's Day. Both deals are with Razorbill Books.

In addition to the above, a number of my blogger clients are working on books or book proposals. Elizabeth Spiers, former Gawker Media writer and editor in chief of MediaBistro, is working on a novel, as is Alex Balk, the anonymous (until now, I guess) author of the sardonic hit blog The Minor Fall, the Major Lift [or TMFTML, at popfactor.com/tmftml]. Meanwhile, Jay Rosen, the head of the journalism department at NYU and proprietor of the PressThink blog [http://journalism.nyu.edu/pubzone/weblogs/pressthink], is working on a nonfiction book proposal about the press, and Matt Welch, who writes for his eponymous blog [mattwelch.com] as well as *Reason* magazine, is also working on a nonfiction proposal.

Then there's Doug Gordon, author of the wedding website PlanetGordon [planetgordon.com], who's doing a guidebook for grooms-to-be; and Heather Hunter, author of the ThisFish blog [thisfish.com], based on the Irina Dunn canard that "a woman needs a man like a fish needs a bicycle." She's working on a young adult novel.

Other blogger clients of mine include Glenn Reynolds, whom everyone probably knows from his InstaPundit blog [instapundit.com], Steve Stanzak, who writes the Homeless at NYU blog [homelessatnyu.com], and Claire Zulkey, who writes a blog called Zulkey.com.

When you're putting together these deals, have publishers voiced any special concerns or issues about working with bloggers?

Not really—other than the same concern that publishers have about all writers, which is can this person actually write a book? You know, I'm constantly amazed at my friends who are writing books, because it's not an easy thing to do. And that's why book deals are not a dime a dozen. It's hard work. It's hard to write a book. And you don't know whether someone, just because he has a great idea, can actually translate that into a two- or three-hundred-page book. Idea and execution are not the same thing.

So I take pretty much the same approach with bloggers that I take with every writer. You know, whether you're a blogger or a professor, you still need a well-thought-out proposal. That's for nonfiction, of course. And for fiction, you usually have to write the novel. There are no shortcuts.

Does the fact that a blogger might already have thousands of devoted fans reading his work help sell his book idea to a publisher?

I think it could. I mean, of course any publisher would be happy if the author already has an audience of dedicated readers for his blog. But does that translate into being able to move books? I myself would be curious to know if, for example, when a blogger writes a positive review of a book he's just read, does the Amazon sales ranking go up? It's just not clear yet how much marketing muscle bloggers have to move books.

Don't get me wrong: word of mouth cannot be underestimated. It can have a powerful effect on the marketing of movies, as the success of *My Big Fat Greek Wedding* showed. And blogs are particularly good at word-of-mouth promotion. But again, I think it's still too early to tell yet how big an effect blogging will have on the marketing of books. It will obviously depend a lot on the blogger and on the book.

Do you think blogging will radically change traditional book publishing?

The short answer is no. I don't think it's going to really change the traditional publishing model. I mean, the time it takes for bloggers to publish something is very short, but I don't think bloggers are going to necessarily speed up the publishing cycle for books. There's a reason that it takes a year or eighteen months from the time an author starts a book to the day it hits the bookstores. That's because it's really hard, and takes a long time, to write a quality manuscript. And to make sure that turns into a quality book, you have to allow time for editing, for copy editing, and for all the back and forth that's needed before the manuscript goes to the printer.

So how does it feel to have discovered a new niche market for agents?

Is it a niche? I'm not quite sure if it's only an invented niche right now. And who can say if it'll turn into some sort of gold mine of talent? Yeah, it remains to be seen how this so-called niche of bloggers will pan out.

In any event, I'm not looking for niches. And I'm not looking for social trends. I'm looking for good writers, and it's very important to remember that. I'm looking for writers who can sustain themselves, who can not only write a book—which is very different than writing a blog—but hopefully can do more than one book.

One-trick ponies are rarely worth the effort for an agent.

Exactly.

CONFESSIONS OF A DISTINGUISHED CULTURAL BLOGGER

An Interview with Terry Teachout

"Woe be to an artist, writer, musician, or fellow critic who incurs Terry Teachout's wrath," warns Publishers Weekly *in its review of* The Terry Teachout Reader, *one of two books that this prolific cultural critic has published just in the last year alone (the other is* All in the Dances: A Brief Life of George Balanchine*). In this collection of essays and reviews from the last fifteen years, Teachout eviscerates some of high culture's most sacred cows: postmodernism is a theory "so patently absurd as to need no refuting"; black studies is a "pitiful and preposterous burlesque of scholarship"; and Norman Mailer is a "nostalgia act" whose work is "noteworthy only for its flaccid awfulness."*

Clearly, Teachout is not shy about his opinions. And, if anything, he is even more hilariously razor-sharp when writing his daily blog, About Last Night *(artsjournal.com/aboutlastnight/). Here the drama critic of the* Wall Street Journal *and the music critic of* Commentary *writes fearlessly on just about every art form under the sun—books, ballet, painting and sculpture, film and TV, and, indeed, whatever happens to catch his eye or ear—in a voice* Publishers Weekly *calls "unapologetically contrarian and morally focused."*

As if all this weren't enough to keep him busy, Teachout also writes "Second City," a column about the arts in New York that appears in the Washington Post, *and in addition to numerous magazine articles, has also written two other books:* The Skeptic: A Life of H. L. Mencken *and his memoir,* City

Limits: Memories of a Small-Town Boy. *He is currently at work on a biography of Louis Armstrong.*

Somehow, Terry Teachout found the time to answer a few questions about the current blogging craze. It should come as no surprise that despite his own dominance as a cultural critic in the mainstream media, he especially likes blogging because it enables "budding young writers to sidestep the traditional media."

What does the blog phenomenon mean to you personally?

I blog every weekday. This means I'm spending a substantial part of my writing life working in a medium that didn't exist a few years ago. You can't get much more personal than that. I also think blogging has brought my work to the attention of at least some people who didn't read me before I started About Last Night. In addition, it's made a great many people who did read me aware that I write about all the arts, not just one or two. Before About Last Night, my audience was stratified—some people read me on music, others on dance, still others on theater, and they were often surprised to learn that I covered more than one art form. Now they know better.

What's so different about blogging versus other forms of expression? Put another way, What can you do with a blog you couldn't do with a more traditional website, newsletter, or article?

You can publish what you write immediately and without editorial supervision. This makes writing less like traditional print-media journalism and more like TV or radio. It also makes the individual writer into an independent agent, free of editorial constraints. He can be as informal—or formal—as he likes. I think these things are on balance more significant than the capacity to link to other pages, though linking is certainly one of the most distinctive and powerful features of blog-style writing.

What sort of impact has About Last Night had?

Self-centered as it sounds, About Last Night makes a difference to me personally because it allows me to market my print-media writings to the readers of my blog. Not only do I plug my books shamelessly, but I post links on the site to everything I write that is accessible via the Web. Before About Last Night, for instance, the only people who read "Second City," my *Washington Post* column about the arts in New York, were Washingtonians. Now it's read—and noticed—far more widely.

And beyond the impact it's had on me personally, I've been told by other bloggers that About Last Night brought a new legitimacy to the medium because I was the first print-media critic with a national reputation to start a blog about the arts. Certainly the number of people blogging about the arts increased noticeably in the wake of About Last Night's launch, though that may be coincidental.

Are blogs empowering new voices? If so who? Will they actually change power relationships in society?

They're empowering amateur writers—thousands of them. And it's already clear that blogging offers a platform to gifted amateur writers—and, just as important, it allows these budding young writers to sidestep the traditional media and win recognition on their own. This can't help but change power relationships in the world of journalism. Specifically, it's diminishing the power of traditional-media "gatekeepers" to shape the cultural conversation, which I think is mostly—but not entirely—a good thing.

Perhaps blogging can best be described as *individual* journalism—the opposite of the "corporate journalism" of the twentieth century. That really says it all.

Does blogging raise significant new issues about privacy, security, ethics, journalistic standards, etc.?

Above all else, blogging makes it possible for writers to commit instantaneous worldwide libel without having access to traditional print media.

That's a hugely serious development whose implications we're only just beginning to grasp.

How does blogging affect the continuum between mass culture and fragmented special interests?

It affects these things in both directions simultaneously: blogging helps to decentralize and fragment the culture, but it also creates new cultural communities in cyberspace. One of the reasons why I started About Last Night was to try to cut across the dividing lines of individual interest and appeal to a wider audience of potential readers. I think I've had some success with this.

Who are the most interesting bloggers in your opinion? Who is using the form in really innovative ways? Who are the most influential bloggers? What are the most insightful blogs? Which blogs are people most passionate about?

In my world, that of art blogging, the most consistently interesting and insightful blogs—to me, that is, and in no particular order—are Maud Newton, Cup of Chicha, Confessions of an Idiosyncratic Mind, PullQuote, Modern Art Notes, Beatrice, The Elegant Variation, Household Opera, The Rest Is Noise, Return of the Reluctant, Tingle Alley, and Something Old, Nothing New. These are the blogs I visit daily without fail. They're "innovative" simply by virtue of the fact that they're blogs, but I think they all use the form idiomatically—as opposed to print-media-style art blogs such as, say, Seeing Things or The Reading Experience, which consist mainly of short- to medium-length essays that are certainly worth reading but could as easily have been published on paper.

Do you have any special insights or opinions regarding the way the blogging phenomenon is affecting or is going to affect literature and the arts?

One of the reasons why I started About Last Night was that I believed the old media were losing interest in the fine arts. It seemed logical to me that serious art journalism and criticism would eventually migrate to the Web, which is the ideal medium for cultural niche marketing. Since I make my living writing about the arts, I thought it'd be a good idea to establish a beachhead while blogging was still comparatively new.

As it turned out, what I predicted is now happening in earnest. And I have no doubt that the trend will continue.

A WEBLOG SAVED MY LIFE LAST NIGHT

An Interview with Ayelet Waldman

Ayelet Waldman's life took a dramatic turn one night in front of more than 2,500 blog readers. Waldman, a novelist, mother of four, and wife of Pulitzer Prize–winning author Michael Chabon, posted a thinly veiled suicide note on her weblog Bad Mother (bad-mother.blogspot.com). "It does not help to know that one's mood is a mystery of neurochemistry when one is tallying the contents of the medicine cabinet and evaluating the neurotoxic effects of a Tylenol, Topamax, SSRI, and Ambien cocktail," she wrote.

Waldman's readers knew that she pulled no punches. During her blog's three-month existence she had discussed intimate details of family life: her genetic termination, her sex life, and her feelings for her children. Two thousand miles away in a hotel bedroom, Waldman's husband read the suicide post, picked up the telephone, and arranged to come home. Waldman's readers posted messages of support. A friend in Israel persuaded her to see a psychiatrist the following morning.

Breaking down in front of an audience of thousands persuaded Waldman to stop blogging. She says that writing so openly about her personal life was draining both her and her husband of story ideas. Plus it was taking up too much spare time—usually two or three hours a day.

Despite that, Waldman believes the blogosphere is the perfect place for women to find advice and support, especially mothers who have sacrificed careers to raise children. But as for Waldman's blogging career, she says she will save her energies for a weekly column at Salon.com and posting comments on other people's weblogs.

You're an accomplished author with six books behind you, and a busy mother with four children to raise. Can you explain why you decided to start a weblog?

I think I have a mild form of hypergraphia. So when I decided last year that I was going to take a couple of months off work I thought now is the perfect time to blog. I had been reading blogs for quite some time but it was the Manolo Shoe blog [shoeblogs.com] that really did it for me. I just thought this is so much fun. I went on to the Blogger website [blogger.com] and I saw how simple it was and how cute the templates were.

What I didn't realize was that it was the perfect form for me; that it fed into the way I write and the way I think. It was almost too good a form. It was so impulsive. I've never kept a journal or diary. I've always written for an audience. This gave me an audience but it was also very easy to be confessional.

The blogosphere has become a way for women to experience a social community that I think has been really rejuvenating, particularly for women that are not working or are not working full-time. It has a whole different meaning than the blogosphere as a political blogosphere.

So the blogosphere has become a place where stay-at-home moms can meet other women without leaving the house. How do they find each other without coming into contact with other men?

Well, they go to places men wouldn't look. For example, the infertility blog world is huge for a group of women. There's a blog called ChezMiscarriage [chezmiscarriage.blogs.com]. She hits about a hundred comments on each post. She's a marvelous writer, way better than most people out there. I would say one of the best in the blogosphere and she's beloved by a large group of women.

She's a survivor of DES, a drug given to women forty years ago so that they wouldn't have a miscarriage. The daughters of those women had malformed uteruses so she could not get pregnant and she has been chronicling the tale of her infertility. But she also does all of this political commentary and social commentary and she's very funny. She's very left wing and she's very bitter. She's huge in this kind of sex-segregated blog universe.

"Very left wing" and "very bitter," that sounds a lot like your weblog. You were a very popular mommy blogger, so why did you stop blogging?

I realized despite how seductive this was it was not something that was good for me as a writer and not good for me as a mother or as a person.

First of all it's unedited and I think this is why the blogosphere has this tone of nastiness that we see so often. I had a piece in the *New York Times* about why I am still having sex with my husband and so many women in contemporary marriages aren't and why that sometimes makes me feel like a bad mother. On the blogs, the reaction to this piece was incredibly vitriolic. Gawker [gawker.com] took off after me and so did Andrew Sullivan [andrewsullivan.com]. I was facedown on the bed weeping.

So many blogs just went to town. But the *New York Times* got one hundred letters and only one or two of them were negative. There were letters from people in forty-year marriages who said this is just how we feel about each other, from children who said this is how my parents feel about each other, and letters from young people who said this is an inspiration.

I said to my husband, "What's the difference between the average *New York Times* reader and the average blogger?" I think there is something about the blogosphere that lends itself to a kind of snarkiness. I know this is true about my own writing when I was blogging. There is a tone that you have to adopt in order to make your voice heard amidst the general cacophony. You have to make it pop. And an easy way to make it pop is for it to be snarky.

Also, there is no second set of eyes, so the first thing that comes into anyone's mind is the thing that comes out on the page, without a cooler head or maybe evaluating it, and that wasn't good for me. I really rely on somebody editing and criticizing.

But, setting aside the snarkiness, aren't weblogs supposed to be that way? Aren't readers willing to put up with some weak writing because the payoff is occasional moments of genius that would never have been published in newspapers or magazines?

I know that's true about the immediacy—that sense that you know me like you wouldn't know me if you read my essays. It's much more personal. But at the same time, all you know is the "squawk." When you blog, you blog about what outrages you or what moves you enough to write. It's more often negative than it is positive. I knew that I just couldn't keep putting out these most extreme parts of my emotional experience.

From the perspective of a writer who works hard at making every word count and being thoughtful, the blogs are true and amazing in some ways but it can bleed over into the rest of your writing. Sometimes I long for the blog now and I wish I could write this stuff in the blog, but I think that if I kept up the blog I would end up blogging where I should be writing a novel. When you are a novelist you take personal experiences and you sit on them until they fester into something totally different.

But Joan Didion said she wrote to find out what she was thinking, what she was looking at, what she saw and what it meant; what she wanted and what she feared. Isn't this the same as what you were doing on your weblog?

Yes. But it really came to a head with a short story my husband wrote called "Along the Frontage Road." It's about a man and his son. They go to a pumpkin patch and the mother is recovering from a genetic termination. If you read my blog you would know that my husband and I terminated a pregnancy because the baby had a genetic abnormality and you would also know just how devastating that was for us emotionally.

My husband wrote this story a good year or two after this happened. He did actually go to the pumpkin patch with Zeke, our son. But if he had come home from the pumpkin patch and he had told me what had happened, I probably would have blogged it. It might have been moving, and it might have been raw and painful and on the nose, but then it would have been gone, and Michael never would have written that short story.

That short story is devastating and beautiful but if I had blogged it I would have taken it from him. That is what I realized about the blog. I was using up my material and his material, too, and I couldn't risk it.

What about this snarkiness that you have been talking about? Is there something more vindictive about men's weblogs and more supportive about women's weblogs?

There are exceptions but as a rule we do fall into these stereotypes. Some women on the infertility blogs express a level of immense pain which is followed by an outpouring of love and support in the community. Maybe I'm reading the wrong men's blogs but I don't see that on any of them. As huge a fan as I am of Juan Cole [Informed Comment at juancole.com] it's not the place to express your emotional side.

True, but you are the mother of four children. Why would you visit infertility weblogs and miscarriage weblogs? Shouldn't you have been visiting mommy blogs or parenting blogs?

I know so many women who are on those blogs that have no fertility issues at all. I went to them because of the outpouring of affection and support. I've been on the Internet as a mother for a really long time. When I was pregnant with my son Zeke eight years ago I was a member of a group email network of people who were expecting babies at the same time. It was for everyone in the world with a baby due in June. There were four hundred people.

There was always the predictable maelstrom, breastfeeding versus bottle feeding, circumcision versus noncircumcision, co-sleeping versus non co-sleeping, the attachment parenting debate, and Ferberizing [a method of sleep training—Ed.]. That is always on the fertility blogs as well, but at the same time there is this level of openness and supportiveness.

It's a remarkable phenomenon to meet thousands of strangers who lend each other emotional support. It's also a phenomenon to see people open up this intimate and heart-breaking aspect of their lives for perusal by strangers.

What about your weblog? That became extremely personal. You wrote about your sex life with your husband, your feelings for your children; by the end you had posted a thinly veiled suicide note. Can you explain why you opened up like that?

That was the second-to-last post I wrote—a suicide note on the Web. In a way, blogging saved me because enough people saw it and said, "Jesus Christ. She's not okay." My husband figured out that I was having a reaction to my medication because he read it on my blog. But that post was a watershed moment for me. I'm pretty proud of the post in a way.

I had never been suicidal before, I have a very mild form of bipolar disorder, but I had switched medications and I had a suicidal reaction to Strattera [antidepressant drug]. My husband was out of town and I had a really, really overwhelming urge to kill myself. I did a bit of research on the Web and I wrote a blog post about suicide rates in people with bipolar II, which is what I have, and about how it feels to have hypomania. I didn't say specifically, "I feel like killing myself," but at the time that I wrote the post, it was the middle of the night and I was really close. I was counting pills.

I got this outpouring of support from the comments. It was three in the morning, and a friend of mine in Israel saw the blog and kept calling until I picked up the phone and she said, "You need to call your shrink, something's going on." She essentially saved me that moment. And that's when I thought, thank God I wrote the post instead of doing something else. I don't know what I would have done if I hadn't had the blog, but I focused all this energy on my blog and I alerted people that I was crying out for help. That morning I called my psychiatrist and one pill and one hour later I was fine.

At that moment I realized I didn't want to be having that kind of a breakdown in front of 2,800 people.

What about your children? Did you ever wonder what it would be like for them to read their mother's suicide note or to read some of the things you say about them?

I think about that a lot. They're a subject of my column, too, and this is something people give me a lot of grief about. But this is what I do. Being a mother is what made me a writer. I write about being a mother, I write about the ambivalence of mothering. It's what consumes me.

There is a level of alienation that so many people, primarily women who stay at home with their children, feel. Betty Friedan wrote about it in the sixties [*The Feminine Mystique*]. It was a revolutionary moment. But it never occurred to any of us that we were going to experience identical emotions, that we were going to feel similarly trapped. Suddenly you're home. You feel as if you should be incredibly happy yet you're not. There's this incredible alienation, incredible low-grade depression and isolation.

I'm not a sociologist and I haven't done any analysis but I imagine there is a certain level of education on the Web. So it's one place where these educated women turn. The Web and the blogosphere has given these people a sense of community. There are women with whom to bond for an hour a day when your kid is napping, to talk to about the sense of despair and loneliness. And they're not women you have to bump into at school the next day or you have to compete with on a day-to-day basis over who makes the best cupcakes for Valentine's Day. They're just voices who can support you. For the women who are on the blogosphere it's an incredibly important source of support.

My real job is as a fiction writer and that has to come first for me, but I do miss the blog.

WHERE HAVE ALL THE JOURNALISTS GONE?

An Interview with Jay Rosen

Jay Rosen has spent most of his career defending journalism as an honored profession. But he often scoffs at its institutions. The associate professor at New York University's Department of Journalism does not care whether the New York Times *or* CNN *sink or swim. He only cares about the survival of the craft and its responsibility to* civitas.

Rosen is an advocate of "public journalism"—where citizens play a role in collecting, reporting, analyzing, and disseminating news, and where news organizations engage with the local community and stimulate debate. Rosen believes the news industry must reconnect with the real concerns that viewers and readers have about their lives, and not just seek the lowest common denominator. His 2001 book asks the question: What Are Journalists For? *And he answers that the media should be democracy's cultivator as well as its chronicler.*

Given this background it is no surprise that Rosen has embraced blogging with a vengeance: with no economic or technological barrier to entry, weblogs have allowed journalism amateurs and professionals to take to the Web, challenging established news organizations for stories and readers. Whether they are stand-alone journalists like Josh Micah Marshall of Talking Points Memo, or the hyperlocal blog Baristanet run by Debbie Galant, Rosen sees an army of civic journalists blazing a trail for future generations.

Since 2003, Rosen has documented this transformation of journalism in the Internet age on his influential weblog PressThink (pressthink.org). He intends to lay out a more structured overview in his next book, Gatekeepers

Without Gates, *to be published in 2006. In the interview that follows, he explains why traditional news outlets are failing in their duty to the public and how the latest generation of Internet journalists is keeping the ideals of journalism alive.*

A few years ago, you were on record as saying that journalists and bloggers were two separate tribes about as friendly with each other as the Yankees and the Red Sox, the Jets and the Sharks, and the Montagues and Capulets. Recently, we read you declared the battle over. What happened?

Well, there were many reasons why this screaming across the barricades went on. The primary reason was one that I spoke about during the first bloggercon in the fall of 2003, in Cambridge, where I spoke about bloggers and journalists as two tribes converging on the same plot of ground. It's a lot like the first scene in *Gangs of New York*, by Martin Scorsese, which shows us preparations for battle between the Irish gang and the natives.

In Scorsese's crosscutting fashion, you see men getting ready to slaughter each other, and over the first fifteen minutes that's what you have. But after that you realize that the movie is not going to be about the fighting but about what happens after these tribes converge. At the time of the bloggercon in October 2003 the tribes were circling each other. As events unfolded and as journalists and bloggers had so much to do with one another it was inevitable that conflicts would arise. So a contest of authority began.

So it's like a blogger gang and a journalist gang doing battle on the Web and in the media?

Exactly. They converged on the same ground. They did battle. But now they have gone a stage further. Now, bloggers are being led towards journalism and journalists are being led towards blogging. One of the primary reasons for that is that the ideal blogger is somebody with a journalist's skill.

Journalists are very well adapted to the blogging form. And it's inevitable that after the shouting people are going to say, "Hey, wait a minute. There's a lot of work to be done here." And that's what's happened.

I try not to make too many statements about the future. But in January I made a statement that the forces of denial are in retreat and I think that was correct. Now we are in a different phase. Blogging is coming into journalism.

So the opposition to bloggers is over—journalists and bloggers are being absorbed into each other's gangs. But you said there was lots of work to be done. What work is there if the battle is over?

Well, there is a lot of work to be done in developing the weblog form, for example. It is in its infancy and has already lapsed into clichés. We need to keep pushing the boundaries of the form. We need people to figure out what this thing can do.

There is also a profound and fascinating question that needs to be answered: What does the weblog form bring to daily journalism? There is so much potential with the powers of the Net, particularly the horizontal communication that the Internet makes possible for a vertical form like journalism. We don't know how to do that yet. We don't know how open-source journalism should work. We don't know how to fund it. We don't know how to organize it. All that work lies ahead.

It sounds like there is a very long way to go. Would it help if we knew how far we had come to arrive where we are today?

Yes. And the story unfolds over a time frame of hundreds of years. The press came onto the political stage at the same time that public opinion came into politics as a force to be reckoned with. It happened in the mid–eighteenth century. And the reason that public opinion started becoming a concern was not anything dreamy and Rousseau-like. It was the fact that the state had grown to the point where people's opinions about it made a difference.

When the king of France fell into a lot of debt, the opinion of the bourgeoisie that held that debt had a large effect on how expensive it was for the crown to raise money. At the same time that opinion outside of the court became important you had the growth of the press. They are two parts of the same historical event.

Now we have reached a new stage because in the modern era we began to imagine the public as more and more of an audience, as a passive recipient of media products, as the people on the other end of what the media was doing. We developed all kinds of derogatory names and visions of these people, like "eyeballs." If you knock on the door of a home in Charlotte, North Carolina, and you ask who lives here? They're not going to yell back to you, "Newspaper readers live here."

In that long history, we arrived at an assumption that the audience would be on the receiving end of a media pipe, perhaps choosing which product to consume but having no more activity than that. The idea that that audience could get up and walk away, could go to the computer and start to become the producer of media never occurred to anybody in this business.

In my work, I call the weblog the "last mile of self publishing." In cable systems they call the final connection from the cable system to the home the last mile. It's who owns the last mile that really controls the cable system. So it's the same thing here. It's like the last mile is the weblog. It's the weblog that did it.

So the weblog is like the vanguard of the revolution. It's taken the power of the last mile of publishing out of the hands of the media elite and placed it in the hands of the people.

Exactly. The idea of the public being capable of media production is totally revolutionary. It adjusts the whole notion of professional journalism to a producing public and shatters what I call *print think.*

Journalists always try to keep citizens in a box that journalists want them in. The classic statement is, "Here's the news and here's a forum you can discuss it in." Well, now people can create their own forum and anything can happen.

What kinds of things are happening?

When 90 percent of the op-ed-style writing was done on actual op-ed pages, editorial page editors had sovereignty over that region of public dialogue.

With blogging and the online space generally, that rule is gone. Opinion in re-action to the news can come from anywhere, and the bloggers are frequently better at it than the sleepy op-ed page ever was. Newspaper op-ed pages can still have influence; they can still be great. But they are not sovereign in their domain, and so their ideas, which never anticipated that, are under great pressure.

When Mark Cuban, owner of the NBA's Dallas Mavericks and a figure in the news, wants to speak to fans, players, or the community, he doesn't do it through the reporters who cover the Mavs. He puts the word out at his weblog. For the beat writers who cover the team this is a loss; Cuban hardly deals with them anymore. Here, however, the balance of power has shifted toward a figure in the news, once known as a source. A weblog helped shift it.

If my terms make sense, and professional journalism has entered a period of *declining sovereignty* in news, politics, and the provision of facts to public debate, this does not have to mean declining influence or reputation. It does not mean that prospects for the public service press are suddenly dim. It does, however, mean that the old political contract between news providers and news consumers will give way to something different, founded on what Tom Curley, the head of Associated Press, correctly called a new "balance of power."

But with this new "balance of power" there will be winners and losers. Don't you worry that the future of traditional news outlets may be in danger?

I look at it a little differently. I don't think it makes sense to say things like "radio is in danger." I don't think media works that way. The tendency is for things to get absorbed into a new combination, not for them to disappear. I never thought it was a serious case that these older forms of news would be replaced. But there are parts of the relationship where the Web is replacing the old world.

Everyone is looking at this canyon from where we are now to what me-dia life is going to be like when the Web platform is more established. It's hard to see traditional news organizations getting across to the other side.

So you think some of them will be left behind. Doesn't that spell the death of traditional media?

Of course. The sources of revenue that they had under the old system just aren't going to be there in the future. The audience is not going to pay anymore for a newspaper. And advertisers are gradually finding that there are more efficient systems for accessing audiences they want to reach.

Traditional media is struggling because it knows that it's producing a high-quality product. But what they find hard to imagine is that the demand today is for something way better than they have ever been. It's a very hard thing to get your mind around, but the world is moving on.

It's not clear that sources of revenue or audience are going to stay with the model that is in place now. But I don't necessarily care if a particular medium or industry has a future. What I care about is whether the social practice of journalism, of service to the public, has a future.

Journalism as a "social practice." We don't hear that term very often. Do you really think public-service journalism has a future?

My opinion is that we cannot rely on the media industry. The public companies system has proven to be a failure. It's failing this very minute because the model cannot produce the recognition of a need to pull back and invest the money, research, and development needed to get over this divide. Instead, we get the opposite: the extraction of monopoly rents from a product that is basically losing market share. That's not the investment you would expect to find in an industry that is trying to get across this canyon.

As somebody who wants to see journalism go on to the next phase of life, I am looking at nonprofit sources, philanthropic sources, individuals who might support great journalism, new models of fund-raising, new models of public support of any kind. I think we have to assume that there are going to be a lot of different answers. This world where the journalists are the professionals and we know where to find them is gone.

But surely we do know where to find them now. They're on the blogs. They're stand-alone journalists.

Yes, we are seeing a growth in stand-alone journalism. Chris Nolan who writes the weblog Politics from Left to Right [chrisnolan.com] coined the term *stand-alone journalist*. It's a category of journalist who isn't affiliated with a company, a network, or a big operation like the AP [Associated Press]. They are sole proprietors of themselves and their work. So a stand-alone journalist is someone who carries out the ideal of independence even more intensely than a mainstream journalist.

Of course, we need to find a way for people to support themselves as stand-alone journalists. There are such people now: freelancers. But freelancers are not self-publishers.

Now the most successful stand-alone journalist is Josh Marshall of Talking Points Memo [talkingpointsmemo.com], whose primary gig is making money off the advertising on his blog. He's an unusual case but that's exactly what you would expect when you have a new category. Chris Nolan herself is another example. And there's Debbie Galant with her hyperlocal thing [baristanet.com].

Those are stand-alone journalists. And the reason it's important is the way no-barriered entry gets put into practice. People simply become stand-alone journalists, stand-alone critics, and stand-alone interpreters.

That's good for individuals but what's the payoff for journalism as a whole?

The payoff is simple. For a long time to be a professional journalist meant surrendering voice and individual talent, especially at the beginning. There's a lot of subordination to norms, rules, procedures, and hierarchies in professional journalism, which is organized as a bureaucracy.

If you say to somebody in network news, "This is a really complicated issue. I am not sure you can do it well in the form you are talking about." They will say to you, "Oh no, we have four minutes. You have to understand four minutes is a long time in television."

Now, if you don't learn to think that way you are never going to make it in television. The very potential of the mediums themselves are constrained by the simple requirements of work. But when you are a lone operator there is nothing to stop you from inventing yourself as a journalist.

The possibility of stand-alone journalism is putting pressure on professional journalism. The kind of blog that works, that's effective with its users, has an influence on journalism.

But what about traditional journalism? Where did it go so wrong?

It just failed to change with the country. In really simple basic ways it just doesn't sound like life. It's disconnected. I have different ways of trusting you as a journalist. One thing I'm going to do is listen carefully to your reports and decide if they are believable, but I am also going to listen to your tone, which will tell me if you seem like a tuned-in person.

One of the problems with newspaper journalism is that it doesn't seem tuned in. The idea that the journalist's connection to the community could help the newspaper tune itself to the people who live there has never been seriously considered in mainstream journalism. It's the opposite. One's connection to the community is feared as a conflict of interest. So over time we have had a model that disconnects a newspaper from its community. Now, you can do that for a while but eventually you start to pay the costs.

So newspapers burned their bridges and now there is no way for them to get back in touch with their readers.

Exactly. Phil Meyer of the University of North Carolina published a book called *The Vanishing Newspaper*, which contains a lot of arguments similar to my own. He says that newspapers gave up on the "influence model." The influence model is a business model for a news franchise in which you put influence in the community, political power, and authority, at the top of your priorities. Ultimately, that is the franchise that enables you to keep the advertising business going.

Now, if you look at newspapers you will see they have abandoned the influence model in favor of costcutting and a very narrow conception of how their business works. For example, the *Des Moines Register* in Des Moines, Iowa, was very proud of itself for circulating in all counties of that state. But when Gannett bought the paper they pulled back from that because they reasoned that the cost of getting the truck out there was less than the amount of whatever revenue the accountant decided was needed. But from an influence model point of view you would never give up that territory because that's political power. Every four years every candidate who wants to be president has to come through that state, making your reporter a national player. You would never give that up because in the long run that is what is going to make the *Des Moines Register* indispensable.

Well that idea lost in American newspapers and the influence model has been abandoned. So maybe the media is not even going to be the steward of journalism into the future. It may be some other institution or a combination of institutions is required to get journalism over the divide and onto the next phase of its life.

It certainly sounds bleak. You make it seem as though the media is staring into the abyss.

Perhaps, but many things will remain the same. I wrote an essay called "Ten Things Conservative About the Weblog in Journalism" and it was an attempt to say that certain things, like accuracy of information and consistency of reputation, will not change. The successful practices on the new platform will resemble successful practices on the old platform. It's like a big experiment because journalism is being reconstituted. To me that's a very exciting thing.

But it doesn't seem very exciting to these major news outlets. What about claims they make that they provide a valuable and expensive service which bloggers could never emulate, like covering wars?

You're right. They're constantly saying that. Therefore what? What are they saying? They don't know how to guarantee that enterprise into the future. I don't know. Neither do bloggers. And neither do media companies.

Journalism has gotten used to a kind of dependence on this media industry that was like some kind of bad big godfather. Now the media industry is just as interested in reality television as it is in actual journalism. Maybe the craft isn't even welcome there anymore.

Certainly, if we look at local television, what you see is the gradual purifying of news until there's almost no journalism at all in it. It's produced with almost no reporting by overstressed staff who have been given fewer people to produce more news. It just presents a parade of calamities that is such a distorted portrait of a community, because it only deals with things that are easily and cheaply made into attention-grabbing news that is closer to reality television programming than anything resembling news. But they call it news and present it with anchors and desks and sets.

So this new gang of bloggers has really shaken up the media?

Yes. But the tensions between the two will remain. There will be tensions between stand-alone journalists and their corporate cousins. And there will be tensions between journalists that are more left aligned and those that are more right aligned or whatever the new divisions turn out to be.

We have had a world with artificially homogenous journalism for a long time and I think that's not going to be true in the future. The infusion of the methods of political attack and of the weaponry of political campaigns into journalism is going to continue. That too will generate conflict. More politicized blogging and politicized fact gathering is ahead. The public is going to have to get used to new forms of politics that take the form of information.

MAKING GLOBAL VOICES HEARD

An Interview with Rebecca MacKinnon

Rebecca MacKinnon spent more than a decade filing news reports for CNN in Asia, reporting from South Korea, North Korea, Pakistan, China, and Japan. But in 2004 she gave it all up for the blogosphere. "Recovering TV reporter turned blogger," is how she describes herself.

MacKinnon's final years with CNN, as Tokyo bureau chief, were increasingly frustrating. Instead of editors allowing her to use the knowledge and experience of years in the region, she was told to cover Japan like a tourist because "that's what a U.S. audience could relate to." She says the news network was doing more to reinforce stereotypes than it was doing to bridge gaps.

In January 2004 MacKinnon went on leave for a semester-long fellowship at Harvard's Kennedy School. She immersed herself in the blogosphere and started up a specialist weblog focusing on North Korea, called NKZone (nkzone.org). After five months she realized that she did not want to return to CNN and news-as-usual. Instead, she resigned her post and continued at Harvard with a fellowship from the Berkman Center for Internet & Society. In 2005 she went on to help launch a new international weblog aggregator called Global Voices. The project aims to draw attention to outstanding weblogs across the globe and to educate and facilitate blogging around the world.

Below, MacKinnon explains how weblogs are stimulating debate in some of the world's most authoritarian societies, and why the blogosphere is better suited to help people in different countries understand one another than global news networks like CNN. What she calls her "current musings" can be found at rconversation.com.

You fulfilled a lifetime ambition working as a foreign correspondent for one of the world's largest news organizations. Can you explain what persuaded you to leave your post as CNN's Tokyo bureau chief to concentrate on the Web?

When I arrived at Harvard I started researching and following the development and impact of blogs not only in the United States but in other countries and I became fascinated. I realized that for better or for worse this is the future of media and that CNN is the past.

I had felt increasingly frustrated in my job for CNN. I was being told that my expertise was getting in the way of covering the kind of stories they wanted. My feeling was that my job, as my bosses envisioned it, was increasingly inconsistent with the reasons why I had gone into journalism, and particularly the reasons why I had wanted to become a foreign correspondent.

The whole point for me was to help people in the United States and around the world get inside the heads of Chinese people or Pakistani people. If I wasn't facilitating greater understanding then what was the point?

There are a lot of problems with blogs, like credibility, but I felt that online social media presented potential that had a lot to do with why I was in this business in the first place.

So you thought online media would give people a better understanding of the world than CNN. Why did you choose to start your new career by focusing on North Korea?

There's almost no firsthand information about what is happening in North Korea, and the media covers that story in a haphazard fashion. It has been labeled part of the Axis of Evil, there are a lot of tensions over its nuclear program, and there are those who make the case for regime change. It's a pretty important story and it's important that there is a more intelligent debate and exchange of information about what is taking place, not only in North Korea but in the surrounding countries.

There are no blogs out of North Korea so I started what one would call a *watch blog*. Basically, it is a group of people outside of North Korea trying to point to and discuss information about what is going on there. We have not been successful in getting people to contribute by email from North Korea; not even diplomats, aid workers, or business people.

Internet access there is very bad but also they're fearful that the government would get so upset that they would cease to be able to do what they are there to do. For instance, if they are trying to distribute aid to save North Korean children it's more important that they do that.

Among North Korean people there's definitely no blogging. There's no email contact with the outside world unless you're a very, very trustworthy member of the high echelons of the party. The Internet within North Korea is basically an intranet.

It seems that North Korea is a very extreme case. How are weblogs affecting other, less stringent but still authoritarian, countries?

Wherever the government or a small elite controls the press, weblogs are emerging as a form of alternative and sometimes dissident press. In China, for instance, you have a situation where all the newspapers and online news sites are controlled. Many of them may be commercially owned but the Chinese Communist Party still has quite a bit of control over what can and can't be said, particularly if it's political or relates to international affairs. Into this mix comes the Internet.

The Internet appeared in China in 1995 and personal websites and bulletin boards started to emerge very soon after. But the government started to control them almost immediately. It required people who operated Internet bulletin boards and discussion forums to delete any comments that the government found objectionable, and it has expected service providers to censor their services. In the past two to three years weblogs have come along and now there are over a million blogs in China.

That's a lot of blogs but, as you say, the Chinese government exerts almost total control over all of them. Can you explain how the government does this over such a vast domain?

There are three Chinese-language blog hosting services that are run by Chinese companies, including one that is run by Isaac Mao [isaacmao.com/meta]. Mao is probably the best known Chinese blogger outside of China because he blogs both in Chinese and in English. To be allowed to run these blog-hosting services, companies are required to police and filter the blogs that they are hosting by key word. For instance, if you set up an account with Isaac Mao's service, which is called BlogBus [blogbus.com], and you post things using certain words that have been keyed into a program as triggering "objectionable content," then you won't be able to post it and/or your blog will be blocked.

Of course, China has thousands of security service people in charge of Internet monitoring, censorship, and filtering who work with the telecoms providers. When bloggers talk about sensitive subjects they have to do it in a very oblique way because there have been quite a lot of Chinese people who have gone to jail for things they have put on websites. I'm not aware of a blogger who has gone to jail yet but that's in part because there has been a lot of self-censorship.

But you do get a lot of interesting speech taking place in the Chinese blogosphere, very lively stories about daily life. There's a very famous Chinese sex blogger who blogged about all the affairs she was having with lots of different men. There are people who are amateur photographers who use their blog to show off their photography and talk about their lives. Last fall a blogger witnessed a murder on the street and reported it first on his blog, and the local newspapers picked up the story from there. So you're starting to see Chinese journalists checking out blogs for story leads on interesting social and cultural stories very much as journalists in the States now follow blogs to get story ideas.

So the blogosphere in China shares many similarities with the blogosphere in the U.S. and, for that matter, the rest of the world. But you mentioned Isaac Mao's blog-hosting service, BlogBus; wasn't this service provider recently shut down, thus blocking Mao's weblog?

Yes. And there were a number of possible reasons for that. Recently there has been a great deal of uproar over the fact that a major Chinese-language discussion forum run out of a Chinese university, the SMTH bulletin board, was effectively shut down. The controls on who could use it were tightened to such an extent that most of the people using that bulletin board couldn't use it anymore. This created a huge outcry because it was the liveliest discussion board in China. It was run out of Tsinghua University, the Chinese equivalent of MIT.

There was a protest at Tsinghua one weekend. People created a little memorial mourning the end of the SMTH bulletin board. No journalist was present but accounts of it came out on the blogs and people had to be very careful about the way in which they talked about it.

Isaac Mao and other bloggers were following this situation on their blogs. Mao had also been documenting what's called the Great Chinese Firewall, China's Internet censoring system. He created a diagram of how he thinks it works and he linked to that on his blog.

Pretty soon afterwards, Mao's blog was blocked and temporarily shut down.

So, if Chinese bloggers—despite the risks—are daring to push their luck and blog critically about their government, there must be many other countries that are seeing challenges to politics or culture on the Web.

Well, Malaysia is not as repressive as China but it's not 100 percent committed to free speech either. The press is controlled by a certain economic and political class, and the mainstream media doesn't like to challenge authority or point out corruption. Now we are seeing the emergence of blogs, particularly by a Malaysian blogger called Jeff Ooi, whose blog Screenshots [jeffooi.com] has become tremendously popular because he dares to criticize the government about corruption. He has become the online voice of a younger generation of more worldly Malaysians who aren't happy with the way the media works, who don't feel the media speaks to their concerns, and who are looking for another outlet. So the blogosphere in Malaysia is emerging as a form of alternative press.

In Iran, you have a situation where blogs are emerging as a dissident press, led by Hossein Derakhshan who lives in Canada and whose nom de plume is Hoder [hoder.com]. He blogs in English and Persian, and is responsible for triggering thousands of Persian blogs both within Iran and amongst the Iranian diaspora. The blogs have become one of the few places where young Iranians can speak their mind and get to know each other online. Of course, they are being filtered and blocked and some Iranian bloggers have gone to jail. The Iranian government is taking it seriously and viewing it as a challenge to its power.

But at the same time you have a reformist presidential candidate, Mostafa Moeen [drmoeen.ir] who has a blog. So at least opposition or reformist politicians are seeing blogs as a way to reach a particular, Internet-savvy, pro-reform audience.

Are there any other ways in which bloggers are changing the international political scene?

Well, there is a Harvard Law School student named Ory Okolloh who is from Kenya. She has a blog called the Kenyan Pundit [blogs.law.harvard.edu/ory] and basically she has become a hub figure who has spawned the growth of the Kenyan blogosphere. These young tech-savvy professional Kenyans are using blogs to criticize the mainstream press, which they find a bit tame.

Kenya does have a free press but these young, educated Kenyans are creating their own alternative information in the blogosphere. According to Ory the Kenyan blog world is growing very, very fast. Plus, she has found that by being involved and by linking to other Kenyan bloggers, she is a solid part of the Kenyan political scene.

It is going to be fascinating to see how this develops and what kind of impact the blogs begin to have on press and politics in various countries. It's still in its very early days but all of these people that I have mentioned are playing historic roles in changing the way political discussion takes place in these countries.

But how do we know if any of these bloggers are having an effect? Have there been any tangible effects of the blogosphere on politics or culture outside of the United States?

In South Korea there is an edited pseudo blog that was set up before blogs really existed. It's a kind of online newspaper called OhmyNews [english. ohmynews.com] which has got a team of professional editors who take in thousands and thousands of submissions every day from ordinary people.

It was largely because of OhmyNews that the current president of South Korea, Roh Moo-hyun, got elected. Early exit polls on election day were showing Roh Moo-hyun's opponent was winning and OhmyNews started reporting that. There were discussion forums attached to the articles and people were saying, "We've got to do something. Text message all your friends and make sure they voted." So all these people started text messaging their friends to vote and younger people started going to the polls at much higher rates later in the day.

People I know who conducted research in South Korea in the wake of this say if OhmyNews had not existed Roh Moo-hyun might not be president. It may not be a blog but it is an example of an online space where alternative media can have a big impact on politics and where alternative information, which is not spreading as quickly through traditional media, spreads much faster online.

But with this growth in online information isn't there a danger that it will be lost in a deluge of weblogs?

My project for the coming year at the Berkman Center is to find better ways to index these conversations that are taking place, so that we can keep track of what's coming out of blogs around the world. Through the Global

Voices project [cyber.law.harvard.edu/globalvoices] we want to point to the most interesting and important information that's coming off the international blogosphere, because if you look at the mainstream media large parts of the world are almost never mentioned.

We are looking to pinpoint people around the world who are emerging as "bridge bloggers," people who blog from a country or about a country who understand what's going on there, like Ory Okolloh, who is able to say, "Here's what the Kenyan blogosphere is talking about and here's why people should care." We're hoping that by creating an index of bridge bloggers it will make it easier to find out what people in Morocco or Indonesia or India are saying.

And what do you hope the effect of finding these bridge bloggers will be?

In one sense we are hoping to, as my colleague Ethan Zuckerman likes to put it, "hack the media." We are hoping journalists will use it as a resource to get tips on stories and realize that there are some stories out there that they might be missing.

But we are also hoping that people will care about those in other countries more if they can get a better insight into what it is like to be Egyptian or Vietnamese. As Hoder likes to put it, if people are able to hear the individual voices and the personalities of Iranian bloggers maybe they will be a little less likely to support a war of regime change against Iran. It might be harder for a population to be demonized when there are so many different voices coming out of the country.

In the past, if you wanted to know what an ordinary Iranian thinks and you didn't happen to know any Iranians and you lived in Iowa, you had to rely on the appearance of quotes or sound bites from Iranians on CNN or in the *New York Times*. You had no other way of finding out what it is like to be an Iranian or what an Iranian thinks about what is going on in the world. But now you can go directly to the blog of an Iranian and you can hear this voice saying, "I'm a twenty-two-year-old Iranian engineering student and here's what I think about my government, and here's what I think about what the United States is doing, and here's what I think about sex and dating and fashion," and you start seeing complex people that you didn't have access to before.

I guess the slightly idealistic hope is that enabling greater access among peoples from vastly different cultures might make a difference. It may be naive, it may be that the cacophony is too great, it may be that people genuinely don't care. But we want to create a vehicle through which those who might want to care can find people, can find voices, can find alternative viewpoints, can find more fine-grained individual personalities and perspectives more easily and more meaningfully than is currently the case.

GAZING AT THE CRYSTAL BALL OF BLOGGING

An Interview with Paul Saffo

It's been said that the danger of gazing into crystal balls is that you can wind up chewing on a mouthful of broken glass. Remember former IBM chairman Thomas Watson, Sr., who in the 1940s famously predicted that the world would never have a need for more than five computers?

Paul Saffo, a director as well as Roy Amara Fellow at the prestigious Institute for the Future, is well aware of the risks inherent in forecasting technology and media trends. Perhaps it is precisely because Saffo combines a deep knowledge of scientific and technological trends with a healthy respect for the limits of human prescience that explains why his services as a futurist are in demand by business and governmental organizations worldwide (he is chair, for example, of Korean giant Samsung's Science Advisory Board). Holding degrees from Harvard College, Cambridge University, and Stanford University, Saffo is also a member of the Royal Swedish Academy of Engineering Sciences and was named one of the one hundred "Global Leaders for Tomorrow" by the World Economic Forum in 1997. Paul serves on a variety of boards and advisory panels, including the Stanford Law School Advisory Council on Science, Technology, and Society. His essays have appeared in Business 2.0, Fortune, *the* Harvard Business Review, *the* Los Angeles Times, Newsweek, *the* New York Times, *and* Wired, *as well as other more specialized periodicals. Saffo is also the author of the books* Dreams in Silicon Valley *and* The Road from Trinity, *available in Japan. He shares his "ideas and destinations" on his website at* saffo.org.

It should be noted that this is not the first time the authors of the present book have had the pleasure of a conversation with Saffo. More than a dozen years ago—and when we were working on the book Road Warriors *at a time when only a small minority of even the computer literate crowd had even heard of the Internet—Saffo predicted that within a very few years a PC without an Internet connection would be "as useful as a paperweight." The reader will therefore understand why we have learned to listen carefully to what Paul Saffo has to say.*

As a futurist, you actually spend a good deal of time looking at the past, don't you?

Well, it helps give you a certain perspective, you know. For example, I saw an article a while back in which some professor talked about bloggers being the cockroaches of media scurrying around the graveyard of failed dot-coms, or something like that. It was this classic sort of hand-wringing over, I guess, the lack of professional editorial management of what's being published on the Web right now. And yet I would say to those who are critical of blogging, and say it's all a bunch of crap, that I can point you to writings in the early 1500s in Venice, after the first modern book was published in 1501, that bemoan the sheer horror of people selling books of untrustworthy origin in the marketplace—you know, unsavory peddlers shoving books at you like bags of cats or something as you walk the canal ways.

Now, I don't want to deny that there's plenty of untrustworthy material in blogs, and on the Internet in general. But the thing to keep in mind is, whenever you have a new technology, you always create an enormous amount of crap. The printing press sounds pretty high falutin' or at least a positive invention to us now. But the fact is, when modern book publishing got started, it was as ragtag and seamy as you can imagine. Even the *Canterbury Tales* is absolutely salacious late-medieval smut. It kind of loses its impact when you have to stop to look up the words, but the "Miller's Tale"? My God, that is racy stuff. And it was the same with the movie business. Even before they invented sound in movies, they invented the keyhole mask and were doing sleazy little movies of mild pornography. Anyway, before the invention of the printing press in 1452, there were some salacious playing cards that a few enterprising merchants sold on the sly. But nothing like what came after the inventing of printing.

Many people aren't aware of this, but the Roman Catholic Church initially opposed the printing press. You'd think they would have favored the mass printing of Bibles, but it was just the opposite. They didn't want that. Reading the Bible was considered solely the job of the priests, and the church published long tracts warning that putting Bibles into the hands of ordinary people would enable them to interpret it anyway they wanted.

In fact, that's where Martin Luther comes in. He was of the opinion that people should read the Bible themselves. That was his revolutionary statement. And his argument with his local bishop was turned into a European-wide revolution. That's what got the church really pissed off at him. The Lutherans were the first ones to print the Bible in vernacular and not in Latin. Very dangerous stuff. You could get burned at the stake back then.

And much the same thing is happening today. As with any new media revolution, we are getting this vast tide of new and different material from blogging. And a lot of it is flotsam and jetsam and crap. It was the same with classical music composing in Mozart's era. We all know about Mozart, and we know about Salieri because of the movie *Amadeus*. But in those days there were a lot of really lousy composers. We've just forgotten about them because they were so bad, nobody wanted to keep their stuff around.

But just as in the past, this new tide of blogging that may indeed be full of lousy writing will eventually recede, and some of the bad stuff will wash away. And in the end, people will be able to appreciate the great new stuff that this revolution has brought us.

So you think blogging will end up a positive addition to our media diet?

I think so, yes. But what particular role it will play—and what particular form as a citizen publishing tool it will actually take—is still very much in doubt. I mean, the most important thing to understand about blogging today is that it's a transitional form.

You could, for example, make the argument—and some do—that blogging as it exists today is merely a license for obsession, with people talking endlessly about their little fixations or their relationship problems. Look at the falloff in blogging. Some very large percentage of blogs are abandoned a few months after they're started.

Right. There's a high churn rate.

Very high churn, exactly. Which suggests that blogging is still in a very early stage. And I think it's really an open question how this phenomenon will evolve exactly. Is blogging going to end up like the CB radio craze of the 1970s and '80s?

You don't really believe that, do you?

No, but I think the question has to be asked. I mean, let's face it, it's still a lot of work to write a blog. So maybe the way it turns out is like Andy Warhol's line about how everybody's famous for fifteen minutes. Maybe everyone blogs for fifteen minutes and then quits.

My point is, we're seeing only the first stage of blogging. We're seeing the big bang of this phenomenon, but I'm wondering what it looks like when it goes steady state. I mean, is blogging like the newsletter era of desktop publishing that was killed by the emergence of the Web—a trend that's bumped aside by some new, unanticipated technology? Or is it like the boys' printing phenomenon of a hundred years ago?

Boys' printing phenomenon?

Yeah, in the late 1900s, they invented these little letterpress printing systems, and you could buy one cheaply and print up whatever you wanted. And little kids were making their own "newspapers" and the like. It was a big phenomenon, very exciting at the time. But it eventually disappeared.

And that's not the only time that new forms and uses of media developed to great enthusiasm from the public only to later morph into something else or disappear entirely. Remember the mimeograph machine? Or how about when cassette tapes were invented, and people were sending audio-tape letters to each other? That's gone, too. And then there was the phenomenon of people cutting their own records, on some sort of Victrola-type machine, and sending them to troops stationed overseas in World War II with everyone in the family's voices on it. That phenomenon died as well.

Each one of these media phenomenon was a big deal in its time. But then it settled down and some of them transformed into something even bigger, like the Internet, and some of them just plain disappeared from the face of the earth.

So assuming blogging doesn't go the way of the mimeograph, how might it evolve?

Well, okay, right now we're in the enthusiast phase. But does blogging really become the citizen voice of the future, a primary means for the masses of ordinary people to communicate with each other and make their voices heard in the larger body politic? Or does blogging settle down to being something that only a few superstars with great voices do, with most people saying, "Oh, that's interesting, but I don't have that many words in me"?

I mean, I love blogging, don't get me wrong. I love the fact that it's now possible for anybody to write something and find an audience. But will all those anybodies really do that? For one thing, I don't care what anybody says about blogging being easy. It's not. Sure, you don't have to be some sort of über-Geek to put up a blog, and millions of relatively nontechnical people have already done it. But it still has to develop a lot further before everyday people decide to jump in. It's got to be as easy as jotting down some notes on a piece of paper or on your little electronic organizer.

Remember, also, that most people don't really know how to write. Even here in Silicon Valley, I am shocked by the number of people who can't even put a sentence together. And then there are the tens and tens of millions of people who can write but hate to write—or at least are afraid of it. Maybe that has something to do with our educational system and how we teach writing. But the fact is, in order to write well you have to start by writing badly, and to write badly you have to actually write. But for many, many people, it's just not a natural act for them. Look at how many more people read blogs than have one of their own.

Also, for some sections of our population, oral culture is more important than written culture. In the inner city of Los Angeles, for example, words spoken have more meaning than words printed. It's almost like a feudal period where fighting words really are fighting words. They have poetry, but their poetry is an oral poetry. It's rap. It's hip-hop. Those kids may not be able to write, but they sure can speak.

So if you look at that phenomenon, then one reasonable question is, does print blogging morph into multimedia blogging? Does it become a sort of free-form collage of video and audio communication, with sound and bits of images and a little bit of text and some pictures all mixed and mashed together like some of the best hip-hop stuff that's happening in music today? I mean, if Hollywood can ever get over its anxiety about showing videos, then I think that, especially for the younger generation, the place where blogging can get real interesting is not when everybody is a writer but when everybody is a video or multimedia producer.

Another thing to consider is the impact that wireless technology is having on media in general—and on blogging in particular—and how that might produce new uses and new varieties of media even in the print sphere. The problem with the Net until recently has been that our portal into this vast new land has been confined largely to our computers, which are located exactly in the one place most of us don't want to be—our desks. Now thanks to wireless and to new classes of wireless handhelds and other devices, cyberspace is not just coming to our desk, it's coming to where we actually live our lives and work and play. So I can envision the growth of new short story forms, for example, where you're sitting on the subway and you've got some time to kill so you pay, say, twenty-five cents to download Stephen King's latest short story abridged and formatted for wireless devices. Or you're sitting in your car, and you know your commute is only going to be twenty-five minutes, so you download an audio version of that short story. I think bloggers may move into the fiction realm, is all I'm saying, since it could be a perfect fit with the wireless technology that's evolving and with people's desire for entertainment.

You present a lot of possibilities, but not much in the way of firm predictions.

I'm a professional forecaster, and if the last twenty years of doing this has taught me anything, it's taught me to know when not to make a forecast. And it's interesting, because I can pretty clearly lay out the road map of technology innovations over the next ten to fifteen years, and identify the big tipping points. But about how it's all going to affect the way we use media in our lives, well the screen goes blank a few years out from now. And I'm trying to figure out why it seems so blank. Hopefully, it's not because I'm going senile, but rather it's because there really are unsettled questions and no matter how much history teaches us about human nature and the trajectory of past media innovations, people really are unpredictable to some degree.

I also think it's important to recognize that blogging is only a piece of a much larger trend in which we are crossing over from a mass media age to a personal media age. You never notice a paradigm shift when you're in the middle of it. You've got to be on the outside looking in. But I suspect this paradigm shift is at least as big as anything in the last fifty years.

How would you define personal media versus mass media?

Imagine two columns. You've got mass media on the left and personal media on the right. Mass media, you're a passive watcher. Personal media, you're an active participant. Mass media, one-way trip—television delivers the world to our living rooms, but all we can do is press our nose against the glass. Personal media, you answer back, you expect an answer back, you take it for granted that you can answer back and you're outraged when you can't. Just as with TV, from print to radio to all other media forms, the citizenry is getting greater control over what media they consume, when they consume it, and what they can do with the media they consume.

So what are you willing to make a prediction about regarding blogging?

Okay, two things. First, blogging as we know it today is an intermediate form, and it will evolve into something more. Secondly, as blogging—or citizen-controlled media—becomes more commonplace and easier to use, I'm reasonably certain that the word *blog* will disappear. And this is a good thing, because it is the most uneuphonious term. And *weblog* isn't much better . . . it's so retro. So good riddance to both of those terms.

And thirdly, I can also say that whatever form it eventually takes, blogging will continue to serve as some sort of new intellectual agora, a new common ground, in response to the failures of traditional Big Media organizations.

What do you mean?

I think there's a real hunger for perspective right now, for shared moments that have genuine meaning, that the established media is no longer fulfilling. Twenty or thirty years ago, in the era of Walter Cronkite, the media had a greater sense of consequences and they took their responsibilities more seriously. Today, you look at Fox and you look at—hell, during the siege of Falluja in Iraq, I happened to turn on one of the morning news shows. And a little bit after finishing a report on what was happening there, suddenly these three anchors got up from their seats and started doing this lambada-like dance. They thought it was so funny. And I'm thinking, Jeez, this is so unseemly. I mean, there are troops getting killed in Falluja!

That's what I think is motivating some of this blogging phenomenon, especially among political and media bloggers. The establishment press can cry all they want about bloggers being the "cockroaches of the media," but they're just whistling in the graveyard. Because their business, the traditional media business, is being destroyed. Not so much by the webloggers, but by themselves. They're slitting their own throats. They're acting like clowns, substituting screaming matches between extremists for so-called balanced reporting, and turning everything into entertainment. You know, I'm appalled by Jon Stewart's *The Daily Show*. It terrifies me, and I happen to agree with its politics. But I'm appalled by it.

Why?

Because all great civilizations fail by turning everything into entertainment, and I'm sorry, but I'm just getting really sick of what the media has become. And so are a whole lot of other people, and I think that's partly what's driving some of the blogging phenomenon.

PUNCHING HOLES IN OLD FADED MIRRORS

An Interview with Arianna Huffington

Author and columnist Arianna Huffington, social and political activist, sought-after television pundit, and onetime candidate for governor of California, has launched a blog propelled by celebrity power. Enlisted in her campaign to "enrich and strengthen the blogs' impact on the national conversation," are some 400 boldfaced names of people who have signed up to contribute occasional musings and insights—from Walter Cronkite to Diane Keaton, from Norman Mailer to Nora Ephron. As the New York Times *put it a few days before her launch in May 2005, she is "about to move blogging from the realm of the anonymous individual to the realm of the celebrity collective."*

Huffington is no stranger to the "big issue" of the day. During the 2000 presidential election she organized shadow Democratic and Republican conventions to highlight issues like campaign finance reform and U.S. drug policy. In 2003, as cofounder of a nonprofit group, the Detroit Project, she helped create a string of television public service advertisements that—albeit in the form of parody—pointedly linked gas-guzzling SUVs to terrorism through lines such as, "And these are the terrorists who get money from those [Middle Eastern] countries every time George fills up his SUV."

She traces her active interest in blogs to her participation on a panel organized by the Hollywood Radio and Television Society in 2003, where she launched into a rant about important stories that she said were not being covered properly by the mainstream media. Fellow panelists like Larry King and Sam Donaldson disagreed, but Huffington says it was at that moment she realized that the blogosphere, with its tendency to focus on a story and not let go, was the way forward.

The "blogazine," as she calls the Huffington Post (huffingtonpost.com), combines a breaking-news section with a group blog. In her interview with us, she talked about why the blogosphere is such a vital part of the media industry and how she hopes the Huffington Post will contribute to the national debate on a wide range of issues. The site "won't be left wing or right wing; indeed it will punch holes in that very stale way of looking at the world."

You have taken on the political establishment in the United States in many different ways during the past twenty years, and you are about to do it again. If campaigning, advertising, and opining haven't changed things the way you would like to see them change, how can a simple blog make a difference?

Blogs have made a huge difference because they have broken the monopoly of the mainstream media. The great majority of journalists head in whatever direction the assignment desk points them. But with blogs an enormous amount of people have become their own reporters. They are driven not by the assignment desk but by passion. When they decide that something matters they chomp down hard and refuse to let go.

As we know from our media right now, that's really what it takes for something to break through the clutter. For me, one of the real indictments of the mainstream media is that 40 percent of the people voting in the last election still believed that Saddam was behind 9/11. Now, what would it take to tell everyone that's not true? It would take a kind of relentlessness, a kind of pit bull nature, which is what the blogosphere has.

That's one of the things I believe has been the greatest influence. You saw it with the demise of Senate Majority Leader Trent Lott. While the mainstream media ignored it, bloggers kept going until Trent Lott had become the former Senate majority leader.

There have been a number of high points for blogs. Do you think there have also been low points?

Yes, absolutely. But the great thing about the blogosphere is that it can be self-correcting. If there's a fact that a blogger puts out that's wrong, the chances of it being corrected quickly are very great. That's one of the things I love about it—the open nature of the forum, the links, the research made visible, the democratic back and forth, the open archives, the conversational nature of it all.

With the mainstream media there are so many constraints. And the biggest constraint, in my opinion, is that the media is suffering from attention deficit disorder. They can only focus on one story at a time. So we have an endless obsession with Michael Jackson, or Scott Peterson, or even the "runaway bride." While the mainstream media is covering the story it's as though nothing else exists. And then, by the same token, when the story stops being on the front burner it's dropped completely. Do you remember Elian Gonzalez?

Elian Gonzalez was a 24/7 story who took up three covers of *Time* magazine, and I don't even think I have read a follow-up story. Does anybody even care what's happened to this child that obsessed the nation? In contrast, in the blogosphere you can stay on a topic and return to it.

So the media has a shorter attention span than even most Americans have and it's obsessed with the story of the day. But there are many blogs with the same characteristics. What is it, then, that makes blogs, in your words, "the most vital news source in our country?"

Its vitality comes from its multiplicity. We thought this vitality would come from a five-hundred-channel universe, but what we ended up with was the same conventional wisdom endlessly repeated.

Paradoxically, in these days of instant communication and twenty-four-hour news channels, it is actually easier to miss information to which we might otherwise pay attention. That's why we need stories to be covered and re-covered, and then re-covered again—until they filter up enough to become part of the cultural bloodstream.

And that's what's different in the blogosphere. The thing that's so exciting is that we don't know where exactly this is going to go. Almost 30 million people got their news online last year. I was at a Society of Newspaper Editors meeting this year and people could not stop talking about bloggers and the blogosphere. That would have been undreamt of even last year.

The impact it's having is accelerating. That's why I found so many willing people when I invited them to join the Huffington Post.

You certainly do have an enviable list of willing contributors: Walter Cronkite, David Mamet, Warren Beatty, Maggie Gyllenhaal, Diane Keaton, and Norman Mailer, to name a few. What kind of reaction did you get when you invited them to join the blogosphere?

Well, one comment from Ed Zwick, who produced a lot of great movies and TV shows like *Shakespeare in Love*, *The Siege*, and *thirtysomething*, summed it up. When I invited him to join our group blog he wrote back to me, "This all sounds suspiciously like writing, but if what you're offering is a bully pulpit for those rare occasions when I feel pissed off enough, or inspired (rarer, still) to actually write for free—then count me in . . ."

The truth is that Ed Zwick could sit down and write an op-ed and get it in the *New York Times*. But would he really do that? Would he take the time to do an op-ed with a beginning, a middle, and an end? Call an editor and take the time to be edited? Now, he can just literally dash off a thought. And in the blogosphere, for better or for worse, first thoughts are best thoughts.

But are they not also dangerous thoughts? I'm thinking particularly of people like New Republic senior editor Gregg Easterbrook, whose rant about the movie Kill Bill and Jewish Hollywood executives who "worship money above all else" cost him a job writing for ESPN.

That's where the self-correcting element of the blogosphere comes in. If you write something dangerous, someone else will shoot it down or point out the falsehood. I don't think contentious views are a problem, but falsehoods obviously are.

What about the people you approached to join the weblog? They are from a wide age range. Did they already know what a weblog was and how it worked?

Most of them were people I knew who were already getting a lot of their news online. But there were other people I approached because I believed their voices were very important and they should be part of the conversation even if they were not particularly computer savvy. So, for example, if Arthur Schlesinger wants to fax me a thought we will take that and turn it into a post. I consider this a great addition to the blogosphere.

In a way, it's the old guard meets the vanguard. We have Walter Cronkite blogging. I just love that. The man was the last great journalist to be trusted by America, and he is in a way paying homage to this new medium by blogging. Bob Blechman, the man who designed our site, is an eighty-two-year-old who has been designing *New Yorker* covers for years. We wanted to bring that old-world sensibility to a new medium. I think it's great to bring these two worlds together.

We also have a lot of young people. Our youngest blogger, Carson Meyer, is eleven. She has a great personality, she's really smart and outspoken, and she live-blogged from the MTV Movie Awards. So, it's going to be intergenerational and across all sorts of professions and time zones.

Everybody's in the same group blog; the people who are eleven-year-olds and the octogenarians, students you've never heard together with Arthur Schlesinger and Larry David. And anytime they post something everyone can comment on it. It can be about food, politics, sex, their children, other people's children—anything that is on their mind. We will also have topics of the day that we will ask them to comment on and we will have some moderated conversations. So it will be a combination of views and styles.

It sounds like what you are creating has not really been attempted before. How would you describe it?

It's a conversation of news and blogs. A blogazine?! All my life I have been very interested in facilitating conversations, whether as a student at Cambridge or having parties around books, or discussing ideas around the dinner table. Ever since I was little, my mother would prepare a meal and we would eat and talk and eat and talk for hours. It's very Greek!

And I've done the same in my wandering gypsy life, whether I was in England, or New York or here in LA. Now, I've added blogging to the ways of starting a conversation.

So how will you know whether the Huffington Post is succeeding?

There are two ways. One is the traffic and the other is having an impact on the national dialogue. You put thoughts and ideas out there and they enter the cultural bloodstream.

You don't need to reach everybody in order to have an impact. Impact comes from a critical mass of people. And I think we have a critical mass of people online. And with the breadth of people we have contributing to the Huffington Post, I hope they will be drawn to what we are offering.

MY SO-CALLED BLOG

by Emily Nussbaum*

The focus for most of this book has been on blogging as a phenomenon related to the adult world of politics, business, media, and culture. But Emily Nussbaum reminds us that of the 10 million plus blogs out there, the vast majority of bloggers are teens and young adults—a full 90 percent, according to some estimates. Teens, especially, says Nussbaum, seem to be aching to share what normally would be considered private experiences: "For a significant number, they become a way of life, a daily record of a community's private thoughts—a kind of invisible high school that floats above the daily life of teenagers."

Nussbaum, an experienced journalist who is now culture editor of New York *magazine and also writes the "Reruns" column in the* New York Times, *provides a great deal of insight into the world of teen blogging, without drawing facile conclusions.*

When M. gets home from school, he immediately logs on to his computer. Then he stays there, touching base with the people he has seen all day long, floating in a kind of multitasking heaven of communication. First, he clicks on his Web log, or blog—an online diary he keeps on a Web site called

*Emily Nussbaum contributes the "Reruns" column to the Arts & Leisure section of the *New York Times.* Copyright ©2004 Emily Nussbaum. Reprinted by permission. This article first appeared in *The New York Times Magazine* on January 11, 2004.

LiveJournal—and checks for responses from his readers. Next he reads his friends' journals, contributing his distinctive brand of wry, supportive commentary to their observations. Then he returns to his own journal to compose his entries: sometimes confessional, more often dry private jokes or koanlike observations on life.

Finally, he spends a long time—sometimes hours—exchanging instant messages, a form of communication far more common among teenagers than phone calls. In multiple dialogue boxes on his computer screen, he'll type real-time conversations with several friends at once; if he leaves the house to hang out in the real world, he'll come back and instant-message some more, and sometimes cut and paste transcripts of these conversations into his online journal. All this upkeep can get in the way of homework, he admitted. "You keep telling yourself, 'Don't look, don't look!' And you keep on checking your e-mail." M. is an unusually Zen teenage boy—dreamy and ruminative about his personal relationships. But his obsessive online habits are hardly exceptional; he is one of a generation of compulsive self-chroniclers, a fleet of juvenile Marcel Prousts gone wild. When he meets new friends in real life, M. offers them access to his online world. "That's how you introduce yourself," he said. "It's like, here's my cellphone number, my e-mail, my screen name, oh, and—here's my LiveJournal. Personally, I'd go to that person's LJ before I'd call them or e-mail them or contact them on AIM"—AOL Instant Messenger—"because I would know them better that way."

Only five years ago, mounting an online journal or its close cousin, the blog, required at least a modicum of technical know-how. But today, using sites like LiveJournal or Blogger or Xanga, users can sign up for a free account, and with little computer knowledge design a site within minutes. According to figures released last October by Perseus Development Corporation, a company that designs software for online surveys, there are expected to be 10 million blogs by the end of 2004. In the news media, the blog explosion has been portrayed as a transformation of the industry, a thousand minipundits blooming. But the vast majority of bloggers are teens and young adults. Ninety percent of those with blogs are between 13 and 29 years old; a full 51 percent are between 13 and 19, according to Perseus. Many teen blogs are short-lived experiments. But for a significant number, they become a way of life, a daily record of a community's private thoughts—a kind of invisible high school that floats above the daily life of teenagers.

Back in the 1980's, when I attended high school, reading someone's diary would have been the ultimate intrusion. But communication was rudimentary back then. There were no cellphones, or answering machines; there was no "texting," no MP3's or JPEG's, no digital cameras or file-sharing software; there was no World Wide Web—none of the private-ish, public-ish, superimmediate forums kids today take for granted. If this new technology has provided a million ways to stay in touch, it has also acted as both an amplifier and a distortion device for human intimacy. The new forms of communication are madly contradictory: anonymous, but traceable; instantaneous, then saved forever (unless deleted in a snit). In such an unstable environment, it's no wonder that distinctions between healthy candor and "too much information" are in flux and that so many find themselves helplessly confessing, as if a generation were given a massive technological truth serum.

A result of all this self-chronicling is that the private experience of adolescence—a period traditionally marked by seizures of self-consciousness and personal confessions wrapped in layers and hidden in a sock drawer—has been made public. Peer into an online journal, and you find the operatic texture of teenage life with its fits of romantic misery, quick-change moods and sardonic inside jokes. Gossip spreads like poison. Diary writers compete for attention, then fret when they get it. And everything parents fear is true. (For one thing, their children view them as stupid and insane, with terrible musical taste.) But the linked journals also form a community, an intriguing, unchecked experiment in silent group therapy—a hive mind in which everyone commiserates about how it feels to be an outsider, in perfect choral unison.

For many in the generation that has grown up online, the solution is not to fight this technological loss of privacy, but to give in and embrace it: to stop worrying and learn to love the Web. It's a generational shift that has multiple roots, from Ricki Lake to the memoir boom to the A.A. confessional, not to mention 13 seasons of "The Real World." The teenagers who post journals have (depending on your perspective) a degraded or a relaxed sense of privacy; their experiences may be personal, but there's no shame in sharing. As the reality-television stars put it, exposure may be painful at times, but it's all part of the process of "putting it out there," risking judgment and letting people in. If teen bloggers give something up by sloughing off a self-protective layer, they get something back too—a new kind of intimacy, a sense that they are known and listened to. This is their life, for anyone to read. As long as their parents don't find out.

It was early September, the start of the school year in an affluent high school in Westchester County, just north of New York City, where I was focusing my teen-blogging expedition. The halls were filled with students and the walls were covered with posters urging extracurricular activities. ("Instant popularity, minus the hazing," read one.) I had come looking for J., a boy I'd never seen, though I knew many of the details of his life. (J., like most of the teenage bloggers I interviewed, insisted he not be identified, in part because his parents didn't know about his blog.) On a Web site called Blurty, he kept an online journal, titled "Laugh at Me." In his user profile he described himself this way: "I have depression, bad skin, weight problems, low self-esteem, few friends and many more reasons why I am angry." In his online outpourings, J. inveighed hilariously against his parents, his teachers and friends who had let him down. "Hey everyone ever," he wrote in one entry. "Stop making fun of people. It really is a sucky thing to do, especially if you hate being made fun of yourself. . . . This has been a public service announcement. You may now resume your stupid hypocritical, lying lives."

I was half-expecting a pimply nightmare boy, all monosyllables and misery. Instead, J. turned out to be a cute 15-year-old with a shy smile. A little bit jittery, he sat with his knees apart, admiring his own Converse sneakers. He had chosen an unfortunately public place for this interview—a stairwell near the cafeteria and directly across from the teacher's lounge—although he insisted that we were in an obscure location.

J. had had his Blurty journal for about a year. He called it "better than therapy," a way to get out his true feelings—all the emotions he thought might get him in trouble if he expressed them in school or at home. Online, he could blurt out confessions of loneliness and insecurity, worrying aloud about slights from friends. Yet despite the fact that he knew that anyone who wanted to could read his journal—and that a few friends did, leaving comments at the ends of his posts—he also maintained the notion that what he was doing was private. He didn't write for an audience, he said; he just wrote what he was feeling.

Writing in his online journal was cathartic for him, he said, but it was hardly stress-free. A week earlier, he left a post about an unrequited crush, and an anonymous someone appended negative comments, remarks J. wouldn't detail (he deleted them), but which he described with distress as "disgusting language, vulgarities." J. panicked, worried that the girl he liked might learn about the vulgar comments and, by extension, his attraction to her. It was a somewhat mysterious concern. Couldn't the girl have read his original post, I asked? And anyway, didn't he secretly want her to read his journal? "Of course," he moaned, leaning against the banister. "For all I know she does. For all I know, she doesn't."

J.'s sense of private and public was filled with these kinds of contradictions: he wanted his posts to be read, and feared that people would read them, and hoped that people would read them, and didn't care if people read them. He wanted to be included while priding himself on his outsider status. And while he sometimes wrote messages that were explicitly public— announcing a band practice, for instance—he also had his own stringent notions of etiquette. His crush had an online journal, but J. had never read it; that would be too intrusive, he explained.

In any case, today he was in a strikingly good mood. After a year of posting his journal on Blurty, which few of his fellow students used, he was switching to a different Web site: LiveJournal, the enclave of many kids in his school's punk set. He'd spent the last day or two transferring all his old posts, setting up a friends list and concocting a new "icon," the tiny symbol that would represent him when he posted: a blurry shot of his face in profile. Unlike Blurty, where accounts are free for anyone who signs up, LiveJournal was restricted. (That policy has since changed.) You either had to pay to join (which J. couldn't afford) or be offered a coveted membership—a private "code"—by someone who already belonged. The policy was intended to make members accountable to one another, but it also had the effect of creating an invisible clique. For J., it was a sign that he might belong at last.

While the sites that are hosts to online journals may attract different crowds, their formats vary only slightly: a LiveJournal is a Blurty is a Xanga is a DeadJournal is a DiaryLand. A typical page shows a dated list of entries, beginning with the most recent. Many posts are short, surrealistic one-liners: "I just peeled a freckle off my neck. Does that mean it's not a freckle?" Others are more like visual poems, featuring a quirky series of scanned pictures (monkeys and robots are popular), a quote from a favorite song or a link to a strange news story. Some posts consist of transcripts of instant-message conversations, posted with or without permission (a tradition I discovered when a boy copied one of our initial online conversations under the heading "i like how older people have grammar online").

But a significant number of writers treat their journals as actual diaries, toting up detailed accounts of their day. "I watched the miracle of life today in bio, and it was such a huge letdown," read one post. "I was expecting it to be funny and sexual but it was way too scientific for my liking, and a bit yucky too, but not as bad as people made it out to be. Although, my not being able to laugh made me feel a bit too old. Current mood: disappointed."

Then there are the kinds of posts that fulfill a parent's worst paranoia. "It was just a nite of lying to my dad," reads one entry posted last fall. "At like 7ish we started drinking, but i didnt have THAT much. And i figured out y i drink so much. Cuz i really really don't like being sober with drunk people. . . . i have more homework to do than imaginable. And to make it better, im hungover and feel sick. Great . . . great. DRINKING IS BAD!!"

Other entries are just plain poignant. "My father is suing my mom on no real grounds. He just wants to 'destroy her' and I am trying my best to stay 'neutral.' Things seem real foggy, but I am told that they should turn out for the best. I just don't know. Affection needed. Current mood: indescribable."

If a journal may look at first like a simple recitation of events, the fact that readers can comment renders it deeply interactive. (On some sites, like Xanga, you can give "eProps" for particularly good posts—the equivalent of gold stars.) Most comments are wisecracks or sympathetic one-liners. Occasionally people respond with hostility. The threads of comments can amount to a public miniconversation, in which a group of friends debates a subject or plans an event or offers advice. "I need your help," one poster wrote. "Yes, your help. You, the one reading this . . . what am i supposed to do when the dynamic of a once-romantic relationship sort of changes but sort of doesn't, and the next week i continually try to get in touch with the girl but she is either not there or can't talk very long, and before this change in the dynamic she was always available?" A string of friends offered suggestions, from "don't call her so much" to "confront her . . . what she's doing isn't fair to you."

In daily life, most bloggers don't talk about what they say online. One boy engaged in vociferous debates on Mideast policy with another blogger, a senior a year ahead of him. Yet the two never spoke in school, going only so far as to make eye contact in the halls.

Silences like this can create paranoia. It may be that friends just didn't read the post. Or it may mean they thought the post was stupid. There's a temptation to take silence—in real life or online—as a snub. "If I get a really mean comment and I go back and I look at it again, and again, it starts to bother me," M. told me. "But then I think, If I delete it, everyone will know this bothers me. But if I respond, it'll mean I need to fight back. So it turns into a conflict, but it's fun. It's like a soap opera, kind of."

It's a drama heightened by the fact that journals are linked to one another, creating a constant juxtaposition of posts among the students. For example, on LiveJournal, you can click a "friends" link and catch up on your friends' experiences without ever speaking, with everyone's accounts posted next to one another in a kind of word collage. For many, this transforms daily life. Teen bloggers are constantly considering how they'll turn a noteworthy moment into an online post. After a party or a concert, these accounts can amount to a prismatic portrait of the evening.

But even this endless linking only begins to touch on the complex ways these blogs are obsessively interconnected and personalized. L. has had an online journal for two and a half years, and it has morphed along with her. At first, her interest list (part of the user profile) consisted of topics like aromatherapy, yoga and Zen—each of which linked to people with the same interest. She deleted that list and started over. In her next phase, she was obsessed with Freudian psychology. Now she lists fashion trends and belongs to the Flapper, Saucy Dwellings and Sex Tips blog rings.

Over the course of the fall, she changed the title of her Web log more than five times. L. relishes the way subtle choices of design and phrasing lend her posts a winking mysteriousness, hinting at feelings without making them explicit. "I don't think I reveal too much; if I'm upset, I don't say why," she told me. "In the beginning, I was just like, there shouldn't be private posts, this should all be public. But then it makes you very vulnerable." And her attitude goes double for her parents. "I don't talk to them about anything. They'll be like, 'How was school?' And I'll be like, 'Fine.' And that was it."

Many of a journal's markers of personal identity are hilariously telegraphic. There are sometimes slots for a journalizer's mood and current music. (Sample moods: "stoned," "restless," "accomplished," "confused" and "braces off Tuesday.") Journal writers link en masse to sardonic identity questionnaires, like "How Indie Am I?" And every once in a while, someone posts a random list of questions, and everyone's journal fills up with simultaneous answers to queries like "Do you believe in an afterlife?" or "Name Four Things You Wish You Had." ("1. A flat tummy; 2. people that would miss me; 3. my copy of 'perks of being a wallflower' back; 4. talent at ANYTHING.")

It's possible to make posts private—or "friends only"—but many journal keepers don't bother, or do so only for selected posts. The general degree of anonymity varies: some bloggers post their full names, others give quirky, quasi-revelatory handles. No wonder everyone is up till 5 a.m. tweaking their font size and Photoshopping a new icon. At heart, an online journal is like a hyperflexible adolescent body—but better, because in real life, it takes money and physical effort to add a piercing, or to switch from zip-jacketed mod to Abercrombie prepster. A LiveJournal or Blurty offers a creative outlet with a hundred moving parts. And unlike a real journal, with a blog, your friends are all around, invisible voyeurs—at least until they chime in with a comment.

For many of the suburban students I met, online journals are associated with the "emo" crowd—a sarcastic term for emotional, and a tag for a musical genre mingling thrash-punk with confessionalism. The emo kids tend to be the artsy loners and punks, but as I spent more time lurking in journals and talking to the kids who wrote them, I began to realize that these threads led out much farther into the high school, into pretty much every clique.

On a sunny fall day, M. and his friends were hanging out in front of a local toy store, shooting photos of one another with digital cameras, when a group of three girls sashayed by. They sported tank tops, identical hairbands and identical shiny hair. I walked over to them and asked if they have Live-Journals. "No," one said. "We have Xangas."

They were all 15, around the same age as M. and his friends. But the two groups had never read the other's posts. M.'s crowd was emo (or at least emo-ish; like "politically correct," "emo" is a word people rarely apply to themselves). These girls were part of the athletic crowd. There was little overlap, online or off. But the girls were fully familiar with the online etiquette M. described: they instant-messaged compulsively; they gossiped online.

With so much confessional drama, I began to wonder if interactions ever swung out of control. Does anyone ever post anything that seems like too much information? I asked. They all nodded intently, tossing nervous eye contact back and forth.

"Yeah," one of the girls replied finally, with a deep sigh. "This one girl, she was really upset, and she would write things that had happened to her that were really scary. Private things that didn't really need to be said on the site—"

Her friend interrupted: "But she knew she was putting it out there. She said, 'I don't care.' "

"It was nice that she was comfortable about it," suggested the third girl.

Her friend disagreed. "It was not nice."

What kinds of things did she write about? I asked. Eating disorders? Sex? "All of it," they said in unison. "All of it."

I walked back to M. and his group. "Those girls are just, like, social girls," said M. dismissively. When I told him they had online journals, he seemed astonished. "Really?" he said. "Huh." He watched with amusement as they walked away.

Blogging is a replication of real life: each pool of blogs is its own ecosystem, with only occasional links to other worlds. As I surfed from site to site, it became apparent that as much as journals can break stereotypes, some patterns are crushingly predictable: the cheerleaders post screen grabs of the Fox TV show "The O.C."; kids who identify with "ghetto" culture use hip-hop slang; the geeks gush over Japanese anime. And while there are exceptions, many journal writers exhibit a surprising lack of curiosity about the journals of true strangers. They're too busy writing posts to browse.

But even diaries that seem at first predictable can have the power to startle. Take J.K., whose Xanga titled "No Fat Chicks" features a peculiar mix of introspection and bully-boy bombast. Some of J.K.'s entries this fall brooded on his bench-warmer status on the football team. "Do the coaches want me to quit?" he worried in one post. "I know that some people have to sit out, that's just the way it works, and I accept that. But does it have to be me when we're down 36 points and the clock is winding down?"

In J.K.'s diary, revelations of insecurity alternate with chest-beating bombast, juvenile jokes and self-mocking claims of sexual prowess. From a teen poet, you expect angsty navel-gazing; it's more surprising to find it in a jock like J.K. In one post, he analyzed his history as a bully during "middle school, the time of popularity," when he did "things too heinous to even mention." In response, a reader posted a long, angry comment, doubting J.K.'s sincerity: "I don't think you understand what hatred I used to have for you because of how you made me feel . . . you can't go back in time, but you can try to make up for what you've done in the past."

Occasionally, a particularly scandalous site will gain a wider readership. It's a social phenomenon made possible by technology: the object of gossip using her Web site as a public stage to tell her side of the story, to everyone, all at once. As I asked around the high school, I found that many other students had heard of the girl the "social girls" had described to me—a student whose confessional postings had became something of a must-read the spring before. Over the course of a monthslong breakdown, she posted graphic descriptions of cutting herself, family fights, sex. It was all documented on her Web log, complete with photos and real names. (She has since removed the material from her site.)

The blog turned her into a minor celebrity, at first among the social crowd, then among their friends and siblings as well. "We were addicted—we would track every minute," one student explained. "We would call each other and go, 'Oh, my god, she wrote again!' " With each post, her readers would encourage her to write more. "Wow u should be writing a book," one wrote. "Ur stories are exactly like one of those teen diary books that other teens can relate to. That might sound corny but its so true."

The girls who read the journal were divided on the subject. Some called the Web site an unhealthy bid for attention—not to mention revenge, since she often posted unflattering details about her ex-boyfriend and former friends. Others were more sympathetic. "I think I empathized with her after reading it, because I'd just heard the stories," one girl explained. "But then she was saying, 'I felt so sad, and I was in this really dark place, and my parents were fighting, and I was cutting myself'—so I could understand it more. Before, it was just gossip. It made her seem more like a person than just, like, this character."

These dynamics are invisible to most adults, whether at home or school. Students occasionally show the school psychologist their journals, pulling up posts on her computer or sharing printed transcripts of instant messages. But the psychologist rarely sought them out herself, she told me, and she was surprised to hear that boys kept them. She called the journals a boon for shy students and admired the way they encouraged kids to express themselves in writing. But she also noticed a recent rise in journal-based conflicts, mostly situations where friends attack one another after a falling out. "They think that they're getting close by sharing," she said, "but it allows them to say things they wouldn't otherwise say, to be hurtful at a distance." When I mentioned the material I'd read about the girl who was cutting herself, she went silent. "You know," she said, "I really should read more into these."

The scandalous journal is an extreme variation, but teen bloggers often joke about the pressure to post with angst; controversy gets more commentary, after all. (Entries often apologize for not having anything exciting to say.) But if there's something troubling about the kind of online scandal that breeds a high-school Sylvia Plath—an angstier-than-thou exhibitionism—there's also something almost utopian at the endeavor's heart. So much high-school pain comes from the sense of being alone with one's stupid, self-destructive impulses. With so many teenagers baring their vulnerabilities, there is the potential for breaking down isolation. A kind of online Breakfast Club, perhaps, in which a little surfing turns up the insecurity that lurks in all of us.

For some journal keepers, the connections made online can be life-altering. In late November, I checked in on J., the author of "Laugh at Me." All fall, his LiveJournal had been hopping, documenting milestones (a learner's permit!), philosophical insights, complaints about parental dorki-ness and plans for something called Operation Backfire, in which he mocks another kid he hates—a kid who has filled his own journal on Xanga with right-wing rants. "I felt happy/victorious," wrote J. about taunting his enemy. "And rightly so."

In the new context of LiveJournal, J.'s posts had become increasingly in-teractive, with frequent remarks about parties and weekend plans; they seemed less purely rantlike, and he was posting comments on other people's journals. When I contacted him via instant message, he told me that he was feeling less friendless than he was when the semester started.

"I feel more included and such," he typed just after Thanksgiving, de-scribing the effect of having switched to LiveJournal from his more isolated Blurty. "All community-ish." He was planning to attend a concert of World/ Inferno Friendship Society, a band with a LiveJournal following. And he'd be-come closer friends in real life with some fellow LJ'ers, including L., who had given J. an emo makeover. He'd begun wearing tight, dark jeans and had "forcibly retired" his old sneakers.

Once J. decided to switch to LiveJournal, LiveJournal began changing him in turn. Perhaps he was adjusting himself to reflect the way he is online: assertive and openly emotional, more than a bit bratty. He'd become more comfortable talking to girls. And if he seemed to have forgotten his invoca-tion not to make fun of anyone, at least he was standing up for himself.

J. had also signed up for a new online journal: a Xanga. He got it, he said, to branch out. He wanted to be able to comment on the journals of other students he knows are out there, including that of bully-boy J.K., where

I was surprised to find one of J.'s comments in early November. "I made a xanga for myself because i keep hearing that that's whats 'cool' now," he wrote on his LJ with a distinctive mixture of rue and satisfaction, the very flavor of adolescent change. "And yet i always try to pride myself on not following status quo. I'm a hypocrite. O yes i am. Current mood: Hypocritical. Current music: Mogwai."

MEET JOE BLOG

Lev Grossman and Anita Hamilton*

"Why are more and more people getting their news from amateur websites called blogs?" ask the authors of this Time *magazine article. "Because they're fast, funny and totally biased," they answer. And why can't we ignore them? Because "blogs not only act like a lens, focusing attention on an issue until it catches fire, but they can also break stories." Grossman and Hamilton here provide the basic who, where, what, and why of this snowballing phenomenon.*

A few years ago, Mathew Gross, 32, was a free-lance writer living in tiny Moab, Utah. Rob Malda, 28, was an underperforming undergraduate at a small Christian college in Michigan. Denis Dutton, 60, was a professor of philosophy in faraway Christchurch, New Zealand. Today they are some of the most influential media personalities in the world. You can be one too.

Gross, Malda and Dutton aren't rich or famous or even conspicuously good-looking. What they have in common is that they all edit blogs: amateur websites that provide news, information and, above all, opinions to rapidly growing and devoted audiences drawn by nothing more than a shared interest

---

*This article first appeared in *Time* magazine on June 21, 2004. Additional reporting by Maryanne Murray Buechner and Leslie Whitaker. Copyright ©2004 Time Inc. reprinted by permission.

or two and the sheer magnetism of the editor's personality. Over the past five years, blogs have gone from an obscure and, frankly, somewhat nerdy fad to a genuine alternative to mainstream news outlets, a shadow media empire that is rivaling networks and newspapers in power and influence. Which raises the question: Who are these folks anyway? And what exactly are they doing to the established pantheon of American media?

Not that long ago, blogs were one of those annoying buzz words that you could safely get away with ignoring. The word blog—it works as both noun and verb—is short for Web log. It was coined in 1997 to describe a website where you could post daily scribblings, journal-style, about whatever you like—mostly critiquing and linking to other articles online that may have sparked your thinking. Unlike a big media outlet, bloggers focus their efforts on narrow topics, often rising to become de facto watchdogs and self-proclaimed experts. Blogs can be about anything: politics, sex, baseball, haiku, car repair. There are blogs about blogs.

Big whoop, right? But it turns out some people actually have interesting thoughts on a regular basis, and a few of the better blogs began drawing sizable audiences. Blogs multiplied and evolved, slowly becoming conduits for legitimate news and serious thought. In 1999 a few companies began offering free make-your-own-blog software, which turbocharged the phenomenon. By 2002, Pyra Labs, which makes software for creating blogs, claimed 970,000 users.

Most of America couldn't have cared less. Until December 2002, that is, when bloggers staged a dramatic show of force. The occasion was Strom Thurmond's 100th birthday party, during which Trent Lott made what sounded like a nostalgic reference to Thurmond's past segregationist leanings. The mainstream press largely glossed over the incident, but when regular journalists bury the lead, bloggers dig it right back up. "That story got ignored for three, four, five days by big papers and the TV networks while blogs kept it alive," says Joshua Micah Marshall, creator of talkingpointsmemo.com, one of a handful of blogs that stuck with the Lott story.

Mainstream America wasn't listening, but Washington insiders and media honchos read blogs. Three days after the party, the story was on *Meet the*

Press. Four days afterward, Lott made an official apology. After two weeks, Lott was out as Senate majority leader, and blogs had drawn their first blood. Web journalists like Matt Drudge (drudge report.com) had already demonstrated a certain crude effectiveness—witness *l'affaire* Lewinsky—but this was something different: bloggers were offering reasoned, forceful arguments that carried weight with the powers that be.

Blogs act like a lens, focusing attention on an issue until it catches fire, but they can also break stories. On April 21, a 34-year-old blogger and writer from Arizona named Russ Kick posted photographs of coffins containing the bodies of soldiers killed in Iraq and Afghanistan and of Columbia astronauts. The military zealously guards images of service members in coffins, but Kick pried the photos free with a Freedom of Information Act (FOIA) request. "I read the news constantly," says Kick, "and when I see a story about the government refusing to release public documents, I automatically file an FOIA request for them." By April 23 the images had gone from Kick's blog, *thememoryhole.org*, to the front page of newspapers across the country. Kick was soon getting upwards of 4 million hits a day.

What makes blogs so effective? They're free. They catch people at work, at their desks, when they're alert and thinking and making decisions. Blogs are fresh and often seem to be miles ahead of the mainstream news. Bloggers put up new stuff every day, all day, and there are thousands of them. How are you going to keep anything secret from a thousand Russ Kicks? Blogs have voice and personality. They're human. They come to us not from some media-genic anchorbot on an air-conditioned sound stage, but from an individual. They represent—no, they are—the voice of the little guy.

And the little guy is a lot smarter than big media might have you think. Blogs showcase some of the smartest, sharpest writing being published. Bloggers are unconstrained by such journalistic conventions as good taste, accountability and objectivity—and that can be a good thing. Accusations of media bias are thick on the ground these days, and Americans are tired of it. Blogs don't pretend to be neutral: they're gleefully, unabashedly biased, and that makes them a lot more fun. "Because we're not trying to sell magazines or papers, we can afford to assail our readers," says Andrew Sullivan, a contributor to *TIME* and the editor of andrewsullivan.com. "I don't have the pressure of an advertising executive telling me to lay off. It's incredibly liberating."

Some bloggers earn their bias the hard way—in the trenches. Military bloggers, or milbloggers in Net patois, post vivid accounts of their tours of Baghdad, in prose covered in fresh flop sweat and powder burns, illustrated with digital photos. "Jason," a National Guardsman whose blog is called justanothersoldier.com, wrote about wandering through one of Saddam Hussein's empty palaces. And Iraqis have blogs: a Baghdad blogger who goes by Salam Pax *(dear_raed .blogspot.com)* has parlayed his blog into a book and a movie deal. Vietnam was the first war to be televised; blogs bring Iraq another scary step closer to our living rooms.

But blogs are about much more than war and politics. In 1997 Malda went looking for a "site that mixed the latest word about a new sci-fi movie with news about open-source software. I was looking for a site that didn't exist," Malda says, "so I built it." Malda and a handful of co-editors run slashdot.org full time, and he estimates that 300,000 to 500,000 people read the site daily. Six years ago, a philosophy professor in New Zealand named Denis Dutton started the blog Arts & Letters Daily *(artsandlettersdaily.com)* to create a website "where people could go daily for a dose of intellectual stimulation." Now the site draws more than 100,000 readers a month. Compare that with, say, the *New York Review of Books*, which has a circulation of 115,000. The tail is beginning to wag the blog.

Blogs are inverting the cozy media hierarchies of yore. Some bloggers are getting press credentials for this summer's Republican Convention. Three years ago, a 25-year-old Chicagoan named Jessa Crispin started a blog for serious readers called bookslut.com. "We give books a better chance," she says. "The *New York Times Book Review* is so boring. We take each book at face value. There's no politics behind it." Crispin's apartment is overflowing with free books from publishers desperate for a mention. As for the *Times*, it's scrutinizing the blogging phenomenon for its own purposes. In January the Gray Lady started up Times on the Trail, a campaign-news website with some decidedly bloglike features; it takes the bold step of linking to articles by competing newspapers, for example. "The *Times* cannot ignore this. I don't think any big media can ignore this," says Len Apcar, editor in chief of the *New York Times* on the Web.

In a way, blogs represent everything the Web was always supposed to be: a mass medium controlled by the masses, in which getting heard depends solely on having something to say and the moxie to say it.

Unfortunately, there's a downside to this populist sentiment—that is, innocent casualties bloodied by a medium that trades in rumor, gossip and speculation without accountability. Case in point: Alexandra Polier, better known as the Kerry intern. Rumors of Polier's alleged affair with presidential candidate Senator John Kerry eventually spilled into the blogosphere earlier this year. After Drudge headlined it in February, the blabbing bloggers soon had the attention of tabloid journalists, radio talk-show hosts and cable news anchors. Trouble is, the case was exceedingly thin, and both Kerry and Polier vehemently deny it. Yet the Internet smolders with it to this day.

Some wonder if the backbiting tide won't recede as blogs grow up. The trend now is for more prominent sites to be commercialized. A Manhattan entrepreneur named Nick Denton runs a small stable of bloggers as a business by selling advertising on their sites. So far they aren't showing detectible signs of editorial corruption by their corporate masters—two of Denton's blogs, gawker.com and wonkette.com, are among the most corrosively witty sites on the Web—but they've lost their amateur status forever.

We may be in the golden age of blogging, a quirky Camelot moment in Internet history when some guy in his underwear with too much free time can take down a Washington politician. It will be interesting to see what role blogs play in the upcoming election. Blogs can be a great way of communicating, but they can keep people apart too. If I read only those of my choice, precisely tuned to my political biases and you read only yours, we could end up a nation of political solipsists, vacuum sealed in our private feedback loops, never exposed to new arguments, never having to listen to a single word we disagree with.

Howard Dean's campaign blog, run by Mathew Gross, may be the perfect example of both the potential and the pitfalls of high-profile blogging. At its peak, blog for america.com drew 100,000 visitors a day, yet the candidate was beaten badly in the primaries. Still, the Dean model isn't going away. When another political blogger, who goes by the nom de blog Atrios, set up a fund-raising link on his site for Kerry, he raised $25,000 in five days.

You can't blog your way into the White House, at least not yet, but blogs are America thinking out loud, talking to itself, and heaven help the candidate who isn't listening.

A BLOGGER'S CREED

by Andrew Sullivan.*

An essayist for Time *magazine and a columnist for the* Sunday Times of London, *Andrew Sullivan is the editor of andrewsullivan.com, a daily blog with commentary on subjects ranging from international affairs and domestic politics to culture, religion, and faith. Sullivan was editor-in-chief of the* New Republic *magazine—the youngest editor in its history. In addition to the* New Republic, *he has written for such publications as the* Wall Street Journal *and* The New York Times Magazine.

In this essay, one of his regular columns for Time, *Sullivan succinctly summarizes the power of blogs but makes no claim that the new medium has slain the dragon of old media. It's just that they keep a sharp eye out toward the beast, adding new voices and forcibly creating a level of transparency heretofore unseen.*

"Bloggers have no checks and balances. [It's] a guy sitting in his living room in his pajamas."

—JONATHAN KLEIN,
former senior executive of 60 Minutes

*This article first appeared in *Time* magazine on September 27, 2004. Copyright ©2004 Time Inc. reprinted by permission.

Well, last week, the insurrectionary pajama people—dubbed "pajama-hadeen" by some Web nuts—successfully scaled one more citadel of the mainstream media, CBS News. One of the biggest, baddest media stars, Dan Rather, is now clinging, white-knuckled, to his job. Not bad for a bunch of slackers in their nightclothes.

You have to ask: Is this a media revolution? In some respects, sure. The Web has done one revolutionary thing to journalism: it has made the price of entry into the media market minimal. In days gone by, you needed a small fortune to start up a simple magazine or newspaper. Now you need a laptop and a modem.

Ten years ago I edited a money-losing magazine, The New Republic, which had 100,000 subscribers. Two weeks ago on my four-year-old blog, AndrewSullivan.com, I had 100,000 readers in one day alone. After four years of blogging, I haven't lost a cent and have eked out a small salary. And I don't even have an editor! Technology did this. And it's a big deal most people have yet to understand.

The results, however, are in. Without blogs, there wouldn't have been a Drudge Report to help speed the impeachment of a sitting President. Trent Lott, hounded by bloggers for a racist remark originally ignored by the big media, would still be Senate majority leader. Blogs played a critical part in the downfall of Howell Raines, former executive editor of the New York Times, in the Jayson Blair scandal. Blogs created a forum where Times insiders could leak and vent, where critics could ridicule and where Raines' editorship could be rattled until it was scuttled by one wayward reporter. The same kind of Web scrutiny added to the forces that brought down the BBC's leadership in the aftermath of a disputed story alleging that Tony Blair's government had "sexed up" evidence of Iraqi WMD. I still wonder if Raines and Rather knew what hit them.

The critics of blogs cite their lack of professionalism. Piffle. The dirty little secret of journalism is that it isn't really a profession. It's a craft. All you need is a telephone and a conscience, and you're all set. You get better at it merely by doing it—which is why fancy journalism schools are, to my mind, such a waste of time.

Blogs prove this. One of the best is a site started by a law professor in Tennessee, Instapundit.com. This "amateur" has earned the trust of his readers simply by his track record—just as the New York Times did a century ago. And after a couple of years, his readership rivals and often eclipses those of the traditional political magazines. Does he screw up? Of course he does sometimes. I've done so many times myself. But the beauty of the blogosphere is that if you make a mistake, someone will soon let you know. And if you don't correct immediately, someone will let you know again. And again. Like Internet Jack Russell terriers, readers grab ahold of your pants and don't let go until you have made amends. Blogs that ignore critics will lose credibility and readers. It's the market at its purest. And readers may have more and better information at their fingertips than the best researcher in the world.

Take the CBS document story. The clues to the alleged forgery were not discovered by the bloggers themselves—but by their readers. While CBS had a handful of experts look at the dubious memos (and failed to heed their concerns), the blogosphere enlisted hundreds within hours. Debates ensued, with different blogs challenging others over various abstruse points. Yes, some of this was fueled by raw partisanship and bias. The blogosphere is not morally pure. But the result was that the facts were flushed out more effectively and swiftly than the old media could ever have hoped. The collective mind also turns out to be a corrective one.

Does this mean the old media is dead? Not at all. Blogs depend on the journalistic resources of big media to do the bulk of reporting and analysis. What blogs do is provide the best scrutiny of big media imaginable—ratcheting up the standards of the professionals, adding new voices, new perspectives and new facts every minute. The genius lies not so much in the bloggers themselves but in the transparent system they have created. In an era of polarized debate, the truth has never been more available. Thank the guys in the pajamas. And read them.

BLOGWORLD AND ITS GRAVITY:
THE NEW AMATEUR JOURNALISTS WEIGH IN

by Matt Welch*

"In the 1960s," write the editors of the Columbia Journalism Review *in introducing this article, "a convergence of cultural, political, and technological circumstances set the stage for the rise of what came to be called the alternative press." At their worst, these early "underground" newspapers were strident and untrustworthy. At their best, they broke new ground in reporting and writing and bore witness to tectonic shifts in our society; and they challenged and altered the dusty mainstream press as well. Something similar is happening now. The circumstances in 2003 include a deep dissatisfaction with Big Media, a hunger for connection and community, and a yearning for political passion and for the writer's voice. Meanwhile, new technology is beginning to honor some of the wild promise of the Web. The result, as we see it, is the emergence of a new age of alternative media.*

While written several years ago, the article continues to be timely, tracing the development and arguing for the significance of the emerging blogosphere. Matt Welch's blog can be read at www.mattwelch.com/warblog.html.

This February, I attended my first Association of Alternative Newsweeklies conference, in the great media incubator of San Francisco. It's impossible

*Reprinted by permission from *Columbia Journalism Review*, September–October 2003, and from the author. Copyright ©2003 by *Columbia Journalism Review*.

to walk a single block of that storied town without feeling the ghosts of great contrarian media innovators past: Hearst and Twain, Hinckle and Wenner, Rossetto and Talbot. But after twelve hours with the AAN, a much different reality set in: never in my life have I seen a more conformist gathering of journalists.

All the newspapers looked the same—same format, same fonts, same columns complaining about the local daily, same sex advice, same five-thousand-word hole for the cover story. The people were largely the same, too: all but maybe 2 percent of the city-slicker journalists in attendance were white; the vast majority were either Boomer hippies or Gen X slackers. Several asked me the exact same question with the same suspicious looks on their faces: "So . . . what's your *alternative* experience?"

At the bar, I started a discussion about what specific attributes qualified these papers, and the forty-seven-year-old publishing genre that spawned them, to continue meriting the adjective "alternative." Alternative to what? To the straight-laced "objectivity" and pyramid-style writing of daily newspapers? New Journalists and other narrative storytellers crashed those gates long ago. Alternative to society's oppressive intolerance toward deviant behavior? Tell it to the Osbournes, as they watch *Queer Eye for the Straight Guy*. Something to do with corporate ownership? Not unless "alternative" no longer applies to Village Voice Media (owned in part by Goldman Sachs) or the New Times chain (which has been involved in some brutal acquisition and liquidation deals). Someone at the table lamely offered up "a sense of community," but Fox News could easily clear that particular bar.

No, it must have something to do with political slant—or, to be technically accurate, political correctness. Richard Karpel, the AAN executive director, joined the conversation, so I put him on the spot: Of all the weeklies his organization had rejected for membership on political grounds, which one was the best editorially? The *Independent Florida Sun*, he replied. Good-looking paper, some sharp writing but, well, it was just too friendly toward the church. "And if there's anything we all agree on," Karpel said with a smile, "it's that we're antichurch."

I assumed he was joking—that couldn't be all we have left from the legacy of Norman Mailer, Art Kunkin, Paul Krassner, and my other child-hood heroes, could it? Then later I looked up the AAN's Web site to read the admission committee's rejection notes for the *Florida Sun* (which was ex-cluded by a vote of 9–2). "The right-wing church columnist has no place in AAN," explained one judge. "All the God-and-flag shit disturbs me," wrote another. "Weirdly right-wing," chimed a third.

The original alternative papers were not at all this politically monochro-matic, despite entering the world at a time when Lenny Bruce was being prose-cuted for obscenity, Tom Dooley was proselytizing for American intervention in Vietnam, and Republicans ruled the nation's editorial pages. Dan Wolf, co-founder of the trailblazing *Village Voice*, loved to throw darts at what he called "the dull pieties of official liberalism," and founding editors like Mailer were forever trying to tune their antennae to previously undetected political frequencies.

The dull pieties of official progressivism is one of many attributes that show how modern alt weeklies have strayed from what made them alterna-tive in the first place. The papers once embraced amateur writers; now they are firmly established in the journalistic pecking order, with the salaries and professional standards to match. They once championed the slogan "never trust anyone over thirty"; now their average reader is over forty and aging fast. They have become so ubiquitous in cities over a certain size, during decades when so many other new media formats have sprung up (cable tele-vision, newsletters, talk radio, business journals, Web sites), that the very no-tion that they represent a crucial "alternative" to a monolithic journalism establishment now strains credulity.

But there still exists a publishing format that manages to embody all these lost qualities, and more—the Weblog. The average blog, needless to say, pales in comparison to a 1957 issue of the *Voice*, or a 1964 *Los Angeles Free Press*, or a 2003 Lexington, Kentucky, *ACE Weekly*, for that matter. But that's missing the point. Blogging technology has, for the first time in his-tory, given the average Jane the ability to write, edit, design, and publish her own editorial product—to be read and responded to by millions of people, potentially—for around $0 to $200 a year. It has begun to deliver on some of the wild promises about the Internet that were heard in the 1990s. Never before have so many passionate outsiders—hundreds of thousands, at minimum—stormed the ramparts of professional journalism.

And these amateurs, especially the ones focusing on news and current events, are doing some fascinating things. Many are connecting intimately with readers in a way reminiscent of old-style metro columnists or the liveliest of the New Journalists. Others are staking the narrowest of editorial claims as their own—appellate court rulings, new media proliferation in Tehran, the intersection of hip-hop and libertarianism—and covering them like no one else. They are forever fact-checking the daylights out of truth-fudging ideologues like Ann Coulter and Michael Moore, and sifting through the biases of the BBC and Bill O'Reilly, often while cheerfully acknowledging and/or demonstrating their own lopsided political sympathies. At this instant, all over the world, bloggers are busy popularizing under-appreciated print journalists (like *Chicago Sun-Times* columnist Mark Steyn), pumping up stories that should be getting more attention (like the Trent Lott debacle), and perhaps most excitingly of all, committing impressive, spontaneous acts of decentralized journalism.

BLOGGING'S BIG BANG

Every significant new publishing phenomenon has been midwifed by a great leap forward in printing technology. The movable-type printing press begat the Gutenberg Bible, which begat the Renaissance. Moving from rags to pulp paved the way for Hearst and Pulitzer. The birth of alternative newspapers coincided almost perfectly with the development of the offset press. Laser printers and desktop publishing ushered in the newsletter and the 'zine, and helped spawn the business journal.

When it burst onto the scene just ten years ago, the World Wide Web promised to be an even cheaper version of desktop publishing. And for many people it was, but you still had to learn HTML coding, which was inscrutable enough to make one long for the days of typesetting and paste-up. By the late 1990s, I owned a few Web domains and made a living writing about online journalism, yet if I really needed to publish something on my own, I'd print up a Word file and take it down to the local copy shop. Web publishing was theoretically possible and cheap (if you used a hosting service like Tripod), but it just wasn't easy for people as dull-witted as I.

In August 1999, Pyra Labs changed all that, with a product called Blogger (responsible, as much as anything, for that terrible four-letter word). As much of the world knows by now, "Weblog" is usually defined as a Web site where information is updated frequently and presented in reverse chronological order (newest stuff on top). Typically, each post contains one and often several hyperlinks to other Web sites and stories, and usually there is a standing list of links to the author's favorite bookmarks. Pyra Labs, since bought out by Google, had a revolutionary insight that made all this popular: every technological requirement of Web publishing—graphic design, simple coding for things like links, hosting—is a barrier to entry, keeping non-techies out; why not remove them? Blogger gave users a for-dummies choice of templates, an easy-to-navigate five-minute registration process, and (perhaps best of all) Web hosting. All for free. You didn't even need to buy your own domain; simply make sure joesixpack.blogspot.com wasn't taken, pick a template, and off you go.

The concept took off, and new blogging companies like LiveJournal, User-Land, and Movable Type scrambled to compete. Blogger cofounders Evan Williams, Paul Bausch, and Meg Hourihan, along with Web designer Jason Kottke, and tech writer Rebecca Blood—these were the stars of the first major mainstream-media feature about blogging, a November 2000 *New Yorker* story by Rebecca Mead, who christened the phenomenon "the CB radio of the Dave Eggers generation."

Like just about everything else, blogging changed forever on September 11, 2001. The destruction of the World Trade Center and the attack on the Pentagon created a huge appetite on the part of the public to be part of The Conversation, to vent and analyze and publicly ponder or mourn. Many, too, were unsatisfied with what they read and saw in the mainstream media. Glenn Reynolds, proprietor of the wildly popular InstaPundit.com blog, thought the mainstream analysis was terrible. "All the talking heads . . . kept saying that 'we're gonna have to grow up, we're gonna have to give up a lot of our freedoms,' " he says. "Or it was the 'Why do they hate us' sort of teeth-gnashing. And I think there was a deep dissatisfaction with that." The daily op-ed diet of Column Left and Column Right often fell way off the mark. "It's time for the United Nations to get the hell out of town. And take with it CNN war-slut Christiane Amanpour," the *New York Post*'s Andrea Peyser seethed on September 21. "We forgive you; we reject vengeance," Colman McCarthy whimpered to the terrorists in the *Los Angeles Times* September 17. September 11 was the impetus for my own blog (mattwelch.com/ warblog.html). Jeff Jarvis, who was trapped in the WTC dust cloud on September 11, started his a few days later. "I had a personal story I needed to tell," said Jarvis, a former *San Francisco Examiner* columnist, founding editor of *Entertainment Weekly*, and current president and creative director of Advance.net, which is the Internet wing of the Condé Nast empire. "Then lo and behold! I discovered people were linking to me and talking about my story, so I joined this great conversation."

He wasn't alone. Reynolds, a hyper-kinetic University of Tennessee law professor and occasional columnist who produces techno records in his spare time, had launched InstaPundit the month before. On September 11, his traffic jumped from 1,600 visitors to almost 4,200; now it averages 100,000 per weekday. With his prolific posting pace—dozens of links a day, each with comments ranging from a word to several paragraphs—and a deliberate ethic of driving traffic to new blogs from all over the political spectrum, Reynolds quickly became the "Blogfather" of a newly coined genre of sites: the warblogs. "I think people were looking for context, they were looking for stuff that wasn't dumb," he said. "They were looking for stuff that seemed to them to be consistent with how Americans ought to respond to something like this."

There had been plenty of news-and-opinion Weblogs previously—from political journalists such as Joshua Micah Marshall, Mickey Kaus, Andrew Sullivan, and Virginia Postrel; not to mention "amateurs" like Matt Drudge. But September 11 drew unpaid nonprofessionals into the current-events fray. And like the first alternative publishers, who eagerly sought out and formed a network with like-minded mavericks across the country, the post-September 11 Webloggers spent considerable energy propping up their new comrades and encouraging their readers to join the fun. I'd guess 90 percent of my most vocal early readers have gone on to start sites of their own. In April 2002

Reynolds asked InstaPundit readers to let him know if he had inspired any of them to start their own blogs. Nearly two hundred wrote in. (Imagine two hundred people deciding to become a columnist just because Maureen Dowd was so persuasive.) Meanwhile, Blogger alone has more than 1.5 million registered users, and LiveJournal reports 1.2 million. No one knows how many *active* blogs there are worldwide, but Blogcount (yes, a blog that counts blogs) guesses between 2.4 million and 2.9 million. Freedom of the press belongs to nearly 3 million people.

WHAT'S THE POINT

So what have these people contributed to journalism? Four things: personality, eyewitness testimony, editorial filtering, and uncounted gigabytes of new knowledge.

"Why are Weblogs popular?" asks Jarvis, whose company has launched four dozen of them, ranging from beachcams on the Jersey shore to a temporary blog during the latest Iraq war. "I think it's because they have something to say. In a media world that's otherwise leached of opinions and life, there's so much life in them."

For all the history made by newspapers between 1960 and 2000, the profession was also busy contracting, standardizing, and homogenizing. Most cities now have their monopolist daily, their alt weekly or two, their business journal. Journalism is done a certain way, by a certain kind of people. Bloggers are basically oblivious to such traditions, so reading the best of them is like receiving a bracing slap in the face. It's a reminder that America is far more diverse and iconoclastic than its newsrooms.

After two years of reading Weblogs, my short list of favorite news commentators in the world now includes an Air Force mechanic (Paul Palubicki of *sgtstryker.com*), a punk rock singer-songwriter (Dr. Frank of *doktorfrank. com*), a twenty-four-year-old Norwegian programmer (Bjorn Staerk of *http:// bearstrong.net/warblog/index.html*), and a cranky libertarian journalist from Alberta, Canada (Colby Cosh). Outsiders with vivid writing styles and unique viewpoints have risen to the top of the blog heap and begun vaulting into mainstream media. Less than two years ago, Elizabeth Spiers was a tech-stock analyst for a hedge fund who at night wrote sharp-tongued observations about Manhattan life on her personal blog; now she's the It Girl of New York media, lancing her colleagues at Gawker.com, while doing free-lance work for the *Times*, the *New York Post*, *Radar*, and other publications. Salam Pax, a pseudonymous young gay Iraqi architect who made hearts flutter with his idiosyncratic personal descriptions of Baghdad before and after the war, now writes columns for *The Guardian* and in July signed a book deal with Grove/Atlantic. Steven Den Beste, a middle-aged unemployed software engineer in San Diego, has been spinning out thousands of words of international analysis most every day for the last two years; recently he has been seen in the online edition of *The Wall Street Journal*.

With personality and an online audience, meanwhile, comes a kind of reader interaction far more intense and personal than anything comparable in print. Once, when I had the poor taste to mention in my blog that I was going through a rough financial period, readers sent me more than $1,000 in two days. Far more important, the intimacy and network effects of the blogworld enable you to meet people beyond your typical circle and political affiliation, sometimes with specialized knowledge of interest to you. "It exposes you to worlds that most people, let alone reporters, never interact with," says Jarvis, whose personal blog (buzzmachine.com) has morphed into a one-stop shop for catching up on Iranian and Iraqi bloggers, some of whom he has now met online or face to face.

Such specialization and filtering is one of the form's key functions. Many bloggers, like the estimable Jim Romenesko, with his popular journalism forum on Poynter's site, focus like a laser beam on one micro-category, and provide simple links to the day's relevant news. There are scores dealing with ever-narrower categories of media alone, from a site that obsesses over the *San Francisco Chronicle (ChronWatch.com)*, to one that keeps the heat on newspaper ombudsmen *(OmbudsGod.blogspot.com)*. Charles Johnson, a Los Angeles Web designer, has built a huge and intensely loyal audience by spotting and vilifying venalities in the Arab press *(littlegreenfootballs.com/weblog)*. And individual news events, such as the Iraq war, spark their own temporary group blogs, where five or ten or more people all contribute links to minute-by-minute breaking news. Sometimes the single most must-see publication on a given topic will have been created the day before.

Besides introducing valuable new sources of information to readers, these sites are also forcing their proprietors to act like journalists: choosing stories, judging the credibility of sources, writing headlines, taking pictures, developing prose styles, dealing with readers, building audience, weighing libel considerations, and occasionally conducting informed investigations on their own. Thousands of amateurs are learning how we do our work, becoming in the process more sophisticated readers and sharper critics. For lazy columnists and defensive gatekeepers, it can seem as if the hounds from a mediocre hell have been unleashed. But for curious professionals, it is a marvelous opportunity and entertaining spectacle; they discover what the audience finds important and encounter specialists who can rip apart the work of many a generalist. More than just A. J. Liebling–style press criticism, journalists finally have something approaching real peer review, in all its brutality. If they truly value the scientific method, they should rejoice. Blogs can bring a collective intelligence to bear on a question.

And when the decentralized fact-checking army kicks into gear, it can be an impressive thing to behold. On March 30, veteran British war correspondent Robert Fisk, who has been accused so often of anti-American bias and sloppiness by bloggers that his last name has become a verb (meaning, roughly, "to disprove loudly, point by point"), reported that a bomb hitting a crowded Baghdad market and killing dozens must have been fired by U.S. troops because of some Western numerals he found on a piece of twisted metal lying nearby. Australian blogger Tim Blair, a free-lance journalist, reprinted the partial numbers and asked his military-knowledgeable readers for insight. Within twenty-four hours, more than a dozen readers with specialized knowledge (retired Air Force, former Naval Air Systems Command employees, others) had written in describing the weapon (U.S. high-speed anti-radiation missile), manufacturer (Raytheon), launch point (F-16), and dozens of other minute details not seen in press accounts days and weeks later. Their conclusion, much as it pained them to say so: Fisk was probably right.

In December 2001 a University of New Hampshire Economics and

Women's Studies professor named Marc Herold published a study, based mostly on press clippings, that estimated 3,767 civilians had died as a result of American military action in Afghanistan. Within a day, blogger Bruce Rolston, a Canadian military reservist, had already shot holes through Herold's methodology, noting that he conflated "casualties" with "fatalities," double-counted single events, and depended heavily on dubious news sources. Over the next two days, several other bloggers cut Herold's work to ribbons. Yet for the next month, Herold's study was presented not just as fact, but as an understatement, by the *Guardian*, as well as the New Jersey *Star-Ledger*, *The Hartford Courant*, and several other newspapers. When news organizations on the ground later conducted their surveys of Afghan civilian deaths, most set the number at closer to 1,000.

But the typical group fact-check is not necessarily a matter of war. Bloggers were out in the lead in exposing the questionable research and behavior of gun-studying academics Michael Bellesiles and John Lott Jr. (the former resigned last year from Emory University after a blogger-propelled investigation found that he falsified data in his antigun book, *Arming America*; the latter, author of the pro-gun book, *More Guns, Less Crime*, was forced by bloggers to admit that he had no copies of his own controversial self-defense study he had repeatedly cited as proving his case, and that he had masqueraded in online gun-rights discussions as a vociferous John Lott supporter named "Mary Rosh." The fact-checking bloggers have uncovered misleading use of quotations by opinion columnists, such as Maureen Dowd, and jumped all over the inaccurate or irresponsible comments of various 2004 presidential candidates. They have become part of the journalism conversation.

BREATHING IN THE BLOGWORLD

Which is not to say that 90 percent of news-related blogs aren't crap. First of all, 90 percent of any new form of expression tends to be mediocre (think of band demos, or the cringe-inducing underground papers of years gone by), and judging a medium by its worst practitioners is not very sporting. Still, almost every criticism about blogs is valid—they often are filled with cheap shots, bad spelling, the worst kind of confirmation bias, and an extremely off-putting sense of self-worth (one that this article will do nothing to alleviate). But the "blogosphere," as many like to pompously call it, is too large and too varied to be defined as a single thing, and the action at the top 10 percent is among the most exciting new trends the profession has seen in a while. Are bloggers journalists? Will they soon replace newspapers?

The best answer to those two questions is: those are two really dumb questions; enough hot air has been expended in their name already.

A more productive, tangible line of inquiry is: Is journalism being *produced* by blogs, is it interesting, and how should journalists react to it? The answers, by my lights, are "yes," "yes," and "in many ways." After a slow start, news organizations are beginning to embrace the form (see page 23). Tech journalists, such as the *San Jose Mercury News's* Dan Gillmor, launched Weblogs long before "blogger" was a household word. Beat reporting is a natural fit for a blog—reporters can collect standing links to sites of interest, dribble out stories and anecdotes that don't necessarily belong in the paper, and attract a specific like-minded readership. One of the best such sites going is the recently created California Insider blog by the *Sacramento Bee's* excellent political columnist, Daniel Weintraub, who has been covering the state's wacky recall news like a blanket. Blogs also make sense for opinion publications, such as the *National Review*, *The American Prospect*, and my employer, *Reason*, all of which have lively sites.

For those with time to notice, blogs are also a great cheap farm system for talent. You've got tens of thousands of potential columnists writing for free, fueled by passion, operating in a free market where the cream rises quickly.

Best of all, perhaps, the phenomenon is simply entertaining. When do you last recall reading some writer and thinking "damn, *he* sure looks like he's having fun"? It's what buttoned-down reporters thought of their long-haired brethren back in the 1960s. The 2003 version may not be so immediately identifiable on sight—and that may be the most promising development of all.

APPENDICES

APPENDIX A
THE BLOG! INDEX

BLOGS, WEBSITES, AND CONTACT INFORMATION
FOR AUTHORS AND INTERVIEWEES

AUTHORS & PUBLISHERS

David Kline   dkline@well.com; BlogRevolt.com

Dan Burstein   info@squibnocketpress.com

PART ONE: POLITICS & POLICY

Joe Trippi   JoeTrippi.com/joesblog

Jon Lebkowsky   Weblogsky.com

Markos Moulitsas Zuniga   DailyKos.com

Ana Marie Cox   Wonkette.com

Roger L. Simon   RogerLSimon.com

Matthew Klam   MatthewKlam.com

Daniel Drezner   DanielDrezner.com

Henry Farrell   CrookedTimber.org

PART TWO: BUSINESS & ECONOMICS

Robert Scoble   Radio.Weblogs.com/0001101

Nick Gall   Radio.Weblogs.com/0126951

Joi Ito   Joi.Ito.com

Nick Denton   NickDenton.org

Jason Calacanis   Calacanis.WeblogsInc.com

John Battelle   BattelleMedia.com

Andreas Stavropoulis	dfj.com/team/andreas_bio.shtml
Christian Sarkar	ChristianSarkar.com
David Teten	Teten.com/brainfood
Michael Cader	PublishersMarketplace.com
Jonathan Schwartz	blogs.sun.com/jonathan
David Kirkpatrick	Fortune.com/fortune
Daniel Roth	Fortune.com/fortune
Stephen Baker	BusinessWeek.com/magazine
Heather Green	BusinessWeek.com/magazine

PART THREE: MEDIA & CULTURE

Wil Wheaton	WilWheaton.net
Colby Buzzell	CBFTW.blogspot.com
Adam Curry	Live.Curry.com
Jeff Jarvis	BuzzMedia.com
Clay Shirky	Shirky.com
Kate Lee	ICMTalent.com
Terry Teachout	ArtsJournal.com/aboutlastnight
Ayelet Waldman	Bad-Mother.blogspot.com
	(no longer writing blog)
Jay Rosen	PressThink.org
Rebecca MacKinnon	RConversation.blogs.com
Paul Saffo	Saffo.org
Arianna Huffington	HuffingtonPost.com
Emily Nussbaum	NYTimes.com
Andrew Sullivan	AndrewSullivan.com
Matt Welch	MattWelch.com/warblog.html

APPENDIX B
THE TECHNORATI TOP 50: A SNAPSHOT IN TIME

Which are the most popular blogs on the Web? The obvious answer would be whichever ones are clicked on the most often. But the problem is that this is actually an impossible question to answer (a very good thing, say privacy advocates). Which is little solace to a society where mass ratings mean everything. We're constantly inundated with statistics: the top one hundred movies by box office; the ten worst-dressed list; the world's richest people; book bestseller lists; the highest-rated cars in a consumer or fan magazine; the biggest audience share for the 10:00 p.m. time slot on network TV.

How, then, to rank the ephemeral world of blogs? The solution—at least for now—is to try and measure "influence," and on those grounds there is general agreement in the blogosphere that one company, Technorati, has found the best way to do this. Yet despite the fact that "everyone" cites it, Technorati's approach remains controversial.

Technorati measures influence across two dimensions: sources and links. The company explains it this way: "Sources tells you the number of people [bloggers] who are linking to the specified URL. Links is the total number of inbound links pointing toward a URL (there can be multiple links from one blog to a URL). The more inbound links and sources to an article or other website, the more that article or site is being discussed."

Put in plain language, *sources* deals with the number of other blogs that have been recommended on people's sites, and for which links have been provided. Say DailyKos.com has a link to AndrewSullivan.com. So does Boing

Boing. The more AndrewSullivan.com is listed as a good source among the other 9 million bloggers Technorati keeps track of, the higher it travels up the list. In other words, Boing Boing is first in the ranking of our snapshot because 14,418 other blogs have put up links to it. We might refer to that as a *passive* measurement.

The second measurement could arguably be called the *active* measurement. If the reader of any blog at all—say of DailyKos.com—submits a comment to fellow readers that says, "Hey, look at what Boing Boing has on its site today," and then conveniently provides a link to Boing Boing as part of their comment, Technorati counts this as a link.

The more sources and links, the more influence a blog has. Here is the ranking, chosen on a random day in May 2005. You will notice a number of our interviewees, Markos Moulitsas Zuniga, Wil Wheaton, Robert Scoble, and Jeff Jarvis among them. Others, like Joi Ito, John Battelle, and Jay Rosen, may have been there the week before or the week after. Who knows, if you check technorati.com/live/top100.html right now, they could be there today.

TECHNORATI TOP 50 ON MAY 5, 2005

1. Boing Boing: A Directory of Wonderful Things—21,933 links from 14,148 sources [boingboing.net; general]
2. Instapundit.com—15,084 links from 10,283 sources [instapundit.com; technology, culture, politics, and law]
3. Daily Kos—15,250 links from 9,136 sources [dailykos.com; politics]
4. Davenetics* Pop+Media+Web—7,566 links from 7,400 sources [davenetics.com; pop, media, Web]
5. Talking Points Memo by Joshua Micah Marshall—10,120 links from 7,297 sources [talkingpointsmemo.com; politics]
6. Engadget—13,006 links from 6,875 sources [engadget.com; technology]
7. AndrewSullivan.com—7,719 links from 5,907 sources [andrewsullivan.com; politics]
8. dooce—6,496 links from 5,701 sources [dooce.com; caustic notes of a stay-at-home mom]

9. GreatestJournal—10,625 links from 5,571 sources [greatestjournal.com; free weblog service]

10. The Best Page in the Universe—6,147 links from 5,417 sources [maddox.xmission.com; creative, hate-filled rants]

11. lgf: anti-idiotarian headquarters—8,098 links from 5,377 sources [littlegreenfootballs.com/weblog; politics]

12. WIL WHEATON DOT NET—6,221 links from 5,282 sources [wilwheaton.net; author and former *Star Trek* actor]

13. kottke.org::home of fine hypertext products—6,823 links from 5,174 sources [kottke.org; Web technology, media, and design]

14. Metafilter|Community Weblog—7,612 links from 5,013 sources [metafilter.com; general interest group blog]

15. lgf: a bunch of scruffy no-names—7,523 links from 4,977 sources [littlegreenfootballs.com; politics]

16. informacão e Inutilidade—6,040 links from 4,934 sources [interney.net; Portugese blog site]

17. The Doc Searls Weblog—5,598 links from 4,881 sources [doc.weblogs.com; technology]

18. Scripting News—5,628 links from 4,564 sources [scripting.com; technology]

19. Wonkette—5,676 links from 4,564 sources [wonkette.com; politics]

20. balmasque—4,540 links from 4,500 sources [balmasque.blogspot.com; an Iranian blog]

21. Power Line—7,209 links from 4,374 sources [powerlineblog.com; politics]

22. A List Apart—5,335 links from 3,792 sources [alistapart.com; Web design and development]

23. Corante—7,349 links from 3,700 sources [corante.com; technology, science, and business]

24. Megatokyo—4,010 links from 3,697 sources [megatokyo.com; online comic/manga]

25. something awful—4,300 links from 3,678 sources [somethingawful.com; general/entertainment]

26. afterall I was the best I ever had—3,603 links from 3,525 sources [serendipityq.com]

27. Arts & Letters Daily: ideas, criticism, debate—3,893 links from 3,488 sources [aldaily.com; culture]

28. The Volokh Conspiracy—5,709 links from 3,432 sources [volokh.com; politics]

29. Michelle Malkin—5,699 links from 3,419 sources [michellemalkin.com; politics]

30. Gawker—4,243 links from 3,419 sources [gawker.com; pop culture and media gossip]

31. This Modern World—3,881 links from 3,333 sources [thismodernworld.com; cartoon]

32. Scobleizer: Microsoft Geek Blogger—5,419 links from 3,332 sources [radio.weblogs.com/0001011; technology]

33. Jeffrey Zeldman Presents The Daily Report—4,021 links from 3,288 sources [zeldman.com; Web design/technology]

34. The Web Standards Project—3,705 links from 3,168 sources [webstandards.org; Web development]

35. Neil Gaiman—3,614 links from 3,101 sources [neilgaiman.com; journal of an illustrated book author]

36. Lileks—3,844 links from 3,089 sources [lileks.com/bleats; writer/columnist]

37. Media Matters for America—5,589 links from 3,089 sources [mediamatters.org; politics]

38. Joel on Software—4,164 links from 3,058 sources [joelonsoftware.com; technology]

39. kuro5hin.org—4,083 links from 3,039 sources [kuro5hin.org; technology]

40. Television Without Pity—3,660 links from 3,010 sources [televisionwithoutpity.com; television critiques]

41. HughHewitt.com—4,521 links from 3,010 sources [hughhewitt.com; politics]

42. BuzzMachine by Jeff Jarvis—4,163 links from 2,930 sources [buzzmachine.com; media]

43. Baghdad Burning—3,453 links from 2,915 sources [riverbend.blogspot.com; Iraq journal]

44. The Lair of the Crab of Ineffable Wisdom—3,552 links from 2,908 sources [rathergood.com; music]

45. Truthout—6,214 links from 2,890 sources [truthout.org; politics]

46. Fleugelz—3,598 links from 2,849 sources [fleugel.com; Japanese blog]

47. Doppler:redefining podcasting—3,014 links from 2,822 sources [dopplerradio.net; podcasting]

48. Informed Comment—3,779 links from 2,821 sources [juancole.com; Middle East, history, religion]

49. Living in the Fairytale—2,830 links from 2,783 sources

50. photojunkie magazine—2,834 links from 2,780 sources [photojunkie.org; photoblogging]

APPENDIX C
THE BLOGROLL

Blogroll is the term used to describe the list a blogger recommends to his or her readers. It usually runs down the right-hand side of the page, and clicking on it will lead the reader directly to the site mentioned.

Here we list some blogs of interest to the authors and contributors.

POLITICS; GOVERNMENT POLICY

A Fistful of Euros (fistfulofeuros.net)

AlterNet (alternet.org)

AndrewSullivan.com (andrewsullivan.com)

Baghdad Burning (riverbend.blogspot.com)

Belgravia Dispatch (belgraviadispatch.com)

Belmont Club (belmontclub.blogspot.com)

DailyKos (dailykos.com)

Daniel W. Drezner (danieldrezner.com/blog)

Edge of England's Sword (iainmurray.org/MT)

Editor: Myself (hoder.com/weblog)

The Flaming Grasshopper (flaminggrasshopper.com)

Global Voices (cyber.law.harvard.edu/globalvoices)

Harry's Place (hurryupharry.bloghouse.net)

HughHewitt.com (hughhewitt.com)

Informed Comment (juancole.com)

InstaPundit (instapundit.com)

Iraq: The Model (iraqthemodel.blogspot.com)

Jim Moore's Journal (blogs.law.harvard.edu/jim)

KausFiles (kausfiles.com)

Little Green Footballs (littlegreenfootballs.com/weblog)

MyDD (mydd.com)

OxBlog (oxblog.blogspot.com)

Passion of the Present (platform.blogs.com/passionofthepresent)

Politics from Left to Right (chrisnolan.com)

Slugger O'Toole (sluggerotoole.com)

Power Line (powerlineblog.com)

BUSINESS, ECONOMICS, TECHNOLOGY

Blogspotting (blogspotting.net)

Blog Maverick (blogmaverick.com)

Brad DeLong's Semi-Daily Journal (j-bradford-delong.net/movable_type)

Doc Searls Weblog (doc.weblogs.com)

FastLane Blog (fastlane.gmblogs.com)

Freakonomics (Freakonomics.com/blog.php)

GoogleBlog (google.com/googleblog)

Marginal Revolution (marginalrevolution.com)

Micro Persuasion (steverubel.typepad.com)

Napsterization (napsterization.org)

Scobleizer (radio.weblogs.com/0001011/)

Scripting News (scripting.com)

Stoneyfield Farm (stonyfield.com/weblog)

Weblogsky (weblogsky.com)

MEDIA, LITERARY, CULTURE

ArtsJournal (artsjournal.com/blogs)

Backstory (mjroseblog.typepad.com)

Blogorreah (ggth.typepad.com/media/book_blogs)

Boing Boing (boingboing.net)

Bookslut (bookslut.com/blog)

Cool Hunting (coolhunting.com)

Chez Miscarriage (chezmiscarriage.blogs.com)

Confessions of an Idiosyncratic Mind (sarahweinman.com)

Dan Gillmor on Grassroots Journalism, Etc (dangillmor.typepad.com)

Defamer (defamer.com)

Doctor Frank (doktorfrank.com)

Dooce (dooce.com)

Engadget (engadget.com)

Gadling (gadling.com)

Galley Cat (mediabistro.com/galleycat)

Kottke.org (kottke.org)

The Litblog Co-op (lbc.typepad.com)

Maud Newton (maudnewton.com/blog)

The Elegant Variation (marksarvas.blogs.com/elegvar)

MobyLives (mobylives.com)

MoorishGirl (moorishgirl.com)

PullQuote (pullquote.typepad.com)

Silliman's Blog (ronsilliman.blogspot.com)

Slashdot (slashdot.org)

Susie Bright's Journal (susiebright.blogs.com)

The Rest Is Noise (therestisnoise.com)

This Fish (thisfish.com)

Tingle Alley (tinglealley.com)

TreeHugger (treehugger.com)

ACKNOWLEDGMENTS

We would like to thank the many people who gave generously of their time and wisdom during the interviews for this book: Scott Allen, John Battelle, Colby Buzzell, Michael Cader, Jason Calacanis, Ana Marie Cox, Adam Curry, Nick Denton, Nick Gall, Arianna Huffington, Joichi Ito, Jeff Jarvis, Jon Lebkowsky, Kate Lee, Rebecca MacKinnon, Jay Rosen, Paul Saffo, Christian Sarkar, Jonathan Schwartz, Robert Scoble, Clay Shirky, Roger L. Simon, Andreas Stavropoulis, Terry Teachout, David Teten, Joe Trippi, Ayelet Waldman, Wil Wheaton, and Markos Moulitsas Zuniga.

We would also like to thank Norman Geras, Dan Gillmor, Bradford Goldense, John Hlinko, Gary Reback, Greg Thomas, Evan Williams, and Maciej Wisniewski for their invaluable insights into the practical advantages as well as limitations of blogging as a political, business, and cultural tool.

Our publisher, CDS Books, was an early believer in our quaint old media notion that it might be a good idea to do a long-form print book about blogs and blogging. We deeply appreciate the vision and indefatigable support of David Wilk, our point person at CDS, Steve Black, COO of CDS, and David Steinberger, CEO of the Perseus Book Group, which acquired CDS as we were finishing this book. Special thanks as well to Donna M. Rivera, George Davidson, Leigh Taylor, and the unsung heroes of the CDS sales force.

David Kline personal acknowledgments: My coauthor, Dan Burstein, was the real source of inspiration for this book. Without his vision and determination—not to mention his extraordinary patience in trying to coax some comprehensible copy out of me—this book would simply not exist. I owe him and contributing editor, Arne de Keijzer, a very large debt of gratitude.

Special thanks also goes to Tiffany Lee Brown, the editor of *2 Gyrlz Quarterly* and blogger at Magdalen.com, whose wise counsel at the beginning of this project set me working in the right direction and doubtless saved a lot of grief.

I'm grateful also to Jim Kennedy and David Kennedy, who gave so generously of their interest and encouragement; Kathy and Fritz Hill, whose warm support helped sustain me along the way; and my mother, Ruth Rothman, who overcame her dread of all things technological to become a one-woman clipping service on my behalf.

Finally, I want to thank my wife, Sarah, whose unflinching love makes all things possible for me.

Dan Burstein personal acknowledgments: It was a special pleasure working with David Kline on another book about a transformative technology a decade after our last collaboration on *Road Warriors*. David is a consummate journalist, narrator, and storyteller, who gets to the essence of business and technology trends and what they mean to real people and to real lives. The canvas that bloggers are painting on today is huge; David was able to find the key spots that help us all interpret the meaning of the painting.

Arne de Keijzer was an extraordinary behind-the-scenes editor of this book, keeping track of all the pieces and pulling them together with his unique ability to create beautiful mosaics out of complex and disparate fragments. In a brief operating history of less than two years, our Squibnocket Partners LLC has been able to accomplish amazing publishing feats, in part because of Arne's constant willingness to scale new heights and his dedication to solving the four-dimensional puzzles that arise along the way.

Paul Berger was my arms, legs, ears, and voice on many aspects of this project, tracking down incredibly busy interviewees and getting us on their calendars for rich and robust interviews in highly compressed periods of time. Paul is a terrific researcher and interviewer and the world will surely be hearing much more from him in his own articles and books to come.

Gilbert Perlman is the true godfather of this book. He saw its importance the first time he heard about it and encouraged us to make it the right book at the right time on this important subject.

Many other people contributed in ways small and large to this book. I am particularly grateful to: Sofie Andersen, Danny Baror, Pamela Cannon, Rose Carrano, Marty Edelston, Steve Etzler, Judy Friedberg, Sam Schwerin, and all my colleagues at Millennium Technology Ventures.

My wife, Julie O'Connor, and my son, David Burstein, were my constant companions on this journey to understand the world of blogs and blogging. Their love, support, and great ideas are integral to all my books and all my life journeys. This one is no exception.

AUTHOR BIOS

DAVID KLINE

David Kline (dkline@well.com) is a journalist, author, and business consultant who has covered some of the world's most important stories over the past twenty-five years.

As a foreign correspondent, Kline reported on the war in Afghanistan and other conflicts, as well as the Bolivian "Coca Nostra," for the *New York Times*, *Christian Science Monitor*, NBC and CBS News, the *Atlantic*, and other major media.

A leading business writer as well, Kline's bestselling book from Harvard Business School Press—*Rembrandts in the Attic: Unlocking the Hidden Value of Patents*—is considered the seminal work in the field of intellectual property strategy within corporate America. He has also written for the *Harvard Business Review*, *Chief Executive*, *Business 2.0*, *Wired*, the *Sloan Management Review*, and other business magazines.

Kline is also co-author, with Dan Burstein, of the 1995 business book, *Road Warriors: Dreams and Nightmares Along the Information Highway* (Dutton).

DAN BURSTEIN

Dan Burstein is an award-winning journalist, an author, and a venture capitalist. He has been writing about new technology trends, as well as investing in emerging growth companies, for more than twenty years. Together with David Kline, Burstein wrote the seminal 1995 book, *Road Warriors: Dreams and Nightmares Along the Information Highway*, which was one of the first books to examine the broad impact of the Internet and digital media on business and society.

Burstein founded Millennium Technology Ventures in 2000 and cofounded Millennium Technology Value Partners in 2004. He currently serves as a Managing Partner of both funds. For many years, he was Senior Advisor at The Blackstone Group, and has also served as a consultant to the CEOs and senior executives of major global corporations. In the last decade, Dan has served on the boards of more than a dozen new technology and media companies.

Burstein has also written books about global macroeconomics, competitive technology and trade strategies, and the financial and political futures of China, Japan, and the European Union. He is a frequent guest expert on television programs ranging from CNBC, CNN, Fox, and Bloomberg to Charlie Rose and Oprah.

Most recently, Dan Burstein and Arne de Keijzer created and edited the *New York Times* bestselling *Secrets of The Code: The Unauthorized Guide to the Mysteries Behind the Da Vinci Code* and *Secrets of Angels & Demons: The Unauthorized Guide to the Bestselling Novel*. These books are also bestsellers in more than two dozen international editions, with well over one million books in the "Secrets" series now in print around the world.

DISCOVER

READ

EXPLORE

LEARN

NEW HANOVER COUNTY PUBLIC LIBRARY

If found, please return to:
201 Chestnut St.
Wilmington, NC 28401
(910) 798-6300
http://www.nhclibrary.org

ML (RR)

1/06